ENGLAND'S OTHER COUNTRYMEN

ENGLAND'S OTHER COUNTRYMEN

Black Tudor Society

ONYEKA NUBIA

BLOOMSBURY ACADEMIC

LONDON • NEW YORK • OXFORD • NEW DELHI • SYDNEY

BLOOMSBURY ACADEMIC
Bloomsbury Publishing Plc
50 Bedford Square, London, WC1B 3DP, UK
1385 Broadway, New York, NY 10018, USA
29 Earlsfort Terrace, Dublin 2, Ireland

BLOOMSBURY, BLOOMSBURY ACADEMIC and the Diana logo are
trademarks of Bloomsbury Publishing Plc

First published in Great Britain in 2019 by Zed Books
Reprinted by Bloomsbury Academic UK in 2022, 2023

A catalogue record for this book is available from the British Library.

ISBN: HB: 978-1-7869-9420-2
PB: 978-1-3503-5430-2
ePDF: 978-1-7869-9422-6
ePub: 978-1-7869-9423-3

Typeset in Bulmer by Swales and Willis Ltd, Exeter, Devon
Index by John Barker
Cover design by David A. Gee

Printed and bound in Great Britain

To find out more about our authors and books visit www.bloomsbury.com and
sign up for our newsletters.

Contents

About the Author

Onyeka Nubia is a pioneering and internationally renowned historian, writer and presenter committed to the study of comparative histories and intersectionalism. Nubia has been a keynote presenter at numerous venues including the Houses of Parliament and the National Portrait Gallery, and has been a consultant and presenter for television programmes including BBC Two's *History Cold Case* and Channel 4's *London's Lost Graveyard*. He is the writer of *Blackamoores: Africans in Tudor England* (2013) and *Young Othello* (2015).

Preface

'We know what we are …'[1] 'cause we know, what we were?

Books are a writer's children – but they need to be read to grow into adults. 'Ay, there's the rub,'[2] because apathy and entrenched political positioning can affect whether and what we read. There is legitimate unease that indifference may be buoyed by the hue and cry of the chat room, and that the one that shouts the loudest and last may blind the eye of reason and drum out the senses. Bloggers have become the new prophets, and social media the new Gods: jealous Gods – that demand obsessive obeisance. Writing a book means taking a stance against the immediacy of the punch line delivered with a shout: tell your audience what they want to hear, how they want to hear it! Authors ask readers to contemplate complicated answers to difficult questions.

As a writer, one's own integrity cannot be compromised by conforming to normatives, simply because they are popular. That would be the equivalent to Nicolaus Copernicus advocating geocentrism[3] because the church and his friends told him to. In modern times, historical normatives are often underpinned by concepts of modernism. This is an idea that 'things' are getting better. Ancillary to this is a conceit that the past is somewhat strange, and the source for most of our ills such as racism and xenophobia. We are told that somewhere, at sometime in history, racist attitudes began, and that is why people have them now. In other words, our prejudices are a legacy of history. Early modern England: the Tudor and early Stuart periods are blamed for being the incubators of modern racism. It is a truism, that European and European-American thinkers from the eighteenth to the twentieth century such as: Arthur de Gobineau, Madison Grant, Karl Richard Lepsius, Samuel George Morton and Charles Gabriel Seligman used anthropology, eugenics, history and theology to validate their claims that Africans were inferior.[4] These writers imagined history. The early modern period was central in that imagination, because it contained the Renaissance: a 'look back' to Europe's classical antiquity. This flourished between the fourteenth and seventeenth centuries and resulted in a 'rebirth' of European creativity. Many European and European-American commentators claimed this metempsychosis or reincarnation was an exclusive European soiree.[5] This book challenges that notion: Africans helped shape European social ethnology and societies. In claiming this, the social history of Africans that lived in Tudor and early Stuart England is revealed. Indeed, this research has been the focus of a twenty-five year sojourn.

By contesting the automatic othering of Africans in the early modern period, a stand is made against long-held narratives on early modern societies contained in post-colonial theories. These conventions have created a mis-memory that Africans had no place in history as protagonists. And that during the early modern period African enslavement defined their impotence and objectification, and is the only major reference point required for any historical investigation. The inference is that the systematic enslavement of African people practised during Georgian and Victorian times can be back-dated to the early modern period, and that there is an unbroken line of English domination of these activities that started with John Hawkins in 1567 and ended in

1807 with its abolition.[6] Often attached to this is a conceit that Africans have not been present in England or the rest of Europe for very long. This latter idea is often contextualised by a suggestion that an African presence in Europe is a modern 'problem' propagated by a failed immigration system. Or that British liberalism and/or imperialism is to blame. So, the only historical methodologies needed to explain the 'Black presence' are tools created by historians of the colonial and post-colonial periods. The result is a narrative caught in a post-colonial praxis. It is a praxis that allows no space for a distinction between modern, systemic, scientific racism and the expressions of early modern indifference and prejudice. It is not a helpful approach. And leaves a panorama in which the African contribution to English, vis-à-vis human history, is veiled. This book pierces that veil, and gives us an impression of African thought present in early modern England. This book is intended to stimulate debates on English identity and how society saw ethnicity, theology and race.[7] Some readers may suffer an emotional reaction. After all, there are still people who are aggrieved with Copernicus: no jittery step forward was ever achieved without disputation and opposition.

Onyeka Nubia, 2018

Note on the Text

The original and irregular spelling contained in early modern books, manuscripts and so on have been maintained, except where the meaning would be lost by doing so. The references in this book to *Blackamoores* are from the revised edition published in 2014. In this book, the words that refer to the 'Proclamation' drafted in 1601 and 'Letters' dated 11 and 18 July 1596 of the same year begin with a capital letter. These words are written in this way because they refer to documents that are distinguished from other proclamations and letters.[1] The term 'trans-Atlantic' is hyphenated and this is congruent with others used in this book such as 'trans-Indian,' 'trans-Pacific,' etc. 'Black' begins with a capital letter when it relates to 'Black Studies'[2] or 'Black people' but not in general. The terms 'African-centred' and 'African-American' are hyphenated because this is the usual way they are written by historians within the field. The term 'post-colonial' is hyphenated rather than written as 'postcolonial' as the historian Imtiaz Habib does.[3] This is similar to the way the phrase 'pre-colonialism' is used. The latter term is being pioneered here to describe the author's methodologies and narratives. Finally, the word 'contemporary' refers to the period in question (1485–1660s circa) and not for example to modern historians.[4]

Introduction

Do we imagine English history as a book with white pages and
no black letters in?[1]

This book had its genesis in my research started over twenty-
five years ago. Only a small part of that work on the presence,
status and origins of Africans in early modern England has
ever been published. Until this moment, it has not been possible to reveal the evidence contained here. Most of the evidence
in this book originates from records written by English people
and other Europeans at the time (primary records). We will
explore the nature of ethnicity in early modern English society
and the social ethnology of the Africans that lived there. The
term African is used here to describe people who have a direct
connection to the continent of Africa and other people who are
of African descent that within the common vernacular may be
called 'Black.' This use of the term African is in fact a standard
approach used by many historians including those influenced
by African-centred historiography and others, who are looking
to set aside definitions that have their root in post-colonial discourses. The ontology (ways of reasoning) and the semantics
of etymology (understanding the meaning of words) about this
approach, are not analysed here to make the narrative accessible
to a general readership, and because many of these issues have

already been examined by the author.[2] Notwithstanding that, in this book some of the language is complex and the rationales may be controversial. But these rationales have not been reached without considerable research. Readers are invited to explore the footnotes to discover some of that research.

However, our ability to comprehend the past has been hampered by prejudice within modern academia. This is because a group of historians of African descent[3] have already questioned the automatic othering of Africans in early modern Europe, but their work has often been ignored.[4] These scholars include: J. A. Rogers, Ivan Van Sertima, Edward Scobie, Runoko Rashidi, John Archer and Duse Mohamed Ali.[5] These scholars have either directly or indirectly implied that the history of Africans in Europe did not begin with enslavement. Too often for non-academic reasons, these authors' works are excluded from mainstream audiences. Sometimes this marginalisation is justified on the basis that they wrote for independent, small or African-centred publishing houses, or their views are dismissed as being divisive or 'polemic.' Of course, books with divisive and polemic contents are already widely circulated and endorsed, often without an appropriate critique of them. So it appears this is not the reason. It seems that this marginalisation is more to do with individual and institutional negligence and/or discrimination, rather than a genuine desire to save readers from being offended.[6] Mainstream academia should have found ways to engage with the evidence that these pioneers provided, and answer the questions they posed, without simply remaining indifferent to this extensive body of work.

Of course there is an acknowledgement that some modern writers have attempted to be inclusive. Through a tradition that is sometimes called the 'Black Atlantic,'[7] academics are attempting to examine the peoples that lived around the geographical spaces such as the Atlantic Ocean. And another group of historians attempt to do something similar with peoples conterminous with the Mediterranean Sea. These researchers tend to consider an African presence as an integrated aspect of geographical historiography. Their work is often insightful and probative, but is still restricted by a post-colonial perspective that ignores evidence provided by historians of African descent.[8]

The post-colonial perspective is challenged in this book as we focus on early modern English society (1485–1660s). The author notes that sometimes the period 1485–1660s is described as being part of a larger era that included the eighteenth century. But here a different approach is offered. This is because the contention is that racism[9] in the eighteenth and later centuries was predicated on a concept which claimed a unified scientific basis. It manifested itself as a science or pseudo-sciences, laws and policies that justified Africans being removed from the 'family of mankind.'[10]

There is a distinction between those kinds of philosophies predicated in that way, and the expressions of early modern prejudice, intolerance, indifference or ethnic chauvinism. The word 'ethnic' as used by the author relates to matters of skin colour or pigmentation, national origins, religion and culture, etc. The author acknowledges that the word 'ethnic' has an inherent Eurocentric bias. But where the terms 'ethnicity' and 'ethnology' are used in this book, it will apply to all people without the hidden subtext of it being associated with terms such as the 'other' or 'stranger.' Whilst the use of the word ethnology refers to the wider social issues pertaining to how ethnicity was seen within early modern society. Of course there is an acknowledgement that the term 'ethnic' in the period in question was prescriptive.[11]

Nevertheless, the question is were Africans in Tudor and early Stuart society (early modern England) subject to an 'anti-African antipathy' that automatically made them into the 'other' or stranger?[12] Many historians have claimed that the early modern period was the origin for racist ideas. But here we question whether the early modern period was the source, and unmask how people in Tudor and early Stuart England actually saw difference. Inevitably that means revealing how ethnology was related to early modern theology; in particular the connection between ethnicity and the 'pathology' of the Curse of Ham.[13] Some modern commentators have claimed that ideas about the Curse were formative in the way in which Africans were perceived in early modern England; such a notion necessitates exploring matters related to theology, but from a historical perspective.

However, the author acknowledges that the reader may find this book contains a certain anti-theological tone. This may especially concern those readers who are adherents to particular religions, and who believe certain religious texts offer the authentic and/or unequivocal 'word of God.'[14] Their objective may be to understand what the word of God is and follow it. Not to attempt to contextualise or historicise it. The difference between that aim and the intention of this book are therefore obvious. Nevertheless, theologians may find this book has value. It is simply that our intentions are different. Pursuant to this intent, discussions on the origins of theological texts have been redacted, as in many ways this important work has been done by authors such as Nicholas Oyugi Odhiambo, and by historians such as: Jonathan Schorsch, Benjamin Braude, David Goldenberg and David M. Whitford.[15] The primary focus here is on answering some specific questions on how Africans were viewed in Tudor and early Stuart societies. Did English people have pejorative views about Africans? What were the views of African people towards their own complexion in early modern England?

In a similar way to theologians, historians may also be challenged by this book's narrative, as it does not utilise established historiographical conventions such as post-colonialism. The post-colonial discourse is one that examines and uses theories to critique colonialism and its consequences. These narratives focus on issues such as racism and the cultural legacies of imperialism. Historians within this field may be diverse, with some enquiring into economics, law or any other areas of 'people activity.'[16] Post-colonial methodologies and narratives are important in analysing evidence and developing arguments of the eighteenth and nineteenth centuries. However, this approach places constraints on investigating primary records in the period in question. This is because most of the continent of Africa had not fallen under European colonial rule and England at the beginning of the early modern period was not a major colonial or imperial power. Of course, Englishmen had established temporary and permanent colonies in Ireland, parts of the Americas and elsewhere. The term 'pre-colonial' is used to describe that England.[17] This pre-colonial approach encourages us to investigate Tudor and early Stuart society and the Africans that lived there, rather than use our imaginations to conjure the past.

Chapter 1 is about how we imagine early modern England. This chapter includes a conceptual analysis of how William Shakespeare has become associated with a fictional mono-ethnic English past. However, Shakespeare's works that include *Othello*, *Titus Andronicus* and the Dark Lady Sonnets are not analysed in detail, as this has been investigated elsewhere.[18] Rather readers are offered a critical perspective on how the writings of Shakespeare may be used to bolster a romantic perspective of Englishness. To counter this romance the case studies of two Africans are presented for readers to consider. One of them was a visitor to early modern England and the other was present in France. Following this the reader is invited to analyse whether English people in early modern times understood the concept of 'race,' and how English identity was shaped at that time.

The second chapter is concerned with whether the momentous events that took place between 1485 and the 1660s changed the way that Africans were seen (social ethnology) in England. Readers are asked to follow the complex interconnected local, national and international changes that occurred. At the beginning of the fifteenth century, England was a small country on the fringe of international politics. But by the middle of the seventeenth century it had become a belligerent and adventuring nation that contested its marginal positioning. Pursuant to this, an analysis is made on whether Englishmen's mercantile aggression altered the status of Africans that lived in England. This analysis is important as some modern historians discuss African ethnology through the history of enslavement. That approach is questioned in this book. Other arguments relate to the similarities and differences between how we view Africans and women in early modern England.

In the third chapter the author investigates whether the early modern period was the source for modern racism. Some historians and political commentators infer that 'England has always been racist' and others argue that there was a 'start' time when racism began. Nevertheless most believe that early modern England was a more 'racist' society than modern Britain is. This chapter explores these notions initially by examining what early modern Bibles said about Africans and ethnicity. Ideas about the Curse of Ham are investigated in some detail, to see whether they were used to explain the blackness of the Africans that lived in England. Englishmen such as George Best, Meredith Hanmer and Hugh Broughton did write about Africans being cursed and their views are anatomised and contextualised here. A new perspective is unearthed about what they wrote, and why they wrote it. There is also an evaluation of whether Best, Hanmer and the others held views that were indicative of their countrymen and women.

The fourth chapter contains an exposition of other views that people had about Africans in early modern society. These views are rarely examined and yet those that wrote and spoke them were powerful and influential people in that society. It includes the commentaries on ethnicity by people such as the Tudor politicians Thomas More and Francis Bacon, the female theologian Juliana Berners, the early modern thinker Thomas Browne as well as the Anglo-Irish academic Robert Boyle. In addition other scholars and writers of the time are discussed, that either questioned the automatic othering of Africans and/or extolled the virtue of Africans and their blackness. From this we get a new perspective on early modern ethnology, theology and national identity.

Chapter 5 includes an exploration of how Africans lived in early modern English society and whether they formed part of local communities there, or whether they were outsiders and strangers. In this chapter our perceptions of Africans in England at this time are set aside as we seek to understand pre-colonial perspectives on ethnology. The ideas of strangeness, community and family are discussed through the writings of Mary Wroth and Edward Herbert, but most importantly through the lives of Africans that lived in early modern England – such as: Maria Mandula, Mary Fillis of Morisco, Dederi Joaquah, Henrie Anthonie Jetto and John Ackame, as well as the community that lived in Lincoln's Inn Fields in 1645 that was derogatorily scandalised in newspaper reports.

In the final chapter the author explores some of the lives and experiences of Africans in early modern England. These lives and experiences indicate a great deal about ethnology in early modern societies and how Africans fashioned their own identity, by interpreting their own blackness. The author proposes that these Africans' perspectives also influenced how English people saw whiteness. Throughout this book, readers are encouraged to question romantic fantasies of Englishness. And we begin this exploration through how and why that fantasy exists.

ONE | Imagining Tudor England

With a hey, and a ho, and a hey hey-nonino.[1]

Telling Tales

Tales of Tudor England connected to William Shakespeare's oeuvre dominate our perceptions of early modern society (1485–1660s). And Shakespeare's written works can provide reference points for our understanding of this period, and be a useful tool to introduce a modern audience to English mores of the time. The famous 'hey-nonino' from Shakespeare's *As You Like It* contains idiomatic phrases strongly associated with Tudor society. These lines may be quoted in the context of discussions on the play *As You Like It*, to illustrate the bawdy language or the humour of early modern England. However, sometimes people use Shakespeare's writings in an unhelpful way, so that the words of *As You Like It* offer a romantic impression that Tudor England was 'little England,'[2] where people only spoke 'strange' sounding words in whimsical alliteration.

'This England'[3] was an imaginary place, but picturesquely portrayed in the hugely popular film *Shakespeare in Love*. It was a place where the people's prime concerns seemed to have been courtly love, speaking poetry in rhyme and courtly romance under the gaze of the queen. The people in 'this other Eden'[4] are often depicted as uniformly Christian, white and happy. In fact, so Christian, so white and so happy that to have Africans as their neighbours would seem to be a figment of political correctness.[5] This idea of Tudor society is within the foreground and background of films and television series such as *The Private Life of Henry VIII, A Man for All Seasons, Ann of the Thousand Days, Elizabeth R, Gunpowder Treason and Plot, Elizabeth, Elizabeth: The Golden Age, The Tudors* and so on.[6] Unfortunately, these programmes leave us with an impression of a mono-ethnic early modern society.

The 'hey-nonino' of *As You Like It* may offer a whimsically quaint perspective of 'little England,' but another speech that is often referred to as 'This England' can have its meaning transmogrified so it becomes the ingredient in a more robust form of exclusive nationalism. This speech originated from the play *Richard II* where John of Gaunt described England as:

> This royal throne of kings, this scepter'd isle,
> This earth of majesty, this seat of Mars,
> This other Eden, demi-paradise,
> This fortress built by Nature for herself
> Against infection and the hand of war,
> This happy breed of men, this little world,
> This precious stone set in the silver sea,
> ...
> Against the envy of less happier lands,
> This blessed plot, this earth, this realm, this England,
> This nurse, this teeming womb of royal kings,
> Fear'd by their breed and famous by their birth,
> Renowned for their deeds as far from home,
> ...
> That England, that was wont to conquer others,
> Hath made a shameful conquest of itself.
> Ah, would the scandal vanish with my life,
> How happy then were my ensuing death![7]

The 'This England' oration by John of Gaunt was a look back to another, earlier, 'happier' time, *before* Shakespeare's lifetime, when the victories against France by Gaunt's father Edward III, and his son the Black Prince, were remembered. The 'This England' speech, along with that of King Henry V's 'St Crispin's Day' and the lines 'We few, we happy few, we band of brothers' etc., can gourmandise our imagination of ethnicity: no 'Black Tudors' could live in 'This England!'[8] As the historian Gretchen Holbrook Gerzina ironically comments, 'there were no black people in England before 1945.'[9] Such ideas arise from juxtaposing Shakespeare's speeches out of context. Shakespeare never wrote 'This England' or 'St Crispin's Day' to reveal the ethnic composition of his society. These speeches were written by Shakespeare as a lament to his past.[10]

The plays of Shakespeare can be conflated into an illusion that Tudor England was mono-ethnically white and that therefore the rest of early modern society was too. This idea may then be reinforced by a cursory reading of Shakespeare's history plays that are missing direct references to Africans living in England.[11] A twenty-first-century post-colonial perspective may infer that any Africans that lived in England during this period must have been so exotically strange that Shakespeare would have felt compelled to explicitly describe or refer to them. Therefore because he did not, they were not. There is an inherent contradiction in such an idea, but the important point is that Shakespeare's plays were not written to show his audience, and certainly not us, a narrative on race and ethnicity.[12]

Of course, in early modern England, people saw difference. And some of those differences were somatic, but we should try to set aside a presumption framed through a post-colonial praxis, that 'colour' would be the most obvious and noteworthy of those differences. In England during this period, the pseudo-science of race, how we now understand it, did not exist. This 'science' was not developed until the end of the seventeenth century – with theories of biological determinism in the eighteenth and nineteenth centuries at the height of European colonialism and imperialism. In early modern England, the books on social Darwinism, 'Whiteman's Burden,' 'Manifest Destiny,'[13] phrenology and cephalometry,[14] had not yet been authored. And the study of physiognomy, even though some early modernists practised it, had not yet morphed into a science.[15]

So in reading Shakespeare through a historiographical lens, we ought to remember that he was a playwright writing to entertain his early modern audiences, even more than he attempted to educate them.[16] Shakespeare was also an astute businessman, who as a 'magpie' rewrote for commercial and political reasons the works of other earlier playwrights such as Christopher Marlowe and authors such as William Painter.[17] To expect in those circumstances, that Shakespeare would objectively provide the answers to questions of diversity in Tudor society would be misplaced. It would be as naïve as believing the films of Quentin Tarantino encapsulate the lives of African-Americans in 1990s America. Certainly films such as *Pulp Fiction*, *Reservoir Dogs* and *True Romance* offer a 'perspective' on race relations in America. But if we looked at Tarantino's films alone, we would end up with a very warped idea of Black America.[18] For a more balanced view we would need to include the artistic opposition to Tarantino's filmography, such as that offered by Spike Lee, John Singleton, the Hughes Brothers and so on.[19] These African-American filmmakers all have authentically different perspectives on the lives of African-Americans in 1990s America.

In a similar manner, to understand Africans in early modern England we need to know the history of the times in which Shakespeare wrote, with qualitative investigations of other primary evidence. This is subsumed in parishes, church reports, early chancery proceedings, books, letters, etc. Only when we have examined and investigated this evidence would we have a broader perspective on early modern society. This would appear to be an admonition we could apply to the study of any historical period. We also need to investigate other contemporary renaissance writers, playwrights, poets etc.,[20] and writers of African descent in early modern Europe. All of this would render us with a wider understanding of the lives of Africans that lived in England. Of course, to find these African writers is extremely difficult, but research has provided us with indications not only of their existence but also their ideas. It soon becomes apparent that if we used Shakespeare to introduce ethnicity in early modern England – we certainly cannot use him to conclude it.

Understanding English Ethnicity

In early modern England, the fears that English people had regarding ethnicity were rooted in the historical relationships they had with their geographical neighbours, especially those in Wales, Scotland, Ireland, France and Spain,[21] and with religious 'others' such as Catholics or Protestants depending on which religion was orthodoxy. These religious and ancient rivalries were at the forefront of ethnic politics in England.[22] English people vocalised in writing and occasionally in laws their fears of the enemy without (the foreigners, be they Welsh etc.) and the enemy within (the religious and 'ethnic' others).[23] Of course, Africans in early modern England could become an enemy by falling into one of the categories just mentioned, in other words by being a member of the 'wrong' class of persons, a foreign spy, or a member of the 'wrong' religion. There are two Africans that illustrate this. These two men appear in the written accounts of Englishmen towards the end of the Tudor period. In those accounts we see glimpses of Africans' voices paraphrased or hidden in the subtext of these English writers' words. Both Africans provide an introduction into how their ethnicity was seen in early modern England, as their blackness was not stigmatised. It was their connections and affiliations that made them 'persons of interest' to English authorities. The first was an African raconteur (teller of tales) described in Tudor records as the 'Negro with a cut on his face.' The second was enigmatically called 'Francis Rumbolo.'

The African Raconteur

The African raconteur: the 'Negro with a cut on his face' appeared in correspondence dated 20 August 1586 by the English politician Edward Stafford (1535–1603). This letter was written to the Principal Secretary of State Francis Walsingham who was also responsible for matters of security and espionage.[24] Stafford's letter referred to the activities of the adventurer Francis Drake, and asked Walsingham to find out if an African that had been present in England, and 'stole away' with Drake, was involved in the debacle that took place in Nombre de Dios in Panama in 1572/3. The letter then revealed how by 1586 this same African was present in Paris (France) and under the protection of the Spanish ambassador:

> There is here [in Paris] a Negro (with a cut on his face) who (sayeth) he came with Sir Francis Drake, and stole away when he landed in England. He gives out that Drake has brought home little or nothing, and has done less, and that his taking of Cartagena, Nombre de Dios and the rest is false. But the man is never away from the Spanish ambassador, and I think is 'supposed' by him to give out these things. I would be glad to know whether any such has escaped from Sir Francis Drake (or no,) and also as much as may be known of the particular successes of his journey. I would make them blown abroad to his honour.[25]

Stafford suggested that the African 'stole away' with Drake, but he does not tell us about the African's origins or how long he stayed in England. There were other Africans strongly connected to Drake that also lived in England at that time. The Symerons accompanied the Englishman on the voyage to

Panama and included people such as Diego Negro that became Drake's 'chief conductor.'[26] Unlike the African raconteur, the Symerons' connections to Drake did not begin in England, but Central and South America. This may mean that the African raconteur became acquainted with Drake independently of the Symerons and joined the Englishman voluntarily. There is no evidence of the African being press-ganged or enslaved.[27]

What happened at Nombre de Dios was a matter of national interest. The stories that adventurers told were propaganda: used to obtain finance for future operations, win over foreign allies, recruit future crews, as well as obtain political and theological dispensation for the acts of terror they often committed. Without this positive palliate, the activities of adventurers could be curtailed by those at court that opposed them. Nombre de Dios was strategically important as a Spanish trading post and was central to Spain's colonial administration of Central America. Drake claimed that he and the privateer Guillaume de Testu robbed a silver mule train in 1572/73.[28] This train operated along an improvised trail which the Spanish used to transport gold and silver they had stolen from their colonies in the Americas. Guillaume was captured and killed as a result of these activities. This left Drake as the principal narrator of the events.[29] Drake claimed to have successfully fought against the Spanish, 'won' renown and buried the swag.[30] Drake's story about the treasure would be used to excite interest among Englishmen for future operations.

Stafford's letter stated that the African provided an alternative narrative of the events in Panama. He wrote that the African said, 'Drake has brought home little or nothing, and has done less, and that his taking of Cartagena, Nombre de Dios and the rest is false.'[31] These seemed to be the paraphrased words of the African. And despite Stafford stating that the African was only repeating what he was 'supposed' to, Stafford was worried by his story. And indeed his narrative seemed to be gaining some sort of international credibility, as he had found an audience in Paris and was protected by the Spanish ambassador. Moreover, Stafford's concerns were emphasised by his request to Walsingham to know more about Drake's version of events. Stafford also seemed to imply that he did not have sufficient knowledge to publicly challenge the African's story. Stafford knew the African's words could jeopardise future operations.

The African raconteur's ethnicity could lend credibility to a European audience that wanted to hear stories about Central America from a person of African descent that may have claimed association with those lands.[32] However, Stafford did not view the African's colour or complexion as inherently dangerous. It was his apparent capacities, knowledge, experience and affiliations with the Spanish ambassador that made him so. It is clear the entire matter was not trivial, but one of official concern. We will return to matters stirred by this African raconteur later, but let us first discuss another 'black man,' whose activities underlined issues regarding ethnicity. The name of this man was Francis Rumbolo and we find him in London, England, in 1595.

The Enigmatic Francis Rumbolo

Rumbolo appeared in a letter by Richard Carmarthen ('Carmarden' 1536–1603) to Robert Cecil. The letter was dated 6 September 1595. By 1595, Carmarthen was Surveyor of Customs for the City of London and a member of the Company of Merchant Taylors. He was a Protestant activist and personally paid for the *Great Bible* to be printed and distributed in Rouen (France) during the latter end of the sixteenth century.[33] In his role, Carmarthen frequently corresponded with Cecil regarding the smuggling of foreign books (including Bibles) into England. His role involved apprehending smugglers, preventing the export of goods from London ports and impounding foreign cargo that arrived in London. In the exercise of his office he was subject to accusations of corruption and nepotism.[34] Carmarthen had an important role, but his correspondent Cecil was one of the most powerful men in England. He was Secretary of State and Lord High Treasurer and by 1595, because of the death of Francis Walsingham, he had authority over matters related to internal and external security as well as espionage and smuggling.[35]

The letter by Carmarthen stated:

the ... [plan] was to lay [in] wait for a suspected person coming from Spain, [to London] *whose physiognomy and shape of body* was in the said paper perfectly described ... It fell out yesterday ... there *came such a man* to sue for four barrels of starch seized by two of the waiters ... he was brought to the Queen's storehouse, and another with him, both Englishmen. [When] ... the writer saw the man, he remembered Burghley's note and reasoned with him: *who confessed* he came from the *southwards* where he had been *six years* in trade ... into the Low Countries, and having *made money* thereby bought the starch there, not knowing but that he might lawfully bring it hither ... He said he had *served some time in the Low Countries*, under what captain the writer remembereth not ... the *black man*, who resembles the *described* [suspected] *person*, [from Spain] ... and many noted him, and the more that he accompanied only with one Forman, an upholsterer, *a known papist* ... They mean to send both men to Cecil for examination ... *The black man* nameth himself Francis Rumbolo, which is counterfeit A copy of the lord Admiral's note is enclosed. – London, 6 September 1595. (Emphasis added.)

According to Carmarthen's letter, Rumbolo was a 'suspected person' and a smuggler who came from Spain. Certainly his name was not English but was common to people from the region of Calabria at the southernmost tip of what is now Italy.[36] By the sixteenth century, this portion of Italy was part of Spain and had been controlled by the Kings of Aragon since 1442. So it is possible that Rumbolo's name was not 'counterfeit' as Carmarthen asserted, but actually pertained to this 'black man's' ethnic roots. In 1595, Spain was at war with England and remained so until 1604. As a Spanish merchant Rumbolo would have been considered suspicious no matter what colour he was. And that may be why Rumbolo had attempted to explain away the 'dangerous' aspects of his ethnicity, by describing his origins with the term 'southwards.' Of course Spain and Calabria are both south of England, but that term was sufficiently ambiguous enough to include other places 'beyonde Spain,' such as North Africa and Asia Minor.[37] The inference being that if he came from anywhere other than Spain, this would have made him less dangerous to the English authorities. Spanish merchants, artisans and professionals ordinarily resident in England during this time were often watched.[38] So, strikingly, the most threatening aspect of this man's ethnicity was his Spanish connections and not his blackness.

In Carmarthen's letter he referred to Rumbolo as a 'black man' twice. In Tudor England this sort of phrase tended to refer to people of African descent, although it was sufficiently wide enough to be an adjective and describe a person of European origin that had a 'darker' complexion. But Carmarthen seemed to use the phrase as a noun: 'a black man.' And the style of the language implied that Rumbolo was a 'black man' from the 'southwards' – and not simply a darker-skinned European from Spain. The fact that Rumbolo had been expected, 'noted,' and his *physiognomy and shape of body* were distinctive implied that his blackness was more than just a suntan. However, Rumbolo's blackness was not so remarkable that it made him an oddity in Tudor society, because of course there were many other Africans that lived there. This may be why Carmarthen used the phrase *physiognomy and shape of body* as this inferred there were other aspects of Rumbolo's appearance that had been 'noted' by Lord Burghley (Cecil's father) in his letter. It was the combination of these attributes that showed he was the 'suspect' they sought. Using a modern term of reference, simply because Rumbolo was Black did not mean 'he fitted the description,' but it did mean that he had the potential to. By contrast some modern commentators claim that through racial profiling suspects are now found guilty simply because 'they are Black.'[39]

Returning to Rumbolo, what crime had he done? It appeared that he was suspected of being part of a group involved in illegal trade between Spain and England. During the Anglo-Spanish War it was illegal to trade with Spain. However, merchants from both countries did precisely that, including exchanging goods and services, people smuggling and trafficking.[40] Carmarthen was aware that these activities took place and his actual function was to monitor and regulate this trade with fines and taxes as well as to recruit foreign merchants as spies.

The goods that Rumbolo was accused of trading were barrels of starch. In the letter Rumbolo was reported as stating he obtained them from the 'Low Countries' (Netherlands, Belgium and Luxembourg) and not Spain. England still legally traded with these countries. Rumbolo seemed to understand the dilemma he was in, and that may be why he suggested that his trade was with those countries and not Spain. This notion was supported by other evidence. Starch was used in the textile industry as a stiffener for clothing and by upholsterers. And that may be why Rumbolo was in the company of an 'upholsterer.' Sometimes this starch was obtained from wheat. But if Rumbolo was from the 'southwards' he may have been in possession of starch made from potatoes or cassava. Potatoes and cassava as tube and root crops became popular in regions of Central and South America, with cassava later being introduced into parts of West and North Africa. The powder made from potatoes and cassava is richer in starch than that made from wheat.[41] If Rumbolo had pioneered the importation of this kind of starch into northern European countries, this would have supported his claim that he had *made money* by that trade in the 'Low Countries,' and he now sought to bring it to England.

However, it was also Rumbolo's connection to this upholsterer (unnamed) – a *'known papist'* – that made him a 'suspected person.' Rumbolo may have tried to set aside any accusation of a Catholic conspiracy by his claim that he had '*served some time in the Low Countries*,' under 'a Captain,' probably as a soldier rather than at sea. This could have been in the bloody conflicts where, for more than eighty years, the Netherlands and Belgium fought together against Catholic Spain.[42] If Rumbolo had been so employed, then as a veteran he would have been rightly offended by an accusation of being involved in a Catholic conspiracy, even if he was in the company of a '*known papist*.' We do not know what the nature of the 'examination' was between Cecil and Rumbolo, nor do we have a record of what happened. In fact, there is a lot about Rumbolo and the African raconteur that we do not know. But we do have an introduction into early modern ethnology. In both circumstances, English writers referred to Rumbolo and the African raconteur's ethnicity by terms such as 'black' and 'Negro.'[43] But these terms did not label them as enemies of the state. That enemy was Spain.

So Englishmen noted the presence of Africans connected to their European rivals. But they feared their European neighbours more than they feared the Africans. At the beginning of the Tudor period the principle objects of this animosity were England's nearest neighbours: Wales and Scotland. Indeed, this anxiety had a logical origin as Africans never ruled England, but Welshmen and Scotsmen did, in the form of the Tudors and the Stuarts, respectively. We now turn our attention to the Tudors that dominated England in the first half of the early modern period, and what their hegemony shows us about ethnicity in early modern society and African ethnology.

Exploring Early Modern Ethnicity: 'Welsh' Kings and English Subjects

The Tudors ruled England through the first half of the early modern period. Their interactions with English nobility reveal how ethnicity was seen in early modern society and why Africans were not the perpetual or automatic enemy. The Tudors originated from a Welsh family called Tudur and their ancestor Ednyfed Fychan established the dynasty. They were Welsh warriors that strategically allied themselves by shifting their allegiances between Norman, English and Welsh kings that included Edward III, Henry V, Llewellyn and Owain Glendower. Through success in war, and negotiated marriages from the thirteenth to the fifteenth centuries, they manoeuvred their way up the feudal pyramid, until Owen Tudor (Owain ap Maredudd ap Tudur) a servant/ soldier transformed himself into a royal courtier. He became the 'Clerk of her Wardrobe':[44] the 'her' in question, was the French Princess Catherine de Valois. She had become Queen of England through her late marriage to Henry V (deceased 1422). As the fifteenth-century *Chronicle of London* stated, 'Oweyn [Tudor] hadde prevyly [privately] wedded the quene Katerine, and hadde iij or iiijor children be here.' The word 'prevyly' suggests that the marriage (1428/29 circa) was quietly arranged without the pomp and circumstance of a marriage of state.[45] For tangible reasons, there was a section of English nobility that was afraid of 'quene Katerine's' marriage. Certainly an idea existed that the queen should have avoided remarriage, and remained a widow dowager bound to King Henry V's memory.[46] There were also rumours that she was pregnant at the time of her betrothal to Owen Tudor, and that her cousin Edmund Beaufort was the father of Edmund Tudor. That may explain the uncertainty in the number of children quoted in the *Chronicle of London*'s account.[47]

As a result of these rumours, stories abounded that sexualised and mythologised Katherine, and provided a peculiar voyeuristic fascination for noblemen throughout the country. For example the English writer Samuel Pepys boasted that he had 'kissed a queen' when in a necrophilic embrace he osculated her corpse.[48] There were legitimate concerns too that the queen's new husband Owen Tudor and their Welsh/French children saw themselves as future rulers of England. The union of the French queen with a Welshman had to be morganatic.[49] The English-born Plantagenets from the paternal line of Edward III held power. It is for these reasons that Owen Tudor's son Edmund Tudor did not press his claim; but his ambition led him to marry another member of the Beaufort family: Margaret Beaufort. She was also a direct descendant of Edward III. Margaret and Edmund's child Henry Richmond (Henry VII) would claim the English throne from his mother's side. But in almost all senses he was from a lesser branch of nobility and the mutilation of Richard III's body at Bosworth Field would not alter that.[50]

The nobility of England during the early Tudor period were rightly obsessed with the matters outlined above because they related to ethnicity, sovereignty and the governance of the state. Ordinary people in Tudor society also kept an eye on events as it determined who ruled them. Many people believed that the king's body represented the body politic of the state, and through the divine right of kings he was God's emissary on earth representing the wealth, health and face of the nation.[51] It is ironic that the Tudor family that had purloined the English throne by killing a king and stealing his crown would be ardent adherents of the divine right of kingship.[52] In this context, Africans that lived in early modern England did not pose an urgent problem that needed to be solved by Englishmen, simply because they were Africans. However, the intrigues between powerful courtiers at the royal court did. Henry VII made a conscientious decision to control these intrigues, whilst legitimising his authority, by contracting suitable marriages for his sons. At the dawn of the Tudor period, Kings and Queens of England zealously pursued closer relations with Iberia as they sought to thwart their English, Welsh and Scottish rivals. The effect of this was to usher in closer relationships between the Tudors and the Crowns of Aragon, Castile and the Habsburgs.

Africans Are Closer Than You Think

As we move away from the romance of Tudor England, matters that may have been obscured become important. Some of these matters are integral to our understanding of how it was plausible that Rumbolo could come from Iberia to England, and why other Africans did. Answers lay in the history of Iberia. The two largest nations in Iberia were Spain and Portugal. But they were fashioned by Christian rulers from smaller nations and principalities such as Aragon, Asturias and Castile.[53] Spain and Portugal were forged as a result of the assimilation of, and war against, various independent kingdoms and peoples that existed in the region. Some of this dis-consanguinity arose because of the presence and influence of Africans in southern Europe. 'Africa is closer than you think.' In fact it is only 12–14 kilometres from the Iberian coastline.[54] This geographical proximity reveals what should be an axiomatic truism: that inter-ethnic exchanges between the continent of Africa and Iberia are/were inevitable. Thus, as England developed connections to Spain and Portugal, so England got closer to 'these Moores beyonde Spain.'[55] These connections led to Iberian Africans (Moors) communing in English villages and towns. By investigating the Iberian connections we draw Africans closer to 'little England.'

These investigations reveal that Africans in Iberia were not just the hoi polloi (the common people);[56] they once ruled in their own right. Research also shows that despite these Africans being joined by other peoples of colour from Arabia and Asia, the initial conquering population owed their origins to an invasion in 711 by Tariq Ibn Ziyad al Zanata (after whom the rock of Gibraltar 'Jebel Tariq' is named). He landed on the Iberian Peninsula with 6,000–7,000 soldiers 'most of whom were Moorish Africans'[57] – 'Black of complexion.'[58] Of course, this was not the first, or the last, African army to invade Europe through Iberia as Tariq followed Hannibal.[59] Nevertheless, the effects of Tariq's conquest lasted longer than Hannibal's did. For almost a thousand years, Moorish incursions meant that Africans jostled with their white counterparts for the mastery of southern Europe. As a military force Moorish armies even ventured as far north as Picardy[60] and Normandy in modern day France. There they founded semi-autonomous communities within European nations.

In southern Europe and Iberia in particular, the opposition to Moorish rule began almost as soon as Tariq set foot on Iberian soil. The Reconquista or Reconquista Crista (Portuguese), as it had been called, started in 722, when Pelagius of Asturias defeated a Moorish army at the Battle of Covadonga. Asturias became the heart of resistance against Moorish rulership in Iberia. In France, the Moors had military losses on several major occasions, the first at Pamplona (now Navarre) in 722[61] and again at the Battle of Tours in 732, the latter was orchestrated by the legendary Roland and Charles Martel the Hammer.[62] The last defeat was immortalised in the *Song of Roland*[63] and appeared to have been a crushing rebuff, of the kind that dissuaded further large-scale military expeditions into France by Moorish armies. However, the Kingdom of Septimania and later Occitania, which included Aquitaine in southern France, remained under Moorish authority,[64] as did the Kingdom of Gallica and other nominally Frankish kingdoms until the eighth century, as Moorish kings still ruled parts of France and most of Iberia until 768. This was despite internal disputes, inter-ethnic rivalries between different non-Christian rulers and further martial conquests under the Almoravids and others, in the eleventh, twelfth and thirteenth centuries. In Iberia, the last independent Moorish kingdoms survived until 1492. As late as the seventeenth century some of these regions in Spain, Portugal and France were still thought of as part of a wider Moorish territory and were referred to by the historian Caelius Augustinus Curio from Basel (Italy) and English writers such as Ben Jonson as the 'land of the blacks,' or 'Swart [Black],' because of the colour of their people.[65]

Africans remained in Spain as they remained in France, although we have little evidence of them coming to early modern England by the latter route. Nevertheless, Africans were present in France in isolated pockets that retained their Moorish sovereignty until they were assimilated into the rest of European nobility and lost their 'Morisco tint.'[66] The 'new European nobility' would inherit from them certain customs, emblems, traditions and practices in culture, language, music, warfare, writing and dance, including the many types of Moorish and Morseca dances[67] known throughout Europe. And perhaps a version of the iambic pentameter[68] that revolutionised the development of the English language.[69]

Some Africans in early modern England had direct links to Iberia, and Spanish/Portuguese nobility; for others it was more indirect. The Spanish nobility included Katherine of Aragon, Mary I and Philip II, who through marriage and descent ruled in England. Henry VII had ushered in this ingress through the matrimony of his sons Arthur and Henry VIII to Katherine – her parents were King Ferdinand of Aragon and Asturias and Queen Isabella of Castile. Katherine, through her parents, was also a direct descendant of Edward III, meaning that she helped to legitimise Henry VII's line. Katherine's daughter with Henry VIII was Mary I, and Mary was therefore also part of this Spanish diaspora.

The Tudors may have initially ruled as a lesser branch of English nobility, but through these complex connections, they were now morganatically part of the most powerful family in Europe. All of these facts made England in certain ways a territory of a greater Spain, emphasised by the fact that Mary I married Philip II and he was crowned King of England.[70] It seems likely that if Philip II had conceived a child with Mary the history of England would have been very different. In Philip's mind he may still have viewed himself as King of England when Elizabeth I came to the throne in 1558.[71] In other words, 'the Spaniard' may have felt that he had been cheated out of the crown by Elizabeth. This idea offers a radically different perspective on the reasons for the Spanish Armada (1588). It was an attempt by the Spanish King to win 'his crown' back from what he considered an illegitimate, heretical usurper.[72]

This history is important for our understanding of why Africans such as Rumbolo and the African raconteur with their connections to Spain could be considered a threat by English authorities. Of course, not every African that came from or via Iberia was dangerous. These Africans travelled along the same paths that Spanish and Portuguese monarchs would traverse. For example, Pero Pedro Alvarez, the 'negro e forro' (meaning the 'Black [African] that came from abroad'), came to England in 1490 from Iberia, and there he negotiated his own manumission from King Henry VII of England on 13 March 1490. This manumission was later upheld by the King of Portugal John II.[73] Pedro's arrival in England was over a decade before Katherine of Aragon set foot on English soil. Pedro was not the only person of colour in King John II's entourage, as, in the 1530s, he and his wife Catherine of Austria had a group of twenty-five 'escravos' that included 'Amerindians' as well as Africans.[74] Portuguese royalty present in England also sometimes had African retainers that lived with them. For example, Katherin 'the negar' was buried on 24 August 1594 at St Stephen's Church, Coleman Street, London. This Katherin was 'dwelling with the prince of Portingal' in London, and she died just one year before he did in 1595. The 'prince of Portingal' in question was Antonio Prior of Crato (grandson of the Portuguese King Manuel I). Despite English assistance he had tried unsuccessfully to capture the Portuguese throne from the Spanish.[75]

The Tudor monarchs Katherine, Mary 1 and Philip II that ruled England had direct connections to the peoples and history outlined above, and this may explain why they also often had Africans living in their English households or within their service. These connections between Iberian nobility and Africans may also illume why Spanish royalty inherited signs and symbols associated with the Moors and why these emblems and motifs became part of English heraldry. This is precisely what happened with the pomegranate. The pomegranate was a fruit/vegetable strongly associated with the Moors of Spain, Granada (Andalucía).[76] At their height the Moorish kingdoms included

Granada, Castile, Leon, Catalonia, Septimania and Aragon, with another province referred to as 'Swarth Lusitania' (a region of Portugal in 1605).[77] Granada was known as the 'last seed of the pomegranate.' The pomegranate was appropriated as a symbol by Katherine's branch of the Tudor family. This was so much the case that when Anne Boleyn became queen and displaced her, her symbol was a dove or falcon pecking at a pomegranate.[78]

Notwithstanding this history, Tudor monarchs did not inherit an ethnology that was automatically anti-African and neither did ordinary English people. But during the same period Spain and Portugal developed a perspective on chromatics (the science of colours) that did include anti-Black symbology. Since Spain was influencing customs, manners and politics in Tudor society it was possible that some of the pejorative ideas we find present in Tudor and early Stuart England arose from Iberian sources.

The thousand years of struggle[79] between the Moors in Iberia and white Christian rulers resulted in the development of Spanish ethno-politics that infected every strata of Iberian society. A tradition emerged that the Moors were the natural enemies of the white man, Christianity and by default God.[80] This tradition could configure the blackness of the Moors beyond somatic colour difference into a symbolic representation of evil. Africans could then become a folklore enemy, typified by their representation in the *Song of Roland* (eleventh century) where they were allies of the Devil. The fact they were 'painted Black'[81] would be an indication of their affinity to evil, as the English writer John Milton's *Paradise Lost* (1667) ascribed. Milton wrote about how the Moorish kingdoms in Iberia were in league with Satan (Lucifer). By contrast, Milton ascribed the white Christian kingdoms of Spain as serving Christ. Such traditions continue today, in the framing and referencing of modern mythology from C. S. Lewis to J. R. R. Tolkien. In Tolkien, the Dark Lord Sauron (who was essentially an archetype for the Devil) had marshalled all kinds of people of colour including Easterlings, Southrons and men 'out of Far Harad black men like half-trolls, with white eyes and red tongues.'[82] In the early modern period some Englishmen had also been influenced by this sort of ethnic chauvinism.

However, in early modern England and the rest of Europe this anti-African antipathy should not be overstated. For example, in Iberia, even after 1492, Africans persisted at various levels in that society, as they did in other parts of Europe as a significant and visible population. Africans were not only an integral element of Iberian society during the early modern period, but they were also among the foremost 'Mudéjar'[83] artisans, merchants, navigators, pioneers, soldiers, craftsmen and so on.[84]

There were positive as well as negative ideas about the colour of Africans in early modern European societies. Even when Ferdinand and Isabella in 1478 instituted the Spanish Inquisition[85] and Charles V in 1516 the system of 'blue blood inheritance.'[86] Moreover, after the Moorish revolt of 1568 that saw many Moors extricated, others remained and flourished throughout the rule of the Habsburgs. For example Benedict the Aethiops (Moor) (1526–1589) – who was born in Messina, Sicily, and died in Palermo (also in Sicily) – became Master of the Novices[87] at Palermo, and was respected within the church there to such an extent that he was later beatified.[88]

For many Iberian Moors it was not until Philip III signed an edict on 4 April 1609 that they were condemned as enemies of the state. On 11 September of the same year, the edict was implemented. Three hundred thousand Moors were expelled from Iberia between 1609 and 1614.[89] It should be noted that some of the earlier expulsions had not been as 'successful' as some historians have speculated, as Moorish people often found ways to secretly return to Iberia.[90] The 1609 persecutions were different, and turned Moorish people into exiles. Jewish and religious non-conformists, including Protestants, were also expelled. Consequently, by the 1630s, the visible 'dark skinned' and non-Catholic populations of the Iberian Peninsula had been ethnically cleansed. Although some people with a Moorish lineage, who had lost their 'Morisco tint,' were converted to Catholic Christianity and remained in Spain. This was despite the purges, the Inquisition and the most obvious ravages of colour persecution. As late as 1727, there were still people who could trace their ancestry to the Moors.[91]

However, this history of the Moors in Iberia has been obscured. This is important as these Moors represented the largest concentration of Africans in early modern Europe. And some of the Africans that lived in England came from and via Spain. But during the twentieth century, fascists in Spain argued that this Moorish or 'gypsy genetic legacy' was a stain on European heritage. This dogma provided an excuse for xenophobic persecutions from the 1930s to the 1970s.[92] A whitewashing of that history then took place. As a consequence, people of African descent were removed from Iberian history and ethnology. By default, this meant that Africans could be erased from early modern English history as well, because any person that came from Iberia that was described as a 'Moor,' 'Aethiopian,' 'Black,' 'Blackamoore,' 'Negro' or 'Niger' could be opined as not being a 'real' African. And if we do find Africans in Iberia, or early modern Europe, they are automatically labelled as temporary visitors, strangers or slaves on the fringes of those societies. By putting Africans into early modern Iberian history we are unravelling that distortion. Africans and Europeans become historic neighbours, Spain becomes the nexus of that propinquity and by association 'little England' becomes a little less little.

TWO | 'little England'

el imperio en el que nunca se pone el sol [the empire on which the sun never sets][1]

but grace was first given to a woman ... women are wise ... therefore, women are wiser then men[2]

Africans in 'little England'

We can now curb our enthusiasm for the romance of 'little England' with what the evidence tells us. Africans lived in early modern England and people such as Rumbolo and the African raconteur indicate there was also a presence in early modern Europe, especially Iberia. Some of the Africans in England were associated with royalty and noblemen. Sometimes these Africans lived in the homes of merchants in English towns. But at the beginning of the Tudor period, mercantile activities did not dominate English society. And England was an overwhelmingly agrarian society – over 94 per cent of the population were connected to the land. Only approximately 6 per cent lived in towns and half of that population (over 250,000 people) were in London. So England in that sense was 'little.'

Nevertheless, by 1660, London had become the largest urban conurbation in Europe. Many historians argue that it was the only 'actual' city in England. This is despite other towns being granted city status. These urban centres included Newcastle and Bristol, which had populations of 15,000, growing to 20,000 by the 1660s, and Norwich, with 10,000 people, which grew to 15,000 (1660s). Coventry and York had approximately 10,000 residents, which rose to 12,000. By 1600, over 9,000 people lived in Exeter. In the same city in the parish of St Mary Major, 'John a More' lived and he was recorded on the 1522 military muster roll. He was described as 'a Billman'[3] and as having 'lands within the parish,'[4] he was not an 'Alien.'[5] Other towns such as Salisbury, Ely, Canterbury, Colchester, Bury St Edmunds and Leicester had populations ranging from 2,550 to 4,000. By the 1660s, 'new' towns such as Oxford, Gloucester, Chester and Peterborough had grown in prominence; many of these places were awarded city status in 1541.[6] The total English population grew rapidly from 2 million at the beginning of the Tudor period to at least 5 million by 1660. Africans in London included people such as 'Henry a Negro' who was baptised at St Pauls, London, on 4 October 1660.[7] Africans also resided in Bristol, Bisley (Gloucestershire), Canterbury, Exeter, Norwich, Salisbury, York and many other urban centres such as Plymouth and Edinburgh (Scotland), as well as rural places that included Blean in Kent, Holt in Worcestershire, Kirkoswald in Ayrshire (Scotland), Hatherleigh in Devon and Eydon in Northamptonshire.[8]

The Africans that lived in towns and rural communities in early modern England resided with Englishmen and women. Many of them would have considered themselves members of local communities, more than subjects of a nation state.[9] Of course there were national pastimes and traditions. But a national identity was always circumscribed by local ones. Often people were born and died in the same local parish. Africans in early modern England breathed that local culture. These Africans were referred to in those records by local chroniclers as: 'Aethiopian,' 'Black,' 'Blackamoore' and 'Moor.' The word Moor meant 'Black,' and could refer to 'dark skinned' Africans, as it was interchangeable with the word 'Negro.' The term 'Blackamoore' was the most popular.[10] These Africans included men, women, children and people of dual heritage whose mothers or fathers were white. Some of these people of African descent were born in England to people that were also born in England; English records sometimes revealed several generations. Other Africans came from Iberia and countries that included Spain and Portugal. Africans also originated from West African kingdoms such as Benin and Kaabu. There were African people from North African countries that included Morocco[11] and occasionally Africans came to early modern England from eastern, central and southern Africa. By 1603–1660s, a significant number also came from or via the Caribbean islands.

Africans in early modern England therefore had diverse origins and included people such as 'Marrion S Soda of Morrisce,' buried on 12 December 1563 in Bodmin, Cornwall. The word 'Soda' was likely to be a reference to blackness with 'suda' meaning Black, and 'of Morrisce' being a reference to the place 'of Morisco,' the same place in Iberia referred to in a later record for 'Mary Fillis of Morisco.'[12] In Mary's record she was also described as 'a blackmore' when she was baptised in London, at St Botolph without Aldgate on 3 June 1597. The word 'Morisco' was also a term used in Spain to describe groups of African people that were forced to convert to Christianity – but it was not so popular in England. Where this sobriquet was used it tended to show a particularly close connection to the Iberian Moorish people. As with 'Moore Robert Tego,' he was taxed as a 'denizen' on 15 December 1567. A 'denizen' was someone that was an 'inhabitant of, or an Alien admitted into the country that now has rights.'[13] Tego was called 'a Morisco, servuant with Thomas Castlyn not denizens.' The word 'Castlyn' was probably an indication that Thomas was from Castile in Spain and Tego may have been from there too. Tego was living in the Vintry St Olave and Old Jewry Ward, London.[14]

There were other Iberian Moors living in early modern England such as the 'needle making Negro' that 'would never teach his art to none.' He lived in Cheapside, which was a thriving London suburb during the reign of Mary I (1553–1558). This African was continuously accredited by early modern English writers as being the first person to bring the art of making 'fine Spanish needles' to England.[15] He maintained a guild-like singular secrecy of his art. He was not the only person of African descent connected to the exclusive needle-making 'profession';[16] Symon Valencia, 'a Blackamoore' who lived in London and was buried in St Botolph without Aldgate on 20 August 1593, was another. He was described as a 'servant to Stephen Driffyn a nedellmaker.'[17] Stephen was still a practising needle maker twenty years later on 11 June 1613 when he was charged to keep the peace.[18] We do not know Stephen's origins, but Symon may have been from Valencia (Spain), hence his name. This was especially as the Moors in Iberia had developed the art of needle-making into a highly skilled profession.[19]

Another very interesting person of African descent that occupied a significant position in his local community was 'Henrie Anthonie Jetto.' He was 26 years old when he was baptised on 3 March 1596 in Holt, Worcestershire, and therefore was likely to have been born elsewhere. His passage to England may have been facilitated by Henry Bromley, an important man that helped restore James I to the English throne.[20] Henrie Jetto wrote his own will, which was one of the oldest authored by an African in England, and he was buried in Holt on 30 August 1627. Jetto had married a woman called Persida that outlived him – she was buried on 7 July 1640. In her will she stated that he held the rank of 'yeoman.' A yeoman held a senior position within the ranks of commonfolk and they were entitled to vote in local elections, although we do not know if he actually did. So significantly, Jetto lived in England more than a hundred years before Ignatius Sancho, a person that many historians claimed was the first person of African descent to vote in an English election.[21]

Of course, Jetto was not the only African to live in rural England. James Chappelle lived on the island of Guernsey.

He was originally a servant of Lord Hatton, until with heroic acts, diligence and determination he became a trusted person at the fort there. He retired to 'The Hatton Arms' in Gretton, Northamptonshire, where some historians claim he ran that public house from 1672.[22] He lived there until he was in his eighties.

Africans such as Chapelle, Mary Fillis, Symon, Marrion and Jetto lived in early modern England and others such as Rumbolo and the African raconteur visited or were temporary residents. The existence of these people has now been acknowledged by a very diverse range of authors.[23] This includes Madge Dresser, Imtiaz Habib, Miranda Kaufmann, Lucy McKeith, J. A. Rogers, Runoko Rashidi, Mike Sampson, Edward Scobie, Ivan Van Sertima, Marika Sherwood and Gustav Ungerer.[24] It is hoped that more historians will begin to acknowledge such a presence. However, fundamental issues remain unanswered regarding African people's impact on early modern society. This is because these Africans rarely appear in the histories written by early modern historians. Historians such as Raphael Holinshed, John Stow, Edmund Howes and William Harrison focused on the *noblis* as most of their patrons were from that class.[25] This causes a problem for anyone wishing to study the social history of Africans in early modern England because, as stated in *Blackamoores*, there is little 'evidence of a resident African group that was powerful enough to commission or sponsor an alternative vision of Tudor England that consistently included them as fully-functioning agents.'[26] In other words, there are no specialised sources that can provide us with all the evidence we need.

Africans were part of local communities and their impact was localised. So to understand this impact requires an examination of local, social and cultural histories. This evidence, however, is not automatically available as contemporary historians consistently failed to record local stories. A researcher is therefore required to be more investigative and insightful in their approach. Local anecdotes can be collected along with comments made by early modern writers as they discuss corollary matters, such as in the private letters of Thomas More that mocked the appearance and ethnicity of the people who travelled with Katherine of Aragon, and arrived with her in London on 2 April 1502.[27] Nevertheless, there is a sparsity of this evidence. This is because the discipline of local studies was not firmly established until the eighteenth century, by historians such as John Nichols and Philip Morant. Nichols did this through his pioneering work as the editor of the *Gentleman's Magazine,* and his historical accounts of local matters in Leicester;[28] Morant through his histories of the county of Essex.[29] However, in early modern England this type of local research was rare. A few writers such as John Nordern, a Tudor cartographer, did include regional tales in his book *Speculum Britanniae* (a 'Mirror of Britanniae'). But Nordern was principally interested in the flora and fauna of geographical topography rather than social history. Only occasionally did he gather stories to embellish his descriptions of the counties he travelled to.[30] Similar issues were connected to other early modern scribes such as George Carew in his *Survey of Cornwall.*[31] Rarely, did other early modern historians such as John Weever provide local history that could help us understand Africans in English society. One instance where that happened was with Weever's revelations about the prelate Meredith Hanmer (discussed later in this book)[32] – these comments helped contextualise Hanmer's diatribe about Africans contained in his sermon on 2 October 1586.[33] This of course was not Weever's intention as he was a poet and antiquarian of funeral monuments.

This paucity of local histories means that we are left with the difficulty of finding the kind of evidence that would inform us about the social history of Africans in England. But we do have another set of records compiled by priests and clerks that reveal moments from local history. These are parish records: bound registers, memorandum daybooks and miscellaneous accounts. Following the dissolution of the monasteries (1536–1541) these documents provide lists of local baptisms, burials and marriages of people in early modern England. They are important because local tax records, subsidy rolls and other local fiscal documents were not maintained with the same efficiency as those managed by the Treasury or the Chancellery.[34] Parish records therefore, for local purposes, provide useful indications of a local area's demographics. In addition, in those records the recorders sometimes made notes about local events, for example in many parishes '1601 was a plague year,' as it was in the parish of St Botolph without Aldgate, and recorders noted it.[35]

In the parishes that do have memorandum daybooks they form an important resource because they are the collected ideas and thoughts of the parish priests or clerks about their local neighbourhoods. This preoccupation with local issues illustrates there was an interest in local matters, despite the scarcity of records. Only occasionally do national matters arise such as the 'death of our sovereign Elizabeth I' in 1603.[36] It is fortunate that we have a series of comprehensively written memorandum daybooks for the ethnically diverse parish of St Botolph without Aldgate. It is these sorts of records that we can draw from for an understanding of the ethnology and social interactions of Africans in early modern England.

Locally created records that reveal people of African descent also include early chancery proceedings such as that for Maria Moriana. She was an African woman that lived in Southampton, England, in 1470. This Moriana spoke little English and was described as an 'innocent,' and was unaware of her employer's intention to sell her as if she were a slave, until those around her intervened.[37] Her employer was a man called Fillipi Cini, a merchant from Genoa (now Italy). He had been a powerful man in Southampton and managed to oust the mayor from office. However, the English courts asserted principles of common law to prevent this influential man from trying to peddle Maria, although they did not categorically rule on the question of the legality of slavery. The case is important for a number of reasons. Not least because it showed an African woman that was sufficiently a member of her community[38] that those around her felt they had a moral obligation to protect her 'innocence.' It is also important that this local community was strong enough to legally oppose Cini, despite him once being part of Southampton's establishment. Cini was not the only merchant in England thwarted in his unscrupulous activities. There were many others and the English courts were forced to adjudicate between common law freedoms and an employer's avarice. During the Tudor period, the English courts were often reluctant to circumscribe rights because of mercantile considerations. Having said that, the oft-quoted and misquoted phrase from the Cartwright case (1569) that 'England was too pure an air for a slave to breathe,' was more of an adage than legal principle, until it was turned into obiter dicta 200 years later.[39]

In early modern society, the primary records show that Africans not only interacted with ordinary local people but with men such as Cini: a 'novo homo' (new man). The novo homo negotiated their place into the Tudor elite through political chicanery, wartime exploits, subterfuge and marriage as Owen Tudor had. Many of them were some of the most well-known people of the age and included David Cecil (the grandfather of William Cecil),[40] Francis Drake, John Hawkins, Thomas Cromwell, Thomas Wolsey, John Lok and so on. Perhaps the Tudor monarchs patronised such men to protect themselves from a hereditary ruling class, many of whom may have felt that they had more authority to rule England than the Tudors did. Historic changes had favoured the creation and recruitment of such men, as by the fourteenth century there was a loosening of the manorial obligations that tied people to the land and a proliferation of commutation through free socage (land tenure) and scutage (payment made in lieu of performing manorial obligations).[41] These methods of commuting were combined with the movement of people into towns. By the fifteenth century many of the new men in those towns were Englishmen that were artisans and skilled workmen, who through acumen and patronage had made themselves independently wealthy. They were powerful enough to combine their interests together in guilds to regulate their professions and protect their livelihoods.[42] However, these independent men were still restricted by law from what trade they could exploit.

'Show Me Adam's Will' (1485-1603)

Some Africans in early modern England were connected to Englishmen of power, politicians, clergymen and adventurers. But tangible limitations were placed on the trade conducted by adventurers. Men such as Wolsey, Richard Rich, More, John Dee, the Dukes of Norfolk, Cromwell, Walsingham, the Cecils and Bacon were wary of privateers and for most of the era 'real' power rested with the politicians. Politics and strategy were the principle methods by which men maintained their positions in Tudor society. Ironically, some of these men of power had dabbled in trade before they took political office. Other Englishmen speculated on mercantile activities, in a similar way as one might now place a bet on a horse race or a card game. But Edward IV prevented John Tintam and William Fabian from being involved in trade in West Africa that involved people smuggling.[43] And William Harrison in 1577 stated, 'As for slaves and bond men we in England have none.'[44] Some historians have even suggested that Elizabeth warned, 'If any Africans should be carried away without their free consent, it would be detestable, and call down the vengeance of Heaven upon the undertaking.'[45] However, Elizabeth and people such as Robert Cecil did intermittently sponsor the privateering and piracy of

Drake, Lok and Hawkins, etc.[46] And foreign merchants resident in England were also occasionally sponsored or claimed noble patronage to carry out people trafficking. This included the Dutch slave trader Casper Van Senden, based in Lubeck in Germany, who attempted to get some Africans in England exchanged for white English prisoners as if they were slaves. His attempts failed because Africans were 'fostered and powered' in English society and too useful to their employers.[47]

Throughout the fifteenth, sixteenth and most of the seventeenth centuries, Englishmen were on the fringe of international trade and only participated in it illegally. The Treaty of Tordesillas on 7 June 1494, with the Pope's blessing, divided the known world between Spain and Portugal. Through lines of exclusive demarcation, traders from all other countries automatically became adventurers. Subsequent wranglings and wars between Portugal and Spain led to the Treaty of Zaragoza in 1529 between King John III of Portugal and Charles V. But the de facto position remained the same. Merchants that were English, Dutch, Lubeck (German), Venetian, Genoese (Italian), French, Ottoman, Mamluk (Egyptian), Moroccan, Barbary (Sale),[48] Benin (West African), Kaabu (West African), Songhai (West African), Kilwa (East African), Mogul (Indian) or Ming (Chinese)[49] now had a common objective in flouting any arbitrary rules that kept them out of international trade.[50] For example, in December 1522 the French King Francis I echoed a sentiment felt by rulers throughout the world when he said:

> The Emperor Charles V and the King of Portugal have divided the new world between them, without allowing me any share; I would desire them to show me Adam's Will, which entitles them to it.[51]

The essence of what Francis meant was that man and not divine providence determined trade relations. The same French king gave the French adventurer Jean-Francois de Roberval

(1500–1560) a commission on 15 January 1541, to carry out trade and explore 'uninhabited [lands] ... not possessed or ruled by any other cultural princes.'[52] This commission was actually a licence to commit piracy, of the kind pursued by English privateers such as Drake and Hawkins. The merchants commissioned in this way were stationed in port towns.[53] They were international and entrepreneurial, and often their activities were part of a policy of aggressive mercantilism that flouted international conventions. English merchants conducted assassinations and co-ordinated acts of terror and sabotage. Many of these merchants operated outside English waters, so that if they were caught – the English government could disavow any connection to them. These English adventurers used the ports in Antwerp (Belgium), Calais (France), Lubeck (Germany), Cadiz (Spain), the Canary Islands, Cape Verde, Sale (now Morocco), São Tomé and Príncipe, and so on.[54]

A number of companies of merchant adventurers were developed, operated and headed by English pirates. One of them in 1551 was the Mystery and Company of Merchant Adventurers for the Discovery of Regions, Dominions, Islands, and Places Unknown. This company was headed by Richard Chancellor, Sebastian Cabot and Hugh Willoughby. It was reconstructed in 1555 as the Muscovy Company. Other Englishmen organised under the authority of Robert Dudley the Earl of Leicester in 1585 were known as the Morocco or Barbary Company, whilst organisations such as the Company of Senegal Adventurers and the First English Guinea Company were established in 1588.[55] Of course there was also the East India Company founded on 31 December in 1600 by George Clifford the Earl of Cumberland. It was originally named the Governor and Company of Merchants of London Trading into the East Indies.[56] And there was the London Company in 1607, whose treasurer Thomas Smythe helped finance the English settlement of Virginia.[57] Interestingly, this Thomas Smythe was connected to an African woman that lived in England called Joanne Marya. She resided in St Philip and Jacob's parish in Bristol. This Joanne Marya had a child called Richard, and Smythe was named on his record: 'Richard a Bastard the sonne of Joanne Marya a Blackemore and was not the wife of Thomas Smythe by the latter (?) was baptised the 15 day of August 1600.'[58] A re-reading of the record suggests that Smythe was more than just an incidental inclusion on the record, especially as no father was named.[59]

Perhaps the most notorious organisation connected to trading during this period was the Merchant Adventurers of Brabant beyond the Sea. They received their charter from Edward VI in 1546. The foremost officers of the company were Henry Anderson and Robert Brandling.[60] Later in 1552, in Bristol, a rival organisation was hatched, simply known as the Society of Merchant Adventurers. This latter group was constituted by John Cabot, essentially as an opposition to others trading under that title from London and elsewhere. Their greatest domestic rival was a ruthless consortium led by Francis Drake and John Hawkins from Plymouth.[61] Holinshed claimed that collectively all these adventurers amounted to 'ten thousand merchants by land and sea,' who had the power to 'purchase lands' and 'make bye-laws.'[62] In reality they 'singed the Spanish King's beard' and 'trouble[d]' and 'annoy[ed]' Spanish traders.[63] The personal reasons why Englishmen joined these organisations revolved around a desire to escape the class-dominated nature of English society. By chicanery they hoped to improve their status. Some succeeded, whilst others failed by not obtaining political or royal patronage.

Africans had various and different connections to these English and foreign merchants in early modern England. However, historians such as Ungerer claim that Africans were only objects or chattels to be traded.[64] It is clear that during the early modern period the status of some Africans in England was uncertain if they had inherited a status from another country, such as Pero Alvarez. But rarely were Africans in England (1485–1603) referred to as slaves, or legally treated as chattels. During the Tudor period some Africans present in England had acted as plenipotentiaries and signed treaties with English merchants. Other Africans were present in England as part of diplomatic missions and so on. English merchants relied on the goodwill of African nations to continue their activities. Most of the English companies mentioned earlier worked in conjunction with the nations mentioned before that resisted the Spanish. In the Tudor period these English merchants needed obsequious diplomacy, as well as ruthlessness, to continue adventuring. For example, with the trade in the Mediterranean, including the Canary Islands, Lanzarote and Madeira, English merchants depended on maintaining effective relationships with Sale, Morocco and other North African states.[65]

Elsewhere, English merchants on the east coast of Africa in Zanzibar were dependent on the patronage of African leadership from the Swahili City States, and they got it, because it helped the Africans oppose Portuguese aggression. And those Englishmen that intercepted trade off the coast of West Africa, such as Hawkins and Drake, and other privateers operating near Cape Verde, São Tomé and Príncipe and the Seychelles, relied on West African kings being tolerant of or acquiescent of their practices.[66] An indication of this relates to a debacle caused by two English merchants called Anthony and Thomas Dassell. They brought two West Africans to England in 1587. In the court case that followed at the High Court of Admiralty in 1592, the Englishmen were accused of kidnapping the Africans and depriving them of liberty.[67] In fact, Anthony Dassell stated that the Africans 'were of some accompt' since they were 'sons to the chiefe justice of their country' and therefore would be treated with 'good entertaynment here.' To this end they were treated as guests in Dassell's home. And he hoped that this hospitality would mean that the Africans 'will be more beneficial and commodious to the Queen [Elizabeth I]' 'in regarde of the trade then all the serva[u]nts of Dom Antonio can do good in going thither.'[68] The Dassells intended to seduce these Africans into being advocates for English interests in West Africa, so that Elizabeth I could dispense with the 'goodwill' of the Prince of Portugal Don Antonio. In other words, the Dassells brought the West Africans to England to become go-betweens, envoys or diplomats – they were not slaves. These wranglings indicate how the aspirations of English merchants were reliant on West African sponsorship.

The activities of other English merchants such as Thomas Sherley, Edward Banes and Francis Drake have been interpreted by historians such as Peter Fryer, Ungerer and others as providing the answer to when and how the systematic enslavement of African people began. It is clear that some English merchants in Tudor England felt that they could interrupt the trade in human beings that had been instigated by the Spanish, Portuguese and Ottomans.[69] And where those activities involved Africans, Englishmen such as Hawkins did sell those Africans elsewhere.[70] But in fact, English adventurers trafficked without scruples and enslaved anyone of any colour or religion, even other Englishmen. They were even willing to sell Englishmen as slaves to the Spanish during the Anglo-Spanish Wars. Their objective was to obtain 'live profits.'[71] In Tudor times, an irrevocable social stigma had not yet been placed on Africans to mark them as perpetual slaves. Foreign merchants found this out too if they felt emboldened to deprive the liberty of their African servants. In England, they often ended up as failed opportunists.

The status of individual Africans connected to men of power was being determined by issues other than race, colour or complexion. Africans lived in the English households or country estates of men such as Cecil, Drake, Frobisher, Hawkins, Leicester, Raleigh and Lok.[72] In some of these households more than one African resided, such as at the estates of Robert Dudley, the Earl of Leicester.[73] And at Robert Cecil's, 'Fortunatus [was] a blackmoor seruant.' He was buried in the church yard at Clement Danes, London, on 21 January 1602.[74] This Fortunatus may have been the same 'Fortunatus A Blackmoore of the age of 17 or 18 years' baptised in Cheshunt on 16 April 1570.[75] This would have made him approximately 49 years old when he died. But this was not certain as there were other Africans called Fortunatus that lived in Plymouth and London at that time.[76]

Trade and Wars Under the Stuarts (1603–1660s)

Fortunatus was buried in 1602. Other Africans lived on into the Stuart period. The question was: did these peoples' status change between 1603 and the 1660s? And were merchants that lived in England the agents of that change? If we are guided by the post-colonial praxis, we may believe that this was the case. It is certain that, during this period, the status of English merchants altered and they acted with greater braggadocio. However, the social fabric of English society did not suddenly transform when the last Tudor monarch Elizabeth I died in 1603. James I became king. He was himself a direct descendant of Henry Tudor on both his paternal and maternal sides. It was just that his last name was Stuart not Tudor. The Stuarts were a Scottish/Danish/French extension of the same Tudor family. This social continuity in the royal family was matched by neighbourhood cohesion in local communities, as Africans that had lived in England at the end of the Tudor period continued into the seventeenth century. These Africans resided within English communities that had existed in much the same way as they had done before.

Nevertheless, from 1603 to the 1660s England became a colonial power and took over significant territories that Spain, Portugal and France once held. This included: Barbados in 1605, St Lucia the same year, Bombay (1608), Bermuda (1609), St Kitts (1623), Nevis (1628), Montserrat (1632), Antigua (1632), Bengal (1633), Madras (1639), Jamaica (1655), Bahamas (1665), Virgin Islands (1666) and the Cayman Islands (1670).[77] Spain declined as a world power because of a number of factors. These included the Thirty Years War (1618–1648), where despite Spain being supported by the Holy Roman Empire, the Catholic League, Hungary, Denmark and Poland it lost to the combined forces of the rest of Europe. The rest of Europe included England and France, and they were emboldened. Matters were concluded at the Treaty of Westphalia in 1648 where the boundaries of Western European states were agreed upon.[78]

Spain was weakened by a proliferation of Anglo-Spanish conflicts from 1625 to 1630 and 1654 to the 1660s; the cumulative effect was the loss of more territories in the Caribbean. Further wars against the Ottoman Empire and resistance from a newly independent Portugal (1640 onwards) and the Netherlands (1568–1648) saw the Spanish retreat from Europe. This sustained opposition was coupled with Spain's own internal dissension, typified by the expulsion of the Moors. The Spanish economy collapsed.[79] Early modern writers such as John Legat (1596) had long acknowledged that 'The Spaniards [white/Christians] were less civilised than their enemies [Iberian Moors]'[80] and Spain was dependent on the latter. Large numbers of non-conformist Protestant merchants were also expelled. These merchants included Englishmen, many of whom had cached considerable wealth for the Spanish state. Spain lost that money.[81]

In the midst of this Iberian recession, the new rulers of Spain – Philip III and Philip IV – were unable to arrest the decline. And their activities, which ranged from feeble impotence to xenophobic zealotry, alienated them from the other 'powers of the earth.'[82] Some commentators at the time suggested that Spain's leaders were insane and that their decision making was debilitated by insanity brought about by centuries of cousins marrying cousins.[83] The aftermath of this atrophy was a crisis in confidence, and the Spain that had once been called 'the Empire on which the sun never sets,' defied its prophecy – by setting.[84]

What Spain left behind was a space that England, France and the Netherlands scrambled to fill. Some of this scramble involved the theft of territories in the Caribbean. In those territories the Spanish and the Portuguese had created a system of indenture that forced whites, Native Americans and Africans to work in harsh conditions. The French maintained these systems under Louis XIV in 1642, and much later developed the 'Code Noir' in 1685.[85] But by the 1660s policies had not yet created a rigid and racially codified legal regime, although political, cultural and religious justifications for such systems had emerged. And by the 1660s, a portion of the English merchant class that ran colonies speculated on ideas about the inferiority of Africans in those colonies. Perhaps, this was a justification for replacing Native Americans with African labour, or because of contact with Spanish and Ottoman traders that already had pejorative ideas.[86]

Colonial Laws and English Freedoms (1603-1660s circa)

By contrast, decades earlier, English judges seemed reluctant to prescribe common law rights when challenged by mercantile demands. As the English merchant Richard Jobson stated in 1623,[87] for most Englishmen it seemed that without an economic imperative, or slave colonies that contained Africans, slavery could be negated as something that other Europeans did. Thomas Roe in 1616 repeated this very idea, 'in England we had no slaves, neither was it lawful to make the image of God fellow to a beast.'[88] Nevertheless, English adventurers had speculated in people trafficking for hundreds of years; John Hawkins was not the first.[89] And by the 1660s, the courts were more willing to set aside the laws and freedoms of indentured workers in England's new territories.[90] By the middle of the seventeenth century, as the economic benefits of colonial expansion became increasingly important, merchants and those connected to them put pressure on the English sovereign (the executive), the legislature (parliament) and the judiciary (courts) to either ignore abuses in the colonies or allow separate legal regimes to exist. English merchants were no longer just adventurers 'annoying' the Spanish. For example, by 1655 state-sponsored privateers such as Robert Venables and William Penn had effectively arrested control of the island of Jamaica from Spain. Nonetheless, Venables and Penn did not directly benefit from their actions, as both were sent to the Tower of London on their return and Venables died penniless.[91] However, the point is that Spain never stole Jamaica back.[92] Later, in 1667, the Treaty of Madrid ratified what the English had already won in the Caribbean.[93]

English authorities had a choice, whether to continue the practices of previous colonial authorities or forge a 'brave new world.'[94] By the middle of the seventeenth century they had chosen the former and governed the indentured workforce by harshness and illiberality. For example, in Virginia (then an English colony) during Bacon's Rebellion (1676), Africans had acted as leaders and instigators of insurrections that included white farmers.[95] The capital of Jamestown was burnt to the ground. This revolt was terrifying to men of power, and from the 1670s onwards anti-African policies, conventions and eventually laws were drafted and implemented. For example, in the case of Butts v Penny in 1671, where a merchant was sent to recover one hundred enslaved people. Obiter dicta of the case stated that these Africans 'are infidels and subjects of an infidel prince and therefore without the rights enjoyed by Christians.'[96] This sort of dicta influenced the ideas of Englishmen abroad. The question is how did these prejudices and events affect Africans that actually lived in England in the seventeenth century?

Most people in England at that time were primarily concerned with domestic matters. The content of early modern
pamphlets can attest to that. These pamphlets were dissemi-
nated by ordinary people on street corners and their popularity
attested to the rising levels of literacy amongst commoners
in England. Most of these pamphlets were political and religious and even though they sometimes included xenophobic,
intolerant and incendiary rants, the local writers rarely mentioned Africans as the enemy or even included them as 'Johnny
foreigner' to be blamed as the French or Dutch present in
England were. By contrast, these pamphlets contained dia-
tribes and sometimes anti-Semitic statements against a range of
other peoples. Sometimes they called the Pope the antichrist;
other pamphlets claimed that the kings of England – James I or
Charles I – were Satan; whilst some pamphleteers defended the
royalist perspective and preached that Oliver Cromwell was
the 'son of the devil.' Each side was vehement in its ideological
angst and violent in its execution. These cultural schisms were
not abated by the introduction of a new King James Bible in
1611. Even though it did become and remains an international
bestseller – it did not stop England being wracked by religious
strife until 1688, when the Glorious Revolution enshrined the
Protestant hegemony.[97]

However, Africans in England were not the prime objects of
hate for any of the major players in English politics during the
events of the early Stuart period. Even when English society
became more political, it did not become more racial. During
the Civil War (1642–1651), as England developed factions such
as the Levellers, Fifth Monarchists and Muggletonians that
wanted to create a new kind of society, ideas about equality
and humanism were spread amongst the lower classes. The
Restoration of Charles II had to coalesce with these ideas. But
during all of these social and international tumults, Africans

lived in English cities, towns and villages. Even those Africans that arrived in England from colonial territories found that no matter what happened abroad, there was no law or force that could compel them to stay shackled to their masters. Many deserted their employers and became part of a growing number of Africans integrated into the English population. It was difficult by law to keep Africans as slaves in early modern England. If they were to be kept as subalterns, it would be by culture and conventions.

Strangers by Design: Othering in Early Modern England

In early modern England, Africans were not the prime victims of discriminatory practices. Furthermore, with the exception of Africans such as the African raconteur and Francis Rumbolo, Africans were not automatically perceived as supporters of or opposition to the real or imaginary plots against the state. By contrast a group of people often referred to as 'Egyptians' were. They had refused to accept the sovereignty of any of the monarchs, oligarchies and plenipotentiaries mentioned in this book. As far as they were concerned the Tudors, Parliamentarians and Stuarts were all equally illegitimate, corrupt and baseless. Egyptians pledged allegiance to separate consanguineous and autonomous states that only happened to be within England, Scotland, Ireland and Wales. They called themselves by a variety of names and sometimes, as Thomas Harman complained in 1566, they claimed a multi-ethnic past.[98]

However, most Egyptians used the Bible, mysticism and paganism to trace their lineages to Africa, via Egypt.[99] As the English poet and pamphleteer Thomas Dekker (1608) stated, they 'walked abroad' as 'tawny Moor's bastards,' but then he added, 'that they are not born so' and 'neither had the Sun burnt them so, but they are painted so.' In other words they were not Black, but 'counterfeit Egyptians.'[100] As the writer Thomas

Browne informed us, 'Artificial Negroes, or Gypsies acquired their complexion by anointing their bodies with Bacon and fat substances, and so exposing them to the Sun.'[101]

Egyptians called themselves by various names, such as Taws and Faws, and were colloquially known as Gypsies. The 'kingdoms' they hailed from were called Little Egypts. Some brigands and petty criminals that sought immunity from the law claimed to be Egyptians.[102] They stated that they had a sovereignty that predated the existing rulers of Europe. They did this to pursue lawless activities, but their attempts to secure that immunity from legal prosecutions over several hundreds of years were hindered. Egyptians were considered a threat to the stability of the state – because they did not recognise the English state.[103] And from the first Egyptian Act in 1512, until the eighteenth century, they could be and were summarily whipped, branded and executed, as the early modern writer Humfrey Dyson reported.[104]

Egyptians were also often accused of witchcraft, so that purges against witchery often resulted in the persecution of Egyptians in England and elsewhere. Moreover, Egyptians tended to have a strong matriarchy and Egyptian women were known to fragrantly assert their rights, at a time when women were not able to do so in the wider English society.[105] This made Egyptian women problematic and troublesome and they were singled out for misogynistic attacks. By comparison, African women were not subject to this kind of institutionalised or sporadic hatred in early modern England. Most African women lived as integrated members of English society.

The matters outlined above touch on issues of gender that require more than a few speculative comments. There are obvious questions that arise, one of them being about whether African women were discriminated against twice, once because of their ethnicity and then again because of their gender. And what was the general status of women in early modern society? As we analyse this we are drawn to the similarities of investigating women's social histories and those of people of African descent. Those writing on these subjects seek to reclaim 'hidden' voices.[106]

Historians such as Susan Broomhall, Patricia Crawford, Laura Gowing and many others revealed the social histories of early modern women even when the men were doing the writing.[107] In the same way, African diasporic social history can be revealed, even when white people are doing the writing. Of course, this method of retrieval has its limitations, since we are hearing the voice of the 'hidden' subject – the woman or the African – through an interpreter. It is therefore an interpretation that may itself need translating. Any bias discovered through this process needs to be revealed, as we did with the letters that described the African raconteur and Francis Rumbolo. Historians have developed their own methodologies to discover these voices.[108] These methodologies are interpretive, and it means setting aside the post-colonial praxis and utilising pre-colonial perspectives.[109] We can then draw similarities between the social history of women and the ethnology of Africans in early modern England.

Therefore, our imaginations may lead us to assume that women in early modern English society were always downtrodden and exploited. But when we look beyond that imagination, we see this notion is as inaccurate as a mono-ethnic perspective of English society. Both approaches ignore the local, national and international complexities that we have been analysing over the last two chapters. However, we should acknowledge that customs and the law, especially in relation to inheritance, routinely discriminated against women.[110] England was a patriarchal society during the early modern period. Men held most of the functions of government. There was a belief that the man should be the master of the public world, but also that 'the house of every one is to *him* [emphasis my own] as *his* castle and fortress, as well for *his* defence against injury and violence as for *his* repose.'[111] When the Scottish firebrand preacher John Knox (1513–1572) claimed that England and Scotland had been bedevilled by a 'monstrous regimen of women,' he referred to the de facto power that women such as Mary of Guise, Mary Queen of Scots and Mary I exercised in noble families across Europe.[112] But Knox was an incendiary ranter because men still ruled in Europe, as evidenced by a church that could ask 'Querelle des Femmes' (the argument or the trouble about women), in a similar way that European and European-American churches and governments later asked 'the Negro Question' or the Nazis, the 'Jewish question.' However, with each of the peoples objectified by such a question, we must not assume that they answered with passive acquiescence or that they went 'quietly into that goodnight.'[113]

Even in the male dominated early modern English society, women privately had the power to legitimatise the authority and power of men. With a word, women could bring down dynasties or raise them up. Often women exercised this power behind closed doors. Only occasionally did they intrude on the public sphere. 'The hand that rocks the cradle is the hand that rules the world' – women raised generations of rulers in England.[114] Women knowing their power found innovative ways to 'retreat behind the powder puff or … petticoat' and still control English society.[115] In a similar way, Africans in early modern England found ways to overcome any prejudice.

Simply because Africans were not always part of the public face of English society does not mean that they did not influence it. The African servants of the 'great' English men of the era must have had some influence on them, just as their wives, daughters and mothers did.

If we look beyond the romance of early modern England, we can see the Africans that lived there. We need to do the same to view women in early modern England. There were positive as well as negative ideas about women that early modern people could and did draw on when they described and thought of them. We know that women writers talked of the 'community of women,' such as the Venetian-French writer Christine de Pizan in 1405 in *The Boke of the Cyte of Ladyes*. Pizan wove the history of women and mythology into a melodious synthesis of womanism that offered an alternative trajectory for historiography; where women were the central constant voice on the history of mankind.[116] Her writing was antagonistic to what she considered the gendering, sexualisation and othering of women in Jean de Meun's *Roman de la Rose*. The latter was of course the most famous book on courtly love written in the thirteenth century and popular in many languages throughout early modern Europe. Meun had portrayed women as objects of courtly love to be admired, won, but also to be controlled and never fully trusted. Pizan followed *Cyte of Ladyes* with the *Treasure of the City of Ladies* and *Joan of Arc*, all of which spoke of the chastity and virtue of women, and claimed that women were superior vessels of divinity. The most famous attempt to assert women's theological centrality was by the Cologne (German) polymath Heinrich Cornelius Agrippa in 1509; he wrote about the superiority of the female sex and his ideas were infused with magic, cabalistic and occultist ideas. He also blended classical humanism and universals into his treatise.[117] And in debates he vocalised his defence of women.[118]

Later English writers such as Thomas Eliot and the woman writer Jane Anger also wrote not only in defence of women, but of the superior aspects of women and their ideas represented an aspect of early modern English thought. For example, Jane Anger, in *Protection for Women* (1589), argued:

> There is no wisdom but it comes by grace, this is a principles
> & Contra principium non est disputandum: but grace was *first*
> [my emphasis] given to a woman, because to our lady: which
> premises conclude that women are wise. Now Primus est
> optimum, & therefore, women are wiser then men.[119]

Women writers such as Marie de Gournay advocated 'woman-ism' and she lectured and spoke at European schools of learning as 'a woman of letters.' From 1591 to 1641, she published a series of books and pamphlets on the equality of women. Other female authors included the Mexican writer Juana Ines de la Cruz and the English writer Rachel Speght, both of whom essentially womanised biblical scripture. The latter engendered a woman's voice in early modern Protestant theology. Other writers, such as Ester Sowerman in 1617, wrote about the inconstancy of men and the virtue of women.[120] We shall see that there are many similarities between the ideas and activities of the writers just mentioned and similar expositions on the constancy of Africans, their blackness and their humanity.

People in early modern England could draw from positive as well as negative ideas about female power and women, as they could about blackness and Africans. However, theological and classical ideas could also be selectively appropriated to foster an idea that women were less than men. In a similar way writers could have their commentaries conflated into concepts that justified Africans being thought of as inferior in early modern society. Eve could be proposed as the originator of sin and menstrual blood as evidence of that sin – God's curse. In a similar way unscrupulous writers could conflate the blackness of Africans with sin, claiming that after the Flood, sin originated from Ham and Africans were his cursed children. These matters are important to our analysis of Africans in Tudor and early Stuart society, as religion and religious beliefs were influential in ordinary people's lives. In untangling these historical and theological issues we will discover notions about the ethnology and social history of Africans in early modern English society.

THREE | The Pathology of the Curse of Ham

> Somebody told a lie one day. They couched it in language. They made everything black ugly and evil. Look in your dictionary and see the synonyms of the word *black*. It's always something degrading, low and sinister. Look at the word *white*. It's always something pure, high, clean. Well I want to get the language right tonight.[1]

The Making of a Myth

We see the myth of the Curse of Ham[2] through the prism of our familiar. This prism means that we think of it as being the cornerstone of a coherent philosophy or theology that stigmatises Africans. We may also believe that it was started by Englishmen in early modern England, and that the myth was believed in that society. As a result, Africans would have lived wretched lives of abject misery, segregated from white people and treated as if they were cursed children of Ham. Furthermore, we may also believe that the myth determined the place of Africans in English society and justified their enslavement.

It is certain that modern legacies associated with the myth still affect racial ideologies and theologies today. Organisations such as the Ku Klux Klan, Aryan Nations, Jesus Christ Church of Latter Day Saints (Mormons),[3] the Christian Identity movement and the Church of Jesus Christ Christians still teach aspects of the Curse of Ham as a political and theological doctrine.[4] In the USA legislators often quoted the myth as starting in early modern England when they created laws such as Slave, Black Codes and Jim Crow legislation which made racial segregation legal. Infamously, on 10 June 1964, Senator Robert Byrd, a former Kleagle of the Ku Klux Klan, gave one of the longest speeches in US Senate history: fourteen hours and thirteen minutes advocating ideas from the Curse of Ham as fact.[5] In South Africa, as the historian Bengt Sundkler stated, Apartheid was supported by theories that had their root in the theory that Africans were cursed children of Ham.[6] The Second and Third Reich also adapted some of the ideas of the Curse of Ham and mixed them with anti-Semitism to justify their views on the 'Aryan race' and Jewish and African people being subhuman. When this was coupled with concepts about evolution, social and anthropological Darwinism and folk or 'volk' philosophy, it was used to legitimise the genocides of Jewish peoples and those of African descent in Namibia and elsewhere.[7]

Organised systems of racist 'thought, speech and action' were associated with the Curse of Ham.[8] Much of these associations originated from interpolations of the myth during the eighteenth and nineteenth centuries. At that time within the British, French and Ottoman empires it underpinned legal, religious, social, as well as cultural concepts and conventions, that Africans were inherently inferior. Therefore, the Curse of Ham provided an apologia or justification for those committing atrocities against Africans during the Maafa, colonialism and neo-colonialism.[9] For these sorts of reasons, Africans living in Britain, such as Ottobah Cugoano (1787), and those in America, including the African-American abolitionist David Walker (1830),[10] fought against the myth and any interpolations associated with it.

This modern history of the Curse of Ham warps our perceptions and does not tell us how the myth was understood in the early modern past; to discover that, we need to go back to Tudor and early Stuart society. What we find is that the Curse of Ham was included in stories about Noah. Noah's stories were popular in England during that period. Some of that popularity was because England was a staunchly Christian country. However, it is helpful to remember that although Christians claimed a religious orthodoxy, even then they were influenced by principles and ideas from other religions. Stories of Noah were written and spoken about by adherents of all three of the Abrahamic religions – Christianity, Islam and Judaism – which meant interpolations on the Curse of Ham are found in all three religions. Within this milieu, the question was, did English Christians believe in any of these interpolations? We need to examine early modern Bibles to find out. This is not as straightforward as it would seem, since there was a multitude of religious texts that were available to Englishmen. These included popular theological tracts, pamphlets, sermons, homilies and letters that although they were not part of any authorised Bible, nevertheless influenced religious thought at that time.

We will later examine some of these theological documents. Here we look at what the most popular Bibles of the early modern period stated about the Curse of Ham. The author makes no apology, even at the risk of repetition, for repeating sections of early modern Bibles that include the myth. It is important for the reader to read in the main body of this book the actual words written by English writers. By reading these words, we may get a clearer perspective on early modern English thought and how this may have affected the ethnology and social interactions of Africans in England.

The early modern Bibles that will help us understand how the Curse of Ham was seen in English society are the: *Wycliffe* (1382–1395), *Latin Vulgate* (fourth century to sixteenth century), *Tyndale* (1523), *Coverdale* (1535), *Matthew's* (1537), *Taverner* (1539), *Great* (1539), *Geneva* (1560), *Bishops* (1568), *Douay Rheims* (1582) and the *King James Version* or *Authorized King James Version* (1611). There were specific reasons for the development of all these Bibles, especially those written in English. These English Bibles were fashioned to fulfil a want for Englishmen to read, hear or understand biblical texts in their own language.[11] Linked to this desire was an interest in having a plain interpretation of biblical stories. Occasionally, the English Bibles were the labour of a single person, but more often they were the combined efforts of groups of people. Some of these texts were created indirectly though the sponsorship of a member of European aristocracy; occasionally a monarch directly commissioned a version, such as with the *King James Version*.[12]

However, throughout most of the early modern period the most popular Bible was the *Wycliffe*. There were at least two versions of this Bible in circulation. The first was written by John Wycliffe, the English dissenter, as early as 1382–1395. This version had initially become popular with the Lollards.[13] The second version of the *Wycliffe* was penned by the Englishman John Purvey under the guidance of Wycliffe and was completed after the latter's death. Purvey's interpretation was a verbatim translation of the *Vulgate Bible*. Both were officially labelled as heretical during the fifteenth century, when England was a staunchly Catholic country; as Archbishop Arundel retorted in 1411, Wycliffe was a person 'of cursed memory,' the 'son of the old serpent [the Devil]' and a person full of 'Malice.'[14] Despite these personal attacks against Wycliffe and public assaults against his work, both renditions of his Bible retained their popularity throughout the early modern period.

In the text of the *Wycliffe* (1382–1395), the Curse of Ham appeared in Genesis 9, verses 18–27.

> Therefore thei that yeden out of the schip weren Noe, Sem, Cham, and Japheth; forsothe Cham, thilke is the fadir of Chanaan./These thre weren the sones of Noe, and al the kynde of men was sowun of hem on al erthe./And Noe, an erthe tiliere, bigan to tile the erthe,

and he plauntide a viner,/And he drank wyn, and was drunkun;
and he was nakid, and lay in his tabernacle./And whanne Cham, the
fadir of Chanaan, hadde seien this thing, that is, that the schameful
membris of his fadir weren maad nakid, he telde to hise tweye
britheren with out forth./And sotheli Sem and Jafeth puttiden a
mentil on her schuldris, and thei yeden bacward, and hileden the
schameful membris of her fadir, and her faces weren turned awei,
and thei sien not the priuy membris of her fadir./And forsothe Noe
wakide of the wyn, and whanne he hadde lerned what thingis his
lesse sone hadde do to hym,/He seide, Cursid be the child Canaan,
he schal be seruaunt of seruauntis to hise britheren./And Noe seide,
Blessid be the Lord God of Sem,/And Chanaan be the seruaunt
to Sem; God alarge Jafeth, and dwelle in the tabernaclis of Sem, and
Chanaan be seruaunt of hym.[15]

This passage is allegorical, but is believed by many Christians
and others to be literal. It recounted the events that occurred after
the Great Flood, when the Earth was destroyed because of the
sins of man.[16] The only living fauna to be saved were Noah's family and two of every species carried into a Great Ark that they
constructed. The family of Noah laboured tirelessly to maintain
all the fauna of the earth. They experienced 150 days of the waters
rising, 150 days of the waters receding, forty days of waiting, and
a further fourteen days of waiting.[17] During the later part of these
events a covenant between God and mankind was established,
signified by a rainbow.

The events described in Genesis 9 happened directly after the
Great Flood. In that context, to a modern reader, these domestic
matters may seem rather absurd or even innocuous, since they
recounted how Noah had laid drunk and naked in his 'tabernacle' or tent. Ham, the youngest son of Noah,[18] saw his father's
'schameful membris,' in other words his father's genitals. Ham
told his brothers about his father's nakedness, but they covered
their heads and walked backwards before covering him. A plain
reading[19] of this biblical text showed that Ham was not an active

protagonist. When Noah woke from his drunkenness he did not curse his son Ham, but his grandson Canaan. The Curse was that Canaan 'schal be seruant of seruauntis' to his 'britheren,' Japeth shall be 'increased' or 'alarged' and will 'dwelle' with Sem (Shem), and Canaan will serve Japeth.

The *Wycliffe Bible* made no mention of the Curse resulting in Ham or anyone else's skin changing colour. In fact, there was not any indication that the Curse had any effect at all. We may remember that Noah uttered the Curse, and he was a man. The Curse did not originate from the 'God of Abraham.' Some early modern commentators suggested that man was not meant to curse – in fact it was a sin.[20] Moreover, this Curse came from a man that had just woken from a drunken state. From a theological perspective Noah was not 'right with God,'[21] or even in 'charge of his faculties,' when he cursed his grandson. The biblical text reveals only one sinner: Noah. Many early modern theologians, as we shall discover, concurred and believed that the important theological aspect of Genesis 9 was the sin of Noah and no one else.

It is often thought that Genesis 9 in early modern Bibles either provided a justification or an apologia for enslaving Africans. And that the punishment given to Canaan and quoted in Genesis 9 effectively made him into a slave. However, the *Wycliffe* included the words that Canaan shall be made into 'a seruaunt of seruantis.' It did not include the word 'slave.' In the Latin *Vulgate*, which formed the basis of both versions of the *Wycliffe*, the words that were used were 'servus servorum.'[22] It is possible to translate the former words as slave. But the point is that these early modern translators did not. The way 'servant' was used in these early modern texts suggested that the English translators wanted to offer a less permanent form of servitude than perpetual slavery. Although there is an acknowledgement that slavery in ancient civilisations and in other early modern societies could be temporary.[23] The issue was that early modern translators used the word 'servant,' and the nature of that service appeared to have meant him 'dwelling' with his older brothers and waiting upon them, not the expiration of all his rights as a perpetual slave.[24]

Perhaps Noah's Curse was only restating family positions and traditions that a youngest son should serve an older one. The difference was that in this case the duty to serve was onerously directed towards the child of the youngest son. This highlights a most important and incongruous issue, which is that the Curse of Ham was not placed on Ham, but Canaan: Ham's son. So it was not really the Curse of Ham, but the Curse of Canaan! The question is why was Canaan named at all? It seemed that Canaan was only cursed for being the son of Ham. He played no part in this debacle and there was no indication in this Bible that he was even there when his grandfather was naked.

So far what we have discussed does not explain how the story of the Curse of Ham could have been used as a source for anti-African antipathy. Readers may assume, therefore, that the *Wycliffe* version of the Curse of Ham varied from others contained in early modern Bibles, and that they and not the *Wycliffe* contained the definitive interpretation of the myth. Let's examine the second *Wycliffe* version. It was written by John Purvey in 1388, but in a similar way to its predecessor it was popular throughout the fifteenth century. It stated in verses 19–27:

These three [Shem, Japeth and Ham] were the sons of
Noe, and all the kind of men was sown of them on all [the]
earth./And Noe, an earth-tiller, began to till the earth, and he
planted a vinery, and he drank wine, and was drunken; and
he was naked, and lay in his tabernacle./And when Ham, the
father of Canaan, had seen this thing, that is, that the shameful
members of his father were made naked, he told his two brethren
withoutforth./And Shem and Japheth putted a mantle on their
shoulders, and they went backward, and covered the shameful

members of their father, and their faces were turned away, and
they saw not the privy members of their father./And Noe waked
of the wine, and when he had learned what things his less(er),
or younger, son had done to him,/He said, Cursed be the child
Canaan, he shall be (a) servant of servants to his brethren./And
Noe said, Blessed be the Lord God of Shem, and Canaan be
the servant of Shem;/God alarge Japheth, and dwell he in the
tabernacles of Shem, and Canaan be the servant of him.[25]

This text of the story is almost identical to that discussed earlier. It is interesting that although other parts of the *Wycliffe* may
vary, when it comes to this story, they share remarkable similarities. Significantly neither contained the anti-African antipathy
we may expect.

Turning to the *Latin Vulgate*, we see a very similar rendering of the myth. The *Vulgate* was written in the late fourth
century but was still used throughout the early modern period.
It was the Bible authorised by the Pope,[26] and was declared as
containing 'authentic' text by the Council of Trent in 1534.[27]
The Curse of Ham appeared in the *Vulgate*, verses 19–27, and
reads as such:

Dixitque Deus Noe hoc erit signum foederis quod constitui
inter me et inter omnem carnem super terram/Erant igitur filii
Noe qui egressi sunt de arca Sem Ham et Iafeth porro Ham ipse
est pater Chanaan/Tres isti sunt filii Noe et ab his disseminatum
est omne hominum genus super universam terram/Coepitque
Noe vir agricola exercere terram et plantavit vineam/bibensque
vinum inebriatus est et nudatus in tabernaculo suo/Quod
cum vidisset Ham pater Chanaan verenda scilicet patris sui
esse nuda nuntiavit duobus fratribus suis foras/At vero Sem
et Iafeth pallium inposuerunt umeris suis et incedentes
retrorsum operuerunt verecunda patris sui faciesque
eorum aversae erant et patris virilia non viderunt/evigilans
autem Noe ex vino cum didicisset quae fecerat ei filius suus

minor/Ait maledictus Chanaan servus servorum erit fratribus
suis/Dixitque benedictus Dominus Deus Sem sit Chanaan
servus eius/Dilatet Deus Iafeth et habitet in tabernaculis Sem
sitque Chanaan servus eius/vixit autem Noe post diluvium
trecentis quinquaginta annis/At impleti sunt omnes dies eius
nongentorum quinquaginta annorum et mortuus est.[28]

An English translation of this text has not been included in
this book as the *Wycliffe* effectively provides that translation.
The *Vulgate* and *Wycliffe* are almost identical. Therefore, the
prevailing issues remain.

The investigation of other Bibles, such as the *Tyndale*, also
show an absence of an overt anti-African antipathy. This is important as the *Tyndale* more than any other Bible was used as the basis
for English Bibles during the middle of the early modern period.
The success of the *Tyndale* was connected to its history as it was
completed in 1521 by the English theologian William Tyndale. His
intention was to create a Bible that 'defy[ied] the Pope and all his
laws.' It was a purpose that he lost his life for.[29] Tyndale wanted
'everyman'[30] even the one that 'driveth the plough [to] ... know
more of the Scriptures than thou [the Pope] dost.'[31] Tyndale
therefore wrote the Bible in plain English.[32] It may be assumed
that because of its plain English it may reveal popular anti-African
sentiments hidden in the text of other early modern Bibles. It says:

These are the .iij. sonnes of Noe and of these was all the
world overspred./And Noe beynge an husbad man went furth
and planted a vyneyarde/And drancke of the wyne and was
droncke and laye vncouered in the myddest of his tent./And
Ham the father of Canaan sawe his fathers prevytees and tolde
his ij. brethren that were wythout./And Sem and Iapheth toke
a mantell and put it on both there shulders ad went backward
ad covered there fathers secrets but there faces were backward
So that they sawe not there fathers nakydnes./As soone as Noe

was awaked fro his wyne and wyst what his yongest sonne had done vnto hym/He sayd: cursed be Canaan ad a seruante, of all seruantes be he to his brethren./And he sayd: Blessed be the LORde God of Sem and Canaan be his seruante./God increase Iapheth that he may dwelle in the tentes of Sem. And Canaan be their seruante.[33]

Readers may notice a pattern with these early modern Bibles. These texts did not reference skin colour, blackness or Africans when they recounted the Curse of Ham.[34] So we can see that in the *Matthew's* and *Miles Coverdale Bibles*[35] the same issues arise. The main difference in the *Coverdale* was that Noah uttered the words, 'Cursed be Canaan a servant of all creation be he to his brethren.' This may imply that the English writers of the *Coverdale* felt that Noah's Curse should be seen as a more permanent status of servileness. In other words that Canaan's servitude meant more than domestic service. We lastly turn to the *King James Version*, Genesis 9, verses 17–27 (1611):

And Noah began to be a husbandman, and he planted a vineyard./And he drank of the wine, and was drunken; and he was uncovered within his tent./And Ham, the father of Canaan, saw the nakedness of his father and told his two brethren without./And Shem and Japheth took a garment and laid it upon both their shoulders, and went backward and covered the nakedness of their father; and their faces were backward, and they saw not their father's nakedness./And Noah awoke from his wine, and knew what his younger son had done unto him./And he said, 'Cursed be Canaan! A servant of servants shall he be unto his brethren.'/And he said, 'Blessed be the LORD God of Shem; and Canaan shall be his servant./God shall enlarge Japheth, and he shall dwell in the tents of Shem; and Canaan shall be his servant.'[36]

The similarity of this text to the other ones should illustrate even for the most sceptical readers that simply by reading Genesis 9 in early modern Bibles we do not get a clearer understanding of why or how the Curse of Ham could stigmatise Africans. We have to look outside of Genesis 9 in early modern Bibles.

How Interpolations of the Curse of Ham Stigmatised Africans

We have learnt that early modern Bibles did not state that Africans were cursed children of Ham. This may be a startling revelation. It means Englishmen in early modern England could not have developed an anti-African antipathy from a plain reading of Genesis 9.[37] In Genesis 9, the relationship between God and Noah's family was ultimately believed by Christians to show that 'all men' are God's children by being descendants of the 'original man' and the 'original family': Adam and Eve. This is known as the theory of monogenesis (one origin).[38] Noah was a descendant of this original family through Adam and Eve's third son, Seth. Ten generations separated Noah from Adam.

In the early modern era, some writers postulated that this 'original family' was white, and the descendants of Ham were Africans. Interpolations were then created that stated that the Curse of Ham made them Black. And some of these fantasies suggested that this blackness was evidence that Africans were cursed. These myth makers interpolated genealogical lists contained in the Bible to justify their ideas. The lists are contained in Genesis 10 and 1 Chronicles 8. In the *Wycliffe*, Genesis 10, it stated:

> These be the generations of the sons of Noël; Shem, Ham, and Japheth (These be the descendants of Noah's sons, Shem, Ham, and Japheth). And sons were born to them after the great flood. Soothly the sons of Ham were Cush, and Mizriam, and Phut, and Canaan.

...

Forsooth Cush begat Nimrod; (and) he began to be mighty in [the] earth,

And he was a strong hunter, *or oppressor, of men* before the Lord; of him a proverb went out, (saying,) As Nimrod, a strong hunter before the Lord. (and he was a strong hunter before the Lord; and a proverb went out about him, saying, Be ye like Nimrod, a strong hunter before the Lord.)

Soothly the beginning of his realm was Babylon, and Erech, and Accad, and Calneh, in the land of Shinar.

Asshur went out of that land, and builded Nineveh, and [the] streets of the city, and Calah, (And he went out of that land to Assyria, and he built the cities of Nineveh, and Rehoboth Ir, and Calah,)

and Resen betwixt Nineveh and Calah; this is a great city.[39]

1 Chronicles 8 contains similar genealogical lists and the text varies very little in other early modern Bibles. So we can work from the premise that the *Wycliffe* version provided an authoritative basis for other early modern theology.

The first issue we may notice was that a plain reading of the text did not state that Africans were cursed. In fact the text did not mention the colour or complexion of any of the people it described. It was only by interpolation and extrapolation that the descendants of Ham: Canaan, Cush, Mizriam and Phut became Africans. However, aspects of the story in *Wycliffe* lack internal logic as the names Cush, Mizriam and Phut are not the names of people, but ancient African civilisations. Cush was the name of the Kingdom of Kush in Ethiopia/ Sudan and Mizriam was another name for Kemet or Egypt; whilst Phut was the Kingdom of Punt in modern day Eritrea, Djibouti and Somalia.[40] But the way that these names were used in the Bible seemed to suggest that they were individual people, or rather the writer/s wanted us to think of them as people that were sons of Ham.

The names of these civilisations are themselves interesting as they are related to cognomens associated with the colour Black that describe the people and/or the land that they came from as Black.[41] However, many modern Eurocentric-historians, and others, are reluctant to claim that Africans were the progenitors of these civilisations.[42] This is because these civilisations are known as 'great civilisations' and to claim that Africans had built them would mean attributing some of that greatness to Africans.[43] This is all the more poignant as the civilisations mentioned in the Bible are not just those in Africa but also Mesopotamia, that included Babylon, Assyria and Nineveh. In other words this would confirm the evidence, arguments and narrative of a global African presence, as proposed by many African-centred historians.[44] So, ironically and in a rather contradictory way for Africans to be 'children of Ham,' they would also have to be 'great' civilisers as well.

The Theological 'Dodgy Dossier'

However, stories about the Curse of Ham were popular with early modern audiences, not because they were associated with issues of colour and ethnicity, but as they contained warnings about sin and redemption, obedience and authority. But it was really the salacious aspects of the story that early modern audiences were attracted to. In teaching about sin a congregation could be outraged, but titillated, when they imagined Noah's nude 'private members' and his naked drunken dance. For these 'conservative' audiences Noah's 'wicked' nudity was shameful, but it was also a source of licentious excitement for readers and hearers.

Initially, early modern writers and pastors wanted to make this risqué and popular story simpler, or provide answers to the questions that parishioners may have asked such as: Who are Ham's descendants? Why did it say in verse 10 of Genesis that they lived in Babylon, Kemet and Ethiopia? And who were the 'real' children of Japheth and Shem? Some Islamic, Christian and Hebrew writers speculated. One of these scholars was Josephus (37–100 CE) the Hebrew/Roman historian. He wrote:

For of the four sons of Ham, time has not at all hurt the name of Cush; for the Ethiopians, over whom he reigned, are even at this day, both by themselves and by all men in Asia, called Cushites.[45]

Josephus did not state that any of the descendants of Ham in Africa and Asia were cursed. He merely offered the Hamitic genealogy to explain the ancestry of some Africans and Asians.

Another writer to create interpolations that did a similar gene-alogical tracing was Ibn Khallikan in the thirteenth century. He was Iranian by birth but Barmakid by extraction.[46] He lived in Cairo (Egypt) and wrote a book known as the *Wafayāt Al-a'yān Wa-anbā' Abnā' Az-zamān* – it was called the *Deaths of Eminent Men and History of the Sons of the Epoch*, but it was better known as the *Biographical Dictionary*. In this book Khallikan stated, 'They [Africans] are all descended [genealogically] from Kush the son of Ham, the son of Noah.'[47] The book has an absence of overt anti-African antipathy and appeared to be offering a genea-logical analysis to decipher the diversity of human beings using biblical/Quranic principles. Khallikan did not state that Africans were cursed. Of course, this genealogical tracing could be used by later scholars that wanted to prove that very thing.

One of those early modern writers that prepared a way for an anti-African interpolation of the Curse was Annius (1432–1502), a Dominican friar and scholar from Viterbo (now Italy). Annius was in the service of the popes Sixtus IV and Alexander VI as a translator and linguist.[48] He imagined and fantasised forger-ies, attributing them to three ancient sources: the Hellenistic Babylonian writer Berosus, the Egyptian writer Manetho and the Roman writer Cato. Annius claimed that these writers had stated that 'Cham [Canaan] of Africa' was the 'corrupter of the world'[49] and that 'Cham [Ham was] … exiled to Africa.'[50] He also sug-gested that Africans were descendants of people that settled in the land of Canaan. Annius therefore attempted to merge an idea that the Mark of Cain was connected to the blackness of Africans. The story of the Mark of Cain was also in Genesis and described how Cain, the son of Adam, became the first criminal after he killed his brother, Abel. Cain was marked by God for his crime and was forced to dwell in the land of Nod.[51] The Mark of Cain was ordained by God. So this was a devious way of trying to convince theologians that Africans had been cursed by God and not by man.[52]

However, Annius did not create a coherent anti-African theology, although he did fabricate a genealogical one that entwined Pan and Canaan's blood lines.[53] Annius, in a similar way to some early modern Christian theologians, wanted to capitalise on a renaissance interest in the classics, including Egyptian and Greek legends. Opportunistically, he saw this as a chance to show how the Bible was modern enough to include the 'new' knowledge that was becoming popular among European elites and some of the common folk. Annius did that by conflating what were essentially pagan stories with biblical ones, with the inclusion of Greek gods such as Pan. Pan was associated with mischief, trickery and malevolence. Of course, Pan was already a notorious character in medieval and early sixteenth-century art, poetry and writings.[54] Annius' fantasies borrowed stories and idioms from this notoriety. However, Greek legends offered a world view of theology, cosmology, morality and history that was incompatible with the Bible. Annius' interpolations therefore created a salmagundi that conflated theologically antagonistic narratives, and collapsed them into an Old Testament timeline. This was a timeline that conjured up a fantastic world that was only 6,000 years old. It was a world in which Greek and Kemetian Gods became part of the biblical 'original family' of mankind. This timeline was known as the Annian genealogy.[55]

Early Modern Interpolations

Some of Annius' ideas were taken up by early modern authors. They interpolated Africans as being the children of Ham and heir to Ham's 'wickedness.' One of the early modern writers to do this was Heinrich Agrippa, the same author mentioned in the last chapter that had defended the rights of women. He claimed Ham, who he called 'Cham … [was] the more wicked than the rest and cruel towards his father.'[56] Agrippa then stated that 'Egyptians' and 'Ethiopians' were Ham's descendants. It is noteworthy that the 'Egyptians' that Agrippa referred to were Ancient Egyptians, and not the 'counterfeit' ones of early modern England. Agrippa also wrote that 'Freers, Monkes and other wandering prowlers' of Rome were children of Ham as well.

For Agrippa, Ham was not the figure that appeared in early modern biblical texts, he was an active protagonist of infamy. This Ham was an amalgamation of classical and mythical characters such as: Ea, who murdered his father Apsu in the Babylonian epic the *Enuma Elish* (1800–1100 BCE); Kronos, who castrated and killed his father with a sickle and later ate his children in the classical Greek writer Hesiod's (750–650 BCE) *Theogony* (700 BCE) (genealogy of the Gods); and the daughters of King Pelias, who killed him in the *Argonautica*, about Jason and the Argonauts, written by the Egyptian-born writer Apollonius of Rhodes (200–250 BCE). Then there was Oedipus, the classical figure that killed his father, Lauis, the King of Thebes, and then married his mother.[57] Through Annius' forgeries, Ham became the father and originator of these acts of terror and patricide.

During the early modern period, despite the lack of biblical justification, other authors also claimed that Ham was the 'father of wickedness' and that Africans were cursed. This included the French linguist and cartographer Guillaume Postel de Etienne in *Cosmographicae* (1561). He wrote:

The name Ethiopia which means black comes from the Greek
and is a hidden etymology for Cush … it signifies servant …
cush is the first son of cham [Ham]. Cham was black coloured
but came from white parents this coloured tinge most certainly
signified a divine punishment.[58]

Postel, despite being a linguist, had managed to conflate several
nominative cognomens together; for example we know that Cush
did not 'signify servant,' but was the name of the ancient African
civilisation south of Kemet. Postel also relied on Greek etymology of
the word 'Ethiopia,' which means 'Aitho' 'ops': 'burnt face.'[59] The
myth it came from stated that the complexion of Africans was caused
by the deity Phaethon (Phaeton) when he lost control of Phoebus'
war chariot. This was a chariot that carried the Sun. The result was
that this cataclysmic act burnt the earth and 'scorched' Africans
Black. This fable was rooted in an adage from Herodotus and the
Roman writer Publius Ovidius Naso (Ovid) that the 'Ethiopians
were the oldest people in the world.'[60] This myth was alluded to
by More, Bacon and Thomas Browne (below) and in early modern fiction such as *Anthony and Cleopatra* (1608) where Cleopatra
described herself as 'Phoebus' amorous pinches black'[61] and in the
Masque of Blacknesse (1605) where the character Niger says:

As of one Phaëton, that fired the world,
And that, before his heedless flames were hurl'd
About the globe, the Æthiops were as fair
As other dames; now black, with black despair:
And in respect of their complexions chang'd[62]

Postel conflated these sorts of myths within the biblical
chronology of Genesis 10 that Cush was the son of Ham. Postel
then emphasised what other authors had not, which was the
blackness of Ham's descendants. It is possible that this emphasis was influenced by the time he spent learning Arabic and

studying in areas controlled by the Ottoman Empire. There he may have absorbed ideas about the inferiority of Africans that were already circulating in that Empire.[63] Postel then appears to have interpreted, confused and exaggerated ideas from authors such as Annius, Khallikan and Josephus. The cumulative effect of these interpolations was to create a myth of a myth that had a completely different theological narrative and trajectory. It is from these interpolations and not from early modern Bibles that the blackness of Africans became synonymous with the Curse of Ham.

However, the prime purpose of these interpolations by Annius was to frame the 'new' knowledge of the Renaissance so that it did not become a theological threat to Christianity. It was certain that the writings of medieval and early modern theologists – such as Thomas Aquinas, William of Ockham, Thomas More, John Dee and Francis Bacon – also infused their narratives with classical ideas such as universals and hermeneutics. Some of these writers even attempted empirical analysis of natural phenomena and attempted to explain them in 'rational' terms.[64] But Annius, unlike Dee or Bacon, was not attempting to move towards empiricism.[65] In fact by Annius adopting the more mythical aspects of Greek culture[66] and philosophy he was taking Christianity nearer to mythology and paganism, and further away from a plain reading of biblical texts. So Annius' intent was to assimilate the teachings of eminent Greek philosophers. Annius wanted Christianity to be strong enough to triumph in the spiritual war against 'heathen' religions – but ironically, with the Pope's blessing, he was willing to absorb aspects of heathenism to do it.

Of course, some Christians had been incorporating aspects of 'heathen,' 'pagan' and animist religions into Christianity since before the early modern period. But that had been done strategically. For example, dates chosen for the commemoration of Christian holy festivals were often placed on the days of pagan holidays to ensure the former's popularity. In some cases this meant rebranding or reinterpreting pagan festivals so they became Christian ones, but with pagan motifs and symbology assimilated within. For example, Easter – the Easter Bunny and Easter eggs are all symbols of pagan fertility. It was not just pagan ideas but places of worship that could also be co-opted into Christian ones, with churches often constructed on the ruined desecration of pagan temples.[67] However, Annius took this a stage further by actually manufacturing his own myths. Consequently, his fantasies on colour and ethnology were only a byproduct of his wider intentions. But once he had manufactured these interpolations they could be used to suggest that Africans were cursed children of Ham.

George Best's 'Infection'

So far in this chapter we have not focused on interpolations of the Curse of Ham written by Englishmen. We will now see that interpolations were penned by some English authors. One such author was the English writer and traveller George Best (d. 1584). The historian David Whitford claimed that George Best had read Postel and this influenced his ideas.[68] This was possible, but Best was actually writing about the Africans he had seen living in Tudor England. He then sought to explain the origins of these Africans' complexions using interpolations.[69] Best says:

> to return again to the Blacke Moors. I myself have seen an
> Ethiopian as black as the father was, although England were his
> native country, and an English woman his mother, whereby,
> it seemeth this blacknesses proceedeth rather of some naturall
> infection of that man which was so strong, that neither native of

the clime, neither the good complexion of the Mother concurring could anything alter.[70]

Best used the terms 'Black Moors' and 'Ethiopian' interchangeably to describe Africans in Africa and those people of African descent born in England. But his nominative nomenclature does not reveal whether he had seen one 'Ethiopian' or many in Tudor England. From the context it appears he would have been unlikely to make a statement about ethnology, if he had only seen one. Best wrote about people of African descent that had African fathers and white mothers. Interestingly, he does not comment on babies born from African mothers and white fathers, although my research suggests that children from those types of relationships were more common.[71]

Best was concerned about Africans born in Tudor England. Best wrote that these 'Ethiopian[s]' were as 'black as the father was.' This made Best question ideas about blackness or 'blacknesse' as he calls it. Best decided that if an African's blacknesse can 'stubborn[ly]' persist in England, despite the person being 'native of the clime,' with a lack of sun, then this meant that blacknesse was not the result of the Sun. This made Best doubt the premise that whiteness was the 'natural inheritance' of those born in England. It may also have meant that African people's inheritance, i.e. their blacknesse, was more dominant than whiteness. The power of blacknesse had to be defined as having a supernatural source – the Curse of Ham – to avoid a conclusion that would make Best part of a 'weaker' people.

Best claimed there was an internal difference between Africans and white people. And this difference was based on a 'naturall infection' that cannot be 'alter[ed]' and 'can not be cured'; a 'Natural infection [that came from] … the first inhabitants of that country.'[72] For a modern reader, the word 'infection' conjures associations of blacknesse with a disease. Some of the experiments on people of African descent undertaken over the next 400 years to 'cure' Africans, by 'washing them white,' may have originated from such fantasies.[73] Best described the blacknesse as something that persists inside the body as a disease does. But in a contradictory way, Best also claimed that this blacknesse was a 'natural' 'blot of infection of blood,' and then theorised that it was a sign of Chus' 'disobedience to God.'[74]

It is interesting that Best focused on Chus, who was another son of Ham, and not Canaan. This may have been a mistake on Best's part, a mistake that other commentators also made. Best believed that this 'infection' of blacknesse was passed on in the blood to all Africans including those in Tudor England, and their English-born children. Best's perspective on blacknesse was contrasted with his position on whiteness. And this reveals his chromatic hierarchy, in which blacknesse was a malady, a problem, and whiteness was 'good.' For a more detailed analysis of these issues as they relate to a hidden hierarchy of colours in human consciousness, readers may wish to examine the work of Brent Berlin and Paul Kay, or that of Frances Cress Welsing.[75]

By making Ham an active protagonist, Best sought to explain the blacknesse of Africans in England. Ham became a sinner and Chus was effectively born from that sin. Best stated that Noah told his sons not to have sex or children during the passage of the Ark, but that they should 'lie in reverence with God.' However, 'Cham [Ham] worked a child to inherit the earth [and] so slept with his wife.'[76] That was why Best said that the child 'Chus was cursed' and born 'blacke and loathsome.' And that Chus and not Ham were cursed Black so: 'that it might remain a spectacle of disobedience to all the world. And of this black and cursed Chus come all these blacke Moores which are in Africa.'[77]

Best's ideas are very important as they were the views of an Englishman that were initiated by his interactions with Africans in Tudor England. It is this familiarity, and not ignorance of Africans in England that was fuelling his ideas on difference. Best's ideas were not formed because he had imagined Africans, as one would unicorns! These Africans were integrated members of English society, and were men that had sexual relations with white English women. Tudor England was not a segregated society in that sense. The people Best was focused on were first-generation English-born 'Ethiopians' and not strangers by birth. It was precisely because these Africans were 'native' and Black that Best resorted to the Curse of Ham to rationalise their blacknesse.

Best struggled to explain how Africans in Tudor England maintained their blacknesse and he questioned why the complexion of Africans was different to other peoples. Best claimed:

> It shall not be fair from our purpose to examine the first original of those blackmen and how by lineal descent they have hither to continue blacke.[78]
>
> ...
>
> [T]he people of Africa, especially the Ethiopians are so cole blacke, their hair like wool curled short, which blacknesse and curled hair, they suppose to come only by parching of the sun, which how it should be possible I cannot see.[79]
>
> ...
>
> [S]o that if the Ethiopians blacknesse came by the heate of the Sun why should not these Americans and Indians also be as blacke as they seeying the Sunne is equally distinct to them both.[80]

Best has revealed the limitation of his geographical and anthropological knowledge. He wrote that only Africans are Black. Most modern Eurocentric anthropologists would disagree, as people with 'dark' complexions and 'nine ether' hair[81]

are to be found throughout the world,[82] whilst many historians, including African-centred historians, state with evidence
there was/is a global African presence.[83] These global peoples
are 'cole blacke, their hair like wool curled short,' as Best
described.[84] And their civilisations were to be found in the
Americas, Asia, Europe and Oceania. But Best claimed that
'Americans and Indians' are not 'blacke.' Perhaps he was only
talking about the Americans that he had heard about or seen.
He may indeed have seen them, since Native Americans were
living in early modern England. Records of their baptisms and
burials are located in cities and towns such as London, Bristol
and Plymouth. William Harrison referred to them and their
customs in his *History of England* and John Stow did the same
in *The Chronicles* where he described the Native Americans[85]
he saw in Bristol in 1502.[86]

Five years after Best wrote his letters in 1584, the sixteenth-century European traveller Lupold von Wedel described the Native
Americans that came to England with Walter Raleigh. Their
names were Wanchese and Manteo, and although they were very
useful to Raleigh in his activities, they were described by Wedel
and other contemporary writers as the epitome of otherness, and
'most childish and silly figure[s],' but also 'fierce and cruel.'[87]
So Best may have observed Native Americans in early modern
England and felt justified to claim that they did not resemble
Africans. This supported his argument that it was not the Sun
but the Curse that was the origin of Africans' complexion.

The Africans that Best had seen in early modern England made
him question the Bible and his own identity. Best believed in the
theory of monogenesis, but if Africans had always been Black as
he proposed, this meant that other people in the Bible were too,
including perhaps the 'original' family. And as a result if man
was made in the image of God, then this would make Africans

divine, God Black, and white people the other.[88] To avoid this conclusion, Best decided that the original man was 'manifestly and plainely appeareth by Holy Scripture ... white, and their wives also, by course of nature should have begotten and brought forth white children.'[89] These ideas were anti-biblical and did not appear in early modern Bibles. It was speculation and interpolation that conjured them, to avoid a troubling theory about the otherness of whiteness.

Best's statements should be seen in context. They are important because they were the comments made by an Englishman that referred to Africans that lived in Tudor England. They also revealed that some Englishmen were willing to use interpolations from the myth to stigmatise Africans. But Best was not writing a sixteenth-century treatise on ethnicity and race, even though the way his comments appear in this book may make it seem so. Best's comments were actually written interspersed over four pages with other observations on various subjects such as travel, politics, religion, fashion, climate and culture. They were more like a stream of consciousness, randomly scribed and often illogically arranged. Best's comments did not form a coherent narrative. And they were not evidence of a well-developed anti-African ideology.

Best lived at a time in England when the study of the sciences was not a profession, but people such as Francis Bacon and John Dee attempted experimentation and empiricism. Best was dissimilar to them and historians such as Joao de Barros, the Portuguese traveller who had extensively explored the northern and southern hemispheres and examined primary documents in the places where he studied.[90] Best was also not an intellectual such as the Ethiopian Monk Abba Bahrey, who had used historiography and ethnology to examine primary documents before he wrote, in 1593, a book on the history of the Oromo people in Ethiopia.[91] Best had not empirically investigated his ideas. He was an observer, a speculator of difference, and he used

interpolations to explain away the blacknesse of his African countrymen. However, Best did not suggest that his ideas should lead
to policies that prevented Africans from having relationships with
white people. Logically, of course, it would seem he was fuelling
such an argument – but logic does not seem to be governing these
ideas, so such a presumption may be misplaced.

Hanmer's 'Moors, Saracens, Nigroes, [and] Barbarians'

Best wrote his letters in the form of a travel diary to stir interest
amongst Englishmen for colonial exploits. Best's intention was to
write an account that inspired Englishmen to oppose Spain and
Portugal and encourage empire building. Best was not the only, or
the first English person to write such accounts, and then to speculate
on Africans being cursed. Another Englishman, Meredith Hanmer,
gave a sermon on 2 October 1586, in London, where he vocalised
similar interpolations to those of Best. Hanmer was an English prelate and the vicar of St Leonard's Church in Shoreditch, London. The
sermon that Hanmer gave was for a man called Chinano, referred to
as a 'Turk.' His entrance into England was the direct result of the
interventions of Drake, who 'rescued' him earlier that year.

In Meredith Hanmer's sermon he digressed to talk about
the Curse of Ham. His ideas are worth exploring because they
were the views of an Englishman that lived in Tudor England.
Moreover, Hanmer was likely to have met Africans around the
parish of Shoreditch and the nearby parishes of St Olave Hart
Street, such as 'Isabell a blackamore' who was buried there on 6
June 1588,[92] or those that lived in Botolph without Aldgate and
Stepney.[93] It is interesting that Hanmer did not refer to these people, nor speculate whether they were cursed. Perhaps this was
because the main focus of his sermon was about how Englishmen
should defeat the Spanish and the 'Great Turk.'[94] Hanmer was
also concerned with the 'victory' of Christ and this was what
led him to say that 'The Moores, the Saracens, the Turkes, are

all of Mahomet' and are 'cursed' because they had received the 'cursed doctrine of Mahomet.' Just to note, the word 'Saracen' was capable of describing Africans, as it did with Bartholomew, an 'Aethiopian' that lived in thirteenth-century England. It was also a term used to describe an African that appeared in the *Flores Historiarum*,[95] who was also known as the 'Ipswich Man'; he was buried in Grey Friar's monastery in the thirteenth century.[96]

Best praised the 'success of Mohammed's religion' and how 'Mohammed wrote in the Arabic tongue and taught them,' when in fact it was well known that 'Mohammed' did not write.[97] However, most of the Africans that have been found that lived in early modern English parishes were not Muslims, but Christians. Hanmer did not mention what effect their baptisms had on the Curse. But his comments on the nature of blackness would seem to suggest that the sacrament[98] did not remove the Curse, as he claimed:

> The Moors called Mauriinhabite Mauritania in Affricke, they are (sayeth Isidor) of the progenie of Cham, whose posterity Noe (Noah) accursed and ... [these] cursed people receive the cursed doctrine of Mahomet.[99]

In other words Africans were twice cursed: by their colour and by their religion. The baptism would only have removed the second curse, and not the first. It is interesting that Hanmer used Isidore the fifth/sixth-century Visigothic theologian to justify his ideas about Africans being maledicted. But it was reckless for Hanmer to paraphrase Isidore's ideas in this way.[100] In fact, Isidore stated:

> Africans are named for one of the descendants of Abraham, who was called Afer. He is said to have led an army against Libya and settled there after he had conquered the enemy and his descendants were named Africans, and the place named Africa, after their ancestor.[101]

Isidore wrote that 'Africa was held initially by the 'Libyans,'' then the 'Africans' and after this the 'Getulians,' and finally the 'Moors and Numidians.' Isidore stated that the 'Moors and Numidians,' 'so the Africans believed,' owed their origins to 'Hercules' and his 'leaderless army.'[102]

Hanmer also misquoted and quoted other classical etymology to describe Africans:

> These people inhabiting Mahomet in Affrike are because of
> their hewe and colour of the Latins called Nigritae, in our vulgar
> speech Nigros and of the Grecians in the same sent for their ...
> blacke colour called maupos and ... Moores. These receiving the
> corruption of Mahomet are called Saracens.[103]

Hanmer had concocted this sermon as political/religious propaganda to champion Protestantism. That intention meant it was difficult to ascertain if, or how, his general observations on 'Nigros' and 'Moores' related specifically to Africans in England. Notwithstanding that, we may note that in the midst of Hanmer's general position, he was not above giving qualified praise to Africans. For example, he praised a nation of Africans who were under the authority of 'Prester John the great King of Aethiopia ... [and stated they] professeth the[ir] faith in Christ.' But this was qualified, because he later stated that these Africans did not practise Christianity as 'purely as it is to be wished.'[104] And in Hanmer's discussion of non-Christian Africans he was not above lauding some of those nations as well. Perhaps because he felt that they could be potential allies, he said:

> Nigros in the kingdom of Senega [Senegal], [despite] being of
> the faith of Mahomet ... are not malicious neither stubbornly
> bent against the Christians: they are delighted with the behaviour
> of the Christians and [regard] ... our faith and religion to be
> holier and the better.[105]

Whether Hanmer believed that the Africans in the Kingdom of Senega were cursed Black by Noah or God he did not say. But his praise of them seemed to show a theological inconsistency in praising those that were actually cursed. And even while Best labelled most Africans as 'infidels,' 'Moors, Saracens, Nigroes, Barbarians, [that are] addicted to Mahomet and obedient to the great Turk,' he acknowledged that there were also 'Jews and Hebrews in Aethiopia.'[106] This same point was also acknowledged by others such as John Legat in 1596,[107] and Samuel Purchas in 1613, who stated: 'The Jewes scattered some violently, some willingly through Asia, Africa and Europe.'[108]

It may be that Hanmer had been influenced by interpolations about the Curse of Ham, but not wholly indoctrinated by them. Hanmer was more likely to see Africans in a 'paternal' way, as Samuel Purchas described: as a 'wandering sheepfold' that could find Christ in the same way as everyone else. In fact Hanmer used these precise words when he said that Englishmen should:

> open the eyes of all Infidels, Jewes, Turkes, and Saracens [this included Africans as stated above], bring into the folde of lost and wandering sheep males of all nations one sheepfolde under the head shepherd and Bissoppe of our … Jesus Christ.[109]

Certainly, there were other less theological and more material reasons for Hanmer's sermon and his views. These reasons were more to do with making money and had little connection to theology or ethnology. Hanmer admitted in the same sermon that Englishmen are 'gredily bent to gete the earthly commodities of Affrike and Asia.'[110] Hanmer may have been talking about himself, as in a similar way to Best he was a supporter of the adventurer and privateer Francis Drake.[111] This support may have influenced his perspectives on ethnicity. Drake was involved in people smuggling and slave trading with his cousin John Hawkins and on his own cognisance.[112] These interpolations of the myth could provide an apologia for any trafficking that included Africans. But Drake and his colleagues such as Hawkins were opportunists, as they themselves admit in their letters and correspondence. Activities along the trans-Indian, trans-Atlantic, trans-Pacific, trans-Mediterranean and trans-Saharan trade routes had not yet been confined to Africans, nor would they be for many decades to come.

The knowledge of the possible wealth that could be obtained from foreign expeditions was known to Hanmer as illustrated by his sponsorship of Drake.[113] Indeed, we know more about Hanmer that suggests he had a dubious character. The sixteenth-early-seventeenth-century historian Weever tells us Hanmer 'converted the brass of several ancient monuments into coin for his own use' and 'plucked up many plates fixed in the gravestones, and left no memory of such as had been buried under them.'[114] Furthermore, in a legal case of 1584 regarding the Earl of Shrewsbury, Hanmer was called to give evidence and may have perjured himself for money. At the court case the recorder William Fleetwood wrote that Hanmer 'regardeth not an oath, surely he is a very bad man.'[115] There is evidence that 'Dr Hanmer vicar of Shoreditch married Richard Turke of Dartford, and Getrude, the wife of John Wynd, without banns and license.'[116] The Richard Turke named in this marriage may be the baptised name for Chinano.[117] What is certain is that Hanmer was capable of committing fraud and telling lies to make money. The nineteenth-early-twentieth-century historian Henry Ellis goes further and says that 'There is a great tradition among the inhabitants of Shoreditch that the doctor [Hanmer] committed suicide [because of his sins].'[118]

Hanmer's statements were an attempt to paint English piratical activities with a theological gloss as if these adventurers were spreading the word of God, rather than seeking pecuniary advancement. Hanmer and Best seemed to have been part of a small group of Tudor Englishmen who felt the need to justify merchant adventuring with theological interpolations. One could see how later English writers may have compounded some of these ideas to claim Africans were the children of the iniquitous Ham.[119]

Early Modern Fantasies

Another Englishman that over thirty years later expressed similar sentiments to Hanmer and Best was Hugh Broughton. But as with Hanmer we do not know whether he applied his strident opinions to Africans living in early modern England. Nevertheless, his views are pertinent because they existed. Broughton was a scholar and theologian, a student of Antoine Rodolphe Chevalier who taught the young Princess Elizabeth (later Elizabeth I) French and Hebrew.[120] Broughton was a famous member of polite English society and was fictionalised and satirised as a sly and cankerous protagonist in Ben Jonson's *Volpone* and *The Alchemist*.[121] His work in *A Breife Discourse of the Scriptures* stated that Africans were cursed. It seemed that in an attempt to develop his ideas Broughton conflated notions such as those expressed by Annius, Postel, Best and Hanmer. He wrote:

> For whatsoever plagues doth befell the Egiptians, the Canaanites, Ethiopians, Blackemores, Babylonians, and *such like* [emphasis my own] contained within Cham's curse … Cham his name signifieth hot or cholericke[122] [Ham] the Prince of Afficke … and those countries did his sonnes … passes, namely in Africa in the South Counties, Cham (the spreader of wickednesse) inhabited the fourth part of the world with his families … Cham had a curse in this world and doubles in the world to come … He had four sonnes the first Cush, of whom came the Ethiopians,[123] or in our tongue Burnt-faces, the second Mizriam of whom the Egyptians came … the third Put, of whom the Libyans and Blackamoores came, and the fourth Canaan of whom the Canaanites come in whom the curse of Cham was pronounced. [And the last line is the important one] notwithstanding that it falleth out also in all his other sonnes.[124]

Of course we now know that none of these ideas came from a reading of the Bible but from a reliance on interpolations that were classical, mythical and fantastically inspired. It is this heady mix that made the myth exciting. A plain reading of the Bible did not have the same impact. That may also be why Broughton extrapolated about Africans being part of a land and inheriting their 'hot and cholericke' nature from it. His inclusion of this idea was lifted from a Greek concept of the theory of the four humors, where human nature could be divided into four types, related to an element, season, colour, organ and temperament.[125] One of those types was 'hot and cholericke.'[126] Broughton's imagination did not extend to question whether Africans that lived in England had that temperament, but he did fantasise that Ham the 'Prince of Affricke' did. He also magnified the profile of some of Ham's descendants, such as Nimrod, whom he called a 'mighty hunter.' But Broughton mistakenly named Ham as the recipient of the Curse, when our close reading of the biblical texts revealed that Noah did not curse Ham at all, but Canaan. Although, interestingly, as with some of the other English writers, Broughton seemed more interested in Cush than Canaan.

In Broughton's earlier book, *A Concent of Scripture* (1588), a map was included which directly contradicted his view in *A Briefe Discourse*. The map may have been based on one created by Jodocus Hondius, the Dutch cartographer, and showed the dispersal of the descendants of the Sons of Ham. The map used colours to represent the sons of Noah. And it appeared to indicate that Noah's descendants were present on all three continents of Africa, Asia and Europe.[127]

In addition to Broughton, there were other early modern English writers that extrapolated ideas about Africans being cursed. They included Thomas Hall in 1661 and Isaac Bassie in 1673. Hall drew on the kinds of ideas discussed earlier, but seemed to have had a desire to make an English theology that supported African inferiority. He wrote:

> The Ethiopians were a vile accursed Nation ... oye children
> of Israel why I should respect you more than the[m] ...
> Ethiopians (that accursed and ... posterity of Cham) I do now
> no more value you then so many Blackmores and Heathens.[128]

Hall postulated that Africans were the enemies of the world. This
is clearly the beginning of a theological scapegoating that could
stigmatise Africans as inherently inferior. But even by 1661 not
many English commentators were willing to extend this metaphor into laws and regulations which could be enforced. That
would not be until the very end of the seventeenth century and
the beginning of the eighteenth. Nevertheless, in 1673, the writer
Isaac Bassie stated:

> above (4000 years) as a foul brand upon Cham and his cursed
> posterity for the Egyptians and Ethiopians or Blackmoores
> are the descendants of cursed Cham ... and ... [are] a
> warning piece to all such young Cham as dare to disgrace
> their parents privately.[129]

Bassie blamed the Africans of posterity for the existence of sin.
He also placed a date on this and suggested that they had only
been in existence for 4,000 years. In other words that their blackness was an aberration placed on a portion of the original family
of mankind to mark their malediction. And Bassie in a similar
way to Broughton mistakenly assumed that Ham was cursed by
his father. Bassie and Hall's ranting resembled the othering of
Africans in the eighteenth and nineteenth centuries. But the last
line from Bassie's quotation seemed to indicate another purpose
for his tirade, which was to warn children not to disobey their
fathers. In other words, he had amplified the nature of Ham's
crimes and punishments so that the whole story of the Curse of
Ham had resonance. His overall aim was to provide a cautionary
tale for English school children.

Shooting the Messenger

I that do bring the news made not the match.[130]

There is an old adage in international relations as vocalised in the play *Anthony and Cleopatra*: 'shoot not the messenger.' In other words messengers are only vessels, without their own opinions. Such an idea may help us understand whether Englishmen in early modern England really believed that Africans were cursed. This is because we need to provide a context for statements written about Africans by Englishmen in the early modern period. Some modern historians have interpreted early modern writers as automatically having the same views as they repeated.[131] However, a more critical perspective enables us to see some of these statements as the repetition of ideas without endorsements. As Samuel Purchas wrote, these English translators worked:

> to help our English Nation, that they might knowe and
> understand many things, which are common in other languages,
> but utterly concealed from this poore Island.[132]

The early modern works in question took the form of books, letters, poems, diaries and so on, that owed their origins to various Hebrew, Greek, Latin, Spanish, Portuguese and Arabic writers that authored them. In some of these writings there were interpolations about Africans being children of Ham, Cush or Canaan. Sometimes these early modern English writers repeated a genealogy of Africans (as Josephus did), without saying whether they considered Africans as cursed. It may also be that these writers wanted to give an authentic or accurate account of the original authors' work. But it did not mean that these ideas were automatically believed by the English writers that wrote them, or by the English people that read and heard them. Good examples of this are the collection of writings contained in the anthology compiled by Samuel Purchas.

Purchas was an English writer that never travelled far from his home in Essex. Instead he collected the accounts and stories of travellers. Purchas added to these with unsorted and random travel entries and miscellaneous collections of essays from the English writer Richard Hakluyt. Some of these works included not only first-hand accounts of what Englishmen had written or seen but the regurgitated interpolations and myths from dubious sources. Purchas writes:

> Cham posteritie was Cush, Mizriam, Put and Canaan. These possessed the south of Asia and Africa of Cham is the name Chemmmu in Aegypt and Amnan the oracle so notorious. Cush gave name to the Aethopians and Arabians known in scripture by that name. Mizriam to the Aegyptians ... Punt to the Libyans sometimes called Phuthaei: the river Fut is mentioned by Pliny not far from Atlas ... Libyans, Ghananim, the Troglodytes, Lebabim, the Cyrenacker, the Napthuhim, Africa the less, Chasluhim, the Saracens, Caphtorim, the Cappadocians [have the same ancestor]. But long before Pliny, the Scripture speaketh of the people of the region [Africa] (not only those which are said to descend of Cush, the sonne of Chem [Ham] but of many others).[133]

We can see that this account from Purchas was not the result of kingdoms and civilisations that an English traveller had visited, but it relied on some of the classical genealogical tracing mentioned in the Bible, with additional references to the works of the Ancient Greek writer Pliny. Pliny wrote about Africans in his writings and sometimes included fantastic fables. The question is how much of the quotation revealed what Englishmen actually thought of Africans, and whether these ideas were capable of being applied to Africans in early modern England. Best did do this, but other English writers seemed reticent.

The English translator Richard Eden also referred to Africans as being descendants of Ham. But it is by no means

clear whether he considered Africans as cursed in the popular and widely distributed *The Decades of the New World*,
published in 1555.[134] Eden also included a Hamitic genealogy
similar to the Annian one, which included references from Pliny
as well as other Greek authors.[135] The terms that Eden used to
describe Africans included classical ones from the Greek and
Latin words such as 'Libya,' which delineated regions and
occasionally referred to the whole continent of Africa.[136] The
same applied to the word 'Cyrneacker,' the Greek name for
the city of Cyrenia in northern Africa. Eden also used the term
'Ghananim,' based on a native African word 'Ghana' used to
describe the warrior kings of the kingdoms of Mauritania and
Mali.[137] Some of the other terms were biblical (Genesis 10, verse
13; 1 Chronicles 1, verse 11), such as 'Napthuhim,' which referred
to the African people that lived west of Kemet. The names
'Charulm' and 'Caphtorim' were the names for the cities mentioned in North Africa and Palestine.[138] The term 'Troglodytes'
defined people that dwelt in caves. This was something that
some commentators suggested the African Garamantes did, so
the term sometimes became synonymous with them.[139]

In 1604, the Welsh writer George Owen Harry adopted a similar approach to Eden in his *The Genealogy of the High and Mighty
Monarch James*. He gifted Ham with a classical and mythical lineage that was illustrious. He claimed:

> Cham called the Saturn of Egypt, the youngest sonne of Noah,
> taking to himself that part of the third world called Africa ...
> booke to wife his sister Rhea, begeat many children of who ...
> was called Mizriam or Osiris father of the Egyptians.[140]

In this interpolation Ham as a 'Prince of Affricke' took a woman
called Rhea as his wife. This Rhea is probably a conflation of the
mythical pagan 'Rhea,' sister and wife of the Greek deity Kronos,
who castrated his father. The commingling of Kronos with Ham

meant that Ham now married a woman that resembled Kronos' wife.[141] Furthermore, in this interpolation Kronos was not only the father of Zeus, but also the ancestor of the Kemetian God Osiris. And Osiris (Ausar) and his wife Auset become part of Ham's lineage. This would ultimately make the Egyptian pharaohs also children of Ham, since the pharaohs claimed direct descent from Ausar and Heru (the son of Ausar). Owen seemed to have muddled an already convoluted fantasy. We shall see that this sort of farrago was why the entire myth was unpalatable to some early modern readers.

The early modern English writers that quoted interpolations of the Curse of Ham fantasised in different ways. Most Englishmen that wrote about difference and ethnology did not believe that Africans' skin colour was the result of the Curse of Ham, but some believed that Africans had a lineage that came from Ham (Hamitic lineage). These Englishmen, such as Edward Leigh, stated that Africans' blackness was the result of the heat. He wrote:

> The Hebrews say Cham ... for black this Cham is named either for his heat or his blackness [and that] ... Cham laboured in excessive heat when he reached Africa, and almost all his descendants are burned or dark skinned by the heat of the Sun.[142]

Leigh's commentary seemed to be a mixture of etymological ideas that originated from interpretations arising from the Latin word 'Aphrike' for Africa meaning 'without cold' and the Greek word 'Aethiopian.'[143]

So far we have not quoted anyone of African descent that suggested the Curse of Ham was a cause of Africans' blackness. One person of African descent that did was the Moorish writer Leo Africanus. He was born in Iberia and wrote about Africans using the reference points of classical writers. Africanus also included mythical aspects in his works, perhaps for the prurient tastes of his European readers. By the time of the completion of Africanus' work, he had converted to Christianity, but he had once been a Muslim. Africanus may have drawn on interpolations from his various theological backgrounds when he suggested that Africans were children of Ham:

> For all the negroes or black Moores take their descent from
> Chus the sonne of Cham who was the son of Noe ... The tawnie
> Moores fetch their pedigree from the Sabeans [and] Saba was
> begotten of Rana which was the eldest sonne of Chus.[144]

Africanus was one of the few writers of African descent in the early modern period to mention the Hamitic lineage. But he did not say that Africans were cursed because they had that lineage.[145]

We have seen that early modern writers such as Africanus were aware of the Curse of Ham, as were some English writers. However, the actual texts of early modern Bibles written by Englishmen did not stigmatise Africans or their skin colour, or mention slavery. The evidence so far revealed there was a disparity between what early modern Bibles said, and what some early modern writers were willing to imagine. Furthermore, the early modern writers appeared to have felt no need to actually change the text of the Bibles they read so that they contained that anti-African antipathy. So no matter how salacious some of these interpolations were, they did not appear to have had the efficacy to alter textual orthodoxy. Any early modern person that quoted or repeated an interpolation would have been relying on words that were extra-biblical or perhaps anti-biblical. It was not the text of early modern Bibles, but a series of interpolations, forgeries and fabrications made by Hebrew, Islamic and Christian scholars.

Moreover, even if early modern English commentators said that they believed in the myth – that did not mean that they automatically believed in an anti-African interpolation. As conceivably they could believe Africans were the children of Ham but not believe that they were cursed. And other English Christians may have studied the Annian genealogy but not professed any anti-African sentiments at all. These realisations may be at variance with our modern perceptions, but we can see that to determine the impact of the myth on Africans in early modern England will not be straightforward. We cannot just quote the Curse of Ham and leave it at that. To understand the social ethnology and wider societal history of Africans in early modern England requires more than this kind of approach. But now at least we know what was not part of that history: a religious biblical orthodoxy that automatically othered Africans. We will now investigate ideas in early modern England that offered different views about the ethnology of Africans, and reveal that some Englishmen revered, venerated and celebrated the Blackamoore's 'blacknesse.'

FOUR | Painting the Blackamoore Black

So that I see not why Blackness should be thought such a Curse to the Negroes.[1]

[T]hey esteeme deformity by other colours, describing the devil, and terrible objects white.[2]

Reflections on Blackness

Africans lived in early modern England at the same time that the documents discussed in the last chapter were being written, published and talked about. Some of the Englishmen that wrote and spoke about Africans had seen, lived near and in some cases lived with these people. Best tells us this, with his notions of ethnology prompted by familiarity with Africans that were born and lived in England. In fact it was these people's proximity to him and not their foreignness that instigated his reflections on their blackness. So no matter how we interpret his work as othering Africans, the Africans he wrote about were part of the same English society he was.

As a modern reader, some of our inability to understand Best's remarks lies in not having the reference points to make sense of how Englishmen saw difference, skin colour, nationhood and so on. Africans lived in an English society where race was not conceptualised as it is now. And yet we have been told that early modern England was a racist society. And that this was the time and place where racism against Africans began. Through that prism we frame the primary evidence we find, to confirm our own prejudices about that society. But we can now see early modern society as it was and appreciate the significance that English Bibles did not state that Africans were cursed. Of course, we have discovered that towards the end of the sixteenth century some English people created and/or repeated interpolations that did refer to Africans in that way. However, these English people did this for a multitude of reasons. In England, a systemic anti-African theology did not exist until much later.[3]

Nevertheless, it is possible for modern readers to use modern notions of logic to interpret ethnology in early modern thought, and claim that simply because an idea about Africans is illogical today, it would have been unbelievable then. Logic is/was not a prerequisite for belief. Some early modern writers' explanations of the blackness of Africans were stranger than Best's asides or Hanmer's sermon, as they metaphorically painted the Blackamoore Black.[4] This is a consideration we may remember as we examine more about how Africans were seen in early modern society. The early modern writers and thinkers discussed in this chapter set aside interpolations of the Curse of Ham. They speculated that the blackness of Africans was the result of climate or heat. Sometimes Englishmen used their own logic, rhetoric or relativism to make sense of the complexion of the people they met. A good example of this relativism can be seen in comments made by the traveller Richard Madox. In 1588 he stated that many 'fantasticall stories' told about Africans were 'illusions' created by the Africans themselves, and then retold to Europeans in 'mockery, sometyme a report of ignorance, sometyme a tale of deceyt.' Madox concluded that these stories were often embellished by rival African merchants and others to 'scare us [Englishmen] away' from 'all the trade' in West Africa.[5] Notable Englishmen adopted a similar scepticism and could not countenance that curses had any power at all.

The Mythology of Cursing

Duke of Buckingham
… for curses never pass
The lips of those that breathe them in the air.
Queen Margaret
I'll not believe but they ascend the sky,
And there awake gods gentle sleeping peace.
…

Duke of Gloucester
What doth she say my Lord of Buckingham?
Duke of Buckingham
Nothing that I respect my gracious Lord.[6]

The biblical Curse uttered by Noah was a 'solemn utterance intended to invoke a supernatural power.' Noah intended to 'inflict harm or punishment' on Ham or his descendant/s.[7] Usually such utterances meant that the one cursing was guilty of a sin. In other words, Noah was the sinner. In early modern England, witches and practitioners of 'black magic' were executed for precisely these types of acts.[8] This was unless their words could be construed as prophetic. To determine this would depend on many matters, including the virtue of the speaker. On this principle, early modern sensibilities can sometimes be gauged through the plays written at the time.

In William Shakespeare's *Richard III*, Queen Margaret was part of a deposed branch of English royalty. She had lost both her family and position. Margaret claimed that she was 'a prophetess.'[9] An early modern audience watching her may believe that she was. But despite this, Buckingham still claimed 'curses never pass/the lips.' Buckingham reflected an early modern scepticism that maledictions were without life. In a similar way, early modern English readers and listeners could read or hear about Noah's utterances and dismiss them. After all Noah was drunk, skyclad[10] and besmirched by his transgressions.

Often this scepticism towards curses was there to dissuade people from cursing. And this was not without reason, as in early modern England 'the poor,' 'the rich,' 'women,' 'Catholics,' 'Protestants,' 'religious dissenters,' 'the French,' 'Egyptians,' 'Germans,' 'Irish,' 'Jewish' people, 'Spaniards,' 'Gentiles,' 'Turkish' people, 'Native Americans,'[11] all 'foreigners,' 'the English' themselves, 'left-handed people' (because they were 'sinister'), 'the Pope,' 'the kings of Spain and Portugal,' 'Elizabeth I,' or 'if she married a foreigner,' those 'that work on the Sabbath,' 'those that took the lord's name in vain,' 'those who read the Koran,' 'those that read the Bible too well,' 'those that do not read the Bible well enough,' 'those that read the Bible in English,' etc. were all cursed.[12] With such a list of 'cursed' people, it is no wonder that the validity of any curse was questioned. And even if Africans were added to this list, they would only be part of, not separate from, the rest of humanity that had also been cursed by somebody.

For people in early modern England to believe that Noah's Curse had any validity at all, a theological case had to be made to prove that the subject of the Curse was sinful enough to deserve it. In this case it was problematic, because Ham's children were not protagonists in the story, and the God of Abraham had already blessed them for saving the fauna of the earth. This may have been why interpolations were created – because plain readings of the Bible did not provide adequate justifications for punishing Ham and his children. As described in the last chapter, outlandish interpolations were imagined. And we now know some of these interpolations drew inspirations from paganism and classical Greek fables, and not from the Bible. These interpolations fabricated sins that Ham, Canaan or Chus committed to make their punishments more deserved. That is why Ham and his children became the 'Princes of Affrike' that delved 'into … evil magical art[s],' as in the stories of Clement of Rome. Some of Clement's stories were translated and read in early modern

England. He claimed that Ham had 'handed down the instruction of ... [the evil magic] to one of his sons, who was called Mesriam ... from whom the race of the Egyptians ... Babylonians and Persians are descended.'[13]

Other writers stated that Ham had done more to Noah than 'uncover' him. Jean de Cartigny stated this in his fifteenth-century work translated by the Englishman William Goodyear. Cartigny wrote that through 'the magical arts' Ham 'disclosed his fathers privites ... he presumed to touch ... his secret parts [genitals] ... and inchanted them by his Magical Arte ... he [Noah] could not joye issue with any women, to beget children.'[14] These stories were created not just to delegitimise Ham or his children, but to theologically legitimise Noah. Other interpolations had Ham or his sons castrate his father and/or be engaged in homosexual acts with him, with the word 'uncover' being a euphemism for those acts. The implication of some of these interpolations was that Ham, through an incestuous union with his own mother, had fathered Canaan, Mizriam and Chus.[15] In this way, Ham and his children were ill-fated and doomed anti-heroes, as in the classical legends. And therefore by default Noah's Curse was vindicated.

We now know that this need to legitimise Noah's cursing was also why some writers conflated it with the Mark of Cain. This provided a theological validation for Noah's Curse which could then be said to come directly from God. Christian writers such as Ambrosiaster (fourth century) and Honorius Augustodunensis (twelfth century) wrote these kinds of interpolations. This idea was also pursued by some English writers in the early modern period such as the popular female author Juliana Berners (Barnes) in *The Book of St Albans* published in 1486. Berners was the female prioress of St Albans and her book was widely read and republished throughout the sixteenth and seventeenth centuries by authors such as Gervase Markham.[16] Berners stated that Ham's descendants lived in the land of Canaan, and then by default the Mark of Cain fell on them too. This meant Ham's descendants were twice cursed.[17] However, Berners did not state that Africans were the recipients of this double curse: in fact she stated something else far more fascinating.

'Europe is the country of churls'

Berners' book did not label Africans in any negative way. Her work stated that English people were children of Ham. Despite Berners' popularity, the implication of this idea for early modern thought is rarely discussed by modern historians.[18] Especially as Berners described the Hamitic lineage as a heritage that many European nobles aspired to be part of. And she stated that either they shared that ancestry with Africans, or it was their sole inheritance. It is a startling revelation, that some English nobility in early modern England wanted Ham and African kings to be their ancestors. It is equally startling that they believed that this lineage would legitimise their authority among other European powers. Moreover, some early modern writers advocated that Ham was the ancestor not only of English nobility but of all Europeans. The English writer Gyles Gadot (1560) asserted this in his *A Brief Abstract of the Genealogy of Late Kings of England* (1560–1562).[19] These notions meant that the European with the 'purest' Hamitic lineage was the one most entitled to rule. This was despite the apparent churlishness (commonness or vulgarity) of Ham. Berners had this to say:

> How gentleman ... first began and How Noe [Noah] divided all the world ... Cham the churl[20] was given the Europe, Japheth the noble ... the occident [Asia] and was the ancestor of Abraham, and Shem *also a gentleman* [emphasis my own] ... shall take that other third part of the world which shall be called Africa ... Europe is the country of churls, the occident countrie of gentleman, Africa is the country of temperance.[21]

Berners' comments on Europeans being 'churls,' and the inheritors of 'Cham['s] ungentleness,' was an idea reiterated throughout later editions of her book.[22] Berners later emphasised the churlishness of Europeans by disenfranchising them from Europe altogether. She wrote: 'Sem my sonne, I make thee a gentleman also to multiply the blood of Abell … to thee. I give the Orient that part of the world which be called Affica, which is the country of temperance.' Seth was given Asia, but Ham and his descendants remained landless,[23] 'vagabonds' and 'runagates' without a homeland.[24] Berners revealed a human hierarchy, one that placed white people at the bottom. White people were a rootless and wandering race, but as we shall discover, some Europeans were willing to tolerate this inscription of inferiority because it served another purpose.

As intriguing as Berners' comments were, she was not the first European to claim that Englishmen were vagabond children of Ham. The Welsh cleric and historiographer Geoffrey of Monmouth (twelfth century) also did. He mythologised an English history that stated the kings of Wales and England owed their origins to a person called 'Brutus.'[25] He was a mythical ruler of Ancient Britannia and a direct descendant of Ham. This Brutus was also purported to be a descendant of Osiris the Egyptian God and 'King in Egypt.' Tudor kings, anxious to prove their legitimacy, claimed this lineage. The Welsh writer Arthur Kelton articulated these apologues in 1547.[26] As did William Harrison with his accounts of the Giants of Albion being the first people in England: 'Albion the giant … repaired hither with … his own race proceeding from Cham … To miserable servitude and most extreme thraldom.'[27] Henry VIII embraced aspects of these legends and presented himself as a descendant of Ham. He commissioned pictures of 'his ancestor' Ham in books that he sponsored. These images resembled those found in Martin Luther's *Deutsch Catechisms* printed and available in England from 1531.[28] Henry transformed the piety of his father's cortege and embraced his 'ancestor' with a pseudo-epicurean panache.[29] Henry became a bearded master of ceremonies that presided over a court of corpulence and greed. To be 'God like,' was to be like Ham the trickster, womaniser, drunkard and glutton.[30]

Ham became Henry's legitimiser, because the English king was the son of a usurper. Other English nobles had a more direct claim to the English throne. So Henry claimed mythical ancestors such as Ham to bolster his royal pedigree. Henry employed scholars and writers to confirm his credentials. These apologues amounted to propaganda, but formed part of the works of early modern thought. Godot declared that the English and Welsh were children of classical figures such as Hercules, the kings of Troy and ancient Kemetian kings.[31] Under Elizabeth I, other Englishmen wrote about how Ham's descendants arrived in England, such as Richard Lynche in his popular 1602 treatise *Travels of Noah into Europe*. Lynche stated, as other English writers had done before, that Ham's lineage was infused with great vitality and that his trickery emulated Bacchus, Dionysus and Pan, who spent much of their time in self-ingratiating hilarity.[32] In 1604 the Welsh writer George Owen Harris proclaimed the same idea when he wrote that James I was the fulfilment of a heritage populated with African gods and Greek heroes.[33]

So these are some of the reasons why Ham and his lineage were desirable to some English, Welsh and Scottish nobility. Ham's trickery became an asset and his schemes a realisation of his vitality. He 'was the mightiest and noblest of his brethren.'[34] However, Henry VIII, Elizabeth I and James I were not the only monarchs in Europe to claim to be children of Ham. Charles V the Holy Roman Emperor, the most powerful man in Europe, also purported to have such a lineage, as did several popes and kings of France. The writings of Hieronymus Gebweiler and the Annian genealogy attest to that, and this lineage was embraced by nobles across Europe. Each one wanted to be the 'King of Kings'[35] and used whatever mechanism they felt could work. This may be why popular images of Ham showed him and his descendants as white in the *Matthew's Bible*.[36] So, when Best and Hanmer claimed that Africans were cursed children of Ham, they were actually opposing a strong and very well established European tradition that claimed the Hamitic lineage as a European heritage. This provided an obvious and powerful reason why there would be theological, political and intellectual resistance to interpolations such as those quoted by Best and Hanmer.

Sins, Folk Devils and Ham's Children

Interpolations, extrapolations and apologues about the Curse of Ham were attached to what was an already popular story. This meant that an early modern understanding of the story was not the same as we have now. The story of Noah remained popular with ordinary people in all three of the Abrahamic religions, but not because it was about the ethnology of Africans or even because it answered a desire among European nobles for classical ancestry. Rather the story of Noah was popular with everyday people because it provided lessons of obedience for children. For many it was temperament and sin, not skin colour that indicated you were a son of Ham. This lore resounds in the work of some classical writers and early church authors, such as Ambrosiaster, whose writings were translated and available in England. A 1516 version of his work stated 'servitude moreover comes from such sin'[37] – your deeds determined whether you were spiritually or metaphorically a child of Ham. Henry VIII alluded to this as a truism in his personal correspondence to Katherine of Aragon in 1532. In the preface with his hand written note,[38] Henry stated: 'No one should be a slave or bound to Christ ... Christ is freedom ... Jesu is the very freedom ... And noble libertie of the spirit ... sin is bondage [and] libertie of conscience.' This may seem ironic bearing in mind his desire to be part of a Hamitic lineage, but Henry was echoing an early modern preoccupation with Christ freeing man from iniquity. As stated by Martin Luther in his *Deutsch Catechisms*, Noah's son 'Cham' was the 'first to merit receiving the title slave,' 'slavery has its origin in sin' and slavery was 'God's punishment' for sin.[39]

We should acknowledge that the theological preoccupation with sin in the Noah story was more important than issues related to ethnology. Theologians in early modern England were obsessed by how even a good man such as Noah, and his children, could fall from grace, as it revealed the 'fragility of man.'[40] English writers such as Gervase Babington (1550–1610) concurred and their ideas were echoed in the works of the influential Dutch humanist Desiderius Erasmus, that sin and slavery could be absolved once one accepted Christ. Others such as Ambrose of Milan, a mentor of St Augustine of Hippo, repeated this notion 'for those who be true and trust in Christ' they are free, 'just as Noah['s] son Cham's sinfulness and imprudent behaviour was the course of servitude,' only 'Christ' of the New Testament could redeem mankind.[41]

English theologians could therefore label Ham and his descendants as the epitome of wickedness: folk devils and the nemesis of mankind. Through political expediency, political opponents could also become children of Ham steeped in infamy. For example, during the English Civil War, Royalists argued that the killers of King Charles I were the children of Ham and Cain. They also stated that 'Caine's bloody race known by their fruits,' had maligned 'the innocent' and were against 'the servants of the living God.'[42] These English writers claimed that the 'sufferings of the servants of the lord in Chester city' during the Civil War were caused by those with 'Cain's Mark.'[43] Moreover, that Charles I was 'Abel … the sacred majesty of the King …

of happy memory.' Evidence of the Mark/Curse was not in the perpetrator having a different skin complexion but: 'Some affix this mark unto Cain's whole body. Others confined it only to some particular part and member thereof.'[44] 'Those who [bore] … this mark to consist on a pararlytical fearful trembling of all his joints, head, hands and whole body';[45] or 'marked' with a 'stigmata' on the forehead.[46] So, to claim that your enemies were marked by Cain or cursed by Noah could be a useful ploy in sanctifying your cause against them.

It appears that for some people in early modern England, Ham's descendants could be anyone you chose to label as such. Nevertheless, some Europeans claimed a Hamitic lineage because they wanted to be associated with what they regarded as spiritual power and the mighty empires of Ham's descendants. Other Englishmen were willing to call other Englishmen sons of Ham, because they denatured them as spiritually wicked. There was not a coherent ethnological or racial agenda, but a spiritually flexible one. This was illustrated by the beliefs of another set of early modern English writers that suggested the Curse of Ham was specific to one person: Canaan.[47] These authors included Englishmen such as John Bale in *Illustrium Maioris Britanniae Scriptorum* (1548),[48] the Bishop of London Edmund Bonner (1555),[49] and the French/German theologian Wolfgang Musculus. In his *Mosis Genesim Plenissimi Commentarii* (1565), Musculus wrote: 'but he [Noah] did not say cursed be Cush, or cursed be Mizriam, or cursed be Put, but cursed be Canaan.'[50] We can see that many English people had a different understanding about the Curse of Ham than we may assume. There were also Englishmen that were willing to refute the interpolations repeated by Best and Hanmer. These Englishmen's connections to Africans in early modern England may have influenced their perspectives.

Thomas More's 'Blacke'

Thomas More was one of the early modern writers that openly questioned interpolations that the blackness of Africans was the result of a myth or curse. More was a social philosopher, politician and thinker and the personal advisor to Henry VIII. He was Lord High Chancellor from 1529 to 1535. He was widely regarded throughout Europe as an important and influential thinker, and his books, which included *Utopia*, are still popular today. More was also a leading Renaissance humanist and part of a small group of elite intellectuals respected for their knowledge of the classics.[51] More's written works were widely available. However, few historians have commented on his writings in the *First Boke* (written in 1528, published in 1557) where he talked about ethnology.[52]

The *First Boke* preceded Holinshed's *Chronicles* and was concerned with many matters including history, religion and culture. For example, on religion More stated how 'Negromacers (Animists) … put faith in their circles,'[53] and in a similar way to the French philosopher Jean Bodin (1530–1596) he examined the similarities that existed between different religions.[54] In the midst of these enquiries More asked: 'What maketh black and white men.' He then attempted to answer that question and make sense of how Africans saw their blackness through their own eyes. In this way, More may have been persuaded by the views and opinions of Africans that lived in Tudor England.[55] More's comments are also very important as he was a politician at the centre of English statecraft. His views may therefore offer an insight to how those in power saw ethnology. More wrote:

> If there were a ma⁻ of Inde[56] that never ca⁻ out of hys country,
> nor never had sene any white ma⁻ or women in his lyfe a sythe
> be seeth innumerable people black, he might were [think] that it
> were against the nature of man to be white. Now if it that because
> nature seemeth to see him to behave therefore that all the world
> iyed if they would say the contrary … that all men should be

blacke, but he believed for against reason and against nature [but
he had no reason to accept this] except that he is not white.[57]
(Irregular spellings have been retained in this quotation.)

More used the word 'Inde' to describe 'Black' people. This
term was significantly wide enough to include Africans as well
as other people of colour.[58] More attempted to explain not only
the origin of blackness but also whiteness. In so doing, he did
something quite remarkable: he articulated an early modern
Black perspective on whiteness, and used it to illustrate the
fallacy of mysticising skin colour. His 'ma⁻ of Inde' became
a translator. A translator that More used to reveal that ethnology was socially constructed. We tend to think of this way of
seeing ethnology as the result of an enlightened modern perspective. And we may consider that such reflections by a white
Englishman in early modern England were impossible – but we
would be wrong.

More used the 'Inde' Black man to question, rationalise and
normalise blackness and whiteness. And by taking the Black
man's perspective, he also proposed that if Black people had
grown up in a 'country blacke,' whiteness could seem 'against
nature.' More proposed that how we see ethnic differences is all
culturally relative. He later commented:

> Whereas ye say, if the man of Inde had learning ne soude
> perceive that it is not against nature but rather consonant with
> nature that some other men should in other countries be white,
> though all his countrymen were black.[59]

These sorts of statements did not just constitute a defence of
blackness, but stood against anyone being othered because of their
colour. However, a modern reader may dismiss this perspective as
evidence of a fantastic imagination – perhaps, as fantastic as interpolations of the Curse of Ham. However, we now know that Africans

and other people of colour lived in Tudor England and that More moved in social circles where they lived. Furthermore, we know that Africans worked and stayed in households where More stayed.[60] His comments, then, provide a reflection of early modern Black thought.

As the historian David Northrup argued, in the early modern period Africans were fully capable of interpreting their own colour without a negative inscription[61] and, it should be added, provide definitive interpretations of their ethnology. More affirmed this with the phrase 'that all men should be black' – a phrase which seemed to reflect the adage that blackness was the de facto colour of humanity. This adage was a classical theory espoused by African theologists such as Origen of Alexandria (Origen Adamantus). Origen proposed that the original man was Black. He also stated in *The Homilies of Origen* (184–253 CE), which consolidated concepts already present in Alexandrian society, that blackness represented 'the primal … image of God.'[62] It is likely that More had read such classical ideas. But what was more intriguing was the notion that the Africans More met in England had these views on colour, and that this influenced what he wrote. More stated:

> And he might by nature perceive if he had learning y the heate maketh his country blacke. And of lyke reason y cold of other countries must make the[ir] people whyte.[63]

More stated that 'heate' makes Black people Black, by default he therefore distanced himself from the magical origins of heliotropic blackness or astronomy.[64]

More also set aside interpolations of the Curse of Ham as a cause of 'blacknesse,' and regarded the idea of the Curse as strange. More stated without 'miracles' we may only 'believe in what we can see,' or prove.[65] In addition, More wrote: 'The cause of his blacknesse but if it be by astronomy, which coning who can lerne that nothing will believe.'[66] More seemed to have interpreted the types of fables associated with the interpolations as 'coning.' A 'con' was often conceived for an ulterior motive related to financial exploitation. Perhaps More implied that those who promoted magic and mysticism to decipher natural phenomenon were doing so for cynical pecuniary reasons. We have seen how this may have been the case with Best and Hanmer. More's comments confirm that some early modern Englishmen were capable of contextualising the question of complexion with social relativism. We have further indications that early modern English society was not automatically anti-African. We explore this as we examine the writing of another early modern writer: Francis Bacon.

'Touching the Coloration of Black and Tawny Moors'

Francis Bacon in 1620 wrote comments on the complexion of Africans that in some ways were similar to those made by More. Bacon's treatise in *Novum Organum* was called 'Experiment Solitary Touching the Coloration of Black and Tawny Moors.'[67] Bacon was a powerful and important man in early modern England. He was a philosopher and author as well as being the legal advisor to Elizabeth I, the Attorney General and the Lord Chancellor of England. He was often regarded by many intellectuals as the architect of the Bacon Method[68] that advocated a methodology of experimentation over faith and mysticism. Bacon wrote:

> The heat of the Sun maketh men black in some countries, as in
> Aethiopia and Guinea, etc. Fire doth it not, as we see in glass-
> men, that are continually about the fire. The reason may be
> because fire doth lick up the spirits and blood of the body, so
> as they exhale; so that I ever maketh men look pale and sallow;
> but the sun, which is a gentler heat, doth but draw the blood to
> the outward parts; and rather concoctech it than soaketh it; and
> therefore we see that all Aethiopes are fleshy and plump, and
> have great lips; all which betoken moisture retained, and not

drawn out. We also see that the Negroes are bred in countries
that have plenty of water, by rivers or otherwise; for Meroe,
which was the metropolis of Aethiopia, was upon a great lake;
and the Congo, where the Negroes are, is full of rivers. And the
confines of the river Niger, where Negroes also are well watered:
and the region above Cape Verde is likewise moist, insomuch
as it is pestilent through moisture: but the countries of the
Abyssenes, and Barbary, and Peru, where they are tawny, and
olivaster, and pale, are generally more sandy and dry.[69]

Bacon had never travelled to the continent of Africa. But he
had visited countries throughout Europe and was familiar with
English colonies in the Americas. Therefore, as with More, the
Africans that Bacon met or saw were those outside Africa. It is
also likely that as with Best, he was writing about Africans present in early modern England and was then extrapolating his
theories on blackness and Africa from these interactions.

Nevertheless, Bacon spoke about Aethiopia and Guinea as
though he knew them. But his opening remarks showed that he
did not. He was ignorant of a global African presence and of other
people of colour that lived throughout the world. This seemed to
indicate that the Africans Bacon had met in England were those
from specific places: Aethiopia, Congo and areas surrounding
the Niger River[70] and Cape Verde. Evidence in *Blackamoores*
proved that Africans from these places lived in Tudor and early
Stuart England. Moreover, this presence included intellectuals,
navigators and literate members of ruling families that were capable of articulating their perspectives on their own origins, identity
and ethnicity.[71]

Bacon attempted to examine the issue of the complexion of
Africans using a methodology of experimentation. He began
with what he believed to be the most logical hypothesis. Not
one based on mysticism or curses, but observations of natural
phenomena: climate and heat. It was likely for this reason that

Bacon, as with More, did not explicitly quote interpolations of the Curse of Ham because he felt they lacked credibility.

In a similar way to More, Bacon's rationalism was based on exploring, discovering and investigating not only ancient texts but established religious doctrine. Bacon then rationalised his hypothesis by what he had observed, that Africans were 'fleshy and plump.' In other words, when compared to white people. In this way Bacon's perspective lacked the relativism of More that deconstructed the socially created normative of whiteness and reflected on ethnology using a Black perspective. Instead, here, Bacon worked from a white normative. Nevertheless, in making such a vivid observational comment Bacon seemed to be talking about Africans with whom he was familiar. Other comments he made on people from the 'Abyssenes,' 'Barbary' and 'Peru' would have been supported by stories from English and foreign travellers present in England. The people of colour from these regions, Bacon suggested, were 'tawny,' meaning lighter in complexion than Black. But what Bacon appeared not to know was that even in the same family, complexion and hair texture may vary[72] – and that in all the regions just mentioned, there were/are people that may be referred to as Black, who had nine ether hair.[73] These African people were also to be found in 'more sandy and dry' places in North Africa, Arabia and elsewhere. Bacon constructed a truism that he promoted as being based on empiricism, but it was in fact limited by a lack of knowledge of anthropology and geography.

We may see, in a similar way, Bacon's comments on water and heat creating blackness: as if being Black was an alchemical[74] reaction to these elements. In his last comments – 'As for the Aethiopes, as they are plump and fleshy, so it may be, they are sanguine and ruddy-coloured, if their black skin would suffer it to be seen'[75] – Bacon noted that African people may be 'plump and fleshy' in outer appearance, but could still be 'sanguine and ruddy-coloured' inside. The 'black skin' covered their true colour.[76] Of course this last statement contradicted everything that he said before. But it may be a kind of affected way of saying that 'colour is only skin deep.'[77]

Bacon's words in *Novum Organum* were part of a wider philosophy of Renaissance humanism that was echoed in the reasoning and philosophy of writers such as Erasmus and Roger Bacon the thirteenth-century philosopher, as well as the fourteenth-century English writer William of Ockham.[78] Ockham was important because his 'device' of investigation, known as 'Ockham's Razor,' was widely used by philosophers and writers of the time. This approach was to analyse competing arguments and theories using logic, with the theory that had the fewest assumptions being the most likely. Returning to Francis Bacon, he wrote: 'And the human understanding is like a false mirror which receiving rays irregularly distorts and discolours the nature of things by mingling its own nature with it.'[79] Bacon believed in distinguishing or cutting away the false distortion to distinguish fact from fiction. A similar perspective was also reflected in the writings of the Frenchman Joseph Justus Scaliger (1540–1609). He was critical of Annius' interpolations although he did use the Annian genealogy.[80] Bacon may have read Scaliger and used it to set aside interpolations connected to the Curse of Ham.

Bacon was critical of myths that claimed the complexion of Africans was caused by fire or magic. But in suggesting heat as a cause he showed his belief in the theory of the four humors, where the humor of the person revealed how a person could be healed.[81] And in his *Essays or Counsels, Civil and Moral of Francis Bacon the Wisdom of the Ancients* he proposed: 'In the warmer climate, the people are generally more wise, but in the Northern climate, the wits … [are] chief[ly] … greater.'[82] Bacon's notions were consistent with the concept that a person's humor provided an indication of their intelligence. But his notions were far from any fixed concept of biological determinism of Africans' inferiority.[83]

In fact, the implication from Bacon's comments was that Africans were 'wiser' because they came from a warmer climate. Moreover, Bacon could contextualise these comments using classical writers such as Aristotle, who stated:

> If, therefore, some men differed from others as much as we think Gods and heroes differ from men, having simply great superiority, first of body and then of soul, so that the superiority of the rulers in respect of their subjects were undoubted and manifest, it is clear that it would be better for those to rule always for life.[84]

By asserting these sorts of ideas, early modernists such as Bacon could suggest that people were not inherently superior to others. It was a controversial sentiment, not necessarily because of ethnology but in trajectory, since it questioned the divine right of kings.[85] Obviously, Greek writers such as Aristotle could have their writings used to justify many different theories.[86] And this does not mean that early modernists such as Bacon were immune from repeating classical myths. For example, he quoted from Aristotle in *Wisdom of the Ancients*:

> Wherefore doth the imagination of the mother, which imagineth of an A Ethiopian or Blackamoore, cause the mother to bring forth a black child: As Albertus Magnus[87] reporteth of a Queene, who in the act of carnall copulation, imagined of a Blackamoore which was painted before her, and so brought foorth a Blackamoore? ... And so in this purpose the imagination is aboue the forming power, and so the child borne followeth the imagination, and not the power of forming and shaping.[88]

These same sorts of fantasies were also written about by classical authors such as the Ancient Greek writer Heliodorus. It was translated by Thomas Underdowne and called *An Æthiopian Historie* (1569):

that the earnest imagination of a woman going great, causeth
often the child to be borne with the qualities & conditions
of the thing imagined [and in Plutarch] that a white woman
conceauing chylde by a vvhite man, was deliuered of an Infant
coale-blacke, because at the tyme that she conceaued, she held
her eyes and imagination fixed vpon the picture of a Black-
Moore which was painted in a cloth vpon the wal, which the
child wholy resembled ... That proceedeth of the imagination
of the mother, which thinketh of the disposition of the father
in the act of carnall copulation. And therefore by reason of
the strong imagination in the time of conception, the children
get the disposition of the father. As it appeareth before of the
Queene which had her imagination on a Blackamoore: and of
an Aethiopian Queene which brought foorth a white child,
because her imagination was vpon a white colour.[89]

These same sorts of fantasies were also written about by the hugely
influential and important early Christian father, the Romanised
African, St Augustine of Hippo (fourth–fifth century CE), in his
book *City of God*.[90] It was discussed in *Blackamoores*:

In this story the principal white character attempts to prove
despite her whiteness that she is part of an Ethiopian royal
family. As the historian Sujata Iyengar states, in this legend 'the
aristocracy is black, and it is the white body which shows up as
aberrant ... cast out and ultimately subjected through battery
and enslavement to control.'[91]

Whiteness was othered by this classical fable. Bacon quoted
such fables, but he distanced himself from advocating them,
and concentrated on what he thought he could prove, which
was that it was heat and water that made the complexion of
Africans, not the dreams of the mother, the imagination of
Gods, fires from a Sun God or curses from Noah. His observations of Africans present in the Diaspora are likely to have
informed his decision making.

Thomas Browne's Blacknesse

Through the work of More, Bacon and others we get an indication
of a Black perspective on ethnology in English society. This early
modern thought appeared to have been initiated by Africans outside Africa that acted as interpreters of their blackness for English
observers. Moreover, this interpretation was so compelling it
meant that some English people questioned their own whiteness.
As a reaction, Englishmen such as Hanmer and Best flirted with
interpolations and mysticism, but even then they did not advocate
discrimination against Africans in England. However, in the case
of More and Bacon the desire for answers led them away from
mysticism towards relativism and rationalism. And More questioned the very nature of how we socially construct identity.

We explore these matters with another English writer who,
more than any other from this period, seemed to have been interested in ethnology and chromatics.[92] This is the polymath and
native of Norwich, Thomas Browne. In his book *Pseudodoxia
Epidemica: or, Enquiries into Very Many Received Tenents* in
1646, he wrote about ethnology and chromatics in three chapters entitled: 'Of the Blackness of Negroes,' 'Of the Same' and
'A Digression Concerning Blacknesse.' These chapters fell either
side of two others that also referred to ethnology: the 'Red Sea'
and a second entitled 'Of Gypsies,' with the overarching title
of that section called: 'Enquiries into the Vulgar and Common
Errors.' So Browne may have acknowledged that to talk about
the blackness of Africans at all was 'vulgar.' It could be that this
title revealed a kind of early modern 'political correctness.'[93] But
without more evidence this is difficult to prove.

Browne's chapters on blackness amounted to seventeen pages
in length. This meant that Browne's discussion on this subject was
one of the most detailed expositions within the early modern period.
Browne's work was very different to the asides of Best or Hanmer.[94]
It is worthwhile examining Browne's ideas, many of which reiterate

what we have already discovered about Africans in early modern England. In 'Of the Blackness of Negroes,' he wrote:

> It is evident not only in the general sense of Nature, that things most manifest themselves into sense, have proved obscure to the understanding ... the faculties of reason most often fail us. Thus of colours in general ... no man has yet beheld the true nature. While some ascribe to the mixture of the elements, others to the graduality of Opacity and Light ... Why is grass green?[95]

Browne began his exposition on the blackness of Africans by framing it within the wider debate of chromatics. In other words, how do colours appear within nature? In examining that question Browne speculates on whether human complexions are the result of natural chromatics. He also queries how colours could be chemically created and suggested that all colours are the result of perception 'or reason.' Browne's approach to chromatics illustrate that he had an inquisitive and critical perspective:

> Why shall the marvel of Peru produce its flowers of different colours, and that not once, or constantly, but everyday and variously? ... And lastly, why some men, yea and they a mighty and considerable part of mankind, should first acquire and still retain the gloss and tincture of blacknesse ... the causes generally received; which are but two in number. The heat and scorch of the Sun; or the Curse of God on Cham and his posterity.[96]

Browne's comments on ethnology are almost a hundred years later than More's. More used the term 'Inde' to describe people of colour. Browne and Bacon used the term 'Negro' to describe Africans. This may be reflective of the more common use of that term by the middle of the seventeenth century.[97] Browne, in a different way to More, described ethnology from a white perspective, and used white as a normative. Nevertheless, it is interesting how Browne described Africans as 'a mighty and considerable part of mankind.' Words are important, and Browne chose these words to convey that he regarded Africans as an integral and intrinsic part of the family of humankind, and not a separate branch of the same. His words 'causes generally received' illustrated that by 1646, the time Browne wrote his book, there appeared to be two popular notions about the blackness of Africans: the first concerned with the 'heat and scorch of the sun'; and the second, the Curse of Ham, which he wrongly stated was ordained by God. The order Browne listed them, and the way that he explained their tenets, reflected that the first was more popular. Browne stated:

> The First was *generally received* [about heat and fire] by the
> Ancients, who in obscurities had no higher recourse then unto
> Nature ... by Strabo. By Aristotle ... why the Sun makes men
> Black and not the fire? ... By the word Aithops it self, applied
> to the memorablest nations of Negroes that is of a burnt and
> torrid countenance. The fancy of the fable infers ... dervieth the
> complexion from the deviation of the Sun, and the conflagration
> of all things under Phareton. But this opinion though generally
> imbraced, was I perceive rejected by Aristobulus a very ancient
> Geographer: as is discovered by Strabo. It has been doubted by
> several modern writers.[98]

Browne summarised what we have already learned about eth-nology in early modern England. Which is that those who wished to achieve a rational understanding of the subject were willing to engage in the critical analysis of classical ideas such as those from Strabo etc. But Browne also proposed less rational explanations for blackness, even though he later discredited them:

> For whilst they make the River Senaga to divide and bound the
> Moors, so that on the south side they are black, on the other only
> tawny, they imply a secret causality herein from the air, place or
> river; and seem not to derive it from the Sun ... nor does he that
> affirmith [the theory] the heat makes black, afford a reason why

> other animals in the same habitation maintain a constant and
> agreeable hue unto those in other parts, as Lyons, Elephants ...
> do yet make good the complexion of their species and hold a
> colourable correspondence unto to those in milder regions.[99]

Browne examined whether the heat was the cause of blackness
and then quoted the mystical idea that the river 'Senega' (Senegal)
in West Africa separates Africans of different complexions.
Browne had never seen it, because he had never been to Africa,
and of course the River Senegal does not divide the people in
that way. But the fact that he felt such a fable was worth repeating
was either a demonstration of his thoroughness to engage with all
ideas, or it revealed he was not entirely immune to fables.[100]

It was also interesting that Bacon used the phrase 'constant
and agreeable hue' to describe a complexion other than Black.
This may mean that he regarded blackness pejoratively as not
being 'constant and agreeable.' Other early modern writers, as we
shall discover, had exactly the opposite view. Browne also wrote:

> Nor did this complexion proceed from heat in man, the same
> would be communicated unto other animals which equally
> participate the influence of the common agent ... Thus Olus
> Magnus relates ... Foxes begin to grow white ... that Hare and
> Partridges turn white in the Winter.[101]

The 'Olus Magnus' whom Browne wrote about was the early modern Swedish writer Olaus Magnus (1490–1557). His book *History
of the Northern Peoples* (1555) was widely available throughout Europe and was translated into many languages. Magnus
was regarded as an authority on the flora and fauna of northern
Europe and Browne quoted from him because the Swedish scribe
was respected for his observations and experiments, although his
work also contained a number of myths. Magnus' book touched
on notions of chromatics and ethnology, but that was not his

intention. For many early modernists Magnus was an authority on how colour could be environmentally determined in animals, and perhaps humans. But then Browne questioned this theory:

> [I]f the fervour of the Sun, or intemperate heat of clime did solely occasion this complexion, surely a migration or change thereof might cause a sensible, if not total mutation; which notwithstanding experience will not admit. For Negroes transplanted, although into cold and flegmatick habitations, continue their hue both in themselves and also their generations.[102]

In a similar way to More, Best and Bacon, Browne revealed in this quotation that the presence of Africans outside Africa had made him question the idea that the Sun made Africans Black. Browne, as with the other authors, may well have met Africans in England and noted that 'Negroes transplanted, although into cold and flegmatick habitations, continued their hue both in themselves and also their generations.' Browne also wrote:

> [E]xcept [Africans] ... mix with different complexions; whereby notwithstanding their only succeeds a remission of their tinctures; their remaining many descents a strong shadow of their Originals; and if theyr preserve their copulations entire, they still maintain their complexions.[103]

In early modern English society some African people appeared to have 'maintain[ed] their color' and Bacon may have seen this. The physician Juan Harte in Spain, in 1588, articulated something very similar when he stated, 'Blacks pass their colour on to their descendants even in Spain away from their homeland.'[104] Browne in England, in 1646, stated that people of African descent, 'maintain their complexion' and 'continued Black.' These comments may have been based on observing Africans and their children in England such as those of Henrie Anthonie Jetto.

Jetto's family lived in Holt, Worcestershire. Jetto himself was described as 'a Black,' a 'Black More,' 'a Black-moor,' and as being 'Jetto' from the French word for 'Black.' When he appeared in English records on 21 March 1596, he was '26 or year aboute.'[105] He married a woman called 'Persida a maid,' whose ethnicity we do not know. He had five children with her, as well as at least one illegitimate son. Some of his descendants, even until the third generation, were referred to through their descent from him, with the word 'Jetto' being a reference to his and their blackness. For example, this was how some of his children were described in their Holt baptism records:

'The same day was Sara the daughter of Henry Jetto A Blackemore servante to Sir Henry Bromley baptised,' 10 December 1598.

'The 29 June was Margaret daughter of Henry Jetto a Blackemore baptised,' 29 June 1601.

'The 26th of April was Ellinor the daughter of Henry Jetto gardener to Sir John Bromley baptised,' 1607.

'The 5 day of March was Richard Jetto sonne of Henry Jetto of Holt baptised,' 5 March 1608.[106]

By 1607 the children's baptism records no longer referred to their father by the term 'Blackemore.' But the ethnic sobriquet Jetto remained as a last name.

The next generation of Jetto's descendants are described accordingly:

'Henry the sonne of John and Isabell Jetto was buried,' 14 March 1641.

'John the sonne of John and Joanne Jetto was baptised,' 2 May 1667.

'Henry the son of John and Joanne Jetto was baptised,' 17 October 1671 [Great-grandson of Henrie Jetto].[107]

Future generations altered the way that they referred to themselves, by changing what was essentially an ethnic term 'Jetto' into 'Jetter' and that is how they continued into the present day:

'Thomas Jetter buried,' 15 May 1717,[108] etc.

Indeed, Thomas Jetter and subsequent generations of the Jetto family may not have retained 'the Morisco tint,' the 'blacknesse,' and therefore the term 'Jetto' or 'Blackemore' may have seemed unnecessary, or even incongruous.[109] It may also have been a reflection of the times. In the Georgian period strong ideas about the science of race had emerged, and Britain was the largest slave trading nation in the world. To live in Britain and have this ethnic ambiguity may have been problematic for the Jetto family.[110] However, in the early modern period where they still retained the 'shadow of their Originals,' that Africanness was self-evident.

We do not know the ethnicity of Persida, Jetto's wife, but in Tudor and early Stuart England many Blackamoore men and women had relationships with white people and some of them had children. But Browne also implied that Africans had relationships with other Africans, when he wrote if they 'preserve their copulations entire, they still maintain their complexions.' We now know there were sexual relationships and marriages between Africans in England, as with Anne Vause, who was buried on 24 April 1618 at St Botolph without Aldgate, London. She was described as 'Anne Vause, a black-more, wife to Anthonie Vause, Trompetter, of the said countrey.'[111] The term 'said countrey' being a reference to more than a geographical nation; rather ethnicity and nationhood.[112] Or as with these London parish records where: 'John Mens of Ratclif a niger & Luce Pluatt a niger' married in September 1610; and 'Salomon Cowrder of Popler a niger sailler & Katheren Castilliano a niger also' were married as well.[113] These same unions continued into the last decades of the seventeenth century and included, in *Holy Trinity Minories*: 8 January 1694, the marriage of 'Thomas Lambert Widower, Mariner and Isabella Bococke, Sp[inster], both Blacks of St Mary Whitechapell.'[114] And in the same parish on 29 September 1694, the marriage of 'Nicholas Armadowe Ba[chelor] and Elizabeth Moore Widdow both Blacks of the p[ari]sh of Stepney.'[115] Finally, also in the same parish, on 17 September 1695 the marriage of 'Peter Daniel Ba[chelor] a mariner and Elizabeth Almeda Wid[ow] both of Stepney, both blacks.'[116] Notwithstanding these records that revealed Africans marrying other Africans, the most common unions for people of African descent in early modern England were with white English people. Evidence that supports this can be found in villages, towns and cities all over the country.[117]

Browne continued:

> And so likewise fair or white people translated into hotter
> Countryes, receive not impressions amounting to this
> complexion, as hathe been observed in many Europeans who
> have lived in the land of Negroes; and as Edwardus Lopes [the
> Portuguese explorer][118] testifieth of the Spanish Plantations, that
> they maintained their native complexions unto his dayes.[119]

Browne here repeated the idea stated by Bacon and Best that people of varying complexions occupied the same position on the earth in relation to the Sun, and that this proved the Sun did not cause complexion in people. Browne later proposed that the 'Moors' that lived in Asia and America came there from Africa. Of course this is too simplistic an analysis. Browne wrote:

> [T]he Negro is properly a native of Africa and that those places
> in Asia inhabited now by Moors, are but the intrusions of
> Negroes arriving first from Africa as we generally conceive of
> Madagascar, and the adjoyning islands, who retain the same
> complexion unto this day. But this defect is more remarkable in
> America, which although subjected unto both the Tropick, but
> are not at all of this hue.[120]

Browne then set about disproving the idea stated by Bacon that
water was the cause of the blackness of Africans. Browne wrote:

> For the parts which the Negroes possess, are not so void of
> Rivers and moisture, as is presumed; ... there are the mighty
> rivers ... [p. 329] which do not only moisten and contemperate
> the air, by their exhalations, but refresh and humectate the earth
> by their annual Inundations.[121]

It is at this point that Browne abandoned finding an answer to the
origin of blackness and tells us so:

> [T]he Sun is not the author of this Blackness; how, and
> when this tincture first began is yet a Riddle and positively to
> determine, *it suppasseth my presumption*. Seeing therefore we
> cannot discover what did affect it.[122] (Emphasis added.)

In desperation Browne repeated the same myths as Bacon, about
certain rivers turning some men Black and others white.[123] He
also continued to quote notions about the power of illusion,
which he called 'the Power and Efficacy of Imagination.' Browne
quoted from the classical legends of:

> Hippocrates ... and Helidore [that spoke] of a Moorish Queen,
> who upon aspection of the Picture of Andromeda, conceived
> and brought forth a fair one. And this perhaps might some say
> it was the *beginning* of *this complexion* ['whiteness' but the
> emphasis my own]; induced first by imagination, which having
> once impregnated the seed, found afterwards concurrent co-
> operations, which were continued by Climes [climate], whose
> constitution advantaged the first impression. [And because of
> the Snow] ... Hawkes, Kites, Bears and other creatures become
> white; And by this way Austin conceiveth the devil provided.[124]

This quotation is significant because it starts with a discussion
of Hippocrates that repeated ideas we have already discussed.

But Browne ends with an idea that Africans are the original and that white people may have been imagined by them. Browne suggested that whiteness could be an 'anomaly' 'continued by [the] Climes,' until it became an adaptation: this being reflective of environmental determinism. The reflective tone of this idea resembled that offered by More, that white was not the norm. Although at key moments Browne still reverted back to using a white standard of normality to discuss ethnicity. For example, when he observed that 'morbosities' have made the 'Chinese [have] little feet, [and] most Negroes great lips and flat Noses.' The normal in each case were the white features, and the 'morbosities' the features of the 'others.'

Browne also believed that the 'original man' was white, as Best claimed. But in a similar way to Bacon, he included Africans within the family of humankind when he queried 'when [did] the seed of Adam ... first receive this tincture [blackness].' Nevertheless, Browne had only begun his exploration of Blackness and having disproved the most popular theory in early modern England, that blackness was caused by the Sun and/or heat/moisture, he then argued against interpolations of the Curse of Ham. This is in Chapter XI entitled, 'Of the Same':

> A second opinion there [that seemed to imply it was less popular than the first] is that this complexion was first a curse of God devised unto them from Cham, upon whom it was inflicted for discovering the nudity the nakedness of Noah. Which notwithstanding is sooner affirmed than proved, and carrieth with it sundry improbabilities. For first ... we shall denigrate a greater part of the earth than was ever so conceived, and not only paint the Ethiopians and reputed sons of Cush, but the people also of Egypt, Arabia, [etc.].[125]

Browne sets aside the Curse of Ham, using history and theology. He did this by stating that it would 'denigrate' 'greater' parts of the human race. He said this denigration would seem illogical bearing in mind the success and mighty civilisations that they created:

> As for Cham and his other sons, this curse attained them not, for Nimrod the son of Chus set up his kingdom in Babylon, and erected the first great Empire; Mizriam and his posterity grew mighty monarchs in Egypt; and the Empire of the Ethiopians hath been as large as either.[126]

Interestingly Browne claimed that for the Curse to be connected to the blackness of Africans, it meant that 'we shall conceive of the travels of Chamese or Cham; [to] ... introduce generations of Negroes as high as Italy, which part [the African] was never capable of deformtie, but hath produced the magnified examples of beauty.'[127] The word 'deformitie' is not used here in relation to physical beauty, but achievements in civilisation. This could mean that Browne believed Africans were not part of an Italian civilisation. But it was more likely that Browne meant as he stated, that Africans in Italy were 'never capable of deformitie' and were part of that civilisation.[128] In the midst of this exposition, Browne then digressed to question whether the Curse could extend to West Africans, as the latter were not mentioned in the Bible. He wrote:

> Phut possessed Mauritania, and the western parts of Africa, and from *these perhaps* [my emphasis] the Moors of the West, of Mandinga, Melegutte, and Guinie. But from Canaan, upon whom the curse was pronounced, *none of these had their original*, for he was restrained unto Canaan and Syria.[129]

This is a very important refutation of a calumny championed by political, scientific and theological racists in the nineteenth and twentieth centuries. They claimed that West Africans were the direct descendants of Ham. That fabrication was the cornerstone for justifications of African enslavement and the Maafa against those people.[130] Browne in the early modern period, however, asserted that these Africans were not the children of Ham. Nevertheless, Browne's most salient point was that the Curse could not apply to any Africans at all, because they did not view their blackness in that way. This approach resembled More and Bacon that used the ideas that Africans had about themselves to determine how they should be viewed, so Browne did the same, perhaps because of his interactions with Africans:

> Lastly, whereas men affirm this colour [of Africans] was a Curse, I cannot make out the property of that name, it *neither seeming so to them*, [my emphasis] nor reasonably unto us, for they take so much content therein, that they esteeme deformity by other colours, describing the devil, and terrible objects white.[131]

Browne then queried any notions of beauty that excluded Africans because of their blackness, and suggested that what we find beautiful is dependent on shape, 'proportion of parts' and what 'custom hath made ... natural.' In other words, 'beauty is determined by opinion' – and is culturally relative.[132] Nevertheless, Browne also acknowledged that some white people may not have had this reflective capacity and said: 'Thus we that are of the contrary complexions [white] accuse the blackness of the Moors as ugly.' But Browne concluded with: 'Now hereby the Moors are not excluded from beauty'; 'Moors escape the curse of deformity.'[133] This time Browne used the word 'deformity' in relation to beauty. Browne asserted that Africans 'hold a common share therein with all mankind.'

Then in a most surprising way Browne wrote:

> [Y]et in the beauty of our Saviour, blackness is commended, when it is said, his locks are bushy and black as a raven. So that to infer this as a curse, or to reason, it as a deformity, is no way reasonable.[134]

Browne has just said that Jesus Christ's 'blackness is commended.' Now to follow his theoretical posturing, Browne cannot claim

that 'our Saviour' was only as Black as a Tawny Moor, because
he had already said that they are distinct from Moors (proper),
Ethiopians, Blackamoores and Negroes. Browne appeared to say
that the blackness of 'our Saviour' was the same or similar to that
of a Moor/Negro. This would illustrate that some English people in early modern times were capable of associating their prime
image of divinity with the blackness of Africans. For Christians,
'our Saviour' was also the 'Son of God,' and Browne's aside was
actually indicative of early modern ideas about the blackness of
Jesus and God. This was echoed in the earlier writings of Juliana
Berners in *Revelations of Divine Love* in 1395 when she wrote:

> His [Jesus'] clothing was full and ample, as befits a lord ... most
> sober and comely. His expression was merciful, the colour of his
> face a comely brown with pronounced features; his eyes were
> black, most comely and handsome, appearing full of tender pity.[135]

Early modern Englishmen and women could envisage Jesus
as 'Black,' 'brown' and 'comely,' their Jesus was a man that
looked like he was from the places where he was born and lived:
Western Asia and Kemet. Of course these representations of a
Black and brown Jesus could be justified from interpretations
in the Bible, but, ultimately, this Jesus was reflective of a certain
English desire to have an authentic face for God – and this was
not a white face.[136]

Finally, Browne's last chapter on blackness (Chapter XII) –
called 'A Digression Concerning Blackness' – admitted that the
two theories on Africans that he had just written about were
'repugnant unto each other, it may not be presumptive or sceptical to doubt of [them] both.' After this statement Browne then
explained how blackness may be the result of a chemical reaction
other than fire. He wrote of bodies that change colour when burnt
and appear Black, he called this an 'infection of their own suffitus,' 'And so do doth fire but cleanse and purify bodies, because

it consumes the sulphureous part.' He explained that 'corroding water will induce blackness … it perfometh by an acid vitriolous.' Browne suggested that this may be why 'the Ethiopians or Negroes become coal-black, from fuliginous efflorescences and complexional tinctures arising from such probabilities, as we have declared before.'[137]

Browne suggested that blackness may be the result of an 'atramentous condition or mixture,' that is 'a vitriolate or copperas quality' similar to what makes ink black. This he called 'vitriol,' which he wrote was 'the active or chief ingredient in ink.' Then Browne claimed that 'I have experimented in plants,' 'copperas, ink,' 'iron' and types of 'vitriol' that only become red and need sunlight. These 'vitriol[s]' he suggested may also be 'salts' 'found in living bodies,' 'the salts of natural bodies do carry a powerful tincture and varnish of all things.' What Browne referred to here was not the 'infection'[138] described by Best, but the chemical melanin, or as some African-centred scholars claim, carbon. Melanin is the substance passed on from generation to generation that reacts according to heat and moisture, etc. It is also the substance that affects pigmentation. There is a science of melanin and readers may wish to examine it.[139] But it is at this point that Browne finally acknowledged the limits to his knowledge:

> Lastly, it is a very injurious method of philosophy, and a perpetual promotion of ignorance, in points of obscurity, nor open unto easy considerations, to fall upon a present refuge unto miracles; or to refer unto immediate contrivance from the unsearchable hands of God … Certainly this is a course more desperate than antipathies, sympathies, or the occult qualities.[140]

Boyle's '… Quite Another Thing …'

To conclude this chapter we include one last early modern writer.[141] He was writing at the end of the period in question and this showed that even by 1664, reflective views on blackness and Africans still persisted in England.[142] This writer was the Anglo-Irish philosopher Robert Boyle. He was an inventor that some regarded as a pioneer in chemistry.[143] Boyle's explanations on the complexion of Africans were nestled within his wider discussions on chromatics. He introduced his treatise by examining the nature of colours. Boyle suggested that even the terms white and black are intrinsically misleading. He questioned whether white actually existed.[144] Of course whiteness is a relative term and is/was often used to refer to skin colour that is lighter than other complexions without actually being white. Boyle suggested that those bodies which 'reflect the lightoutwards' more than they absorb should be called white,[145] and that any attempt to create the 'sensation of whiteness' with liquor and oils etc. was difficult, because whiteness fades.[146] Black bodies receive and 'retain all the motion' of the Sun, and 'black bodies reflect but little of the light which falls on them.'[147] Boyle had taken this argument further along the trajectory than Bacon and Browne, as ultimately he claimed that all colours are illusions.[148]

Boyle then wrote:

> The cause of blackness, in whole nations of Negroes, has long since been disputed by learned men, who possibly had done well to have considered why some whole races of other animals, as foxes and hares, are distinguished by a blackness unusual to the generality of the same species.[149]

Boyle continued, 'It is *commonly presumed*, [my emphasis] that the heat of the climates, inhabited by Negroes, is the cause of their colour.' Boyle drew from ideas we have already seen in the work of Best and Browne, that some Asian people that lived at the same longitudinal position from the Sun were 'tawny.' Boyle then compared different white people that lived side by side in England and stated that in Greenland the 'natives' were 'olive coloured' or 'darker' 'and this is a cold climate.'[150] Therefore disproving the theory that people of colour cannot live in a cold 'clime.'

Boyle next switched his attention to curses and myths:

There is another opinion as to the complexion of the Negroes,
not only embrac'd by many of the *vulgar* [my emphasis] writers,
but by men of eminence and learning; who would have their
blackness an effect of Noah's curse upon Cham ... But though
a Naturalist (may without disparagement believe all the Miracles
attested by the Holy Scriptures,) ... yet in this case to flye to a
Supernatural Cause, will, I fear, look like Shifting off the Difficulty,
instead of Resolving it ... And not only we do not find expressed
in the Scripture, that the Curse meant by *Noah* to *Cham*, was the
Blackness of his Posterity, but we do find *plainly* enough there
that the Curse was quite another thing ... Nor is it evident that
Blackness is a Curse, for Navigators tell us of Black Nations, who
think so much otherwise of their own condition, that they paint
the Devil White ... Nor is Blackness inconsistent with Beauty ...
which even to our European Eyes consists not so much in Colour,
as an Advantageous Stature, a Comely Symmetry of the parts of
the Body, and Good Features in the Face. So that I see not why
Blackness should be thought such a Curse to the Negroes.[151]

Boyle was reiterating all that we have read from the early modern
writers in this chapter. What Boyle added was that navigators say
there are 'Black Nations ... that paint the Devil White.' And later
Boyle noted that 'the inhabitants [of certain African countries] ... are
so fond of their blackness, that they will not suffer the whites to be buried in their land.'[152] Boyle tells us these Africans were afraid that the
whiteness of these bodies would pollute the earth! And that this pale
complexion was caused by some sort of disease that was contagious,
and the Africans did not want to catch it. Boyle reminded his readers,
and reveals to us, that there was not a universal hierarchy where
whiteness was superior.

Boyle, as with More and Browne, had shown a remarkable
capacity to write with relativism and even empathy of a Black perspective, this empathy being prompted by what we have already
discussed. Boyle wrote:

for Black children, brought over into these colder climates,
lose not their colour. And credible authors inform us, that the
offspring of Negroes, transplanted out of Africa above a hundred
years ago, still retain the complexion of their progenitors.[153]

Boyle, Browne and Best were talking about Africans that lived
in England and the rest of Europe: the 'colder climates.' These
Africans were not the distant stranger 'but here amongst us.'[154]
But Boyle had also read the work of the Brazilian naturalist Willem
Piso, *Historia Naturalis Brasiliae*, written in 1648. This Piso
had dissected the bodies of Africans in Brazil and found that their
complexion was only in the upper epidermis of their skin. Boyle
admitted that '[the] like has been confirmed to me by a physician, who dissected a Negro in England.'[155] He did not reveal the
name of this 'physician,' perhaps because in early modern England
there were strong religious, moral and legal oppositions to human
autopsies.[156] Of course when we understand this, we realise that
the 'physician' could be Boyle. Whoever it was that actually performed these 'experiments' they proffered sameness, and not
difference. The results of these experiments were quite different to
similar ones engineered in the nineteenth and twentieth centuries
that were used to justify scientific racism.[157]

Making Sense of More, Bacon, Browne and Boyle

Twenty-first-century readers may be a little overwhelmed with
the early modern writers discussed in this chapter. We have
found out that early modern reference points used to make sense
of ethnology were often different to what we have now. And even
when they offered ideas that we may consider as modern, such
as ethnicity being socially constructed, this may not be what we
expect. We should question the praxis that English people in the
early modern period would automatically have a negative perspective on Africans, or that they imagined them from afar, as if
they were mythical beasts. A greater understanding enables us

to read the works of English writers contextually. Early modern writers – whether they were Best, More, Bacon, Browne or Boyle – seemed to have had their ideas on ethnology prompted by contact with Africans in the Diaspora, including those in England. But the statements and treatises of ethnology by More, Bacon, Browne or Boyle were different to the asides of Best and Hanmer. Writers such as More attempted to write a coherent account about the subject and not just offer a stream of consciousness. We may bear that in mind when we compare the efficacy of their written words.

In early modern England, English people that advocated mysticism to vitiate blackness would discover that their Bibles did not support such interpolations. And often Englishmen found that their own intellect led them away from anti-African fantasies. Moreover, most of the early modern writers in this chapter had not travelled to Africa. They were not the initiators of any question on ethnology: it was Africans present in Europe that prompted that enquiry. And this presence questioned blackness, but also whiteness. These Africans also seemed to have provided Englishmen with a view about the naturalness and persistency of their own colour, even whilst they lived in the 'cold and phlegmatic' 'climes.' And that retention made some English people understand that blackness was more than just a result of the Sun.

So we now know that Africans outside Africa initiated an aspect of English early modern thought. This aspect was a reflective perspective infused with relativism that echoed tenets of Africans in the Diaspora. English people lived in a society that was quite capable of rationalising and normalising ethnic differences.

FIVE | Black Strangers and Slaves Turn'd African Neighbours

> This say Penelope Ockamy the daughter of John Ockamye
> a Moor lyeth idely at Home with her father ... will not
> work for reasonable wages.[1]

Africans lived in Tudor and early Stuart England but it is difficult to fully understand the part they played in societal development, because our perceptions of them are distorted by a post-colonial praxis. This distortion encourages us to see Africans through two extremes: either we marginalise them, or we distort them so that they become folk devils.[2] When we marginalise Africans, they lose their humanity and they are metamorphosed into 'fantastic,' 'fabulous,' 'beasts' and 'unicorns' that can be mythologised and fantasised about. We do not see them as an integral aspect of early modern societies in either a contextual or an intertextual way.[3]

It is not by chance that the most famous African we know from early modern England is a fictional character called Othello, whose blackness is still disputed and who never set foot on English soil![4] Even so, we select stories and poetry from characters such as Othello, Aaron, the Prince of Morocco, Eleazar and Caliban that feed our diet for fantasy. A fantasy fed by the prurient aspects of our own imaginations. Any evidence that does not fuel our prurience is re-interpreted so that it does.

Those that wrote and talked about Africans, such as Kenneth Little in *Negroes in Britain* (1948)[5] and Peter Fryer in *Staying*

Power (1984), suggested that Africans were not neighbours to people in early modern England, because they were either slaves or a few 'strolling players' – isolated, strange and transient. It was an idea that had its origins in much earlier comments by Samuel Parsons Scott in *History of the Moorish Empire in Europe* (1904).[6] Of course this does not negate the robustness of Fryer's research on a later African presence,[7] but it was unfortunate that his comments on Africans in early modern England were based on speculation. Other historians such as Nabil Matar (1998) suggested that 'sub-Saharan African[s]'[8] were less frequent visitors to early modern England than 'Muslims,' without examining whether 'sub-Saharan' Africans could also be Muslims, or the evidence for an African presence in England that included many 'sub-Saharan' Africans.[9]

The term that Matar used – 'sub-Saharan' – is unfortunate and has not been utilised to describe Africans in this book as it was not contemporaneous in Tudor and early Stuart society. The word 'sub' comes from the Latin word meaning 'under,' 'beneath or within.' The phrase surmises that in some ways the Sahara Desert alchemically changed the anthropology of Africans, so that magically they became two separate peoples separated by it. This idea is reminiscent of the kind of fantastic speculations set aside by Browne. Although when modern scientists, historians, etc. use the term 'sub-Saharan' they contend that it is an accurate phrase that defines more than the geographical origins of Africans, in fact, it is a euphemism or 'proxy' to describe 'dark-skinned Africans.' This terminology, generated through the post-colonial praxis, does not help us understand Africans in early modern society.

Most modern historians seem to be influenced by the post-colonial praxis that discounts Africans as English neighbours. Writers such as Kim Hall (1996) stated that Africans in Tudor England were 'too accidental and solitary to be given a historical statistic.'[10] More recent historians, such as Gustav

Ungerer (2008) and Imtiaz Habib (2008), also attempted as the author does to make sense of an African population that lived in England at this time.[11] But, unfortunately, they sometimes reflect the second distortion. That is to perceive Africans as the perpetual other, dangerous slaves or folk devils. As folk devils, the blackness of Africans can be purported as a threat to early modern England, as if that society was so fragile that theologically, culturally and politically it would be endangered by an African presence. But this perspective has more to do with the way that modern racists view Africans as psychological and symbolic enemies, than early modern English ethnology.[12]

This perspective may also influence how we perceive the activities of Englishmen such as John Hawkins, John Lok, Martin Frobisher, Francis Drake, Thomas Lovell and William Towerson, and Dutchmen such as Casper Van Senden. They are often blamed as the originators of an anti-African antipathy. Certainly, these men were involved, often sporadically, in people smuggling and slave trading. Some of these men were even sponsored by Elizabeth I and members of her government to carry out their activities. But an African presence in Tudor and early Stuart England was not just a 'byproduct' of their 'trade,'[13] nor did Englishmen use 'science' to justify their banditry, piracy and freebooting.

Nevertheless, evidence may be used to support this othering of Africans in early modern England that includes two Letters, one written on 11 July 1596 with another on 18 July of the same year, and a Proclamation drafted in 1601. As outlined in this book, and as discussed in *Blackamoores*, these documents can be portrayed as confirming systemic hatred directed towards Africans. In fact they were bungled, opportunistic and failed forays to obtain African people from speculators that had little power or authority.[14] In Tudor England there was an absence of Black laws, Black codes or legalised anti-African discrimination. Although during the Stuart period, in the

Caribbean Islands and some states in the Americas, piecemeal provisions were enacted to make Africans into slaves.[15]

All of this may be difficult for us to comprehend, so we look for other evidence and sources for early modern prejudice that proves Africans were outsiders in English society. One of those sources is religion. Early modern Bibles can be portrayed as the originators of anti-African antipathy. But this book challenges that proposition. We find that early modern Bibles did not contain explicit statements about Africans being cursed or inferior. And we discover that most of the Englishmen that stated Africans were children of Ham did so for reasons other than engrafted hate. We have seen too, that many English people believed that they were 'churlish' children of Ham and Africans were 'gentlemen' free of sin. And we have found that the Curse of Ham was used as a label, that could be applied to anyone you chose, including Catholics, or even the murderers of Charles I. Furthermore, we now know Englishmen were willing to be reflective and view whiteness as other, and Africans as the original. And there were even some Englishmen and women that were capable of seeing the primal image of Christ as a Black man. We are now faced with the reality that English society was very different from what we may have presumed. And to understand Africans in it means using different tools from those that come from post-colonialism.

We need to ask ourselves new questions reflective of pre-colonial notions. One of those questions is whether Africans were neighbours to the people they lived with in early modern England? An examination of the record of Maria Mandula may help:

'Maria Mandula, Stranger, Advena[e] [stranger or foreigner] and Aethiops,' buried in Calne, Wiltshire, England, 10 December 1585.[16]

Maria Mandula's last name may be an echo of her continental African past, or owed its origins to the Latin or Arabic words for almonds.[17] Her record from the market town of Calne[18] in

Wiltshire seemed at first glance to offer the epitome of strangeness. Perhaps, we may presume it was impossible for an African woman that died in Wiltshire in 1585 to have been a neighbour to the white English people that lived around her. After all, this woman was described as a 'Stranger' twice, once in English and again in Latin 'Advena[e],' with the word 'Aethiops' embellishing her foreignness. These terms could be interpreted as prescriptive labels placed on her after her death that proved she was not a neighbour. These presumptions require examination.

What the Word 'Aethiop' Means in Mandula's Record

Mandula was buried on 10 December 1585.[19] She was described by the colloquial term 'Aethiops,' a sobriquet that conveyed she was an African. It comes from the Greek words: 'Aitho' and 'ops': burnt faces.[20] Despite the fantastic origin story around this term it could be used to describe Africans without a prescriptive aspect to it.[21] In fact there were positive connotations to the term in early modern society. Translated works of the writer Herodotus were available in early modern England that stated Ethiopians were the oldest people on earth and that they descended from the classical heroes Perseus and Andromeda in Greek legends.[22] Other stories had these Africans as part of the legendary kingdom of Prester John. This fabled king originated from the line of Solomon and Sheba. And Sheba herself was sometimes referred to as an Aethiopian. Letters were written by European kings to Ethiopian kings because they believed the African potentates were Prester John. This included English monarchs from the 1390s that established diplomatic relations with Ethiopian authorities.[23] Pursuant to this, King Henry IV of England on 20 October 1422 wrote a letter to the Ethiopian king, earnestly seeking his aide in the spreading of Christianity.[24] The letter praised and congratulated Prester John and sought communications and a relationship with Ethiopia, saying that the world should hear more of its Christian king.[25] There was no way of knowing if the letter actually reached the then emperor of Ethiopia, Dawit I.[26] But communications continued between European and Ethiopian authorities. So, the key point was that the term 'Aethiop' was associated with an African nation that for Europeans could represent positive aspects of Africanness and humanity. The inclusion of that term in Mandula's record was therefore not necessarily negative.

There are other positive associations attached to the term 'Aethiop' that was used in Mandula's record. Some of those early modern connotations are specifically related to the word, others are connected to the blackness associated with the term. Important biblical figures were referred to by English writers as Ethiopians. This included Moses' wife Zipporah,[27] and painted images of them can be seen in the work of Jacob Jordaens (1650). These images formed part of early modern nomenclature.[28]

Other early modern writers pointed to the Ethiopian Eunuch in the Bible as one of the first converts to Christianity.[29] These Ethiopians became a generic representation of all Africans. This is despite some early modernists such as Browne that claimed the Ethiopians mentioned in the Bible were not Africans in the same way as Blackamoores, etc. Most early modern writers were vocal in stating the exact opposite. For them the biblical and classical stories of these legendary Ethiopian personalities proved that the Ethiopians of antiquity were archetypal representations of all Africans: 'I am dark and beautiful' and 'black is beautiful'[30] were the phrases repeated by these English writers.

Africa in the form of Ethiopia and Africans in the guise of Ethiopians could also personify much more. Their blackness could represent the 'new' religion and the English Protestant Church.[31] As the English theologian Anthony Gilby (1581) wrote, quoting from Origen: 'Ethiopia – that is, the people of the Gentiles – outstrips and precedes in its approach to God these to whom first his oracles were given.'[32] As 'Ethiopia shall stretch forth her hands unto God and Princes shall come out of Egypt,' Ethiopia became a metaphor for all Gentiles – 'Ethiopia is all of us.'[33] Gilby wrote, 'I am that Ethiopia. I am black indeed by reason of my lowly origin, but I am beautiful through penitence.'[34]

These same theological concepts, which mix negative and positive connotations, were within the early modern idea that the 'new' Protestant Church was an African woman, as in Scheltco Geveren's *Of the End of the World* (1583). The apocalyptic book was edited by the radical English theologian Thomas Rogers[35] and included this phrase:

> The chaste daughter of Sion and beloved spouse of Jesus Christ …
> thou art blacke and browne, by reason of the extreme heate of the
> Sunne … For thy blacknesse by his holy spirite he hath turned into
> beautifulnesse.[36]

The 'blacke' and 'browne' of the 'daughter of Sion,' the 'pure and unspotted Virgin,'[37] was literal and symbolic. This Black 'Bride of Christ'[38] was in fact a theological archetype and metaphor inherited from the classical theologians from North Africa, such as Origen.[39] For early modern scholars she could then become an ethnological projection of the new Church. Her blackness became a way of distinguishing Protestantism from the 'false' gaudy colours of old Catholicism. The latter could be portrayed as a white woman with 'tainted white flesh.'[40] As the English poet Richard Barnfield (1574–1620) wrote:

> White is the colour of each paltry miller,
> White is the ensigne of each common woman;
> White is white vertues for blacke vyces piller,
> White makes proud fooles inferiour unto no man:
> White is the white of body, blacke of minde,
> Vertue we seldome in white habit finde[41]

Barnfield later went on to claim that blackness in people was superior to whiteness. In his poem *The Affectionate Shepherd* (1592), he wrote:

> The snow is white, and yet the pepper's blacke,
> The one is bought, the other is condemned:
> ...
> So white compared to blacke is much condemned.
> ...
> And yet the silver-noted nightingale,
> Though she be not so white, is more esteemed;
> ...
> Yet this I say that blacke the better is,
> In birds, beasts, frute, stones, flowers, herbs, mettals, fish.
> And last of all, in blacke there doth appeare
> Such qualities as not in yvorie;
> Black cannot blush for shame,[42] looke pale for feare,
> Scorning to weare another livorie.
> Blacke is the badge of sober modestie,
> The wonted weare of ancient gravetie.[43]

These poetic comments that Black is 'better' than white, could reflect on African women – such as Mandula – that lived in early modern England, 'Scorning to weare another livorie.' Their 'sober modestie' could ichnographically represent not just their neighbourhood, but the English Church itself.[44] In an actual or metaphorical way, Mandula, as an 'Aethiop,' had the 'vertue and gravity' the new Church coveted. As Barnfield stated:

> But true religion doth such toyes refuse [whiteness or colours]:
> Vertue and gravity are sisters growne,
> Since blacke by both, and both by blacke are knowne.[45]

These theological allusions of blackness to sobriety and virtue were associated with the term 'Aethiop' and could compete in a field of ideas with any negative associations of the same word.

The blackness of Mandula and other people, such as 'Johanna Joaneson an Ethiopian turned Christian[,] dwelling at Mr Samuell Dassall,' who was baptised on 7 May 1654 in St Andrew Undershaft (City of London), was praised by famous writers such as Lady Mary Wroth (1587–1651). Wroth was probably the most famous female poet of her times and she wrote *Urania* and *Pamphilia to Amphilanthus*.[46] In her poetry she often explored womanness and blackness, and expressed a desire to be concealed or cloaked in both. Ironically, during the production of Ben Jonson's *Masque of Blacknesse* (1608), she played one of the daughters of Niger and was blacked up.[47] This blackening was so complete that she was unable to become white again to fulfil the 'washing' required in the masque's finale.[48] This may have had a cathartic effect, which she felt compelled to write about: 'once you go Black you never go back' is the perverse euphemism.[49] But more likely Wroth was exploring in her poetry the general ideas present in early modern English society on female power and blackness. Wroth's desire to explore blackness echoed in her sonnet *Like to the Indian* (1621):

> Like to the Indians scorched with the Sunne,
> The Sunne which they doe as their God adore:
> So am I us'd by Love, for ever more [play on the word Moor] …
> *Better are they* [my emphasis] who thus to blacknesse run,
> And so can onely whitenesse want deplore:
> Then I who pale and white am with griefes store …
> Then let me weare the marke of *Cupids* might,
> In heart, as they in skin of *Phoebus* light[50]

The desire of Wroth, an English aristocratic, to be 'scorched with the Sunne' should not be dismissed as merely a poetic and translucent fantasy. We have seen these notions written about too often to ignore them. They were an aspect of early modern ethnology.

Some of the ideas suggested by Wroth were echoed in a perspective that the blackness of the 'Aethiop' contained a hidden

Black power. Edward Lord Herbert of Cherbury also wrote about this, in 1665, in a *Sonnet of Black Beauty* where he stated:

> Black beauty, which *above* that common light,
> Whose Power can no colours here renew …
> That we may know thy blackness is a spark
> Of light nináccessible, and alone[51]

In *Another Sonnet to Black Itself*, Herbert emphasised the nature of this 'hidden power.' He wrote:

> Thou Black, wherein all colors are compos'd,
> And unto which they all at last return,
> Thou color of the sun where it doth burn,
> And shadow, where it cools, in thee is clos'd,
> Whatever nature can, or hath dispos'd
> In any other hue: from thee do rise
> …
> Of that thy hidden power; when thou dost reign
> The characters of fate shine in the skies[52]

In a third poem, *To Her Face*, Herbert wrote, 'Sure Adam sinn'd not in this spotless Face.' Herbert here implied that while the original man was not Black, that blackness was purer than whiteness and free from 'original sin.'[53]

Barnfield and Herbert were writing in the midst of the investigations discussed in the earlier chapters. We may remember that the most common adage repeated throughout the early modern period was not to do with Africans being cursed, but from the idiomatic phrase 'a leopard cannot change his spots, nor can an Aethiop change his skin.'[54] In the light of these perspectives on blackness, he may not have wished to. This hackneyed phrase of course was contrite, but it pointed to an idea that the divinity of blackness was constant and unchanging. Mandula was an 'Aethiop' and her blackness could be seen as constant and sober.[55] That blackness could also represent not just all Africans but an aspect of the English Church, 'the Christ' and a part of the universe infused with the 'light nináccessible.'

Mandula's Strangeness

Maria Mandula was also called a 'Stranger.' This term was also not as pejorative as it first may appear. The term did not mean that those described as 'Strangers' were automatically strange in the way that we may now surmise.[56] The term 'Stranger' was movable and described people who were perceived as not being 'native citizens' or born in England, hence they were not 'natural citizen[s].' If Mandula had been domiciled – treating England as her 'permanent home, or [having a] substantial connection with [it]' – this may have been written on her record. In other words, Maria was probably a recent arrival and had not been 'naturalised.' 'Naturalisation' was often achieved through the Church, from being baptised and/or by being resident for a certain amount of time in a parish. Local considerations tended to determine the process, despite national protestations. One could also be acculturalised by becoming a 'denizen,' that was an 'inhabitant of or an alien admitted into the country that now has rights' granted by that state.[57]

So Mandula was a 'Stranger,' and that term could refer to specific groups or individuals. Sometimes strangers were blamed for economic problems.[58] For example many strangers were violently attacked by 'unruly youths' – many of whom were apprentices of various guilds – during the 'outrages' called the 'Strangers Riots' of 1517, 1592, 1595 and 1666. But the term 'stranger' was colloquial and it could be used to describe lots of different people. For example, the victims of the 'Stranger Riots' were predominately white European Protestants. These were immigrants that had come from France, Holland and Germany and lived in London and other major towns. Africans did not seem to have been singled out during these outrages,[59] for the reasons mentioned in this book and because they were not perceived as offering a numeric, economic or political threat. In early modern England, most Africans were integrated members of English society, and did not live separately from white English people as some European migrants did. Africans such as Mandula were not automatically folk devils in early modern England, even if they were sometimes labelled 'strangers.'

Mandula was buried in an English church with her name. She must have been known to her neighbours and fellow parishioners. The English Church was not adverse to burying people without a name if parishioners did not know them, as with 'an Irish child [that] died at Wm Knaps,' buried on 22 April 1591. This record from the Malmesbury parishes in Wiltshire listed neither the name of the mother, nor the name or sex of the deceased child. Or priests could use the word 'Stranger' without any other explanation, as happened with 'a Stranger woman' that was buried in Truro, Cornwall, on 12 April 1606.[60] Churches could even refuse to bury people at all, if they were too strange or not Christian. Ergo, Mandula's record offered the likelihood that she was a Christian as she was buried in the churchyard, and was considered enough of a neighbour to be buried by her Church despite what she was labelled.[61]

As we have seen with Mandula's record, the question of whether Africans were neighbours to people in early modern England was connected to broader issues. One of those issues was neighbourliness. Neighbourliness is a wide term that explicates the capacity of a person to be accepted as a member of a neighbourhood (community). But English tort lawyers simplify this by asking through the 'neighbour test': 'Who is my neighbor?'[62] The answer for many in early modern England was, 'All that dwelt round about them' (The Bible, KJV, Luke, 1611).[63] As these words from the Bible written in the common style aver, proximity could engender neighbourliness. The historian Keith Wrightson reminds us that in early modern England there could be 'near' neighbours as well as 'far' ones. 'Near' ones being those that you knew, family, friends, acquaintances and so on; 'far' ones being people more distant, remote.[64] Residents in different geographical locations cultivated diffuse notions of neighbourliness.

There were also heterogeneous and multifarious networks of neighbourly activities functional within the public and private spheres.[65] Core principles of neighbourliness were central to early modern life and how English people related to each other. Some Englishmen preached it. Others wrote about it and ensured that the way religious scriptures were translated and interpreted, the word 'neighbour' was included. This happened with the *Church of England Book of Common Prayer* (1549). There the question was catechised 'What is thy dutie towards thy neighboure?' The answer: 'My dutie towards my neighboure is, to love him as myself. And to do to all men as I would they should do to me.'[66] Significantly, this phrase endured in various versions of the book from 1549 to 1604, evincing that its meaning had a persistent place in early modern thought.[67]

Of course, a critical perspective may query whether the terms 'him' and 'men' were sufficiently inclusive enough to include Mandula – a woman of African descent – or whether she would have been excluded along with other peoples such as religious minorities etc. A post-colonial interpretation may encourage us to question whether such Tudor phrases resembled those in the American Declaration,[68] where the words 'all men are created equal' only gave birth to inchoate (not complete) rights that did not extend to Africans, women and so on.[69] We may then believe that similar issues would apply to deny neighbourliness to an African woman in early modern England. But early modern England was not colonial America or the Antebellum South. In England, at this time, ideas of neighbourliness were vocalised without the systematic contradiction that the chief proponents were also slave owners. By contrast, the USA was economically and socially reliant, and politically and morally hamstrung, by the systemic enslavement of African people. Most of the founding fathers who spoke of their own rights and justice were owners of slaves, such as George Washington, Thomas Jefferson and Benjamin Franklin.[70]

Furthermore, as we have discovered in this book, although English early modern historiography was steeped in war, it was war directed against those who geographically threatened them – not Africans. Early modern Englishmen did not inherit a racialised anti-African ethnology. This meant that English preachers such as John Hooper the Bishop of Gloucester (1551) did not insert the equivocation that neighbourly love should be restricted to white people when he talked about what a man 'is bound to believe of God, Hys King, His Neighbour, and Hymselfe.'[71] Other authors such as Berners (1480) and Markham (1595) associated neighbourliness not only with the parable of the Good Samaritan, but with good housemanship. These writers included Africans among the family of man and therefore deserving of neighbourly considerations. Whilst some, such as the English authors Richard Mulcaster (1581) and Hugh Broughton (1614) (despite what the latter theologically postulated about 'Egyptians' and 'Blackamoores'), still advocated that being a 'good neighbor' was explicit in being human.[72] And perhaps this was implicit in the theory of humanism that was spreading across Europe.[73]

A neighbour was a member of society and helped to shape it. When modern historians automatically belie that Africans could have been neighbours in early modern society, they avoid the possibility of 'intersectionality.' 'Intersectionality' is a term coined by Kimberle Crenshaw which states that various and seemingly divergent histories can be connected. Applying this, we can see that Africans in early modern society can have apparently conflicting but co-existing 'belongings.'[74] Through an intersectional lens the burial record for Mandula revealed that she was a woman, an African and labelled as a 'Stranger.' But also that she was probably a member of her parish, and a neighbour to those people around her, despite her being labelled a 'Stranger.' We can apply these same principles to other Africans that lived in early modern England.

Early Modern Africans Surpass 'Our' Expectations

'One Tobye a Blackamore and Traveller by the way' was an African that lived in Barley, a small village in North Hertfordshire. He was buried there on 6 June 1596.[75] This record revealed an African that had a connection to the village of Barley but was not a resident, because he was 'a Traveller by the way.' This probably meant that he was of 'no fixed abode.' We may think this would have been one of the prime qualifications for being an 'Egyptian.' But we now know that this term had cultural and, by association, political ramifications. So Tobye was probably not an Egyptian. But he was 'a traveller,' and yet he was still buried in the churchyard at Barley. And as with Mandula he must have been known by the priest or the parishioners because he was buried with his name.[76]

There are other examples of Africans that had similar burials, and some of these people seemed to have had even fewer connections to their parishes than Tobye. For example, there is the African whose name nobody apparently knew, who was buried in St Olave Hart Street, London, on 29 June 1588. He was simply called 'a man blacamore' who 'laye in the street.'[77] But both Tobye and the 'man blacamore' were not so alien that they were interlopers. And despite them being of no fixed abode and perhaps having no full-time occupation, that did not disqualify them from a Christian burial. They are likely to have been people that were considered by their parishioners as locals even if they were not assimilated into their neighbourhoods.

Another African that lived in early modern London also challenges our presumptions about neighbourliness. This was 'the Negro that would never teach his art to any.' He lived and worked in the capital between the years of 1553 and 1558. This African was referred to by William Harrison (1577)[78] and many others, and he probably originated from the Iberian Peninsula. He had a skill in making 'fine Spanish needles' but 'would never

teach his art,' and therefore, to quote the historian Thomas
Fuller (1662), the art 'dyed with him':

> [T]he first Spanish needles in England were made, in the Reign
> of Queen Mary, in Cheapside, by a Negro but such his envy, that
> he would teach his art to noone, so that it dyed with him. More
> charitable was Elias Crowse.[79]

This African was a pioneering craftsman ensconced in the hub-
bub of Cheapside, at that time a London suburb. He lived near
white English people and he was their neighbour, even if he had
chosen not to pass his skills onto them. This African had left his
mark on his community and chroniclers noted his presence until
the beginning of the nineteenth century when he disappeared
from the history books.[80]

Another person of African descent that was part of a neighbourhood like the needle-maker, but differently to him had familial
connections to her community, was a young woman called Mary
Fillis of Morisco. Mary was a neighbour to those in proximity to
her and a functional member of her neighbourhood. Mary's long
and detailed records illustrated how her African identity and foreign origins did not automatically 'other' her. Mary was 'abowt 20
yeares owld' when she was baptised in St Botolph without Aldgate,
London, on 3 June 1597. She was described in contemporary parish registers, churchwarden's accounts and the Memorandum Day
Books written by priests and clerks. In those records her ethnicity
was described as being 'black,' 'a Moor,' 'a blackamoore' and 'of
Morisco.'[81] The latter was a reference to Morisco as a place (the
Iberian Peninsula) and a definition of her individual identity.

As we now know, the Moriscos were forced to convert to
Catholic Christianity and became subjects of the kings of Spain
and Portugal. These people were made to wear badges to show
their conversion and these badges marked them as strangers in
their own land. Many of these Moriscos endured in Iberia, even

during the xenophobic outrages of the Spanish Inquisition that targeted them, highlighting that for them they still regarded Spain as home. And as a result of matters arising from the Morisco Revolt of 1568–1571, the Moriscos allied themselves with Protestants and other religious non-conformists to oppose the rulers of Spain. The revolt failed and for many Moriscos life in Spain became intolerable. The last expulsions of Moriscos occurred in 1609 under King Philip III.[82] Use of the term 'Morisco' from the 1560s to 1620s tended to be specific and related to these particular groups of peoples of African descent that inhabited the Iberian Peninsula. This background highlights that Mary's life offers the possibility of intersectionality in action.

It seems likely that Mary and her father, who was referred to as 'Fillis of Morisco,' were directly connected to the early modern history just described. The word 'Morisco' was rare in English records, thus, in this case, Fillis and Mary had probably been the active participants of the adaptive acculturation of this term into their parish records. So, it would seem that Fillis and Mary remembered their past and had offered the term 'of Morisco' to define their own identity. This seemed to have been accepted by members of their neighbourhood.

So there were aspects of Mary and Fillis of Morisco's identity that would seem to make them automatically strangers – but they were not. Some of the reasons for this may have been because Mary's father had the profession of 'a basket and shovel maker,' which may have meant he was a metal worker too. Moorish metalworkers were famous throughout Europe.[83] Such a skill and trade would have made him a useful member of his neighbourhood. Fillis' baptism was not recorded with Mary's, so it seems plausible that Fillis brought his daughter with him from the Iberian Peninsula, after all she was too young to have travelled to England alone.[84] But by the date of her baptism on 3 June 1597 he had died. Interestingly, there was no mention of her mother.[85] Mary had been a 'servant with one

M(ist)res Barker in Marke Lane, a widdowe,' but by the time of her baptism she was 'dwelling with Millicent Porter a seamester of the libertie of Eastsmithfield.'[86] Mary's baptism seemed to have sealed her position as a neighbour within her neighbourhood.

The historian Habib offers an antithetical perspective and suggests that Mary was a stranger begirded by dubious people on the margins of society. While it appears likely that Millicent Porter was a woman with a questionable reputation, there is nothing in the records to prove that Mary was.[87] Rather Mary's very long entry, which detailed her conversion to Christianity and her 'very Christian lyke' pronouncements, indicated that her decision to 'be made a lyvely member of the same [Church and community]' was celebrated.[88] The long list of attendees at her baptism attested that she was not only part of a neighbourhood, but 'a lyvely member of' it. Mary 'was desyrous to becom a Christian,' and her conversion appeared to have been voluntary. This voluntary conversion seemed to have been a further indication of her neighbourliness. According to her parish records the decision to convert took thirteen years. Thirteen years was a long time to spend as a non-Christian in a sixteenth-century English parish and this reveals a great deal about the religious tolerance of her neighbours. And it indicates what we know from other evidence, that she came from a multi-ethnic local community.[89]

Mary's baptism may also provide an alternative explanation for why many Africans in early modern England had adult christenings. Hitherto it had been postulated that adult baptisms proved that all Africans were converted on arrival. But some early modern parish records may actually reveal the last stage in a conversion of an African that began years earlier. Therefore, some of these Africans may have been living in England for many years before they were baptised. Just as with Mary, these records may not indicate guileless recent arrivals herded to the parish font, but cognisant adults that had taken time to convert. Certainly, the early modern English Church had an investment in adult baptisms and celebrated them.

An individual who became part of his or her church willingly, and a 'good neighbour' by choice, offered something special to their neighbourhood. As Samuel Purchas wrote, the 'victory over that Beast' seemed nearer when an adult mind willingly chose Christ. These sorts of conversions offered the prospect, as Purchas promulgated in 1613, that 'the tawney Moore, blacke Negro, duskie Libyan, ash-coloured Indian, olive-coloured American should with the whiter European become one sheep-fold under a Christian God.'[90]

This theoretical belief in all the colours of mankind being one family under God meant that the neighbourhood could include people with diverse origins. Of course that did not mean there were not ideas about difference in early modern society – we know there were. It also did not mean that early modern England was without prejudice. The point was that in Tudor and early Stuart society negative notions were competing with the realities of neighbourliness and community. Most Africans that lived in early modern England were not strangers, because the fact of their neighbourliness mattered more than any interpolations about the colour of their skin.

Another woman of African descent called Grace of Hatherleigh illustrated this idea of neighbourliness. She lived in Hatherleigh, a village in Devon, during the early modern period. Her records start from 1604:

Grace a Negyer, [baptised, 13 May 1604.]

Rebecca, a base daughter of Grace, a negyer, [baptised, 10 August 1606.]

Rebecca a blackmore base daughter of Grace, [burial, 23 December 1607.]

Honour a Negro ... a base daughter of Grace, [baptised, 8 May 1611.]

Honour [described as] an illegitimate child of Grace, [burial, 6 June 1613].[91]

These records provide snapshots in the life of a family of African descent that lived in Hatherleigh. This was a family whose female head, Grace, was referred to in every entry but one by terms such as 'Negro' or 'Negyer.'[92] In early modern England, these sobriquets[93] did not automatically imply Grace's servility, or stop her from being part of a neighbourhood or her local church being 'her' church.

Grace was baptised as an adult in 1604 and conceived two years later. As a recipient of an adult baptism it was likely that she had come from another country, because those born in England were traditionally baptised soon after birth as Grace's children seemed to have been. Grace's records indicate what other evidence has shown, that people of African descent were being born in early modern England. These people were christened in the same churches and at the same fonts as white people were. Africans were not segregated to 'Coloured only' churches or 'Coloured only' fonts, as people of African descent were later to be in the Antebellum South and elsewhere.

In Tudor and early Stuart England the common law, statute, orders in council, under the prerogative, by declaration or decree, did not legally justify segregation. The local means of establishing neighbourliness had not yet been subverted by special race laws.[94] Interestingly, Grace's two 'illegitimate' or 'base' children had been baptised without any reference to who the father was, or whether Rebecca had the same absentee parent as Honour. Both of Grace's children died early, Rebecca after just a year and four months, Honour after two years and one month.[95] We do not know the cause of death for either child.

Grace's family's records apprise a number of issues that reflect on their status in early modern England. They were not strangers; Grace and her children were baptised members of their church. The family's situation appeared to have been determined by Grace being a single mother and not because of considerations based on her ethnicity.[96] Grace, despite her predicament, survived amidst her neighbours and appeared not to have been ostracised from her church after the birth of her children[97] as in both cases she was able to get baptisms and burials for them.

Grace's situation was different to how African women were stigmatised, abused, raped and in some cases mutilated in the Americas in the eighteenth, nineteenth and twentieth centuries because they were labelled as 'chattels,' 'breeders' and 'mammies.' As the prolific African-American author bell hooks stated, these women were subject to a white male patriarchy that was racist, elitist and sexist.[98] They were stigmatised as the stranger and other, despite their proximity and interactions with white Americans.[99] They never became part of the 'neighbourhood,' but formed separate societies at the base of the American nation. In early modern England, Grace was vulnerable as a single mother, but not as African-American women were in the Antebellum South. Grace's vulnerability in Hatherleigh society appeared to have stemmed from an absence of a strong extended family that could contest her rights, find a surrogate husband, or coerce an absentee father to marry her and pay alimony. She remained visible at least until 1613 when she disappeared from the records.[100]

Similar matters to those outlined with Grace are raised with the records for another African called 'Mark Antonio.' He was from the parish of St Olave Hart Street in London. He was baptised on 26 January 1616, but he died just two days afterwards and was buried on 28 January 1616. In those records he was described as 'a Negro baptised' and 'a negro Christian.'[101] He had become a member of the 'sheepfold' of his neighbourhood even if he had only lived there for a short time. In fact, members of his parish may have considered that his baptism was 'a victory over the Beast' for all the reasons stated.

Another person of African descent that we know more about than Antonio and who was a neighbour within his community was Henrie Anthonie Jetto. As we know from previous chapters Jetto came to England as an adult and was baptised at the age of 26 in 1596 in Holt, Worcestershire. He lived in Holt on the estates of Henry Bromley, where at first he assumed a lowly status. The term the recorder used to delineate his station was 'belonging to Henry Bromley.'[102] Jetto remained in Holt, and he was later referred to by his profession as 'the gardener' of Henry Bromley. By the time Jetto wrote his will on 20 September 1626, he had become an independent man of property and was a fully functional member of his neighbourhood. He was described as 'Jetto of Holt' and also described himself in the same manner.[103]

Jetto died in 1627, but in his wife Persida's will in 1640 he was recorded with one final title 'Johnanes Jetto of Holt in the country of Worcestershire yeoman.'[104] As a yeoman, Jetto was part of a distinct class: 'a commoner who cultivated his own land.' It was a class that Thomas Fuller (1642) chronicled as being 'most happy [men] for living privately in [their] own lands,' and this land had to be worth more than 'forty shillings.' Fuller refers to yeomen as the representations of the best of 'English customs' and as having a 'free and plentiful manner.' A yeoman's neighbourliness was demonstrated by them being 'bountiful both to strangers and poor people.'[105] A yeoman could vote in local elections, and serve as Fuller writes 'as a main man in juries' during court cases.[106] For Jetto to have been a 'good yeoman' he would also have been a good neighbour.

We know that Jetto and his wife Persida had five children together. Jetto also had a son called 'John the Cuthbert' out of wedlock, with an unknown woman, but whose last name was probably Cuthbert. He was also named in Jetto's will. In addition, Jetto's will included the kinds of dispositions over property and chattels that one would have expected from a yeoman of Holt. Persida was named in Jetto's will as the executive trustee for the disposition of the equitable interests of their various children. The will even contained a warning to two of Jetto's recalcitrant children:

> It is my will that if my sonne Richard and my daughter Margaret
> will not be ruled and doe after theyr mother's commandment for
> to have ... 20, shillings[107] a piece and no more and theyre portion
> to [the estates] ... to their two sisters.[108]

What makes this will so important are not the startling revelations
in it – there are none. The ordinariness of the language and the
nature of the dispositions point to an idea that Jetto's presence
in Holt society was natural, and his neighbourliness was without
question. Although these sorts of documents are rare, because they
were written by an African that lived in early modern England,
they do provide a clear perspective on matters of neighbourliness.

Jetto's descendants may have formed an influential stratum
of Holt society, as he had over twenty-four grandchildren, most of
whom lived in the local area. We may remember that Holt was a
relatively small village, so this would have made Jetto's family
a very significant population in their neighbourhood. In Holt, it
must have been quite common to be a neighbour of one of Jetto's
relations. This is especially as Jetto's family included the Woods
and Cuthberts. Significantly, most of Jetto's descendants, even
up to the third generation, referenced themselves in regard to
their African ancestor and emphasised his, and hence their,
African roots by the sobriquet 'Blackamoore.' Perhaps this was
because the Jetto ancestry gave them a place among their neighbours and kudos in Holt society. This process continued until
well into the seventeenth century. However, by the beginning of
the eighteenth century the Jettos began calling themselves 'Jetter'
as a last name – it was no longer a description of blackness.[109]
Jetto's descendants are alive today and include many families
from Holt such as the Blucks. The Blucks live in Worcestershire,
South Wales and parts of the USA. They did not know that they
had this African connection until this research became public,
and up until that moment they had 'reckoned' themselves as
'nothing but English.'[110]

The Jetto family shows how far we have come from assuming every African in early modern England was a 'Black stranger.' In this case, the Jettos, Jetters, Woods, Cuthberts and Blucks of Holt could all call Henrie Anthonie Jetto the Blackamoore a neighbour, but something more as well: eponymous ancestor or ancestral patriarch perhaps.[111]

There is another African present in early modern England who has not been discussed before, whose presence and family reveal that Africans lived in communities and that they were neighbours to people in their neighbourhoods. This is John Ackame (sometimes written as Abercombie, Accome, Acomy, Ockamy, etc.).[112] He lived in Little Hadham, a village in Hertfordshire. He was recorded on 17 June 1599 in the *East Hertfordshire Muster Book* as 'a servant to Mr Capell Hadham Hall.'[113] 'Mr Capell' was Henry Capell and he was a member of a powerful Hertfordshire family that helped host Elizabeth I at Little Hadham in 1578. Ackame was part of their household. In July 1603, Ackame was baptised.[114] He later married Marye Personell, a widow, but we do not have the date for this. Ackame may then have moved with her from Little Hadham to Brickendon, also in Hertfordshire, perhaps to be independent of his former employer.[115] Mary died and was buried in May 1613. After she died, Ackame married another woman, Temperance Swain, a year later on 9 May 1614.[116]

John Ackame had a number of children. The first, called 'Gyles Sonne of Accomy,' was baptised on 25 October 1618.[117] Another son, 'John Sonne of Abercombie,' was baptised on 22 January 1622.[118] Other children included 'Elizerbchyely,' recorded as a 'daughter of John Acomy,' and she was baptised on 25 March 1625. Six years later, in another set of records, John Ackame and his other daughter appeared in *The Returns of the Constables of Brickendon*, with a very interesting entry. It was dated 26 July 1631, and stated:

This say Penelope Ockamy the daughter of John Ockamye a
Moor lyeth idely at Home with her father@ y … [for six years]
They have not any other with those Hamlett y … ye be … owill
not work for reasonable wages.[119]

Other members of Ackame's family, such as 'Gyles Ockamey,'
were fit for work and apprenticed. Thirteen years after his baptism, Gyles went to work for a John Halstead, a local Hertfordshire
man. But it is interesting that with Penelope, Gyles' sister, we
have a case where a person of African descent was being sought
out to be apprenticed. This may indicate that Penelope was so
much part of her neighbourhood that she was expected to participate within it, as other young women of her age were. This
fact opposes what some historians claim, that Africans would
have been considered strange and not the kind of people that
would make desirable apprentices. The irony is that Ackame and
Penelope were reluctant to allow this apprenticeship to happen.
By 1631, Ackame's wife was not living with him and we do not
know whether his daughter was actually apprenticed. The last
record we have for Ackame is from 1638, 'John Abercombie to
was buried this day April 4.' The record of his burial appears to
be the first recorded burial for that year.[120]

The Ackame family of Little Hadham and Brickendon is
important for the same reasons as Jetto's was in Holt. They
were people of African descent that were members of their
neighbourhoods. The local interest shown in the Ackame family's circumstances illustrated that. But there are a number of
unanswered questions arising from the records of the Ackame
family regarding why Ackame (the father) was separated from
his second wife Temperance Swain and why had he lived for
six years alone with his daughter. We also do not know why the
constables were so keen to have Penelope Ackame apprenticed.
Should we read more into the words 'They have not any other
with those Hamlett'? It may be that the constables considered

the relationship between father and daughter inappropriate. Or that the local officials had merely an ordinary concern for the welfare of Penelope because she was a young girl 'of age' that lived in their neighbourhood. The important point for our deliberations was that these sorts of matters could have affected any family in early modern England. These issues did not arise because the Ackame family were of African descent, but because they were members of their neighbourhood.

Early modern English neighbourhoods that included Africans such as Ackame could also extend beyond England's shores. For example, some West Africans were neighbours to English people and part of English communities. Some of these West Africans came to England via overtures between West African rulers and English merchants.[121] In the early modern period, most West African kingdoms were independent of European control and had never been conquered by a European power. This was very different to the modern period, where by the end of the nineteenth century almost the entire continent of Africa had fallen under either European or Ottoman domination.

In Tudor and early Stuart times, continental Africans in England had a status connected to the power of the African kingdoms from which they came. In those situations not only was neighbourliness offered to most of them once in England, but was retained by them once they returned to their own kingdoms. Some West African dignitaries were even able to guide that process and, for their own reasons, foster international neighbourliness. There are numerous examples of this such as the Africans that stayed as 'guests' with the Dassells in the sixteenth century, despite being called 'slaves' in some accounts.[122] The idea was that on their return they would continue their familial connections with England. This was consistent with an early modern perspective that advocated extending neighbourliness abroad to expand trade or promote proselytisation.

To explore this we may examine a dignitary called Dederi Joaquah from the country of Cestos in West Africa.

Dederi was baptised in St Mildred's Poultry, London, on 1 January 1611.[123] Dederi travelled to England because of international interest from West African kings in European affairs. They sought to foster relations with western European countries outside of Spain and Portugal. The Empire of Songhai had claimed authority over the nation Cestos of which Dederi was part. West African kings were not allowed to enter into treaties with Europeans except under the permission of the Emperors of Songhai. This provided a restraint and limitation on European infiltration into West Africa, but also curtailed the trade in which West African kings could be involved. Once the Empire of Songhai was conquered in 1591,[124] West African kings increasingly sought relations with European nations. What occurred from the 1590s to the 1620s was a mini scramble – not for Africa but out of Africa, as many West African kings became opportunistic and sought diplomatic relations with European and Ottoman potentates.

Some of these West African kings were expansionist and wanted the 'magic' and power of European guns and cannons. They postulated that this 'magic' was linked to the religion of Christianity. In the early modern period some West African princes, such as Dederi, converted to Christianity to use this 'magic.' It was for strategy's sake. These West Africans were seeking Englishmen as their neighbours pursuant to matters of local, regional and international expediency.[125] At this time, when these West African princes returned to Africa they rarely turned their states into Christian ones, proselytised or even practised the 'new religion.' Their neighbourliness had a limit. As is suggested in this book, and by authors such as David Northrup, this era was more about Africans' agency in Europe rather than the other way round.[126]

What we have learned about Africans, such as Dederi, in local and regional English records corroborates that neighbourliness could extend to them as they communed in their localities. Of course not every African in early modern England was blessed with hubris and sagacity, the diversity of their roles was as byzantine as their origins. But in early modern England, Africans' ethnicity did not prevent them from negotiating their neighbourliness in a similar way to other people. And that innate capacity was not interrupted, even if they had inherited a servile status from another country as with Pero Alvarez, or even if conspiracies were concocted to trick them into a lowly status while in England as with Maria Moriana. These Africans, whether foreign-born or not, were not omitted or ostracised from their neighbourhoods.

If we tell the story of England's early modern neighbourhoods without these Africans it diminishes our comprehension of this period of history. We should also remember that the people of African descent included in this chapter are only a part of a much larger population that lived throughout England, Scotland, Wales and Ireland from 1485 to the 1660s. It is not possible at this stage, because early modern records do not provide that amount of statistical verification, to know how many Africans lived in these societies. But they were certainly more than a 'few strolling players.'[127]

Africans lived throughout early modern England. In London, evidence proves that Africans resided in the multi-ethnic and multi-religious parish of St Botolph without Aldgate (London). There the Africans constituted 5 per cent of that parish's population.[128] During the early modern period this parish was much larger than it is now and extended all the way to the River Thames. It was a parish noted by early modern historians – such as Raphael Holinshed, William Harrison, John Stow and Edmund Howes – for its diverse and cosmopolitan nature. It housed French traders, Italian musicians, Irish Travellers, Huguenot craftsmen and members from urbane Iberian communities that included Sephardi Jewish artisans.[129] Interestingly, many of the parishes close to

St Botolph including Bishopsgate, East Smithfield, Shoreditch and Stepney also had a diverse commonality that included Africans. A further set of parishes with a significant and visible African presence included those of St Olave Hart Street (London) and St Andrews in Plymouth where the population was 4 per cent.[130] This prospect of Africans as a significant presence in parishes in early modern English neighbourhoods leads us to an interesting article written in 1645.

Black Neighbours, White Strangers
At Lincoln's Inn Fields, London, Sunday 13 April 1645:

> It being not upon the subject of Mars[131] which is our business, but of Venus and Bacchus, It's a strange custome in Lincolne's Inn-Fields, not far from the Portugall Ambassadours house, the practice we conceive every way as bad as any that were used when the book of Recreations commanded or permitted maygames, and revellings: … There gathers many hundreds of men, women, maids, and boyes together, then comes Negers, and others of like rankes, these make sport with our English women and maids, offer in the Venetian manner by way of introduction to that used in their Stewes: why these black men should use our English maids and women upon the Lord's day, or any other in that manner, we no reason for: but the truth is, the fault is wholly in these loose persons that come there, and in the officers of those parishes where it is done.[132]

This extract is from an article in the *Moderate Intelligencer*. It reported on events that took place in London on 13 April 1645 at Lincoln's Inn Fields. Africans were described as active participants in these forays. The writer described these Africans as morally culpable: because they had sexual relationships with 'our [white] English women.' As Thomas Rymer later reported in 1692, 'With us in England a Moor might marry some little drab, or small-coal wench.' The English do not feel 'hatred and aversion to the Moors and are therefore willing to marry them.'[133] And we know that in England throughout the early modern period marriages and relationships did occur between people of African descent and white English people.[134] But Rymer prescribed and limited the class of white women that married African men to: 'drab[s]' and 'coal wench[es].' But these terms did not reveal the diversity of white women involved in inter-ethnic unions in early modern England, and ironically, the writer of the *Intelligencer* confirms this. However the writer in the *Intelligencer* was not complaining about marriages between Africans and white people, but unsolemnised relationships. The writer called these activities a 'practice' and he pejoratively described those Africans involved as: 'Negers' and 'blackmen.' But he did not blame them. Instead, the writer accused the other 'loose persons' that attended, and criticised the 'officers of the parish' for not stopping the immodesty.

However, a re-examination of the article reveals that the writer was less concerned with ethnology and more interested in questioning the morality of his early modern society. The reason for this was because the *Moderate Intelligencer* was anything but moderate. It was a puritan and republican periodical that pioneered what we may now call the tabloid press. During the English Civil War, it sought to encourage opposition against King Charles I with its tales of military victories against the Royalist forces. This same publication was later to call for the execution of the king.

The events here, that the writer described, were part of customary activities that happened throughout England. Some of these events were part of spring or May Day festivities, which were an integral and popular aspect of English culture, and had been for a long time. John Stow wrote about them in his *Survey of London* and described that on 'the Lord's day' people revelled all day and absconded from church.[135] These events were linked to Morris, Morens and Moorish dances that had become part of English culture; as the *Diary of Henry Machyn* tells us, 'the Mores dance and then many minstrels and after came the sergantes and yeoman on horse-bake ... then came the dullo (devil) and a Sowdan.' This spectacle was all presided over by a 'Lord of Misrule.'[136]

By the middle of the Tudor period, a certain theological licence was given to these activities because of their popularity, as attested to in early modern books such as the popular *The Husbandman's Recreations* that the writer colloquially referred to as the '*book of Recreations*.' This book was written by John Rhodes the Minister of Enborne in 1588.[137] Rhodes wrote about how dance was permissible in spring to celebrate the Creation. But by the Stuart period, spring revels had become an opportunity to loosen morals in a Bacchanalian fashion, with sexual licentiousness exercised in public parks and spaces. The notorious libertine John Wilmot proffered precisely this sort of revelling in his poem 'A Ramble in St James Park.'[138]

These dissipations were features of early modern English society and persisted even when puritans took over the government. In December 1644, this government had enacted ordinances to limit, restrict and curtail 'Festivall Dayes' that included spring celebrations and Christmas: 'as a feast giving liberty to carnall and sensuall delights' that had 'no warrant in the word of God.' However, the opposition to these ordinances saw spring and Christmas events celebrated with greater vigour, sometimes on an ad hoc basis that flouted the government's restrictions.[139] The libidinous prodigality at Lincoln's Inn Fields can be seen as an example of that resistance. The fact that they chose the largest public square in London may have underlined that intent.[140]

These sorts of revels that mocked these ordinances were common throughout England, so why had the writer focused on events at Lincoln's Inn Fields? The answer lay in the fact that the Fields were opposite the Portuguese ambassador's house. The writer attempted to incriminate the Portuguese ambassador, Antonia de Sousa, with the activities in question, perhaps to tarnish his reputation. The ambassador was a Catholic and a Marrano (a Jewish convert to Christianity),[141] and more importantly he was a personal friend of Charles I.[142] The writer of the article may have sought to stir up xenophobia, not necessarily against Africans, but the ambassador as a foreigner and a religious other, and in turn smear the King. Lincoln's Inn Fields were also located near government offices, so it may be that this frolicking was being portrayed as a danger to the moral health of the state.

The writer described hundreds of men, women and children, in other words families and communities that revelled together. Then he reported how Africans arrived – we are not sure why they arrived later than the rest; and the way that he described them suggested they were all African men. The writer then stated that these Africans all 'make sport' with English women. When this is happening, it is unclear what the white English men were doing. Perhaps, the writer wanted us to use our imagination to assume that the English men were voyeurs (as he is), pimps or only interested in having sex with other men. The last point is not as speculative as it seems, as during the early modern period Lincoln's Inn Fields was frequented by men who engaged in homosexual acts.[143]

However, the events described by the writer were not what they seem. The writer accused the Africans of lewdness in the 'Venetian style.' The last phrase was a euphemistic way of labelling as 'foreign' the sexual activity that occurred there. Of course we know that these types of revels were congruent with English mores. The writer tried to manipulate his readers' emotions by proposing that white English women would be enticed by African men into more sexual activity in their 'stewes.' These stewes were the secret, private dwellings located in the poorer sections of London where some African men lived. Nevertheless, despite the offer of illicit sex in the future, the actual gregarity of the soiree offered a public spectacle. That was a spectacle that did not seem to have included rape and/or sexual abuse, even though we do not know how young the 'boyes' and 'maids' were. Setting that equivocation aside, these activities seemed to be very different to those carried out by masters and overseers on plantations in the Americas and elsewhere. On those plantations, in the masters' houses, and along the byways, systemic abuse was profligated. White men were the chief protagonists and patriarchal purveyors of that abuse. However, by contrast, in early modern England, in Lincoln's Inn Fields, African men were the central figures in a sexual cornucopia, predicated on voluntary lasciviousness. It did not appear to have been an expression of male patriarchy, but something else.

The communities that attended these jollies may have actually been bound together by these 'strange custome[s]' that took the form of 'low ritual.'[144] Low rituals are particular to their communities and show who belongs. The Africans did belong to a community, or communities of peoples, that according to the writer were numbered in the 'hundreds.' The writer (we presume a white man) did not belong. He was an outsider, the other, the stranger that stood on the fringes of this ethnically diverse neighbourhood in London's seventeenth-century England, as a frigid bystander.

In order for us to see Africans such as those portrayed in the *Intelligencer* clearer, we need to contextualise them into the times in which they lived. More than three hundred years ago, the writer of the article, despite his prejudice, had acknowledged Africans as present in English society. That is something that many modern writers are yet to do. And this myopia creates a mis-memory that erects insurmountable barriers to the notions that Africans and Europeans could be historic neighbours and share the same living spaces. As the author Siobhan Kattago states, 'mis-memory is not necessarily forgetfulness, nor it is an outright lie. However, a mis-memory borders dangerously on mythology.'[145] This mis-memory can be buttressed by a fascination with the romance of Tudor and Stuart England, not the history of early modern societies. We have many books intoxicated by the romance of this period, and few on the history of multi-ethnic communities such as that described at Lincoln's Inn Fields. This is not just neglecting the history of Africans, women, the poor, etc. It is actually indifference towards the real history of England. Many of the historic peoples that have populated these islands are ignored – we make them into strangers. We do not know them. Perhaps they were never as strange as we made them. When we commit to understand them, they become less strange and more familiar to us.

Conclusion

Antony a poore ould Negro aged 105 years, [buried] on 18
May 1630 Hackney [London].[1]

Antony was described in his parish burial record as an African
centenarian. He died in England almost four hundred years
ago and was buried in the cemetery of St Augustine's Church,
Hackney. Was Antony really 105? We may never know, but this
record reminds us how most Africans were an integral part of
their neighbourhoods in early modern England. Antony's age
was significant for the priest that wrote his obsequies. Perhaps
in his community, his seniority assured him some respect. He
would have been one of the oldest people in Hackney and perhaps in England. His record was written posthumously, so fellow
parishioners must have known him. He was probably a Christian
(otherwise that would have been stated), and part of a community
that cared enough to bury him in a Christian graveyard. Antony
was not a stranger. His poverty meant that his fellow parishioners
may have paid for his burial expenses and there is no indication
that Antony was a slave. This record illustrates how an African
presence is undeniable even if their voices are hidden.

Africans such as Antony dwelt in urban areas throughout England
such as London, Plymouth and Bristol. They rubbed shoulders
with Scots as far north as Ayrshire in Scotland, were employed
as stevedores in ports as far south as Portsmouth in Hampshire,

looked out across the Atlantic as far west as Truro in Cornwall, and nestled in towns as far east as Norwich in East Anglia. Africans breathed the rural air in villages and hamlets such as Brickendon in Hertfordshire, Calne in Wiltshire, Eydon in Northamptonshire, Hatherleigh in Devon and Holt in Worcestershire.[2] Most of these Africans were nestled in neighbourhoods and were part of the communality of early modern England. We cannot dismiss them by simply stating that the religion and mores at the time othered them. Only a few audacious Africans were deemed a danger to the English authorities, such as the African raconteur and Francis Rumbolo. But they were not dangerous because of the colour of their skin, it was their activities and affiliations that made them so.

However, we have gone much further than that in this book and we ourselves have been audacious enough to challenge the idea of an anti-African antipathy, at what some readers may have considered would be subjects most likely to reveal this kind of systemic prejudice: early modern ethnology, religion and chromatics. We have discovered there was no unified anti-African theology. We now understand that the Curse of Ham and fables about cataclysmic acts causing blackness could offer negative ideas about Africans. But they did not reveal the extent of early modern English thought, not just because interpolations of the Curse of Ham were discordant.[3] Rather this was because some people in early modern English society were sceptical about the Curse's validity. And even those that did speculate on the Curse's efficacy often doubted that the story had anything to do with a change of skin colour. Moreover, some English monarchs claimed a Hamitic heritage as a spiritual lineage, to gain or legitimise their earthly power. Other Europeans claimed that all Europeans were churlish descendants of Ham and Africans were gentlemen free of sin.

We also now know that Englishmen in the early modern period were capable of writing and talking about Africans in Africa and elsewhere without reference to myths. In dictionaries which English people used to make sense of the world, there was no reference to Africans' blackness being mystical. This included the *Dictionary* written by the English diplomat and scholar Thomas Eliot (Elyot) in 1538: Africans and Africa were described as 'Affricanus, man of Affricke ...' 'Affrica the third part of the worlde ...'.[4] The same approach was adopted by William Salesbury in *A Dictionary in English and Welsh* (1547) and by the English writer Andrew Boorde in *Introduction to the Book of Knowledge* (1555), where he wrote that Moors are 'blake,' 'infydels and unchritened' and that they 'do kepemuche of Maconites lawe as the Turkes do.'[5] Boorde may have included negative allusions towards Africans when he claimed they were not Christians, but he did not suggest that they were cursed. In John Withal's *Short Dictionary* (1581), Africans were defined in relation to their colour, but not necessarily negatively.[6] And in John Minsheu's *Spanish English Dictionary* (1599), the blackness of Africans was emphasised, but it was never postulated that it was the result of a curse. He wrote: 'Moro – a blacke Moore of Barberie or a Neager ... Moronez – a blackish swartie colour.'[7]

Readers using the evidence and rationales in this book may now contextualise and examine with circumspection early modern books that contained fables and fantastic stories about Africans. Especially as it is often unclear whether the English writers were merely regurgitating stories. As the Ethiopian writer Abba Gorgoryos (1595–1658) remarked, 'Europeans were sick of a certain itch of writing and did both write and publish whatsoever they heard, whether true or false.'[8] The Tudor traveller Richard Madox (1546–1583) warned us about such gullibility.[9] And we have ascertained that their remarks were germane regarding some of the English authors discussed in this book. For example it is unlikely that the 'illusions' in Philemon Holland's translation of Pliny's books,[10] of 'satyrs and 'limberlegged' Africans, were used as ciphers to define the mores of Africans that lived in early modern England.[11]

Negative interpolations about Africans were not so widely believed that they were felicitous to Englishmen or others that attempted to treat people as unequal. Some Englishmen that were involved in people smuggling did use interpolations to justify their actions, but most did not. Their activities were based on opportunism, not a theology authenticated by textual orthodoxy. These opportunists used ideas they thought would work such as to claim that Africans were not liege, domiciled or Christian – when in fact, many were liege, domiciled and Church goers. And even during the seventeenth century, when English merchants became capriciously aggressive and the economy was more reliant on their trade, Africans remained within the fabric of early modern English society untransformed by England's new international bumptiousness.

In early modern England, only occasionally did Englishmen use inferences drawn from myths or interpolations to stigmatise the Africans that lived among them. But for each negative connotation about Africans, there were opposing and often more popular positive ones. The 'noble,' dignified, 'blameless' and 'long lived' Africans were part of early modern English nomenclature. Such symbolic representations of blackness could be subsumed into a Christian allusion that embellished a chromatic idea that blackness was plain and simple: without gaudiness. As such it offered an unsullied representation of the new English Protestant Church. Catholicism was 'tainted' by colours. Blackness was pure. This nomenclature was symbolic but also literal and applied to Africans as representations of a people innately 'steered by truth.'[12] For example, iconography and artistic representations of Balthazar in early modern paintings of the *Adoration of the Magi* illustrated this. Balthazar represented the new youthful Church that arrived last, but was the future of Christendom. In that sense Balthazar could personify, often with early modern European dress, the new 'modern' Church. He was portrayed in this way in a considerable number of paintings, etchings and so on created throughout Europe: from the Czech Republic to Portugal (including England). And many of the famous Renaissance artists of the time depicted Balthazar accordingly, including the early Netherlandish painters Hieronymus Bosch and Hans Memling.[13]

It was not just Balthazar that could be lionised as a representation of the new Church; but the nation of Ethiopia as a whole that could betoken all Gentiles. After England's schism from the Church of Rome this kind of metaphorical concomitance would become more important. The virtue of African nations and the divine status of African saints, and peerless men and women of pulchritude were an aspect of early modern English Protestantism. Of course this inclusion of African magis, saints and even of the 'comely' 'Black' and 'brown' Christ had additional benefits. They could be a vehicle to promote and entice Animist or Muslim Africans into being allies or even converting to Christianity. For a new Protestant Church that initially struggled to find legitimacy,[14] finding theological allies was important no matter what colour they were. We may remember that Christianity either in the form of Protestantism or Catholicism has only recently become the most dominant religion in the world with more than two billion followers.[15] In early modern times Protestants belonged to a small struggling faith.

Africans were not just symbols in early modern England but also real people employed by English nobility – people such as Catalina de Motril, an Iberian Moor, who was part of Katherine of Aragon's entourage,[16] and John Blanke the Kings' 'black trumpeter' who lived in London in 1507.[17] In Plymouth, 'Bastien, a Blackmoore of Mr Willm Hawkins,' was buried on 10 December 1583.[18] And 'Fortunatus a blackmoor seruant to Sr Robert Cicill' was interred in St Clement Danes Churchyard in Westminster on 21 January 1602.[19] Elizabeth I herself also had a 'littel black a More.' She commissioned 'Henry Henre to make for him a garcon coat ... of white taphata cutt and lyned ... striped with gold and silver with buckeram bayes ... knitted stockings [and] white shoes.' This African boy was employed until at least the next year, 13 April 1575, when a further warrant granted this 'littel black a More' a further set of fine attires. This time the garments were to be made by the designer Thomas Ludwell.[20] With this diversity in Elizabeth's entourage, it was not surprising that debacles to deport Africans 'lost ... the note of her Majesty's pleasure therin'[21] or that Elizabeth was alleged to make protestations against slavery.[22] These rumoured protestations may have had their roots in Elizabeth's closeness to the Africans in her retinue.

These ideas were alluded to at the time in scandalous accusations reported in Venice by the English ambassador on 23 August 1609. These allegations were contained in an anonymous book that circulated in Rome that stated:

> [T]alking of Queen Elizabeth, who styled herself Head of
> the Anglican Church and Virgin, the writer accuses her of
> immodesty, of having given birth to sons and daughters, of
> having prostituted her body to many different nationalities, of
> having slept with blackamoors; of Henry VIII that he gave out
> that Anna Boleyn was his wife whereas she was his daughter.[23]

We are not in any position to verify these accusations and some are very incogitable, such as Anne Boleyn being the daughter of Henry VIII,[24] but for these accusations to be truly salacious, some of them had to have the possibility of plausibility. Looking at the claim that Elizabeth had 'slept with blackmoors,' for this to be conceivable she was likely to have had more than one 'little Blackamoore' in close proximity to her. And this must have been known. Moreover, there was evidence of personal affiliations between Elizabeth and Africans. This was connected to the overtures between the Moroccan leadership and the queen that had even seen the idea promulgated that she should marry

North African princes such as Ahmad al-Mansur (1549–1603).[25] John Stubbs foreshadowed that sentiment. And we may remember that he was a man that had little tolerance for foreigners or foreign marriages. Nevertheless, he suggested that if the queen was to marry a foreigner, it would be better that she marry one of 'these Moores beyonde Spain,' rather than a French man.[26]

Therefore, the truly scandalous aspect of the accusation that Elizabeth had relationships with Africans may not have been related to ethnology, as we know marriages and unions of that kind occurred in early modern England. It would have been the inference that Elizabeth behaved manlike, by selecting men for coitus, as if she were a man lusting after women. Men of power in early modern England could and did engage in various morganatic sexual unions with people, including African women and those of 'other nations.'[27] For example, the Englishman Cuthbert Holman had a 'supposed' relationship with 'Christian the negro svant to Richard Sheere,' and their illegitimate child 'Helene,' was baptised on 2 May 1593.[28] Other relationships have been proved by the records such as those from St Philip and Jacob's parish, Bristol, when 'Richard a Bastard the sonne of Joanne Marya a Blackemore' was baptised on 15 August 1600. Joanne was described 'as not the wife of Thomas Smythe by the latter.'[29] This statement implied Smythe had a closer connection to Joanne than merely being the sponsor of her child's baptism and he was in fact Richard's father. The nature of their relationship was confirmed by a later record on 14 December 1603, in the same parish that reads 'Joane Smyth the wife of Thomas Smyth beinge a blacka-moore was Buried also the xiiij th day of the plague.' Thomas Smythe had married Joane before her death, even if he had been involved in an unsolemnised relationship with her three years earlier.[30] Of course as the *Intelligencer* article suggested and the accusations made against Elizabeth inferred, women of high status in early modern England were not supposed to engage in sex in that way, even if they got married afterwards. Perhaps African men in England, outside a traditional white male patriarchy, offered the opportunity for white women to exercise their sexuality in non-prescribed ways. It was this invitation to sexual liberty that the writer of the *Intelligencer* and the English ambassador were really objecting to.

It may have been scandalous for Elizabeth I to have promiscuous relationships with Blackamoores. However, it was not surprising, controversial or calumnious that Africans lived with and near her or other English people throughout the early modern period. Africans were born, baptised, married, died and were buried in England. Africans persisted in England through all the major events that shaped early modern English society. And we have some records written by white English people that provide indications of African people's words and thoughts. For example, we have the comments by Thomas More, Francis Bacon, Thomas Browne and the Anglo-Irishman Robert Boyle. These early modern writers tell us that Africans had perspectives on complex concepts such as ethnology and chromatics. And we can deduce that these ideas may have proved useful tools for Africans to exercise their agency as they navigated their way through English society. The exchanges that took place in English neighbourhoods were less exotic or strange and more frequent and culturally immediate than what happened abroad. The ideas Africans brought to English towns and villages helped shape an aspect of early modern thought that extolled the virtue of the perfect blackness in people, objects and theological precepts.

However, most Africans lived as other people did in their early modern neighbourhoods. Africans were just as capable of speaking and writing about everyday life, on matters that were necessary, practical and commonplace. For example, Mary Fillis of Morisco's words appeared to have expedited her full access into a Christian community. These words seem similar to those that other people involved in adult baptisms would have articulated. Henrie Anthonie Jetto wrote about the dispositions of his property, in a similar way as any yeoman in early modern England would. This tells us a great deal about Africans in early modern England. That many of these people had very different concerns from those that we may have about them. We want to know how their colour would have been seen, and whether they were integrated into English society. Many of these preoccupations are prompted by a post-colonial praxis that has been shaped by future historical events. Africans that lived in early modern England did not have these proclivities because they dwelt in their own time and space, and that was not a post-colonial circumvolution.

Having said that, this book does not offer an apologia for racism – either historical or modern. Nothing here is intended to diminish the horrors of the Maafa, colonialism, imperialism, the devastating effects of the implementation of the 'Science of Race,' scientific racism, 'Manifest Destiny,' 'The White Man's Burden' and 'The Bell Curve,' etc.[31] Nor does the author claim that there was not prejudice against Africans in early modern societies. As we have discovered, there was. It is just that this prejudice was not state sponsored.

Africans had voices in early modern England, enough to offer perspectives that challenged early modern prejudices. We are just beginning to interpret the voices of these Africans in early modern England and link this to a wider African diasporian perspective, as Africans also lived in early modern Europe. Some of these Africans were vocal and influential in developing European culture. One of them was Juan Latino (1518–1596), an African professor at the University of Granada who was chair of the School of Grammar and the Latin Language between the years 1573 and 1596. He published three volumes of poems.[32] Then there was Julian de Valladolid whose official title was 'steward for the blacks.' In Seville he acted as a spokesperson for people of African descent in Iberia,[33] although many of his words have been lost. There were also painters of African descent in early modern Europe such as Higiemonte Indianer (c. 1675), he was included in portraits from the Teutsche Academy in Germany in 1675.[34] The portrait of another artist of African descent, Juan de Pareja (1606–1670), became a renowned 'classic' of the Renaissance in its own right.[35] Much of what was written about Pareja by modern historians tends to belittle him as a mere slave, but this presumption is open to a rebuttal.[36] As we have seen, some find it easier with casual reasoning to call everyone that they have not researched a stranger and slave, and then apply theories to justify their presuppositions.

During the fifteenth and sixteenth centuries the intellect of African Christians from Ethiopia also filtered into early modern European ontology. And the works of Ethiopians such as Gorgoryos' were popular with European students. Gorgoryos was a sixteenth-century Ethiopian intellectual who co-authored several important translations in Amharic of the Ge'ez script with his much younger German colleague Hiob Ludolf.[37] Ludolf wrote, quoting Gorgoryos:

> The Ethiopians are pleased with their own Blackness, and prefer it before the White Colour … Some Authors write, that the Ethiopians paint the Devil white in disdain of our Complexions.[38]

We know that Englishmen in England were persuaded by these sorts of ideas, not just to make sense of blackness but to query their own whiteness. These Africans' aphorisms were part of early modern English thought. Not least because some of these African writers translated Greek and Roman texts in their communities in Ethiopia, Egypt, Morocco, Tunisia and so on. This African sagacity included the classical African early fathers such as Origen, Tertullian and Julius Africanus. Africanus wrote about the 'harmony of colours' and peoples long before Samuel Purchas was later to attest to this through his metaphor of the 'sheepfold' of Christ.[39]

Other African scholars included the Egyptian Abba Mikael, who translated from Arabic *The Book of the Wise Philosophers*,[40] and the Ethiopian writer Zera Yacob (Zära Yaqob) (1599–1692), who philosophised on the meaning of history and theology.[41] African Christians as religious minorities also lived in the Swahili City States and West African kingdoms such as Timbuktu. They lived along the coastal trading routes of civilisations such as Songhai and Benin, and in the kingdoms of Bakonga (Congo/ Zaire), Matamba and Kidogo (Angola). Many of these Africans in Africa lived in early modern societies that were religiously pluralistic and polytheistic in their religious practices. Their religions were practised differently to the imposed colonial orthodoxy of the nineteenth and twentieth centuries. In the early modern period West Africans could attend a Madras and offer Ṣalāh al-Fajr (Islamic prayers) in the morning, study the Torah in the afternoon because of its lessons for life and moot biblical stories in the evening because of their efficaciousness, but when night fell return to the old (Animist) gods.[42] We now know that these Africans' views on ethnology and theology were not unfamiliar to literate Englishmen. But, the fact that they may be unfamiliar to us is because modern research has been preoccupied with postcolonial, rather than pre-colonial matters.

It is hoped that readers will continue to demystify the Africans of early modern England and countervail any post-colonial praxis. Through examining records intertextually Africans can be appreciated without being automatically othered. They then emerge as more than strangers – rather neighbours that lived, and were not just present, in their neighbourhoods. So the reader is invited to examine one last record in the light of the rationales and evidence presented in this book. It does not describe an African in early modern England, but Ireland, and reminds us that we need to do further research there. The record for this African was contained in the *Irish Digest* dated October 1641. It talked about a siege at the Castle of Blagall in Kildare (Ireland) that occurred during the Irish Rebellion. This rebellion was where Felim O'Neill of Kildard, with a significant number of Irish gentry, raised a force that attempted to overthrow English and other Protestant landowners. These events helped initiate the English Civil War (1642–1651) as many Englanders became involved. In the article it is the army raised by the rebellion that is referred to as 'The enemy':

> The enemy was 1,500 men, with artillery and other engines for war, … among the rest *was a blackamoor, an old beaten soldier*, and *(as was thought)* was either possessed by -a devil or a witch … [elsewhere he was referred to as] 'a stout blackamoore' 'with strong faith' … for he would aduance soe farr in sight of the deffendants, that he neuer desired the benefitt of any shelter from the bullett, the deffendants aimed at him, as theire butt, receauinge many in his bodie, not soe much hurt receaued, as once to stumble, nor did he shew the least motion of cowardize or feare, or gaue an ince of grounde, rather recouered, cryinge out vpon the deffendants, that the poore dastardly folke did spend theire labour in vaine, that he cared not for theire shott, and accusinge his owne partie of timerous and imbecilitie, for not aduancing and follow him; the defendants did spend a great quantitie of theire amunition and shott against this onely man, but all in vaine, which obsearved by a yongeman, spoke to his comrade, that they should make crosses on theire bulletts, and aime at that blackamoore together, and I vndertake said this yongman, if we hitt this rogue, his charmes or black art will litle auayle him against the crosse, the other condescended … both charginge and aiminge, as aforesaid, they both killed and tumbled him presently starke deade to the grounde, to the *great*

greefe of the assay Hants, and *vnspeakable joy of the deffendants* ... wounded men; of deade was founde 7 score and 20, with the blackamoore, and seuerall officers and comaunders, and many wounded ... [they later found the unnamed African had armour woven into his clothing and that was how he had been able to resist their attacks].[43]

Can we see this *'old beaten' 'blackamoor' 'soldier'* with a clear unfettered perspective? And what do we learn of his social ethnology and societal relationships? Did they differ from the communality of Africans in early modern England? Readers are invited to engage in an exciting process of discovering their own narrative for this African.

Appendix 1

Thomas More
The Works of Sir Thomas More Knyght … The First Boke …

If there were a ma⁻ of Inde that never ca⁻ out of hys country, nor never had sene any white ma⁻ or women in his lyfe [p. 125] a sythe be seeth innumerable people black, he might were [think] that it were against the nature of man to be white. Now if it that because nature seemeth to see him to behave therefore that all the world iyed if they would say the contrary … that all men should be blacke, [p. 125] but he believed for against reason and against nature [but he had no reason to accept this] except that he is not white … And he might by nature perceive if he had learning y the heate maketh his country blacke. [p. 125] And of lyke reason y cold of other countries must make the[ir] people whyte … [p. 125] [The cause of his blacknesse] … [If he be] reasonable … but if it be by astronomy, which coning who can lerne that nothing will believe. [p. 127] Whereas ye say, if the man of Inde had learning ne soude perceive that it is not against nature but rather consonant with nature that some other men should in other countries be white, though all his countrymen were black. [p. 127][1]

Thomas Browne
Pseudodoxia Epidemica

Chapter X: Of the Blackness of Negroes

It is evident not only in the general sense of Nature, that things most manifest themselves into sense, have proved obscure to the understanding; But even in proper and appropriate objects, wherin the sense cannot erre, the faculties of reason most often fail us. [p. 322] Thus of colours in general ... no man has yet beheld the true nature. While some ascribe to the mixture of the elements, others to the graduality of Opacity and Light ... [the principles of colours according to Chemists] ... [examining the relationship between salt, sulphur and mercury with colour]. Why is grass green? ... Moreover, beside the specifical and first digressions ordained from the Creation, which may be urged to salve the variety in every species ... [he questions whether this is true].

Why shall the marvel of Peru produce its flowers of different colours, and that not once, or constantly, but everyday and variously? ... [p. 322] And lastly, why some men, yea and they a mighty and considerable part of mankind, should first acquire and still retain the gloss and tincture of blacknesse ... the causes generally received; which are but two in number. The heat and scorch of the Sun; or the Curse of God an Cham and his posterity. [p. 323]

The First was generally received by the Ancients, who in obscurities had no higher recourse then unto Nature as may appear in a discourse concerning this by Strabo. By Aristotle ... why the Sun makes men Black and not the fire? Why it whitens wax but blackens skin? By the word Aithops it self, applied to the memorablest nations of Negroes that is of a burnt and torrid countenance. The fancy of the fable infers also the antiquity of the opinion, which dervieth the complexion from the deviation of the Sun, and the conflagration of all things under Phareton. But this opinion though generally imbraced, was I perceive rejected by Aristobulus a very ancient Geographer: as is discovered by Strabo. It has been doubted by several modern writers, particularly by Ortelius, but amply and satisfactorily discussed as we know by no man ... which rightly understood, may it, not overthrow, yet showdly shake the security of this Affection.

And first, Many which countenance the opinion in this reason, do tacitly and upon consequence overthrow it in another. For whilst they make the River Senaga to divide and bound the Moors, so that on the south side they are black, on the other only tawny, they imply a secret causality herein from the air, place or river; and seem not to derive it from the Sun. The effects of whose activity [p. 324] are not precipitously abrupted, but gradually proceed to their cessations ... nor does he that affirmith [the theory] the heat makes black, afford a reason why other animals in the same habitation maintain a constant and agreeable hue unto those in other parts, as Lyons, Elephants ... do yet make good the complexion of their species and hold a colourable correspondence unto to those in milder regions. Nor did this complexion proceed from heat in man, the same would be communicated unto other animals which equally participate the influence of the common agent ... Thus Olus Magnus relates ... Foxes begin to grow white ... that Hare and Partridges turn white in the Winter.

Thirdly if the fervour of the Sun, or intemperate heat of clime did solely occasion this complexion, surely a migration or change thereof may might cause a sensible, if not total mutation; which not withstanding experience will not admit. For Negroes transplanted, although into cold and flegmatick habitations, continue their hue both in themselves and also their generations; except their mix with different complexions; whereby nothwithsanding their only succeeds a remission of their tinctures; their remaining many descents a strong shadow of their Originals; and if theyr preserve their copulations entire, they still maintain their complexions. As is very remarkable in the dominions of the Grand Signior [Sultan of Turkey] and most observable in the Moors of Brasilia, which transplanted about hundred years past continue the tinctures of their fathers unto this day. And so likewise fair or white people translated into hotter Counrryes, receive not impressions amounting to this complexion, as hathe been observed in many Europeans who have lived in the land of Negroes; and as Edwardus Lopes testifieth of the Spanish Plantations, that they maintained their native complexions unto his dayes.

Fourthly, if the fervour of the Sun were ten soul cause hereof in Aethiopia, or any land of Negroes, it were also reasonable that Inhabitants of the same latitude, subjected unto the same vicinity of the Sun, the same diurnal arch, and direction of its rayes, should also partake of the same hue and complexion, which [p. 327] notwithstanding they do not. For inhabitants of the same attitude in Asia are of a different complexion, as are the inhabitants of the Cambogia and Java, insomuch that some conceive the Negro is properly a native of Africa and that those places in Asia inhabited now by Moors, are but the intrusions of Negroes arriving first from Africa as we generally conceive of Madagascar, and the adjoyning islands, who retain the same complexion unto this day. But this defect is more remarkable in America, which although subjected unto both the Tropick, but are not at all of this hue either under or near the Northern. So the people of the Gualata, Agad, Garamantes and Goaga, all within the Northeren Tropicks are not Negroes; but on the other side about Capo Negro, C Falo and Madagascar, they are of a Jetty black. [Browne then begins a digression about the effect of the Sun and discussing the longitude and latitude of its movement. And the effect of the Dog Star.]

[T]here are Negroes in Africa beyond the southern Tropick, and some so far removed from it, as Geographically the clime is not intemperate ... Whereas in the [p. 328] same elevation Northward, the Inhabitants of America are fair; and they of

Europe in Candy, and Sicily and some parts of Spain, deserve not properly so low a name as Tawny.

Whereas the Africans are perceived to be more peculiarly scorched and terrified from the Sun, [Browne then discusses an idea that Africans are Black because of a lack of water ...] it will not execute the doubt. For the parts which the Negroes possess, are not so void of Rivers and moisture, as is presumed; ... there are the mighty rivers ... [p. 329] which do not only moisten and contemperate the air, by their exhaltations, but refresh and humectate the earth by their annual Inundations. Besides, in that part of Africa, which with all disadvantage is most dry ... the people are not esteemed Negroes; and that is Lybia, which with the Greeks carries the name of all Africa. A region so desert, dry and sandy, that travellers (as Leo reports) are fain to carry water on their Camels ... Yet is this Countrey accounted by Geographers no part of terra Nigritarum, Ptolomy placeth herein the Lenco Aethiopes, or pale and Tawny Moors.

But how far they were mistaken in this apprehension, modern Geography hath discovered; ... whose complexions descend not so low as unto blackness ... produce this deep and perfect gloss of Blackness. [p. 329]

Thus having evinced, at least made dubious, the Sun is not the author of this Blackness; how, and when this tincture first began is yet a Riddle and positively to determine, it suppasseth my presumption. Seeing therefore we cannot discover what did affect it, it may afford some piece of satisfaction. It may be therefore considered, whether the inward use of certain waters of peculiar operations might not at first produce the effect in question. For of the like we have records in Aristotle, Strabo, and Pliny ... of two fountains in Boeotia, the one making sheep white, the other black; of the water of Siberis which made Oxen Black, and the like effect it had on men, not only dying their skin, but making their hairs black and curled. This was the conceit of Aristobulus, who received so little satisfaction from the

other [idea] ... that he conceived it as reasonable to impute the
effect into water. [p. 329]

Secondly, it may be perpended whether it may not fall out the
same way as Jacob's cattel, became speckled, spotted and ring-
straked that is, by the Power and Efficacy of Imagination; which
produceth effects in the conception correspondent unto the phancy
of the Agents in generation; ... in Hippocrates we read of one, that
from the view and intention of a Picture conceived a Negro; and
in the History of Helidore of a Moorish Queen, who upon aspection of the Picture of Andromeda, conceived and brought forth a
fair one. And this perhaps might some say it was the beginning of
this complexion [whiteness]; induced first by imagination, which
having once impregnated the seed, found afterwards concurrent
co-operations, which were continued by Climes [climate], whose
constitution advantaged the first impression. Thus Plotinus conceiveth white Peacocks first came in: Thus many opinion that from
aspection of the Snow, which lyeth long in Northern Regions and
high mountains, Hawkes, Kites, Bears and other creatures become
white; And by this way Austin conceiveth the devil provided, they
never wanted a white spotted Oxe in Aegypt; for such a one they
worshipped, and called Apis. [p. 329]

Thirdly ... which meeting with congenerous causes might
settle durable inclinations, and advance their generations into
that hue, which were naturally before but a degree or two
below it. ... [this change has occurred] in organical parts and
figure the Symmetry being actually or purposely perverted,
their morbosities have vigorously descended to their posteri-
ties and that in durable deformities. ... Thus have the Chinese
little feet, most Negroes great lips and flat Noses, And thus may
Spaniards, and Mediterranean inhabitants, which are the race
of Barbary Moors (although after frequent commixture) have
not worn out the Camoys Nose unto this day.

Artficial Negroes, or Gypsies acquire their complexion by
annointing their bodies with Bacon and fat substances, and so

exposing them to the Sun. In Guinie Moors and others, it hath
been frequently observed that they mosyten their skins with fat
and oyly materials, to temper the irksome driness thereof from the
parching rayes of the Sun. Whether this practise at first had not
some efficacy toward this complexion, may also be considered.

Lastly ... and when the seed of Adam did first receive this tincture; we may say that men became black in the same manner that
some Foxes, Squirrels, Lyons, first turned of this complexion ...
All of which mutations however they began, depend on durable
foundations; and such as may continue forever. [But what was
the original man?] ... deduct the administration of Angels ... [we
should consider those in] ... Noah's Ark ... [he then writes about
anthropology ... But states from these discussions.] ... I receive
no greater satisfaction.

However, therefore this complexion as first acquired, it is evi-
dently maintained by generation, and by the tincture of the skin
as a spermatical part traduced from father unto Son; so that they
which are strangers contract it not, and Natives which transmigrate,
omit it not without commixture, and that after divers generation.
And this affection (if the story were true) might wonderfully be
confirmed, by what Maginus and others relate of the Emperor of
Aethopia, or Prester John, who derived from Solomon is, not yet
descended into the hue of his Country, but remains a Mulatto,
that is, of Mongril complexion unto this day ... yet we are not of
Herodotus conceit, that their seed is black. An opinion long ago
rejected by Aristotle, and since by sense and enquiry ... that all
seed was white ... [in nearly all animals, some plants and men] ...
And thus it may also be in the generation and sperm of Negroes,
that being first and in its naturals white, but upon separation of
parts ... there arising a shadow or dark efflorescence in the outside; whereby ... are also dusky, before they have felt the scorch
and fervour of the Sun. ['turning white' suggests that white is not
natural or the original but a result of a reaction to nature.]

Chapter XI: Of the Same

A second opinion there is [second may imply less popular] that this complexion was first a curse of God derived unto them from Cham, upon whom it was inflicted for discovering the nudity the nakedness of Noah. Which notwithstanding is sooner affirmed than proved, and carrieth with it sundry improbabilities. For first, if we derive the curse on Cham, or in general upon his posterity, we shall denigrate a greater part of the earth than was ever so conceived, and not only paint the Ethiopians and reputed sons of Cush, but the people also of Egypt, Arabia, Assyria, and Chaldea; for by this race were these Countreys also peopled. And if concordantly unto Berosus ... Halicarnassus, Macrobius ... Leandro ... Annius, we shall conceive of the travels of Camese or Cham; we may introduce generations of Negroes as high as Italy, which part [those Africans] was never capable of deformtie, but hath produced the magnified examples of beauty.

Secondly, the curse mentioned in scripture was not denounced upon Cham, but Canaan his youngest son, and the reasonsthereof are divers. The first from the Jewish Tradition, whereby it is conceived, that Canaan made the discovery of nakedness of Noah, and notified it unto Cham. Secondly, to have cursed Cham had been to curse all his posterity, whereof but one was guilty of the fact. And lastly he spared Cham because he had blessed him before. Now if we confine this curse to Canaan ... then do we induce this complexion on the Sidonians, then was the promised land a tract(/) of Negroes. For from Canaan was descended the Canaanites, Jebusites ... which were possessed of that land. [p. 331] ... nor is it distinctlie determinable from whom thereof the Ethiopians are proceeded. For whereof these of Africa are generally esteemed to be issue of Chus, the elder son of Cham, it is not easily made out. [He then argues that Blackamoores come from Arabia and that the land of Chus forms no part of Africa. But is part of Asia and the Asian Ethiopians are the ones mentioned in the Bible, this includes the wife of Moses, the Queen of Sheba and other Aethopians that came from Arabia. And were not negroes. He goes onto explain that many African nations that he knows, do not appear to be easily descended from any of the sons of Noah.] ... Phut possessed Mauritania, and the western parts of Africa, and from these perhaps the Moors of the West, of Mandinga, Melegutte, and Guinie. But from Canaan, upon whom the curse was pronounced, none of these had their original, for he was restrained unto Canaan and Syria.

Fourthly, to take away all doubt or any probable divarication, the curse is plainly specified in the Text, nor need we dispute it, like the Mark of Cain ... [in other words it is specific] cursed be Canaan, as servant of servants ... [p. 331] As for Cham and his other sons, this curse attained them not, for Nimrod the son of Chus set up his kingdom in Babylon, and erected the first great Empire; Mizriam and his posterity grew mighty monarchs in Egypt; and the Empire of the Ethiopians hath been as large as either. Nor did the curse descend in general upon the posterity of Canaan ... But why there being eleven sons, five only were condemned, and six only escaped the malediction, is a secret beyond discovery.

Lastly, whereas men affirm this colour [of Africans] was a Curse, I cannot make out the property of that name, it neither seeming so to them, nor reasonably unto us, for they take so much content therein, that they esteeme deformity by other colours, describing the devil, and terrible objects white. And if we seriously consult the definitions of beauty, and exactly perpend what wife men determine men thereof in the proportion of parts, conceiving it to consist in a comely [p. 332] commensurability of the whole unto the parts, and the parts between themselves: which is the determination of the best and learned Writers. Now hereby the Moors are not excluded from beauty: there being in this description no consideration of colours, but an apt connexion and frame of parts and the whole. Otheres there be, and those most in number, which place it not only in proportion of parts but also in grace of colour. But to make Colour essential unto Beauty, there will arise no slender difficulty; for Aristotle in two definitions of pulchritude, and Galen in one, have made no mention of colour. Thus horses are handsome under any colour, and the symmetry of parts obscures the consideration of complexions. Thus in colour animals and such are confined unto one colour, we measure not there beauty thereby: for if a Crow or Black-bird grow white, we generally account it more pretty; And in almost a monstrosity to descend not to opinion of deformity. By this way like-wise the Moors escape the curse of deformity: there concurring no stationery colour, and sometimes not any unto Beauty.

M Leo the Jew ... in his Genealogy of Love: defining beauty a formal grace which delights and moves them to love that comprehend it ... And by this consideration of Beauty, the Moors are also not excluded, but hold a common share therein with all mankind. [p. 332]

Lastly ... if ... we allow the common conceit of symmetry and of colour, to descend unto singularities, or determine in what symmetry or colour it consisted, were a slippery designation. For beauty is determined by opinion, and seems to have no essence that holds one notion with all ... [p. 333] according as custom hath made it natural, or sympathy and conformity of minds shall make it seem agreeable. Thus flat noses seem comely unto the Moor, an aquiline or hawked one unto the Persian, a large prominent nose unto the Roman; but none of all these are acceptable in our opinion ... Thus Homer to set off Minerva called her ... that is, gray or light blue eyed, now this unto us seems far less amiable than the black. Thus we that are of the contrary complexions accuse the blackness of the Moors as ugly; but the spouse in the Canticles excuses this conceit, in that description of hers, I am black, but comely. And howsoever Cerberus, and the furies of hell be described by the poets under this complexion, yet in the beauty of our Saviour, blackness is commended, when it is said, his locks are bushy and black as a raven. So that to infer this as a curse, or to reason, or to reason it as a deformity, is no way reasonable ... receiving such various apprehensions, that no deviation will be expounded so high as a curse or undeniable deformity, without a manifest and confessed degree of monstrosity.

Lastly, it is a very injurious method of philosophy, and a perpetual promotion of ignorance, in points of obscurity, nor open unto easy considerations, to fall upon a upon a present refuge unto miracles; or to refer unto immediate contrivance [p. 334] from the unsearchable hands of God ... Certainly this is a course more desperate than antipathies, sympathies, or the occult qualities.

Chapter XII: A Digression Concerning Blackness

There being therefore two opinions repugnant unto each other, it may not be presumptive or sceptical to doubt of both ... we shall deliver at present a short discovery of blackness ... deducing the causes of blackness from such originals in nature ... for, art being the imitation of nature, or nature at the second hand, it is but a sensible expression of effects dependent on the same, though more removed causes: and therefore the works of the one may serve to discover the other.

[Browne then digresses to talk of how bodies change colour when burnt and appear black] infection of their own suffitus, ... And so do doth fire but cleanse and purify bodies, because it consumes the sulphureous part ... also corroding water will induce blackness ... it perfometh by an acid vitriolous.

These are the advenient and artificial ways of denigration, answerably whereto may be the natural progress ... being either fuliginous concretions in the earth, or suffering a scorch from denigrating principles in their formation ... And so may the Ethiopians or Negroes become coal-black, from fuliginous efflorescences and complexional tinctures arising from such probabilities, as we have declared before. [pp. 335-338]

The second way wherby bodies become black, is an atramentous condition or mixture, that is, a vitriolate or copperas quality conjoining with a terrestrious and stringent humidity; for so is atramentum scriptorim, or writing ink commonly made by copperas cast upon a decotion or infusion of galls ... for vitriol is the active or chief ingredient in ink ... partaking chiefly of iron and copper ... I have experimented in ... [plants, copperas, ink, iron and types of vitriol that only become red and need sunlight etc.] ... iron and vitriol are the powerfuel denigrators. [Looks for scientific answers] atramentum ... Such an atarmentous condition may be found sometime in the blood, when that which some call acetum, vitriolum, concurs with parts prepared for tincture. And so from these conditions [he explains how Africans may become Black] ... receiving atramentous impressions in some of those ways.

[Vitriol, salts etc. found in living bodies, etc. sometimes giving a] grateful sharpness ... or an austere and inconcotted roughness ... that not only is vitriol the cause of blackness, but the salts of natural bodies do carry a powerful tincture and varnish of all things.

[A]lthough in this long journey we miss the intended end, yet are there many things of truth disclosed along the way.[2]

Appendix 2

Letter from King Henry IV of England, to Prester John, 20 October 1422.

Henry IV. to the Emperor oe Abyssinia./Henrieus, Dei gratia Bex Anglice et Francia, et/Dominus Hibernice, magnijico et potenti Principi, Regi/Abassice, sive Presbytero Johanni, amico nostro in/Christo dilecto, salutem in omnium Salvatore./Magnifice Princeps, amice in Christo dilecte./Talia nobis nova de vestra Majestate jampridem nun-/ciata fuere, quae menti nostrae perimmensum gaudium/attulerunt, et [praecipue] cum honorem Dei necnon/utilitatem Ecclesiae concernant, et proficuum animarum./Et utinam ipsa nova fuerint pro consolatione Fidelium/latius expressata/Nunciatum est namque nobis per venerabilem in/Christo Patrem, Johannem, Archiepiscopum Orientis ac/Ethiopiae per Sedem Apostolicam, Petri videlicet, or-/dinatum, necnon et per alios fidedignos qualiter ex/devoto benevolo ac singulari zelo, Dominum nostrum/Jesum Christum, Fidemque Catholicam, et Fideles,/necnon et sacrosanctam et immaculatam Ecclesiam/Beatorum Petri et Pauli, scilicet Ecclesiam Romanam,/vestra Magnificentia persequitur gratiose; et quantam/gerit affectionem ipsa Sublimitas circa Sepulchrum/Dominicum ab hostili potentia redimendum. Unde/revera, magnifice Princeps, gaudemus in Domino, et/gratias agimus Jesu Christo, Qui de fideli devotione/CXLVII.

(MS. Cotton. Nero, B. xl fol. 172. –
On vellum; an original draft)

tanti Principis et suorum, ut speramus, Suam dignatus/est
Ecclesiam ampliare; Ipsumque suppliciter exoramus/ut quod
incepit in vobis Ipse perficiat, ut caritas vestra/magis ac magis
abundet in Domino Jesu Christo.1/Et scire velitis, magnifice
Princeps, quod ob honorem/et reverentiam Crucifixi, necnon
et devotionem specialem/quam ad Suum Sepulchrum a diu
gessimus et gerimus,/ut tenemur, Illud jamdudum in persona
nostra duximus/visitandum quod etiam iterato proponunus,
vita comite/per Dei gratiam, ad impendendum Sibi servitium,
per-/sonaliter visitare, velut praefatus Archiepiscopus
de/intentione nostra in hac parte, necnon de affectione/quam
erga Majestatem vestram gerimus et habemus,/experienter
instructus, per quem de statu vestro prospero/speranms
imposterum effici certiores, vestrae Celsi-/tudini noverit
lucidius explicare; cui velitis in suis/ex parte nostra dicendis
sedulam dare fidem, ipsumque/tanquam fortem Ecclesiae
pugilem et pastorem, vobis ut/asserit multipliciter obligatum,
qui pro visitanda Majes-/tate vestra ad ejusdem pnesentiam
jam decedit, suscipere/velitis nostrae considerationis intuitu
recommissum;/significantes nobis, si placeat, in quibus
vestrae Dilec-/tioni poterimus complacentiam exbibere./Dies
vobis adaugeat in prosperitate fecundos ad Sui/Nominis
gloriam et honoris, Qui pro nobis de sacra-/tissima Virgine
dignanter voluit incarnari./Datum, etc./1 Pliilippians, i. 6. | –
Cedulam, MS.

HENRY IV. Se Abyssiuia to the emperor./Henrieus by
the grace of God King of England and France,/The Irish,
magnijice and Prince, King/Abassice, whether it be a priest
named John, as the friend of our God unto the/Beloved Christ,
in the salvation of all the Savior./A magnificent leader in
Christ, my friend./Such are the new version of your Majesty,
the first nun/ciata were other things which the mind of the
joy of our perimmensum/brought it, and [especially] as well
as the honor/Church concerning the utility and benefit of
souls./But they wish the new comfort for the faithful/widely
expressed/And it was for us with respect to the/Christ, the
Father, John, of the East and of the Archbishop of/Ethiopia by

the Holy See, Peter, that is, OR-/dinate, as well as trustworthy
men by means of others, and how the/a devout tone of
benevolent intention, but extraordinary in his zeal to the Lord
our/Jesus Christ, and our Catholic and faithful/They also took
the sacrosanct and inviolate/Peter and Paul, that the Church
of Rome/your Magnificence thus pursue after his graciously;
the amount/represents the height of affection around the
Tomb/Sunday from hostile power redeeming. Therefore,/In
fact, the magnificent Prince, revel in the Lord;/We give thanks
to Jesus Christ, He who comes from the devotion of the
faithful/147.

(MS. Cotton. Nero, B. xl fol. 172. –
On vellum; an original draft)

of so great a prince and of their fathers, as we hope,
vouchsafed to His/Church to increase And when we humbly
beseech/He himself, as he has begun in you, to complete it, so
that your love may abound/may abound yet more and more in
the Lord Jesus Christo.1/Then you will know the magnificent
prince is an honor/shame of the cross, as well as a special
devotion/His grave for a long time and done and is doing/as
we long ago that a person is fit to/The visit also recalled
proponunus life;/By God's grace, rendering him the service
per-/personally visit, as named archbishop of/our intention,
in this respect, as well as concerning that affection,/And as for
your Majesty, we have/The experience of a trained, by means
of which he wrote concerning your state with a prosperous
speranms for the future, to become a more certain, it will be
Celsi-/should know that is brighter than the total amount be
to explain; to whom you want to in their own sedulam give
faith on our part will be said presently, and should be/Church
pastor brave like a boxer, you should/in many states bound
for the visit Majes-/pnesentiam your hearts to the reality of
already ceases to be, the same, to support the/are willing to
our consideration and with a view to recommissum;/which
signify to us, if it pleases God, in the which yours dilec-/ll be

able to pleasing fitting./In time you add it into a success for decades/Of the name of honor, and glory, and, He who speaks for us, by the sacraments/Virgin-worthiness of the most wanted incarnate./Given, etc./1 Philippians i. 6. | – schedules, MS.[1]

Notes

Preface

1 Quotation from William Shakespeare, *The Tragedy of Hamlet, Prince of Denmark*, Act IV, Scene V, L. 43, 1599–1602, in Richard Proudfoot, Ann Thompson, David Kastan, David Scott (eds.), *The Arden Shakespeare Complete Works* (Walton on Thames: Thomas Nelson and Sons, 1998), p. 320.

2 Shakespeare, *Hamlet*, Act III, Scene I, L. 65, 1599–1602, in Proudfoot et al. (eds.), *The Arden Shakespeare*, p. 309.

3 Geocentrism is the idea that the earth is the centre of the Universe.

4 For a commentary on these ideas see Maghan Keita, *Race and the Writing of History: Riddling the Sphinx* (London: Oxford University Press, 2000), pp. 15–27; Some of these ideas are quoted and advocated in John R. Barker, *Race* (Dallas, TX: Ostara Publications, 2016), passim; Charles Benedict Davenport, *Heredity in Relation to Genetics* (New York: H. Holt, 1911), passim; Ostara is a press devoted to a Eurocentric world view and contains many books that include these sorts of perspectives.

5 There is an acknowledgement that some writers claim Europe had a Renaissance in the twelfth century see Susan Wise Bauer, *The History of the Renaissance World: From the Rediscovery of Aristotle to the Conquest of Constantinople* (New York: W. W. Norton, 2013), passim; Robert L. Benson, Giles Constable, Carol D. Lanham (eds.), *Renaissance and Renewal in the Twelfth Century* (Cambridge, MA: Harvard University Press, 1982), passim; Charles Homer Haskins, *The Renaissance of the Twelfth Century* (Cambridge, MA: Harvard University Press, 1927), passim.

6 The enslavement of African people did not begin in 1567; it was not a 'trade' in the strictest sense of the word; it did not end in 1807; nor did Britain's participation stop in 1807 or even by 1833.

7 The idea of 'race' is complex and in some ways controversial. It is often used as Jonathan Schorsch does in *Swimming the Christian Atlantic:*

Judeoconversos, Afroiberians, and Amerindians in the Seventeenth Century (Leiden/Boston, MA/Biggleswade: Brill Extenza Turpin, 2008), p. 5 (6), 'Without wishing to enter into an enormous and dangerous topic, race/ethnicity is real, i.e., "natural" insofar as different population groups often manifest different biological conditions [genotype] … Different population groups may also manifest statistically-notable somatic uniqueness [phenotype]: eye shape, particularly light skin, height, etc.' In this book these notions of race and the post-colonial discourses that rely on it are subject to continuous analysis.

Note on the Text

1 Authors various, Letter to Lord Mayors, signed by Queen Elizabeth, National Archives, Kew, London, PC 2/21, f. 304, 11 July 1596; Authors various, Letter signed by Queen Elizabeth, National Archives, Kew, London, PC 2/21, f. 306, 18 July 1596; and Authors various, Proclamation ca January 1601, National Archives, Kew, London, *Tudor Royal Proclamations*, 1601/ 804.5–805.

2 The term 'Black History' is often used to describe 'Black Studies,' 'Africana,' 'African History,' 'African Diaspora studies,' etc. In the USA such programmes are well developed; in Britain they are not, see Kehinde Andrews, Black Studies degree programme. It is one of the first university programmes in Britain: Kehinde Andrews, 'At Last the UK Has a Black Studies University Course: It's Long Overdue,' *Guardian*, 20 May 2016, www.theguardian.com/commentisfree/2016/may/20/black-studies-university-course-long-overdue, accessed 06/09/2016.

3 Imtiaz Habib, *Shakespeare and Race: Postcolonial Praxis in the Early Modern Period* (Lanham, MD: University Press of America, 1999), pp. 157–205; for more on post-colonialism as a historiographical discipline see Bill Ashcroft, Gareth Griffiths, Helen Tiffin (eds.), *The Post Colonial Studies Reader* (London/New York: Taylor & Francis, 2006), pp. 28–38, 44–62, 73–77, 84–93 (Euro-centrism and otherness).

4 There is an acknowledgement that some historians include the eighteenth century when talking about the early modern period, see John Cannon, *The Oxford Companion to British History* (Oxford: Oxford University Press, 2002), introduction; James Sharpe, *Early Modern England: A Social History, 1550–1760* (London: Bloomsbury Academic, 1997), introduction; Alison Wall, *Power and Protest in England, 1525–1640* (London: Bloomsbury Academic, 2002), introduction; but in this book the author suggests a different historiography in relation to the social history of Africans in England.

Introduction

1   Onyeka, *Blackamoores: Africans in Tudor England, Their Presence, Status and Origins* (London: Narrative Eye, 2013, 2014), p. vii.

2   Onyeka, 'What's in a Name: Africans in Tudor England.' *History Today* 62:10 (October 2012), www.historytoday.com/onyeka/tudor-africans-whats-name#sthash.G2xe8vO4.dpuf.

3   These historians' works encompass a range of different and very diverse sets of studies conducted throughout the world, for a view on this see Molefi Keti Asante, Ama Mazama (eds.), *The Encyclopedia of Black Studies* (London: Sage Publications, 2005), pp. 1–15.

4   The books that claim to offer a comprehensive approach to this period but appear to do this are many, but include: Geoffrey Rudolph Elton, *England Under the Tudors* (London: Oxford University Press, 1995), pp. 1–25; Robert Tittler, *Townspeople and Nation: English Urban Experiences, 1540–1640* (Stanford, CA: Stanford University Press, 2001), pp. 1–43; and Robert Tittler, Norman Jones (eds.), *A Companion to Tudor Britain*, Blackwell Companions to British History (Oxford: Oxford University Press, 2004), pp. 1–32.

5   Edward Scobie, *Black Britannia: A History of Blacks in Britain* (Chicago, IL: Johnson Publishing Company, 1972), pp. 190–203; Joel Augustus Rogers, *World's Great Men of Colour*, Volumes 1 and 2 (1931, new edition, New York: Touchstone Books, 1995), pp. 1–7; Joel Augustus Rogers, *Sex and Race*, Volumes 1–4 (St. Petersburg, FL: Helga Rogers, 1941/2), Volume 1, pp. 151–160, 196–220; and Ivan Van Sertima (ed.), Edward Scobie, *African Presence in Early Europe* (Piscataway, NJ: Transaction Publishers, 1985), pp. 12–15, 190–223; the references for Runoko Rashidi, John Archer and Duse Mohamed Ali are contained in the bibliography.

6   Stephen Howe is one of those writers who claim most of the African-American and Caribbean historians noted above are polemic fantasists in *Afrocentrism: Mythical Pasts and Imagined Homes* (1998, 2nd edition, London: Verso, 1999), pp. 1–16, 215–229; others include: Mary Lefkowitz, *Black Athena Revisited* (Chapel Hill, NC: University of North Carolina Press, 1996), pp. 113–120; Mary Lefkowitz, *Not Out of Africa: How Afrocentrism Became an Excuse to Teach Myth as History* (New York: Basic Books, 1996), passim.

7   All the following books are passim unless otherwise stated: Kate Lowe, Thomas Earle (eds.), *Black Africans in Renaissance Europe* (Cambridge: Cambridge University Press, 2005); Michael Guasco, *Slaves and Englishmen: Human Bondage in the Early Modern Atlantic World*, The Early Modern Americas (Philadelphia, PA: University of Pennsylvania Press, 2014); Jonathan Schorsch, *Jews and Blacks in the*

Early Modern World (Cambridge: Cambridge University Press, 2004); Schorsch, *Swimming the Christian Atlantic*; Francois Soyer, *The Persecution of the Jews and Muslims of Portugal: King Manuel I and the End of Religious Tolerance (1496–7)*, Medieval Mediterranean (Leiden/ Boston, MA: Brill, 2012); Francois Soyer, *Ambiguous Gender in Early Modern Spain and Portugal: Inquisitors, Doctors and Transgression of Gender Norms*, Medieval and Early Modern Iberian World (Leiden/ Boston, MA: Brill, 2012); Francois Soyer, *Popularizing Anti-Semitism in Early Modern Spain and Its Empire*, Medieval and Early Modern Iberian World (Leiden/Boston, MA: Brill, 2014); David Wheat, *Atlantic Africa and the Spanish Caribbean, 1570–1640* (Chapel Hill, NC: University of North Carolina Press, 2016); David Wheat, 'Mediterranean Slavery, New World Transformations: Galley Slaves in the Spanish Caribbean, 1578–1635.' *Slavery & Abolition* 31:3 (2010), pp. 327–344, reprinted in Philip D. Morgan, *Maritime Slavery* (London: Routledge, 2012); David Wheat, 'Global Transit Points and Travel in the Iberian Maritime World, 1580–1640,' in Peter C. Mancall, Carole Shammas (eds.), *Governing the Sea in the Early Modern Era: Essays in Honor of Robert C. Ritchie* (San Marino: Huntington Library, 2015), pp. 253–274; David Wheat, 'The First Great Waves: African Provenance Zones for the Transatlantic Slave Trade to Cartagena de Indias, 1570–1640.' *The Journal of African History* 52:1 (2011), pp. 1–22; David Wheat, 'Garcia Mendes Castelo Branco, *Fidalgo* de Angola y Mercader de Esclavos en Veracruz y el Caribe a Principios del Siglo XVII,' in María Elisa Velázquez (ed.), *Debates Históricos Contemporáneos: Africanos y Afrodescendientes en México y Centroamérica*, (Mexico: D.F.: INAH, CEMCA, UNAM-CIALC, IRD, 2011), pp. 85–107; David Wheat, 'The Spanish Caribbean in the Colonial Period,' in Ben Vinson (ed.), *Oxford Bibliographies in Latin American Studies* (New York: Oxford University Press, 2012); these authors also include William D. Phillips, *Slavery in Medieval and Early Modern Iberia*, The Middle Ages Series (Philadelphia, PA: University of Pennsylvania Press, 2013), passim; and Stephen Hornsby, Michael Hermann, *British Atlantic, American Frontier: Spaces of Power in Early Modern British America* (Lebanon, NH: University Press of New England, 2005), passim.

8 Subaltern studies have also been useful because they reveal the hidden subject: see Gayatri Chakravorty Spivak, 'Can the Subaltern Speak?' in Cary Nelson, Lawrence Grossberg (eds.), *Marxism and the Interpretation of Culture* (Urbana, IL: University of Illinois Press, 1988), pp. 271–313; and Stephen Morton, 'The Subaltern: Genealogy of a Concept,' in Gayatri Spivak, *Ethics, Subalternity and the Critique of Postcolonial Reason* (Cambridge: Polity, 2007), pp. 96–97.

9   Racism is distinct from prejudice or statements of ethnic chauvinism; it relies on a belief in separate and distinct races, a hierarchy, with some races automatically being inferior to others, and most importantly on the power to enforce one's perspectives. Some argue that racism is constructed, but prejudice is a natural phenomenon that occurs because of difference and a desire to protect one's 'grouping.' Those that offer these views include a diverse set of people, some of whom are included in this book.

10   The quotation is from the *Dred Scott Case, Scott v Sandford*, Chief Justice Roger B. Taney, United States Supreme Court (1857), 60 U.S. 393.

11   For a wider discussion on these matters beyond what is included here, please see Onyeka, 'What's in a Name?,' pp. 34–39.

12   The term 'anti-African antipathy' is used here as a generic phrase that describes what we may now call ethnic prejudice, chauvinism etc. that is directed towards Africans because they are Africans. This antipathy may not be supported by law or policies.

13   'Pathology' comes from the Greek word 'pathos' to know or understand, it is usually used to describe diseases. In this book 'pathology' will include a diagnosis of the cause and effect of ideas associated with the Curse of Ham, in relation to an anti-African antipathy. A few historians use the word pathology in this way including: Veena Das, 'Collective Violence and the Shifting Categories of Communal Riots, Ethnic Cleansing and Genocide,' in David Stone (ed.), *The Historiography of Genocide* (New York: Springer, 2008), pp. 93–99; and Gareth Steadman Jones, 'The Pathology of English History.' *New Left Review* 46 (1967), pp. 29–43.

14   On the different methodological tools used in each discipline see Nimi Wariboko, *Methods of Ethical Analysis: Between Theology, History and Literature* (Eugene, OR: Wipf Stock Publishers, 2013), passim; Darren Sarisky, *Theology, History, and Biblical Interpretation: Modern Readings* (London: Bloomsbury Publishing, 2015), passim; and Robert M. Doran (ed.), Bernard Lonergan, *Method in Theology* (Toronto: University of Toronto Press, 2017), passim.

15   Nicholas Oyugi Odhiambo, *Ham's Sin and Noah's Curse and Blessed Utterances: A Critique of Current Views* (Bloomington, IN: Author House, 2014), pp. 39–47; Schorsch, *Jews and Blacks in the Early Modern World*, pp. 16–48, 135–166; Benjamin Braude, 'The Sons of Noah and the Construction of Ethnic and Geographical Identities in the Medieval and Early Modern Periods.' *William and Mary Quarterly* 65 (1997), pp. 103–142; David M. Goldenberg, *The Curse of Ham: Race and Slavery in Early Judaism, Christianity, and Islam* (Princeton, NJ: Princeton University Press, 2003); David M. Whitford, *The Curse*

of Ham in the Early Modern Era: The Bible and the Justifications for Slavery (London: Routledge, 2016); all passim.

16 The term 'people activity' was coined by Neely Fuller in *The United Independent Compensatory Code/System/Concept a Textbook/Workbook for Thought, Speech and/or Action for Victims of Racism (White Supremacy)* (Place of publication unknown: Neely Fuller, 1957–1980), passim.

17 The subject of the colonialism of Ireland and the Americas has been widely written about, some authors include: Audrey Horning, *Ireland in the Virginian Sea: Colonialism in the British Atlantic* (Chapel Hill, NC: University of North Carolina Press, 2013), passim; Roger Lockyer, *Tudor and Stuart Britain, 1485–1714* (New York: Pearson Education, 2005), pp. 477–506; Kenneth R. Andrews, *Trade, Plunder and Settlement: Maritime Enterprise and the Genesis of the British Empire, 1480–1630* (Cambridge: Cambridge University Press, 1984), passim; for more on the travellers who participated in colonial exploits see Claire Jowitt, Daniel Carey, *Richard Hakluyt and Travel Writing in Early Modern Europe* (London: Ashgate, 2012), passim; other authors are included in the bibliography.

18 These matters have been written about extensively, see: George Bagshawe Harrison, *Shakespeare at Work 1592–1603* (London: Routledge, 1933), pp. 310, 311; Ivan Van Sertima (ed.), *African Presence in Early Europe*, pp. 201, 207, 292; Ivan Van Sertima (ed.), *Black Women in Antiquity* (Piscataway, NJ: Transaction Publishers, 1984), p. 140; Ivan Van Sertima (ed.), *Golden Age of the Moor* (Piscataway, NJ: Transaction Publishers, 1992), pp. 342–345; Scobie, *Black Britannia*, p. 6; Imtiaz Habib, *Black Lives in the English Archives, 1500–1677: Imprints of the Invisible* (Farnham: Ashgate, 2008), pp. 308, 326, 327 (Dark Lady Sonnets and prostitutes); Marika Sherwood, 'Blacks in Elizabethan England.' *History Today* 53:10 (2003), pp. 40–42; Simon (Samuel) Schoenbaum, *William Shakespeare: A Compact Documentary Life* (Oxford: Clarendon Press, 1977), p. 125; Schoenbaum, *Shakespeare's Lives* (London: Clarendon, 1991), p. 688; Gustav Ungerer, 'Recovering a Black African's Voice in an English Lawsuit,' *Medieval and Renaissance Drama in England* (Madison, WI: Fairleigh Dickinson University Press, 2004), pp. 255–271 (note 4); Joel Augustus Rogers, *Nature Knows No Colour-Line* (St. Petersburg, FL: Helga Rogers, 1952), pp. 76, 77, 81; Hugh Calvert, *Shakespeare's Sonnets and Problems of Autobiography* (Braunton: Merlin, 1987), pp. 203–206, 220; Brenda James, *Henry Neville and the Shakespeare Code* (Bognor Regis: Music for Strings, 2008), pp. 150–154; and Robert Nye, *The Late Mister Shakespeare: A Novel* (London: Chatto and Windus, 1998), pp. 281–285, 289–297 (a fictional retelling of Lucy Negro legend).

One

1 William Shakespeare, *As You Like It*, Act V, Scene III, L. 16, 1599, in Proudfoot et al. (eds.), *The Arden Shakespeare*, p. 186.

2 Quotation from Shakespeare, *The Famous History of the Life of King Henry the Eighth*, Act II, Scene III, L. 47, 1601, in Proudfoot et al. (eds.), *The Arden Shakespeare*, p. 580 – 'little England,' or 'little Englander' are terms used to describe an idea of Englishness that is exclusive.

3 Quotation from Shakespeare, *The Tragedy of King Richard the Second*, Act II, Scene I, L. 49–50, 1597, in Proudfoot et al. (eds.), *The Arden Shakespeare*, p. 679.

4 Ibid., L. 42.

5 The Selected Bibliography contains a list of the books that appear to offer this impression and may also include: Elton, *England Under the Tudors*; Tittler, *Townspeople and Nation*; and Tittler, Jones (eds.), *A Companion to Tudor Britain*, all throughout; for a contrary view see Marika Sherwood, in 'In This Curriculum, I Don't Exist,' The Institute of Historical Research, University of London School of Advanced Study, www.history.ac.uk/resources/history-in-british-education/first-conference/sherwood-paper, accessed 27/07/2011.

6 This idea can also be inferred by the way that documentaries tell the 'British story,' see Simon Schama et al., *A History of Britain*, 2 Entertain Video, 2000–2002; this impression is present in films and TV series such as: Alexander Korda, *The Private Life of Henry VIII*, United Artists, 1933; Fred Zinnemann et al., *A Man for All Seasons*, Columbia Pictures, 1966; Charles Jarrott et al., *Anne of the Thousand Days*, Universal Pictures, 1969; Roderick Graham (dir.) et al., *Elizabeth R*, BBC2, 17 February 1971; Shekhar Kapur et al., *Elizabeth*, Polygram, 1998; Gillies Mackinnon, *Gunpowder Treason and Plot*, BBC 2, 14 April 2004; Shekhar Kapur et al., *Elizabeth: The Golden Age*, Universal Studios, 2007; Michael Hirst et al., *The Tudors*, Showtime/Reveille/Working Title, 1 April 2007; this trend is rebutted by Gareth Roberts (writer), Charles Palmer (dir.), 'The Shakespeare Code,' *Dr Who* series, BBC, 7 April 2007; and Josie Rourke (dir.), *Mary Queen of Scots*, Universal Pictures, 7 December 2018.

7 Shakespeare, *The Tragedy of King Richard the Second*, 1597, Act II, Scene I, in Proudfoot et al. (eds.), *The Arden Shakespeare*, p. 679.

8 The term 'Black Tudors' is used by the author Miranda Kaufmann, *Black Tudors: The Untold Story* (London: Oneworld Publications, 2017).

9 Quoted in Maghan Keita, 'Race, What the Bookstore Hid,' in Celia Chazelle, Simon Doubleday, Felice Lifshitz, Amy G. Remensnyder (eds.), *Why the Middle Ages Matter: Medieval Light on Modern Injustice* (London: Routledge, 2012), p. 130.

10 For this kind of conflation see the popular pulp book, George Courtauld, *The Pocket Book of Patriotism* (Halstead: Halstead Books, 2004), pp. 49 ('This England'), 50 ('St Crispin's Day'), 53; and see George Courtauld, *Pocket Book of Patriots: 100 British Heroes* (London: Random House, 2010), pp. 39 ('St Crispin's Day'), 79–80 ('This England'), 92, 134, 155, 273; Hereford Brooke George, Arthur Sidgwick, *Poems of England* (London: Macmillan, 1896), pp. 5–7; for a wider discussion see David J. Baker, Willy Maley (eds.), *British Identities and English Renaissance Literature* (London: Cambridge University Press, 2002), pp. 11–23, 69–71, 81–99; Max Meredith Reese, *The Cease of Majesty: A Study of Shakespeare's History Plays* (London: Edward Arnold Publishers, 1961), passim.

11 A commentary on this idea is in Habib, *Black Lives*, pp. 35, 49, 74; Nabil Matar, *Islam in Britain, 1558–1685* (Cambridge: Cambridge University Press, 1998), pp. 50–70; Leslie A. Fiedler, *The Stranger in Shakespeare* (New York: Stein and Day, 1972), pp. 139–199; Kim Hall, *Things of Darkness: Economies of Race and Gender in Early Modern England* (1995, 2nd edition, New York: Cornell University Press, 1996), p. 211; Margo Hendricks, 'Surveying "Race" in Shakespeare,' in Catherine M. S. Alexander, Stanley Wells (eds.), *Shakespeare and Race* (Cambridge: Cambridge University Press, 2000), pp. 1–23; George Kirkpatrick Hunter, 'Othello and Colour Prejudice.' *Proceedings of the British Academy* 53 (1967), p. 153; Jose Piedra, 'In Search of the Black Stud,' in Louise Fradenburg and Carla Freccero (eds.), *Premodern Sexualities* (New York: Routledge, 1996), pp. 22–44; Braude, 'The Sons of Noah and the Construction of Ethnic and Geographical Identities in the Medieval and Early Modern Periods,' pp. 103–142; Joyce Green MacDonald, 'Black Ram, White Ewe: Shakespeare, Race and Women,' in Dympna Callaghan (ed.), *A Feminist Companion to Shakespeare* (Oxford: Wiley Blackwell, 2001), pp. 188–207. Other authors, including Jonathan Burton, Ania Loomba and Patricia Parker, are listed in the Selected Bibliography.

12 For a Eurocentric anthropologist perspective on race see Ashley Montagu (ed.), *UNESCO Statement on Race: An Annotated Elaboration and Exposition of the Four Statements on Race Issued by the United Nations Educational, Scientific, and Cultural Organization* (1st edition not known, 3rd edition, New York: Oxford University Press, 1972), p. 78.

13 On 'social Darwinism' see John P. Jackson (jr.), Nadine M. Weidman, *Race, Racism and Science: Social Impact and Interaction* (Santa Barbara, CA: ABC CLIO, 2004), pp. 75, 76, 84–127; 'Manifest Destiny,' see Nell Irvin Painter, *The History of White People* (New York: W. W Norton and Company, 2010), pp. 188, 235; the term

'Whiteman's Burden' comes from a poem by Rudyard Kipling written in 1899, in Winthorp D. Jordan, *The Whiteman's Burden: Historical Origins of Racism in the United States* (Oxford: Oxford University Press, 1974), pp. 26–65; on 'white supremacy' and 'white power' see Fuller, *The United Independent*, passim; also see Ashley Montagu, *Man's Most Dangerous Myth: The Fallacy of Race* (Redditch: Read Books, 2013), passim.

14 Phrenology is the study of the brain and was pioneered by Franz Joseph Gall in the eighteenth century, see David B. Baker, *The Oxford Handbook of the History of Psychology: Global Perspectives* (Oxford: Oxford University Press, 2012), pp. 182–184, 468–485; cephalometry, the generic term used to refer to the study of the human head and which includes craniometry, is essentially a modern enquiry, but was speculated on in the early modern and classical periods.

15 Physiognomy is the study of the outward appearance of a person, especially their face. Readers may wish to consult the work of Giambattista Della Porta (1535–1615), *Magia Naturalis* (Naples: publisher unknown, 1558, 1559). Images are shown that equate the physiognomy of human groups with animals as evidence of both of their temperaments; one image in this book appears to show an African compared to a bull and a European to a greyhound, see Giambattista Della Porta, *Magiae Naturalis …* (Antverpiae: Ex officina C. Plantini, 1564), p. 59.

16 Of course sometimes Shakespeare's written works and the productions of his plays were overtly political. This is revealed in the desire of conspirators supporting the Earl of Essex's rebellion of 1601. They believed that a performance of *Richard II* by the Lord Chamberlain's men would initiate the uprising. It did not. See Rebecca Lemon, *Treason by Words: Literature, Law and Rebellion in Shakespeare's England* (New York: Cornell University Press, 2005), pp. 52–79.

17 The term 'magpie' was applied posthumously by Ben Jonson to Shakespeare in *Preface to the First Folio*, 'To the memory of my beloved, Mr William Shakespeare and what he hath left us' (London: Ifaac Iaagard, 1623), preface. A magpie steals 'shiny' things from others and makes them his own; Christopher Marlowe's work is well known but see Fredson Bowers (ed.), Christopher Marlowe, *The Complete Works of Christopher Marlowe* (Cambridge: Cambridge University Press, 1973), passim; and William Painter (1540?–1595), *The Palace of Pleasure: Beautified, Adorned and Well Furnished, with Pleasaunt Histories and Excellent Nouelles, Selected Out of Diuers* (London: Henry Denham, 1566), passim. His work contained stories upon which Shakespeare based many of his tragedies.

18 Sean Tierney, 'Quentin Tarantino in Black and White,' in Michael G. Lacey, Kent A. Ono (eds.), *Critical Rhetorics of Race* (New York: New York University Press, 2011), pp. 81–97; Adilifu Nama, *Race on the QT: Blackness and the Films of Quentin Tarantino* (Austin, TX: University of Texas Press, 2015), passim.

19 An excellent book on these filmmakers and this idea is Manthia Diawara, *In Search of Africa* (New York: Harvard University Press, 2009), pp. 237–279; see also Olivier Barlet, *Contemporary African Cinema* (East Lansing, MI: Michigan State University Press, 2016), n.p. 'The Burden of Hollywood.'

20 On this comparative perspective on Shakespeare and Italian writers of the period see Michele Marrapodi (ed.), *Shakespeare and the Italian Renaissance: Appropriation, Transformation, Opposition* (London: Routledge, 2015), passim; on contemporary writers in performance see Sarah Annes Brown, Robert I. Lublin (eds.), *Reinventing the Renaissance: Shakespeare and His Contemporaries in Adaptation and Performance* (New York: Springer, 2013), passim.

21 Spain was not England's enemy at the beginning of the period in question. This is illustrated by the fact that Katherine, a Spanish princess and England's queen, helped organise the defeat of a Scottish monarch that had invaded England in 1513 at the Battle of Flodden. James IV King of Scotland was killed, see George Goodwin, *Fatal Rivalry, Flodden 1513: Henry VIII, James IV and the Battle for Renaissance Britain* (New York: Hachette UK, 2013), passim.

22 For more on this see Benjamin Bradshaw, Peter Roberts (eds.), *British Consciousness and Identity: The Making of Britain, 1533–1707* (Cambridge: Cambridge University Press, 1998), pp. 2–13, 110–112, 142; Hans Kohn, Craig J. Calhoun, *The Idea of Nationalism: A Study in Its Origins and Background* (New York: Macmillan, 1944), pp. 6–12, 156–162; Philip Schwyzer, *Literature, Nationalism, and Memory in Early Modern England and Wales* (Cambridge: Cambridge University Press, 2004), pp. 49–76, 126–151.

23 Of course other nations, peoples and entities within and outside the nation were portrayed as threats including the Devil, Spain, Egyptians, Huguenots, Jewish people, heretics and heathens; some modern historians, quoting the letters dated 11 and 18 July 1596 and the 1601 Proclamation, claim Africans were too. This shall be explored later.

24 Robert Hutchinson, *Elizabeth's Spy Master: Francis Walsingham and the Secret War That Saved England* (London: Weidenfeld and Nicolson, 2006), passim.

25 Sophie Crawford Lomas (ed.), Edward Stafford, *Calendar of State Papers, Foreign Series*, Volume 21 (London: Her Majesty's Stationery,

1927), p. 73; Edward Stafford, Letter to Francis Walsingham, Secretaries of State; State Papers Foreign, France (June–December 1586), 20 August 1586, National Archives, Kew, ref. SP 78/16, f. 90–91: added in parentheses ( ) the missing sections from Lomas' entry, but contained in the primary records, and my words in [ ] for the reader's sense.

26 Francis Drake, William Davenant, *The History of Sir Francis Drake, Expressed by Instrumentall and Vocal Musick* ... (London: Henry Herringman, 1659), pp. 12, 14, 18, 19 (quotation); Pedro Sarmiento de Gamboa, Nuna da Silva, *New Light on Drake: A Collection of Documents Relating to His Voyage of Circumnavigation, 1577–1580* (London: Hakluyt Society, 1968), introduction, p. 302.

27 This is a revised position from that stated in Onyeka, *Blackamoores*, pp. 155–160, which includes more on the Symerons. They were a group of people of African and Native-American descent that separated from their Spanish colonisers and formed independent communities and kingdoms in North, Central and South America. Sometimes these same people are called Maroons, see Richard Price (ed.), *Maroon Societies: Rebel Slave Communities in the Americas* (New York: Anchor Books, 1973), pp. 11–15.

28 John Sugden, *Sir Francis Drake* (London: Random House, 2006), p. 72.

29 Andrews, *Trade, Plunder and Settlement*, p. 131; Peter Whitfield, *Sir Francis Drake* (New York: New York University Press, 2004), p. 34.

30 See previous note.

31 Stafford, Letter to Francis Walsingham, 20 August 1586, f. 90–91.

32 An African narrator's ethnicity could add authenticity to what they said, see Onyeka, *Blackamoores*, pp. 155–160.

33 *The [Great] Bible in Englyshe of the Largest and Greatest Volume ... According to the Translation Apoynted by the Queen Maiesties Iniunctions to be Read in Churches with in her Maiesties Realme ... At the Coste and Charges of Richard Carmarden* (Rouen: C. Hamillon, 1566), passim.

34 Authors various, 'A Brief, Listing a Series of Complaints against [Richard] Carmarden of London, Surveyor of the Customs to Queen Elizabeth, and the Damage Caused by his Misbehavior to Shipping, Trade, and Receipt of Customs,' (sixteenth century), ref. Hench # 5a.7 (6435-a), Folder 2 : 13 (Charlottesville, VA: University of Virginia Library, Special Collections Library, Charlottesville, Virginia, Medieval and European Manuscripts).

35 Walsingham had died in 1590, see Hutchinson, *Elizabeth's Spy Master*, introduction.

36 On Spain's influence in Calabria and the Kingdom of Naples see Thomas James Dandelet, John A. Marino (eds.), *Spain in Italy: Politics, Society, and Religion 1500–1700* (Leiden/Boston, MA: Brill, 2007), pp. 14, 263, 277, 426, 471.

37 John Stubbs, *The Discoverie of a Gaping Gulf, The Discoverie of a Gaping Gulf Whereinto England is like to be Swallowed by an other French Marriage, if the Lord Forbid not the Banes, by Letting her Maiestie see the Sin and Punishment Thereof* (London: H. Singleton, 1579), pp. 4, 32, 35, 42 (quotation): Stubbs was referring to the Moorish dominated parts of Iberia as well as Northern and Western Africa etc.

38 See Pauline Croft, 'Trading with the Enemy, 1585–1604.' *Historical Journal* 32 (June 1989), pp. 281–302; Pauline Croft, 'English Commerce with Spain and the Armada War, 1558–1603,' in Simon Lester Adams, M. J. Rodriguez-Salgado (eds.), *England, Spain and the Gran Armada, 1585–1604: Essays from the Anglo-Spanish Conferences* (1988, new edition, Edinburgh: Rowman and Littlefield, 1991), pp. 236–263; and Albert Loomie, 'Religion and Elizabethan Commerce with Spain.' *The Catholic Historical Review* 50 (April 1964), pp. 27–51.

39 This is sometimes referred to as 'racial profiling' and there are many books on this, see Stanley Cohen, in *Folk Devils and Moral Panics* (St Albans: Paladin, 1973), passim; Stuart Hall, in C. Critcher, T. Jefferson (eds.), *Policing the Crisis: Mugging, the State and Law and Order* (London: Macmillan, 1978), passim; Jeff Shantz, *Racism and Borders: Representation, Repression, Resistance* (New York: Algora Publishing, 2010), pp. 37–56; Jack Glasser, *Suspect Race: Causes and Consequences of Racial Profiling* (Oxford/London: Oxford University Press, 2014), passim; a great read on this subject is Bruce Wright, *Black Robes, White Justice: Why Our Legal System Does Not Work for Blacks* (Secaucus, NJ: Lyle Stuart, 1987), passim.

40 Croft, 'Trading with the Enemy, 1585–1604,' pp. 281–302; Croft, 'English Commerce with Spain and the Armada War, 1558–1603,' pp. 236–263; and Loomie, 'Religion and Elizabethan Commerce with Spain,' pp. 27–51.

41 James N. BeMiller, Roy L. Whistler (eds.), *Starch: Chemistry and Technology* (Orlando, FL: Academic Press, 1984), pp. 2–4, 337–373, 601–629; of course, potatoes in the sixteenth century were still a 'new' crop for most Europeans, see Redcliffe N. Salman, *The History and Social Influence of the Potato* (Cambridge: Cambridge University Press, 1985), pp. 34–51, 73–101, 142–159, 424–434, 563–572; for the use of starch in textiles see Ann Rosalind Jones, Peter Stallybrass, *Renaissance Clothing and the Materials of Memory* (Cambridge: Cambridge University Press, 2000), pp. 59–75.

42 This was known as the Eighty Years War, it started in 1568 and ended in 1648, see Geoffrey Parker, *The Army of Flanders and the Spanish Road 1567–1659* (London: Cambridge University Press, 1972), passim;

James D. Tracy, *The Founding of the Dutch Republic: War, Finance, and Politics in Holland 1572–1588* (Oxford: Oxford University Press, 2008), passim.

43   These epithets and descriptive terms are discussed later.

44   See Terry Breverton, 'The Marriage of Owen and Catherine and the Births of Edmund and Jasper Tudor, 1428–1436,' in *Owen Tudor: Founding Father of the Tudor Dynasty* (Amberley: Amberley Publishing, 2017), n.p.

45   Quotations from Nicholas Harris Nicolas, Edward Tyrrell (eds.), *A Chronicle of London: From 1089 to 1483* ... (London: Longman, Rees, Brown Orme and Green, 1823), p. 123; see also, Melita Thomas, 'Scandalous Tudor Weddings: 7 Tudor Women That Married for Love,' *History Extra*, www.historyextra.com/feature/tudors/scandalous-tudor-weddings-7-women-who-braved-royal-wrath-marrying-love, accessed 21/01/2018; on marriages in Tudor England in general see Diana O'Hara, *Courtship and Constraint: Rethinking the Making of Marriage in Tudor England* (Manchester: Manchester University Press, 2002), passim; on royal or 'state' marriages see Patricia Fleming, 'The Politics of Marriage Among Non-Catholic European Royalty.' *Current Anthropology* 14:3 (June 1973), pp. 231–249.

46   A dowager owes her title to her deceased husband – for more on this legal position see William Blackstone, *Commentaries on the Laws of England*, Volume 1 (London: William Walker, 1826), p. 223; for the political and cultural implications see Sue Sheridan Walker, *Wife and Widow in Medieval England* (Ann Arbor, MI: University of Michigan Press, 1993), pp. 17–59.

47   As father of Edmund Tudor, Beaufort would therefore be the grandfather of Henry VII.

48   This happened on 23 February 1669, see Phil Gyford (ed.), Samuel Pepys, 'The Diary of Samuel Pepys, Daily Entries from the 17th Century London Diary,' at www.pepysdiary.com/diary/1669/02/23/, accessed 18/01/2018; for more on this see Thea Tomaini, *The Corpse As Text: Disinterment and Antiquarian Enquiry, 1700–1900* (Martlesham: Boydell and Brewer, 2017), pp. 69–74.

49   A morganatic union is one where one party may not inherit their spouse's title – for how this worked with widows see Walker, *Wife and Widow in Medieval England*, pp. 17–59.

50   On this mutilation see David Hipshon, *Richard III and the Death of Chivalry* (Stroud: History Press, 2009), p. 25.

51   On the divine right of kings see James I speech to Houses of Parliament, Whitehall, London, 21 March 1610, reported in Joseph Robson Tanner, *Constitutional Documents of the Reign of James I A.D. 1603–1624*

(Cambridge: Cambridge University Press, 1960), p. 15; John Burrell, *The Divine Right of Kings Proved from the Principles of the Church of England, In a Sermon Preached* … (London: John Hayes, 1683), passim; John Neville Figgs, *The Theory of the Divine Right of Kings* (London: Creative Media Partners, 2015), passim; Ernst H. Kantorowicz, *The King's Two Bodies: A Study in Medieval Political Ideology* (Princeton, NJ: Princeton University Press, 2016), passim; Edmund Plowden Law Report, 1571, from a legal case in 1550 reported in Kantorowicz, *The King's Two Bodies*, p. 7.

52 Constance Jordan, *Shakespeare's Monarchies: Ruler and Subject in the Romances* (Ithaca, NY: Cornell University Press, 1999), pp. 8–33; Albert Rolls, *The Theory of the King's Two Bodies in the Age of Shakespeare* (Lewiston, NY: Edwin Mellon Press, 2000), passim.

53 See Onyeka, *Blackamoores*, pp. 107–151.

54 On the distance between Iberia and North Africa any atlas will attest this. The following electronic resource was useful, Author Unknown, 'Straight of Gibraltar – Map & Description,' *World Atlas*, www.world atlas.com/aatlas/infopage/gibraltar.htm, accessed 25/12/2016; and Allan Richard Robinson, Paola Malanotte-Rizzoli, *Ocean Processes in Climate Dynamics: Global and Mediterranean Example*s (New York: Springer, 1994), p. 307.

55 The quotation and other references to Africans are in Stubbs, *The Discoverie of a Gaping Gulf*, pp. 4, 32, 35, 42.

56 The 'hoi polloi': a Greek word meaning 'the masses' or 'the common people'; see *Oxford Dictionary of English* (Oxford: Oxford University Press, 2003), p. 826.

57 Quotation from Edward Blount (tr.), Ieronimo Conestaggio, *The Historie of the Uniting of the Kingdom of Portugal to the Crowne of Castill* … (London: A. Hatfield for E. Blount, 1600), pp. 1, 5–7, 39; see John Legat, *A Watch-worde for Warre Not so New as Necessary … Against the Spaniard* (London: Printer to the University of Cambridge, 1596), pp. xxv, 29, 121; Tarif Abentarique, *The History of the Conquest of Spain by the Moors. Together with the Life of the Most Illustrious Monarch Menesh Almanzar and of the Several Revolutions of the Mighty Empire of the Caliphs and of the African Kingdoms … Now Made English* (London: Fleach, sold by T. Fox, 1687), p. 36; Stanley Lane-Poole, *Story of the Moors in Spain* (London: G. P. Putnam and Sons, 1886), pp. 13, 36, 53.

58 See Samuel Purchas, *Purchas His Pilgrimage; or Relations of the World* … (London: William Stansby for Henrie Fetherstone, 1613), pp. 193–195; Ivan Van Sertima (ed.), *African Presence in Early Europe* (Piscataway, NJ: Transaction Publishers, 1985), pp. 140, 152, 166, 171; Abentarique, *The History of the Conquest of Spain by the Moors*, p. 51; and Rogers, *Nature Knows No Colour-Line*, pp. 55–57.

59 Of course, there are many books on Hannibal – for those that contain important matters which relate his invasion to Tariq's see Carl Skutsch, *Encyclopedia of the World's Minorities* (London: Routledge, 2013), pp. 29–31; Joel Augustus Rogers, *Sex and Race*, Volume 1, pp. 151–154.

60 On the Moors of Picardy see David Mac Ritchie, *Ancient and Modern Britons*, Retrospect, 2 Volumes (1884, 3rd edition, 1985, reprint, Los Angeles, CA: Preston, 1986), p. 341, and an article in *The Spectator*, 27 September 1884, p. 21, http://archive.spectator.co.uk/article/27th-september-1884/21/ancient-and-modern-britons.

61 'By the Goths,' see Sylvanus Urban (ed.), 'An Account of the Several Orders of Knighthood ...,' *Gentleman's Magazine* (London: Edward Cave, 1753), pp. 613–614.

62 See Caelius Augustinus Curio, *A Notable History of the Saracens ...* (London: William How and Abraham Veale, 1575), pp. 31, 46–51, 121 (Africans in France), 67, 68, 79; Legat, *A Watch-worde for Warre*, p. 121 'Saracens of Lybia,' 'captaine of the Saracens of Africa,' 'Syrians' distinguished from them; Ben Jonson, *The Character of Two Royall Masques, the One of Blacknesse. The Other of Beautie ... 1605 and 1608 at White hall* (London: Thomas Thorp, 1605), pp. 3–5, 9 (Aquitania); John G. Jackson, Willis Nathaniel Huggins, *An Introduction to African Civilisation* (New York: Avon House, 1937), n.p. 'Arab-Moorish Civilisation and Culture'; John Bagnall Bury, *The Cambridge Medieval History*, Volume 2 (London: The University Press, 1964), pp. 374–375.

63 As in Arthur Sanders Way, *The Song of Roland Translated into English Verse* (Cambridge: Cambridge University Press, 1913), p. 78; in the early modern period the words and sentiments were translated in many ways, see John Harrington's translation of *Orlando Furioso in English Heroical Verse* (London: publisher unknown, 1591), passim.

64 This has been written about by many early modern writers including Legat, *A Watch-worde for Warre*, p. 31 'Aquitania' was 'taken by the Moors,' p. 50 'the Moors were driven out of Aquitaine.'

65 Curio, *A Notable History of the Saracens*, pp. 31, 46–51, 121; Jonson, *The Character of Two Royall Masques*, pp. 3–5, 9.

66 The term 'Morisco tint' was a derogatory one used in the eighteenth century to refer to the skin colour of Africans, from Samuel Martin, *An Essay upon Plantership, Humbly Inscribed to His Excellency George Thomas Esq; Chief Governor of the Leeward Islands* (London: T. Cadell, 1773), quoted in *London Chronicle*, XXIII:2537 (13–16 March 1773), p. 250.

67 For the Moorish influence on Moorish and Moresca etc. dances see Jonathan Eastwood, *The Bible Word-Book: A Glossary of Old English Bible Words* (London/Cambridge: Macmillan and Co, 1866), pp. 323–324;

for a different view see John Forrest, '*Morris and Matachin*': *A Study in Contemporary Choreography* (London: English Folk Dance and Song Society, 1984), p. 19; and John Cutting, *History and the Morris Dance: A Look at Morris Dancing from the Earliest Days until 1850* (Alton: Dance Books, 2005), pp. 18, 19, 20, 169.

68 Iambic pentameter is the term used to describe the rhythm and feet in the most popular and famous poetry of the Renaissance. The idea that it has Moorish origins is a contested subject, see Robert Briffault, *The Troubadours* (Bloomington, IN: Indiana University Press, 1965), passim; for another view see Francesco Ramondo, *Ideal of the Courtly Gentleman in Spanish Literature, Its Ascent and Decline* (Bloomington, IN: Trafford Publishing, 2013), pp. 45–46.

69 For the Moorish influence on English names, etc. see Mark Anthony Lower, *English Surnames: Essays on Family Nomenclature* (London: John Russell Smith, 1842), pp. 11–13 (Roman African influence on names), 34–35 (Iberian Moors).

70 An excellent book on this is by Harry Kelsey, *Philip of Spain, King of England: The Forgotten Sovereign* (London: I.B. Tauris, 2012), passim.

71 A similar perspective is offered in Geoffrey Parker, *Imprudent King: A New Life of Philip II* (New Haven, CT: Yale University Press, 2014), pp. 310–365; and Parker, *The Grand Strategy of Philip II* (New Haven, CT: Yale University Press, 2000), passim.

72 See previous note; albeit that Philip II also considered marrying Elizabeth I despite these matters.

73 Evidence in Pedro De Azeved (ed.), *Archivo Historico Portuguez* (Madrid: Libano da Silva, 1903), p. 300; and Antonio Vieyra, Jacinto Dias do Canto, *A Dictionary of the Portuguese and English Languages, in Two Parts* ... (1773, 2nd edition, London: J. Collingwood, 1827), p. 351. (Definition of the word 'forro'). 'Forro' is also a language spoken in São Tomé and Príncipe in West Africa and this may indicate that Pero originated from there, see Albert Gerard (ed.), *European-Language Writing in Sub-Saharan Africa*, Volume 1 (Budapest: Akademiai Kiado, 1986), p. 432.

74 Evidence in Gustav Ungerer, *The Mediterranean Apprenticeship of British Slavery* (Madrid: Verbum Editorial, 2008), pp. 75, 137, 124; Rogers, *Nature Knows No Colour-Line*, pp. 63, 66, 76, 77, 82–93, 100–110, 119, 121–123, 143, 144–145; and Anne Marie Jordan, 'Image of Empire, Slaves in the Lisbon Household and Court of Catherine of Austria,' in Lowe, Earle (eds.), *Black Africans in Renaissance Europe*, pp. 155–181.

75 GL Ms 4448 (Katherin's record); Richard Wernham (ed.), Public Record Office, *List and Analysis of State Papers, Foreign Series:*

January to December 1595 (London: Her Majesty's Stationery Office, 1964), p. 208 (the Prince's death).

76   There are many definitions of the words 'Al Andalus' in Jere L. Bacharach, Josef W. Meri (eds.), *Medieval Islamic Civilization: An Encyclopedia*, Volume 2 (New York/London: Routledge, 2006), pp. 43-44. The standard one is 'land of light.'

77   Primary evidence that supports this comes from a range of sources including Caelius Augustinus Curio, *A Notable History of the Saracens*, pp. 18, 26-28, 29, 121, 134; and secondary sources include Franz Heinrich Ungewitter, *Europe, Past and Present: A Comprehensive Manual of European Geography* … (New York: Putnam, 1850), p. 67. The quotation is from Jonson, *The Character of Two Royall Masques*, p. 9. The contention in this article is that even though Jonson's Masque is fictional, it belies an underlying truism of his time – that there was a 'Black' population living in the Iberian Peninsula who had originated from Africa. This matter is discussed in some detail in Onyeka, *Blackamoores*, pp. 41-106.

78   On the pomegranate see Susan Brigden, *New Worlds, Lost Worlds: The Rule of the Tudors, 1485-1603* (London: Allen Lane, 2000), p. 111; The British Archaeological Society Association and Royal Archaeological Institute of Great Britain and Ireland, *Archaeological Journal*, Volume 69 (London: Royal Archaeological Institute, 1912), p. 485; and Robert Chambers, William Chambers, *Chambers Miscellany of Useful and Entertaining Tracts* (Edinburgh: William and Robert Chambers, 1846), pp. 26, 30 (Mary I of England later readopted the pomegranate as one of the symbols of her branch of the Tudor royal family).

79   See James F. Powers, *A Society Organized for War: The Iberian Municipal Militias in the Central Middle Ages, 1000-1284* (Berkeley, CA: University of California Press, 1987), passim.

80   The negative aspects about the 'blackness' of Africans in Renaissance Europe is well documented, see Samuel Parsons Scott, *History of the Moorish Empire in Europe* (New York: Lippincott, 1904), p. 355; Hall, *Things of Darkness*, p. 13; Peter Fryer, *Staying Power: The History of Black People in Britain Since 1504* (London: Pluto Press, 1984), pp. 4, 5, 8; Virginia Mason Vaughan, *Performing Blackness on English Stages, 1500-1800* (Cambridge: Cambridge University Press, 2005), pp. 57-60; Emily Carroll Bartels, *Spectacles of Strangeness: Imperialism, Alienation, and Marlowe* (Philadelphia, PA: University of Pennsylvania Press, 1993), introduction.

81   For the concept of blackness in skin colour as a 'kind of paint' and the idea of painting faces see Annette Drew-Bear, *Painted Faces on the Renaissance Stage: The Moral Significance of Face-Painting*

Conventions (Lewisburg, PA/London: Bucknell University Press, 1994), pp. 102–104; Ania Loomba, Jonathan Burton, *Race in Early Modern England: A Documentary Companion* (Basingstoke: Palgrave Macmillan, 2007), preface, introduction; and Tony Bennett, Lawrence Grossberg, Meaghan Morris (eds.), *New Keywords: A Revised Vocabulary of Culture and Society* (Oxford: Blackwell, 2005), pp. 249–250.

82 In C. S. Lewis, *Chronicles of Narnia*, they are the 'Calormene' with 'dark faces' that live in the desert and are cruel and wicked, see *The Horse and His Boy* (London: Geoffrey Bles, 1954), passim; Michael Boyce, 'The Uncomfortable Racism of C. S. Lewis,' *Geekdom House*, https://geekdomhouse.com/the-uncomfortable-racism-of-c-s-lewis/, accessed 28/01/2018; quotation from, J. R. R. Tolkien, *The Lord of the Rings: The Return of the King* (London: George Allen and Unwin, 1954; new edition, London: Harper Collins, 1997), p. 828; Brian Rosebury, 'Race in Tolkien Films,' in Michael D. C. Drout (ed.), *J.R.R. Tolkien Encyclopedia: Scholarship and Critical Assessment* (Abingdon: Taylor & Francis, 2007), pp. 555–561; John Milton, John S. B. Dolle, et. al. (eds.), *Paradise Lost: A Poem in Twelve Books* (London: S. Simmons, 1st edition 1667, 1674), passim.

83 'Mudejar' was one of the names given to the Moors that stayed in Iberia after 1492. See Francisco Marquez Villanueva, 'On the Concept of Mudejarism,' in Kevin Ingram (ed.), *The Conversos and Moriscos in Late Medieval Spain and Beyond*, Volume 1: Departures and Change (Leiden/Boston, MA: Brill, 2009), pp. 23–51; it is also the name for a certain type of architecture and art associated with the Moors, see University of Wisconsin, 'Casselman Archive of Islamic and Mudejar Architecture in Spain,' *Digital Collections University of Wisconsin-Madison Libraries*, https://uwdc.library.wisc.edu/collections/arts/casselmanimage/, accessed 28/01/2018; for more on Moorish craftsmanship see Onyeka, *Blackamoores*, pp. 107–151.

84 See previous note; Africans were not just 'slaves' in Iberia as is sometimes suggested, even when they were called 'escravos.'

85 The prime target of the Inquisition were the Moors: in Granada for example, according to the author Henry Kamen, between 1560 and 1571, 82 per cent of those targeted were Moors, see *The Spanish Inquisition: A Historical Revision* (New Haven, CT: Yale University Press, 1998), p. 217; Thomas Bourke, *A Concise History of the Moors in Spain from the Invasion of That Kingdom to Their Final Expulsion from It* (London: Rivington Hatchard, 1811), p. xviii; and Janet Lloyd, *The Spanish Inquisition: A History* (London/New Haven, CT: Yale University Press, 2006), pp. 44–46, 54, 105.

86 On 'blue blood' inheritance see Robert Lacey, *Aristocrats* (London: Hutchinson, 1983), p. 67; David Brewster, *Brewer's Dictionary of Phrase and Fable* ... (London: H. Altemus, 1870), p. 131; Barbara Fuchs, *Exotic Nation: Maurophilia and the Construction of Early Modern Spain* (Philadelphia, PA: University of Pennsylvania Press, 2008), pp. 116, 124–128, 170; Conestaggio, *The Historie of the Uniting of the Kingdom of Portugal to the Crowne of Castill*, p. 6; Susan Adams et al., 'The Genetic Legacy of Religious Diversity and Intolerance: Paternal Lineages of Christians, Jews, and Muslims in the Iberian Peninsula.' *The American Journal of Human Genetics* 83:6 (4 December 2008), pp. 725–736.

87 Master of the Novices was in charge of teaching the novices (or potential new priests). It was a trusted and important role, see James Frances Lover, *The Master of Novices: An Historical Synopsis and a Commentary* (Whitefish, MT: Literary Licensing, 2013), passim.

88 Margaret Jean Cormack (ed.), Giovanna Fiume, *Saints and Their Cults in the Ancient World* (Columbia, SC: University of South Carolina Press, 2007), pp. 16–51. He was beatified in 1743 and canonised in 1807.

89 Bourke, *A Concise History of the Moors in Spain*, pp. 252–253; Scott, *History of the Moorish Empire in Europe*, p. 355; Philippus Limborch, *The History of the Inquisition* (London: Samuel Handler, 1731), pp. 129–132.

90 A similar perspective on this is offered by Trevor J. Dadson, 'Un Ricote Verdadero: El Licenciado Alonso Herrador de Villarrubia de los Ojos del Guadiana – Morisco Que Vuelve,' in Francisco Domínguez Matito, María Luisa Lobato (eds.), *Memoria de la Palabra: Actas del VI Congreso de la Asociación Internacional Siglo de Oro*, Burgos-La Rioja 15–19 de julio 2002, Volume 1, 2004 (2007), pp. 601–612; Trevor J. Dadson, 'Los Moriscos de Villarrubia de los Ojos (siglos XV–XVIII). Historia de una Minoría Asimilada, Expulsada y Reintegrada, Tiempo Emulado,' *Historia de América y España* (Madrid: Iberoamericana, 2007), pp. 1299–1328; Trevor J. Dadson, *Tolerance and Coexistence in Early Modern Spain: Old Christians and Moriscos in the Campo de Calatrava* (Rochester, NY: Tamesis, 2014), passim.

91 Kamen, *The Spanish Inquisition*, pp. 351–395; Limborch, *The History of the Inquisition*, Volumes 1–3 (1731), passim.

92 The fascist writer Ernesto Gimenez Caballero does this in *Genio de Espano* ... (Madrid: Ediciones Jerarquía, 1938), in Nil Santianez, *Topographies of Fascism: Habitus, Space, and Writing in Twentieth Century Spain* (Toronto: University of Toronto Press, 2013), p. 76; an excellent book on these persecutions is by Paul Preston, *The Spanish Holocaust: Inquisition and Extermination in Twentieth-Century Spain* (London: Harper Press, 2012), passim.

Two

1 Fray Francisco de Ugalde (1520), in Jean-Benoit Nadeau, Julie Barlow, *The Story of Spanish* (Oxford/London: Oxford University Press, 2013), p. 172.

2 Jane Anger, 'Her Protection for Women' (1589), in Randall Martin, *Women Writers in Renaissance England: An Annotated Anthology* (London: Routledge, 2014), pp. 80–97, quotation at p. 93; Stephanie Hodgson Wright, *Women's Writing of the Early Modern Period, 1588–1688: An Anthology* (Edinburgh: Edinburgh University Press, 2002), pp. 2–5, 29, 461.

3 A bill was a military weapon: a polearm similar to a halberd, see George Silver, *Paradoxes of Defence* (London: Edward Blount, 1599), pp. 19–20.

4 Margery M. Rowe (ed.), Devon and Cornwall Record Society, *Tudor Exeter Tax Assessments 1489–1595: Including the Military Survey 1522* (Torquay: The Devonshire Press, 1977), p. 17.

5 The term 'Alien' was movable and could describe someone that was resident in a parish, non-resident, baptised or simply born elsewhere. But the point was that 'John a More' was not an Alien. For more on 'Aliens' see Cyril Coffin, 'Aliens in Dorset 1525,' *The Dorset Page*, www. thedorsetpage.com/history/Aliens/Aliens.htm, posted 2000, accessed 02/01/2007. Also see the registering of Aliens in *Lay Subsidy Records, Returns for the City of London in 1292–1392* …, National Archives, Kew, London, PRO E179/144/2 and E179/144/3; and Lara Hunt Yungblut, *Strangers Settled Here Amongst Us: Policies, Perceptions, and the Presence of Aliens in Elizabethan England* (1996, new edition, London: Routledge, 2003), p. 55.

6 John Beckett, *City Status in the British Isles 1803–2002* (Aldershot: Ashgate, 2005), pp. 9–19.

7 'Henry a Negro,' baptism, City of Westminster Archives Centre, p. 236, 1660 October/4/St Pauls/Volume1Burials/MF 1; also found by the historian John Ellis, personal email 28/01/18.

8 See Onyeka, *Blackamoores*, pp. 242–264; Habib, *Black Lives*, pp. 274–334.

9 Writers with a similar view include: Anthony P. Cohen, *The Symbolic Construction of Community* (Chichester: Ellis Horwood, 1985), p. 85; Joshua Phillips, *English Fictions of Communal Identity, 1485–1603* (Farnham: Ashgate, 2003), pp. 11–22, passim (on local 'belonging'); and Joyce A. Youings, *Sixteenth-Century England* (London: Allen Lane, 1984), pp. 88–102. More evidence is to be found in: London Metropolitan Archives, Registers of St Dunstan; and All Saints Church, Stepney, LMA P93/DUN/255. See primary documents

in: London, GL Ms 9243–9245, GL Ms 4310, GL Ms 9222; author unknown, *St Martin in the Fields Parish Register*, Volume 1 (London: publisher unknown, 27 September 1571), p. 116; Plymouth and West Devon Record Office, Plymouth, St Andrews/MF1–4; Devon Record Office, East Allington/20/08/1577 PR; and Northampton Records Office, Northampton, Microfiche 120, pp. 1–3.

10 For a wider discussion see Onyeka, 'What's in a Name?,' pp. 34–39; Onyeka, *Blackamoores*, pp. 41–90.

11 For more on Moroccans in early modern England see Nabil Matar, *Islam in Britain, 1558–1685* and Matar, *Turks, Moors and Englishmen in the Age of Discovery* (New York: Columbia University Press, 2000), passim; Daniel Vitkus, *Turning Turk: English Theatre and the Multicultural Mediterranean, 1570–1630* (New York: Palgrave Macmillan, 2003), pp. 21–50; Habib, *Shakespeare and Race*, pp. 157–205.

12 Cornwall Record Office, Old County Hall, Truro, Cornwall, TR1 3AY, Registers of Bodmin, ref Mf 12 FP 13/1/11, Burials 1558–1757, 12 December 1563, 'Marrion S Soda of Morrisce'; on Mary Fillis, Miranda Kaufmann has a different view in *Black Tudors*, pp. 134–168, and suggests that Mary originated from Morocco.

13 *Oxford Dictionary of English*, pp. 515, 1171 (definitions of 'native' etc.); on who is 'native' and 'liege' see Lien Luu, *Immigrants and the Industries of London, 1500–1700* (Aldershot: Ashgate, 2005), pp. 142–144; and Harry Lee Faggett, *Black and Other Minorities in Shakespeare's England* (Prairie View, TX: Prairie View Press, 1971), pp. 1–6.

14 The record of 'Moore Robert Tego' is with St Michael Paternoster Church, Vintry Ward, London, ref. Vintry Ward MF 0574365; and Habib, *Black Lives*, p. 303.

15 For more on him see John Stow, *The Annales of England, Faithfully Collected Out of the Most Authenticall Authors* (London: R. Newbery, 1592), pp. 1037–1045; John Stow, Edmund Howes, *The Annales, or Generall Chronicle of England, Begun First by Maister Iohn Stow, and After Him Continued ... Unto the Ende of This Present Yeere 1614, by E. Howes* (London: Thomas Dawson for Thomas Adams, 1615), p. 948; Frederick James Furnivall, John Norden et al. (eds.), William Harrison, *Harrison's Description of England in Shakespeare's Youth* ..., Volumes 2 and 3 (1577, 1584, 1877, new edition, London: New Shakespeare Society, 1878), p. 34; and in *Blackamoores*, pp. 132–135.

16 For more on how the term 'profession' was used see Rosemary O. Day, *The Professions in Early Modern England, 1450–1800: Servants of the Commonweal* (Harlow: Longman, 2000), pp. 13–14 (definition of profession), 21–23 (exclusive nature of most guilds and professions in Tudor England).

17 GL Ms 9222/1, p. 288.

18 William Le Hardy (ed.), 'Sessions of the Peace and Gaol Delivery A.D. 1613, Sessions Roll,' *County of Middlesex, Calendar to the Sessions Records, New Series, 1612–1614*, Volume I (London: Clerk of the Peace, 1935), pp. 117–154.

19 Onyeka, *Blackamoores*, pp. 132–135.

20 Will of Henrie Jetto, Will number 102, dated and signed on 20 September 1626, but executed 13 September 1638, Worcestershire Archives, Worcester.

21 For more about Sancho see Onyeka, 'The Black Equestrians Africans in Georgian Britain.' *History Today* 64:7 (July 2014), www.historytoday.com/onyeka/black-equestrians#sthash.E8iWMY82.dpuf.

22 Records in: National Archives, Prerogative Court of Canterbury, Prob 11/492, Poley Quire Numbers: 1–44 (dated 19 February 1707); Habib, *Black Lives*, pp. 226, 227, 228, 358; local historian Peter Hill claims 'he just helped out' at 'The Hatton Arms,' as he can find no record of his name on a licence, see *A History of Hostelries in Northamptonshire* (Amberley: Amberley Publishing, 2010), pp. 23–24.

23 A selection of other authors offering evidence and commentaries on this includes: Lowe, Earle (eds.), *Black Africans in Renaissance Europe*, pp. 1–17; Barbara Fuchs, 'A Mirror Across the Water: Mimetic Racism, Hybridity, and Cultural Survival,' in Paul Beidler, Gary Taylor (eds.), *Writing Race Across the Atlantic World* (New York: Palgrave Macmillan, 2005), 26–59; Guasco, *Slaves and Englishmen*, pp. 1–6, 44, 91–93, 121–155; Philip D. Morgan, 'Maritime Slavery.' *Slavery and Abolition* 31:3 (2010), pp. 311–326; Schorsch, *Jews and Blacks in the Early Modern World*, pp. 1–17, 70–102; Schorsch, *Swimming the Christian Atlantic*, pp. 6, 25–46, 480–490; David Wheat, 'Mediterranean Slavery, New World Transformations,' pp. 327–344; David Bindman, Henry Louis Gates, Frank M. Snowden, *The Image of the Black in Western Art*, Volumes I–IV (New York: Harvard University Press, 2010–2014), pp. 1–93, has very detailed paintings and images of these populations.

24 Habib, *Black Lives*, passim; Kaufmann, *Black Tudors*, passim; Sherwood, 'Blacks in Elizabethan England,' pp. 40–42; Lucy MacKeith, *Local Black History: A Beginning in Devon* (London: Archives and Museum of Black Heritage, 2003), p. 35; Rogers, *Nature Knows No Colour-Line*, pp. 55–57; Rogers, *Sex and Race*, pp. 86–88; Mike Sampson, 'Friends of Devon Archives: The Black Connection,' *Friends of Devon Newsletter*, 25 (May 2000), pp. 12–15; Edward Scobie, *Black Britannia*, pp. 190–203; Sertima (ed.), *African Presence in Early Europe*, pp. 12–15, 190–223; Ungerer, *The Mediterranean Apprenticeship of British Slavery*, pp. 1–62; Gustav Ungerer, 'The

Presence of Africans in Elizabethan England and the Performance of *Titus Andronicus*, at Burley-on-the-Hill, 1595–96,' *Medieval Renaissance Drama in England Annual*, 21 (2008), pp. 19–56; a larger list of authors is included in the bibliography of Onyeka, *Blackamoores*, pp. 297–340.

25 Onyeka, *Blackamoores*, pp. xxiv, xxv; on writers pleasing their patrons see David Cressy, *Literacy and the Social Order: Reading and Writing in Tudor and Stuart England* (Cambridge: Cambridge University Press, 2006), p. 1; Francis Bacon, *The Two Bookes of Francis Bacon of the Proficience and Advancement of Leaning, Divine Humane* (London: Henrie Tomes, 1605), p. 1; and Antonia Gransden, *Historical Writing in England, c. 550–1307* (1970, new edition, London: Routledge, 1996), introduction.

26 See Onyeka, *Blackamoores*, pp. xxiv, xxv.

27 Onyeka, *Blackamoores*, pp. 113–116; Miranda Kaufmann has a different view in *Black Tudors*, pp. 14–16.

28 For more on Nichols and the *Gentleman's Magazine* see William Bowyer, John Nichols, *Literary Anecdotes of the Eighteenth Century*, Volumes I–III (London: Nichols and Son Company, 1812), passim.

29 Philip Morant, *The History and Antiquities of Colchester in the County of Essex* (Colchester: J. Fenno, 1789), passim.

30 John Norden, *Speculum Britanniæ. The First Parte. An Historicall and Chorographicall Discription of Middlesex. Therein are … Sett Downe, the Names of the Cyties, … Parishes, etc.* (London: John Norden, 1593), passim; Norden, *A Chorographicall Discription of the Severall Shires and Islands of Middlesex, Essex, Surrey, Sussex, Hamshire, Weighte, Garnesey & Jarsey. Performed by the Traveyle and View of John Norden. [With his Dedication to Queen Elizabeth, an Address to the Lords of the Privy Council, and Maps of Essex and Hampshire]* (London: John Norden, 1595), passim; Other counties included those listed in the publication.

31 Carew's works include: Thomas Stafford (ed.), George Carew, *Pacata Hibernia. Ireland Appeased and Reduced. Or, an Historie of the Late Warres of Ireland, Especially Within the Province of Mounster vnder the Government of Sir G. Carew … Illustrated with Seventeene Severall Mappes …* (London: Aug. Mathewes for Robert Milbourne, 1633); Carew, *The Survey of Cornwall. And an Epistle concerning the Excellencies of the English Tongue. Now first Published from the Manuscript … [written in 1602 and 1605 respectively]* (London: Samuel Chapman, 1723).

32 John Weever, *Ancient Funeral Monuments within the United Monarchie of Great Britain … Intermixed and Illustrated with Variety of Historical Observations …* (London: Thomas Harper, 1631), p. 427;

and Thomas Cromwell, *Walks Through Islington; Comprising an Historical and Descriptive* ... (London: Sherwood Gilbert and Piper, 1835), pp. 78–79.

33 Meredith Hanmer, *The Baptizing of a Turke: A Sermon* ... (London: Robert Walde-Grave, 1586), p. E2.

34 See Onyeka, *Blackamoores*, pp. xix–xxxv.

35 Quotations from records in parish records from: London, GL Ms 9243–9245 (St Botolph without Aldgate), GL Ms 4310, GL Ms 9222; Author unknown, *St Martin in the Fields Parish Register*, Volume 1 (London: publisher unknown, 27 September 1571), p. 116; Plymouth and West Devon Record Office, Plymouth, St Andrews/MF1–4; Devon Record Office, East Allington/20/08/1577 PR; and Northampton Records Office, Northampton, Microfiche 120, pp. 1–3.

36 London, GL Ms 9243–9245 (St Botolph without Aldgate), GL Ms 4310, GL Ms 9222; Plymouth and West Devon Record Office, Plymouth, St Andrews/MF1–4.

37 The phrase 'innocent' was used several times to describe Moriana's knowledge of her employer's intentions, in National Archives, Kew, London, *Early Chancery Proceedings* (ECP), C1/148/67; and Alwyn Ruddock, *Italian Merchants and Shipping in Southampton 1270–1600* (Southampton: University College, 1951), pp. 126–127, 138.

38 On the meaning of community see Philippa Maddern, '"In Myn Own House": The Troubled Connections between Servant Marriages, Late Medieval English Households Communities and Early Modern Historiography,' in Susan Broomhall, Stephanie Tarbin (eds.), *Women, Identities and Communities in Early Modern Europe* (Aldershot: Ashgate, 2008), p. 62; The ideas of 'belonging' and 'community' in Tudor England are of course complex subjects and are discussed by Cohen, *The Symbolic Construction of Community*, p. 85; Phillips, *English Fictions*, pp. 11–22, passim (on how medieval and Tudor fiction saw 'belonging'); and Youings, *Sixteenth-Century England*, pp. 88–102.

39 *In the Matter of Cartwright*, 11 Elizabeth, 2 Rushworth's College (1569), p. 468, the case concerned a Russian slave severely beaten by his master. There is some doubt of the exact wording of this famous quotation, as it is reported as obiter dicta in cases such as *Somersett's Case, R. v. Knowles, ex parte Somersett*, 20 State Tr (1772), 1; the Somersett case was about an enslaved African in Georgian Britain; 'obiter dicta' is a legal phrase that refers to a decision in a legal case that does not form part of the rule of the case, but nevertheless is important and persuasive, rather than legally binding on judicial precedent.

40 David Cecil (1460–1540) was himself of Welsh origins – his father was Richard Cecil, the son of Phillp Seisyll. They rose to prominence under Henry VII and the family settled in Lincolnshire. The name 'Cecil' was anglicised from 'Seisyll,' as with the name 'Tudor,' see T. J. Morgan, Prys Morgan, *Welsh Surnames* (Cardiff: University of Wales Press, 1985), pp. 191–192.

41 An excellent article on scutage and commuting of manorial obligations is Stephen Alford, 'Urban Safe Houses for the Unfree in Medieval England: A Reconsideration,' *Slavery and Abolition*, 32:3 (September 2011), pp. 363–375.

42 On guilds see Maarten Roy Prak (ed.), *Craft Guilds in the Early Modern Low Countries: Work, Power and Representation* (Aldershot: Ashgate, 2006), pp. 111–125; Day, *The Professions in Early Modern England*, pp. 21–23 (exclusive nature of most guilds and professions in Tudor England); John Bromley, *The Armorial Bearings of the Guilds of London: A Record of the Heraldry of the Surviving Companies with Historical Notes* (London: F. Warne, 1960), passim.

43 Evidence can be found in John Green, Ashley Thomas (eds.), *A New General Collection of Voyages and Travels … in Europe, Asia, Africa and America …* (London: Thomas Astley, 1745), p. 138; a commentary is contained in Joseph Tracy, *Colonization and Missions: An Historical Examination of the State of Society …* (Boston, MA: Massachusetts Colonization Society, 1846), pp. 11–12; however, Englishmen elsewhere were involved in enslaving people, see Ungerer, *The Mediterranean Apprenticeship of British Slavery*, pp. 17, 32, etc.; Anthony Gerard Barthelemy, *Black Face, Maligned Race: The Representation of Blacks in English Drama from Shakespeare to Southerne* (London: Louisiana State University Press, 1987), p. 20.

44 William Harrison, in Furnivall, Norden et al. (eds.), *Harrison's Description of England in Shakespeare's Youth …*, Volumes 2 and 3, p. 134.

45 The primary record for this quote is difficult to locate, but the phrase is repeated by Luther Porter Jackson, *Journal of Negro History*, 9:1 (January 1924), p. 15; and by James Bandinel, *Some Account of the Trade in Slaves from Africa: As Connected with Europe* (London: Longman Brown, 1842), p. 36; Thomas Clarkson, *Thoughts upon Slavery* (London: Joseph Crukshank, 1778), p. 44; John Hill (ed.), George Berkeley, *The Naval History of Britain from the Earliest Periods of Which There Are Accounts in History* (London: T. Osborne and J. Shipton, 1756), p. 239. There is an acknowledgement, of course, that members of her government sponsored the enslavement of many peoples including Africans.

46 On the effects of this sponsorship and piracy see, Robert Greene, *The Estate of English Fugitives under the King of Spain and His Ministers* (London: John Drawater, 1595), pp. 1–2; Thomas Purfoot, *The Historical Discourse of Muley Hamet's Refining the Three Kingdoms, of Moruecos Fes and Sus. The Religion and Policies of the More or Barbarian* ... (London: Clement Knight, 1609), chapter 15.

47 Some of these matters are discussed later in this book, but for a more detailed analysis see Onyeka, *Blackamoores*, pp. 1–40.

48 This was the Republic of Sale in what is now Morocco.

49 Of course this list of traders is not finite, but does include those that English merchants wrote about in their correspondence.

50 These are just some of the peoples, kingdoms and trading centres that defied Spanish and Portuguese hegemony – of course there were many more. To see how African traders became pivotal in these international relationships see E. W. Bovill, *The Golden Trade of the Moors* (London: Oxford University Press, 1958), pp. 156–157, 169–179, 201–209.

51 Reported in John Francis Gemelli Careri (1651–1725), *A Collection of Voyages Travel, Some Now First Printed from Original Manuscripts, Others now First Published in English* (London: Henry Lintot, John Osborn, 1744–1746), p. 563; Giovanni Gemelli Carei, *A Voyage Round the World in Six Parts* (1728), p. 563, reported differently as, 'The Sun shines on me as well as on others. I should be very happy to see the clause in Adam's will which excluded me from my share when the world was being divided,' in Lewis Hanke, *The Spanish Struggle for Justice in the Conquest of America* (Philadelphia, PA: University of Pennsylvania Press, 1949), p. 148.

52 Quoted in Adam Shortt, Arthur G Doughty (eds.), *Canada and Its Provinces: A History of the Canadian People and Their Institutions* (Toronto/Edinburgh: Publishers Association of Canada, 1913), p. 39.

53 An article that includes a list of ports such as Bruges and Hamburg, with some excellent maps, is Catia Antunes, 'Early Modern Ports 1500–1750,' *European History Online*, 3 December 2010, http:// ieg-ego.eu/en/threads/crossroads/courts-and-cities/catia-antunes-early-modern-ports-1500-1750, accessed 01/02/2018.

54 For more on the use of these and other ports see Robert Kerr (ed.), *A General History Collection of Voyages and Travels, Arranged in Systematic Order: Forming a Complete History of the Origin and Progress of Navigation, Discovery, and Commerce, by Sea and Land, from the Earliest Ages to the Present Time*, Volume 7 (Edinburgh: W. Blackwood and Sons, 1824), pp. 331–338; John Maclean (ed.), David Watkin Waters, *The Art of Navigation in England in Elizabethan and Early Stuart Times* (London: Hollis and Carter, 1958), p. 84; and

George Carew, *Letters from George Lord Carew to Sir Thomas Roe, Ambassador to the Court of the Great Mogul 1615–1617* (London: Camden Society, 1860), pp. 116, 117.

55　George Cawston, Augustus Henry Keane, *Early Chartered Companies, A.D. 1296–1858* (Manchester: Ayer Publishing, 1968), pp. 228–229; and Ungerer, *The Mediterranean Apprenticeship of British Slavery*, p. 12.

56　See previous note.

57　Of course much later the Royal African Company was founded, see Robin Law (ed.), Great Britain Record Office, *Correspondence from the Royal African Company Factories at Offra and Whyda on the Slave Coast of West Africa in the Public Record Office 1678–1693* (Edinburgh: Centre of African Studies Edinburgh University, 1990), passim.

58　Bristol Record Office, Bristol, P/ST PJR/1/1/CMB 1576–1621, n.p.

59　For more on the power and influence of Thomas Smythe see Edward Foss, *Biographia Juridica. A Biographical Dictionary of the Judges of England: From the Conquest to the Present Time* ... (New Jersey: Law Book Exchange, new edition, 1999), p. 617; Maine Historical Society, *Collections of the Maine Historical Society*, Volume 18 (Portland, ME: Maine Historical Society, 1831), pp. 34–36; and Robert Brenner, *Merchants and Revolution: Commercial Change, Political Conflict, and London* ... (London: Verso, 2003), pp. 96–100, 109, 154, 216, 223, 433, 434, 526, 529; on the capacity of such men to get their names expunged from official records etc. see Laura Gowing, 'Giving Birth at the Magistrates Gate: Single Mothers in the Early Modern City,' in Broomhall, Tarbin (eds.), *Women, Identities and Communities in Early Modern Europe*, pp. 137–150.

60　See Lawrence Stone, 'Social Mobility in England 1500–1700.' *Past and Present* 33 (April 1966), pp. 16–17 (they were also known as the 'Fellowship of Merchant Adventurers of the Town and County of Newcastle upon Tyne' and 'Merchant Venturers in the Ports of Brabant beyond the Seas'); and Eneas Mackensie, 'Incorporated Companies: Merchant Adventurers,' Historical Account of Newcastle-upon-Tyne: Including the Borough of Gateshead, 1827, *British History Online*, pp. 662–670, www.british-history.ac.uk/report.aspx?compid=43401, accessed 18/01/2008.

61　This consortium was particularly ruthless, see Carole Levin, *The Reign of Elizabeth I* (Basingstoke: Palgrave Macmillan, 2001), pp. 119–121; W. E. Miller, 'Negroes in Elizabethan London.' *Notes and Queries* 8 (4 April 1961), p. 138; and Emeka Abanime, 'Elizabeth I and Negroes.' *Cahiers Elizabethans* 19 (19 April 1981), p. 2.

62　Quotations from Holinshed, *The Chronicles* (1577), pp. 1531, 1550, 1572, 1865; Other evidence in Douglas Bisson, *The Merchant*

Adventurers of England: The Company and the Crown, 1474–1564 (London: Associated University Press, 1993), introduction; and William Ezra Lingelbach, *The Merchant Adventurers of England: Their Laws and Ordinances with Other Documents* (New York: B. Franklin, 1971), pp. 1–12.

63 First quotation attributed to Francis Drake, 19 April 1587, in Adrian Spear Mott, Richard Hakluyt, *Hakluyt's Voyages* (Boston, MA: Houghton Mifflin, 1929), p. 179; from original: Richard Hakluyt (ed.), *The Principal Navigations* …, Volume 6 (London: Christopher Barker, 1598), n.p.; 'trouble' and 'annoy' were terms often used to describe the activities of adventurers, see John Hawkins, *Declaration of the Troublesome Voyage, of John Hawkins to the Parties of Guynea and the West Indies in the Yeares of Our Lord, 1567–1568* (London: Thomas Purfoot, 1569) passim; Richard Eden, *Decades of the Newe World West India* (London: William Powell, 1555), passim; and Philip Gosse, *Hawkins Scourge of Spain* (New York: Harper and Brothers, 1930), p. 290.

64 Ungerer, *The Mediterranean Apprenticeship of British Slavery*, p. 76; Ungerer, 'Recovering a Black African's Voice in an English Lawsuit,' pp. 255–271; and Ungerer, 'The Presence of Africans in Elizabethan England and the Performance of *Titus Andronicus*, at Burley-on-the-Hill, 1595–96,' pp. 19–56.

65 See Matar, *Islam in Britain*, passim; Matar, *Turks, Moors and Englishmen in the Age of Discovery*, passim; Vitkus, *Turning Turk*, pp. 21–50; Habib, *Shakespeare and Race*, pp. 157–205.

66 See Robert Baker, *Travails in Guinea/Robert Baker's 'Brefe Discourse'* (1568), in Hakluyt (ed.), *The Principal Navigations*, pp. 7–8, 27 (African resistance), 24, 37 (surrender to Africans); for a longer exposition on this see Onyeka, *Blackamoores*, pp. 152–194.

67 Quotations from the case, High Court of Admiralty, 1592, at National Archives, Kew, London, HCA 24/39/49–51; also discussed in Kerr (ed.), *A General History Collection of Voyages and Travels*, Volume 7, pp. 342–349; Onyeka, *Blackamoores*, pp. 176–177.

68 The quotations are from primary court case records at the National Archives, Kew, London, HCA 24/39/49–51; and in Kerr (ed.), *A General History Collection of Voyages and Travels*, Volume 7, pp. 342–349; but Ungerer says these Africans were slaves in 'The Presence of Africans in Elizabethan England and the performance of *Titus Andronicus* at Burley-on-the-Hill, 1595/96,' pp. 19–56.

69 On the dominance of Spain and Portugal in the trade in human beings during the sixteenth century, recent research by David Richardson, David Wheat and Marc Eagle corroborates the systemic

nature of it, see David Keys, 'Details of Horrific First Voyages in Transatlantic Slave Trade,' *The Independent*, 17 August 2018, www. msn.com/en-gb/news/world/details-of-horrific-first-voyages-in-transatlantic-slave-trade-revealed/ar-BBM2ycN?li=BBoPWjQ&oc id=mailsignout, accessed 17/08/2018; but we should set aside the slightly misleading phrase the 'First;' And see that some of these matters had been suggested before, see Ungerer et al.

70 Hawkins, *Declaration of the Troublesome Voyage*, p. 8.

71 Quotation from James Walvin, *Black Ivory: A History of British Slavery* (London: HarperCollins, 1992), p. 19; the complicated question of what impact English adventurers had on the African presence in England is also examined in Onyeka, *Blackamoores*, pp. 1–40, 211–231.

72 Evidence in Onyeka, *Blackamoores*, pp. 249–260; Habib, *Black Lives*, pp. 274–368.

73 Payments and references to Africans can be found in the Earl of Leicester's accounts in Simon Adams (ed.), *Household Accounts and Disbursement Books of Robert Dudley, Earl of Leicester* (London: Cambridge University Press, 1995), pp. 178, 210.

74 City of Westminster Archives Centre, London, 1601/2 January/21/St Clements Dane/ Volume1Burials/MF 1.

75 Hertford Archives, Hertford, Fortunatus' record can be found at: www.hertsmemories.org.uk/content/herts-history/people/african-caribbean-people-in-herts-before-1830/fortunatus.

76 As artistically suggested in the enigmatic play by Rex Obano, *The Moors of England*, rehearsed reading 16 April 2015.

77 See Courtauld, *The Pocket Book of Patriotism*, pp. 60–61.

78 Authors various, *The Articles of the Treaty of Peace, Signed and Sealed at Munster, in Westphalia, 24 of October, 1648 … As also the treaty of peace between France and Spain, concluded at Nimmeguen, the 17 of September, 1678* (London: W. Only, 1697), passim.

79 Helen Rawlings, *The Debate on the Decline of Spain* (Manchester: Manchester University Press, 2012), passim; Richard Anthony Stradling, *Europe and the Decline of Spain: A Study of the Spanish System, 1580–1720* (London: Allen & Unwin, 1981), passim; Carlo M. Cipolla, *The Economic Decline of Empire* (London: Routledge, 2013), pp. 121–196.

80 John Legat, *A Watch-worde for Warre*, p. xxxii.

81 See Croft, 'Trading with the Enemy, 1585–1604,' pp. 281–302; Croft, 'English Commerce with Spain and the Armada War, 1558–1603,' pp. 236–263; and Loomie, 'Religion and Elizabethan Commerce with Spain,' pp. 27–51.

82 The phrase 'powers of the earth' was used by Thomas Jefferson, John Adams and Benjamin Franklin, *In Congress, July 4, 1776. A Declaration by the Representatives of the United States of America, In General Congress Assembled* (London: publisher unknown, 1776), passim, to describe precisely the power that Spain had in the early modern period and that Britain and France had in the eighteenth century.

83 See Kenneth L. Campbell, *Western Civilisation: A Global and Comparative Approach*, Volume 2: Since 1600 (London: Routledge, 2015), pp. 9–11; William James Maloney, *The Medical Lives of History's Famous People* (New York: Bentham Science Publishers, 2014), pp. 145–148; Razib Khan, 'Inbreeding and the Downfall of the Spanish Hapsburgs,' *Discover: Science of the Curious*, created 14 April 2017, http://blogs.discovermagazine.com/gnxp/2009/04/inbreeding-the-downfall-of-the-spanish-hapsburgs/#.WnC9XXzLgdU, accessed 30/01/2018.

84 This famous phrase was borrowed from similar classical ones interpreted or recorded. But it was first used in its present form to describe the Spanish not the British Empire, by Fray Francisco de Ugalde in 1520, quoted in Nadeau, Barlow, *The Story of Spanish*, p. 172.

85 On the 'Code Noir' and similar laws in the United States of America during the nineteenth century known as 'Black codes' or 'Black laws' see Richard Juang, Noelle Morrissette (eds.), *Africa and the Americas: Culture, Politics, and History: A Multidisciplinary Encyclopedia* (Santa Barbara, CA/Oxford: ABC-CLIO, 2008), pp. 277–279; Junius Rodriguez (ed.), *Slavery in the United States: A Social, Political, and Historical Encyclopedia*, Volume 2 (Santa Barbara, CA/Oxford: ABC-CLIO, 2007), pp. 7, 13, 230–231, 541–543; and Asante, Mazama, *Encyclopedia of Black Studies*, pp. 188–189.

86 Bartolome de las Casas (1484–1566), the Spanish colonist and priest, advocated the enslavement of Africans to replace Native Americans. He later retracted some of those ideas, see Robin Blackburn, *The Making of New World Slavery: From the Baroque to the Modern, 1492–1800* (London: Verso Books, 1998), passim; Sujata Iyengar, *Shades of Difference: Mythologies of Skin Colour in Early Modern England* (Philadelphia, PA: University of Pennsylvania Press, 2008), pp. 7–13, 67, 76–78; and Goldenberg, *The Curse of Ham*, pp. 4–8, 107, 132, 133, 138 (Ottoman Empire).

87 Richard Jobson, *The Golden Trade: Or, A Discovery of the River Gambia, and the Golden Trade of the Aethiopians. Also, the Commerce with a Great Blacke Merchant, Buckor Sano, and his Report of the Houses Covered with Golde, and Other Strange Observations for the Good of Our Owne Countrey; Set Down as They were Collected in Travelling, Part of the Yeares, 1620 and 1621* (London: Nicholas Oke, 1623), passim.

88 Thomas Roe, *An Account of the Embassy of Sir Thomas Roe to the Great Mogul … Collected from his own Journal, 23 March 1616*, pp. 150, 445, in John Harris (ed.), *Navigantium atque Itinerantium Bibliotheca*, etc. Volume I (London: Bennet, 1705–1764), passim.

89 See Gustav Ungerer and Anthony Gerard Barthelemy: Ungerer, *The Mediterranean Apprenticeship of British Slavery*, pp. 17, 32, etc.; Barthelemy, *Black Face, Maligned Race*, p. 20. They both name English merchants working in Iberia such as Thomas Malliard and Robert Thorne. Barthelemy suggested that Malliard showed John Hawkins how to conduct the enslavement of peoples.

90 Leon Higginbotham, *In the Matter of Colour: Race and the American Legal Process. The Colonial Period* (1978, new edition, New York: Oxford University Press, 1980), pp. 320–329; for the development of the law see Author unknown, *A Forensic Dispute on the Legality of Enslaving Africans Held at the Commencement in Cambridge New England July 21, 1773* (Boston, MA: John Boyle, 1773), pp. 1–16; and Blackstone, *Commentaries on the Laws of England*, Volume 1, pp. 332–335.

91 William Penn, Robert Venables, *A Great … Victory Obtained by the English Forces, Under the Command of General Penn and Gen. Venables Against the French and Others, in the West Indies …* (London: publisher unknown, 1655), passim; on William Penn see Howard Malcolm Jenkins, 'The Family of William Penn.' *The Pennsylvania Magazine of History and Biography* 20:1 (The Historical Society of Pennsylvania, 1896), pp. 1–29.

92 On further conflicts that ensured English control see Alexandre Olivier Exquemelin, *Bucaniers of America: or, a True Account of the Most Remarkable Assaults Committed of Late Years Upon the Coasts of the West-Indies, by the Bucaniers of Jamaica and Tortuga, Both English and French. Wherein Are Contained … the Unparallel'd Exploits of Sir Henry Morgan, Our English Jamaican Hero, Who Sack'd Puerto Velo, Burnt Panama, &c …* (London: William Crooke, 1684), passim.

93 Authors various, *Articles of Peace, Commerce, & Alliance, Between the Crowns of Great Britain and Spain Concluded in a Treaty at Madrid the 13/23 Day of May, In the Year of Our Lord God, 1667/ Translated out of Latin. Treaties, etc.* (London: publisher unknown, 1667), passim.

94 The phrase originates from William Shakespeare, *The Tempest*, Act V, Scene I, L. 203–206, 1610–1611, in Richard Proudfoot, *Arden Shakespeare: Complete Works* (London: Thomas Nelson and Son, 2001), p. 1093.

95 Michael Leroy Oberg (ed.), *Samuel Wiseman's Book of Record: The Official Account of Bacon's Rebellion in Virginia, 1676–1677* (New York/Oxford: Lexington Books, 2005), passim; Steve Martinot, *The Rule of Racialization: Class, Identity and Governance* (Philadelphia,

PA: Temple University, 2003), pp. 28–75, at 60 (the rebellion); for more on colonial America see Higginbotham, *In the Matter of Colour*, pp. 320–329; Aaron B. Wilkinson, *Blurring the Lines of Race and Freedom: Mulattoes in English Colonial North America and the Early United States Republic*, unpublished (Berkeley, CA: University of California, 2013), pp. 1–27, 27–54; Jordan, *The Whiteman's Burden*, pp. 26–65.

96 Butts v Penny, (1677), 2 Levinz, p. 201; reported in Colin Bobb-Semple, *English Common Law, African Enslavement and Human Rights* (Charleston, SC: CreateSpace, 2012), pp. 19–20. The quotation was obiter dicta. It was not the rule of the case. There is some doubt as to whether this case actually made the enslavement of African people legal, see James Dowling, Archer Ryland, *Reports of Cases Argued and Determined in the Court of Kings Bench* (London: S. Sweet, R. Pheney, A. Maxwell, 1822), pp. 688–689, 697–698, 721–727. But the fact that this statement was made at all is nevertheless significant.

97 For more on the idea of a Protestant hegemony see Alison Margaret Conway, *The Protestant Whore: Courtesan Narrative and Religious Controversy in England, 1680–1750* (Toronto: University of Toronto Press, 2010), passim, Conway's references at pp. 188, 274–275 may be particularly useful.

98 Thomas Harman, *A Caveat or Warning for Common Cursetors, Vulgarly Called Vagabonds* … (1566, new edition, 1573); quoted in Julia Wardhaugh, *Sub City: Young People, Homelessness and Crime* (1999, new edition, London: Taylor & Francis, 2017), pp. 49–53.

99 See David Mayall, *Gypsy Identities, 1500–2000: From Egipcyans and Moon-men to the Ethnic Romany* (London: Routledge, 2004), pp. 5–11, 45; Judith Okely, *The Traveller-Gypsies* (Cambridge: Cambridge University Press, 1983), pp. 2–7.

100 Thomas Dekker, *Lanthorne and Candlelight. Or the Bell-Mans Second Nights Walke. In Which he Brings to Light, a Broode of More Strange Villanies, Than Ever Were Till This Yeare Discovered* (London: Iohn Busbie, 1608), n.p.; quoted in Faggett, *Black and Other Minorities in Shakespeare's England*, pp. 96–98; and Wardhaugh, *Sub City*, pp. 49–53.

101 Thomas Browne, *Pseudodoxia Epidemica: or, Enquiries into Very Many Received Tenents and Commonly Presumed Truths* (London: Edward Dod, 1646), p. 329.

102 See Mayall, *Gypsy Identities, 1500–2000*, pp. 5–11, 18–24; James Andrew Scarborough MacPeek, *The Black Book of Knaves and Unthrifts* (Storrs, CT: University of Connecticut, 1969), pp. 1–21, 252–262; Ian Hancock, 'The Struggle for the Control of Identity,' *Perspectives*,

www.osi.hu/rpp/perspectives1f.htm, accessed 06/07/2007; and Paul
Slack, *Poverty and Policy in Tudor and Stuart England* (London:
Longman, 1988), pp. 91–99.

103 Evidence and further references are to be found in *The Oxford English
Dictionary*, p. 351; Charles Knight, *The English Encyclopaedia*
(London: Bradbury Evans, 1868), pp. 613–616; and suggested by
David MacRitchie, *Scottish Gypsies Under the Stewarts* (Edinburgh:
D. Douglas, 1894), pp. 25–33, 42, 51; Gypsy Lore Society, *Journal of
the Gypsy Lore Society*, 2:2 (1891), pp. 34–37.

104 Humfrey Dyson (collator), *A Book Containing all such
Proclamations as were Published by the Reigine of the Late Queen
Elizabeth 1559–1602* (London: Bonham Norton and John Bull,
1618), pp. 1–6, 300, 324, 356, etc.

105 Wardhaugh, *Sub City*, pp. 49–53; Brian Belton, *Questioning Gypsy
Identity: Ethnic Narratives in Britain and America* (Walnut Creek,
CA: Altamira Press, 2005), pp. 74, 176.

106 See Broomhall, Tarbin (eds.), *Women, Identities and Communities*,
passim; Patricia Crawford, 'Public Duty, Conscience and Women
in Early Modern England,' in John Morrill, Paul Slack et al. (eds.),
*Public Duty, and Private Conscience in Seventeenth-Century England:
Essays Presented to G. E. Aylmer* (Oxford: Clarendon Press, 1993),
pp. 201–234; Patricia Crawford (ed.), *Exploring Women's Past: Essays
in Social History* (Carlton South, Vic.: Sisters Publishing, 1983), passim; other writers include: Laura Gowing, Philippa Maddern and Jodi
Mikalachki, some of whose work is discussed throughout this book or
listed in the Selected Bibliography.

107 Laura Gowing in Broomhall, Tarbin (eds.), *Women, Identities*, p. 2.

108 On women, this is discussed extensively by a range of historians who
include Patricia Clarkson, Laura Gowing and Philippa Maddern;
also see Selene Scarsi, *Translating Women in Early Modern England:
Gender in the Elizabethan Versions of Boirado, Ariosto and Tasso*
(Farnham: Ashgate, 2001), pp. 1–13, 73–123 (on translating, interpreting and identifying the 'hidden' or women subject).

109 Similar ideas are expressed by Onyeka in 'The Missing Tudors: Black
People in Sixteenth-Century England.' *BBC History Magazine* 13:7
(July 2012), pp. 32–33.

110 On this subject see Broomhall, Tarbin (eds.), *Women, Identities
and Communities*, passim; Crawford, 'Public Duty, Conscience and
Women in Early Modern England,' pp. 201–234; Crawford, *Exploring
Women's Past*, passim; other writers include: Laura Gowing, Philippa
Maddern and Jodi Mikalachki, some of whose work is discussed
throughout this book or listed in the Selected Bibliography.

111 Quotation from Edward Cooke, in the common law case, *Semayne's Case* (January 1st, 1604) 5 Coke Rep. 91; it is often transcribed as 'Everyman's home is his castle,' but owes its origins to older phrases, see Richard Mulcaster, *Positions Which Are Necessarie for the Training up of Children* (London: T. Vautrollier, 1581), n.p. 'He is the appointer of his owne circumstance, and his house is his castle.'

112 John Knox, *The First Blast of the Trumpet: Against the Monstrous Regimen of Women* (Edinburgh: Andrew Steuart, 1571), passim.

113 Few writers have drawn an analogy between 'Querelle des Femmes' (1500s circa), 'The Negro Question' (1849) and the 'Jewish Question' (1753–1754), please see Heinrich Cornelius Agrippa (below); Thomas Carlyle, 'Occasional Discourse on the Negro Question,' *Fraser's Magazine for Town and Country*, 40 (1849), pp. 670–679; John Stuart Mill, 'The Negro Question,' *Fraser's Magazine for Town and Country*, 41 (1850), pp. 25–31; for George Padmore and the 'Negro Question' see *The Life and Struggles of Negro Toilers* (London: International Trade Union Committee of Negro Workers …, 1931), passim; Otto Duv Kulka, *The 'Jewish Question' in German Speaking Countries, 1848–1914, A Bibliography* (New York/London: Garland Publishing, 1994), passim; A. Guibbory, *'The Jewish Question' and 'The Woman Question' in Samson Agonistes: Gender, Religion, and Nation* (Cambridge: Cambridge University Press, 2004), passim; W. Brown, *Tolerance and/or Equality? The 'Jewish Question' and the 'Woman Question'* (Urbana, IL: University of Illinois Press, 2004), passim; R. A. Hill, *Black Zionism: Marcus Garvey and the Jewish* Question (Columbia, MI: University of Missouri Press, 1998), passim; the last quotation is from the poem by Dylan Thomas, 'Do Not Go Gentle Into That Goodnight' (1947), published in Marguerite Caetani (ed.), *Botteghe Oscure* (Roma: Marguerite Caetani, 1951), n.p.

114 The phrase is an often quoted phrase, but comes from a poem by William Ross Wallace, 'What Rules the World' (1865), in *New 5 & 10 Cent Store, Musical Hand-Bill: The Hand That Rocks the World, Poetry by William Ross Wallace* (Toronto: Imrie & Graham, 1865 circa), n.p.

115 From the play: Jerome Lawrence, Robert Edwin Lee, *Inherit the Wind* (1955, new edition, New York: Dramatists Play, 2000), p. 60.

116 Although written in 1405, the book was widely available in English throughout the early modern period see Bryan Anslay (tr.), Christine de Pizan, *Begin. Here Begynneth the Boke of the Cyte of Ladyes, the which Boke is Deyded in to iij partes. End …* (London: H. Pepwell, 1521), passim; see Maureen Quilligan, *The Allegory of Female Authority: Christine de Pizan's Cité Des Dames* (Ithaca, NY: Cornell University

Press, 1991), passim; Margaret Brabant, *Politics, Gender, and Genre: The Political Thought of Christine de Pizan* (Boulder, CO: Westview Press, 1992), passim; and Kate Langdon Forhan, *The Political Theory of Christine Pizan* (London: Routledge, 2017), passim.

117 Concepts of 'humanism' and 'universals' are not the same, but both were influenced by Neoplatonic teachings, some aspects of Roman natural law, and offered an idea that all living things had 'substantiality' and the potential for divinity, see Paul Vincent Spade (tr. ed.), *Five Texts on the Mediaeval Problem of Universals: Porphyry, Boethius, Abelard, Duns Scotus, Ockham* (Indianapolis, IN: Hackett, 1994), passim; more on these matters and 'magic' are discussed later in this book.

118 Albert Rabil (ed.), Henricus Cornelius Agrippa, *Declamation on the Nobility and Preeminence of the Female Sex* (Chicago, IL: University of Chicago Press, 1996), passim.

119 Anger 'Her Protection for Women,' pp. 80–97, quotation at p. 93; Hodgson Wright, *Women's Writing of the Early Modern Period, 1588–1688*, pp. 2–5, 29, 461.

120 For more on Agrippa, Cruz, Speght, Sowerman and many others see Patricia Demers, *Women's Writing in English: Early Modern England* (Toronto: University of Toronto Press, 2005), passim; Kate Aughterson, *Renaissance Woman: A Sourcebook. Constructions of Femininity in England* (London: Routledge, 2003), passim; Stephanie Merrim, *Early Modern Women's Writing and Sor Juana Ines de la Cruz* (Nashville, TN: Vanderbilt University Press, 1999), passim.

Three

1 Speech, Martin Luther King, 1967, quoted in Herbert Robinson Marbury, *Pillars of Cloud and Fire: The Politics of Exodus in African American Biblical Interpretation* (New York: New York University Press, 2015), p. 228; this section of the speech can be seen at Martin Luther King, 'Somebody Told a Lie – MLK That's Never Quoted,' www.youtube.com/watch?v=UGtjAaJeUWY, published 09/06/2011, accessed 12/02/2018.

2 In this book the Curse of Ham is referred to as a myth; the author acknowledges that not every reader will regard it as such.

3 Some sections of the Mormon Church have moderated their perspective on this in recent years. But see statements such as that by Brigham Young, the second President of the Church of Jesus Christ of Latter Day Saints, 'You must not think, from what I say, that I am opposed to slavery. No! The negro is damned, and is to serve his master till God chooses to remove the curse of Ham.' Brigham Young, *New York*

Herald, 4 May 1855, p. 8; For more on this see Lester E. Bush, *Neither White Nor Black: Mormon Scholars Confront the Race Issue in a Universal Church* (Salt Lake City, UT: Signature Books, 1984), passim.

4   On the law and organisations that relied on the Curse of Ham see Charles B. Copher, Gayraud S. Wilmore (eds.), *African American Religious Studies: An Interdisciplinary Anthology* (Durham, NC: Duke University Press, 1989), pp. 117–127.

5   See ibid., pp. 117–127; a 'Kleagle' is a senior rank in the Klan, Senator Robert Byrd's speech was given in Washington on 10 June 1964, 'Noah apparently saw fit to discriminate against Ham's descendants in that he placed a curse upon Canaan,' in Authors various, *Congressional Record: Proceedings and Debates of the Congress ...*, Volume 110, Part 10 (Washington, DC: US Government Printing Office, 1964), p. 13207. It was a speech against the Civil Rights Act 1964.

6   Bengt G. M. Sundkler, *Bantu Prophets in South Africa* (London: Lutterworth Press, 1948), p. 57.

7   On this matter see William A. Dyrness (ed.), *Global Dictionary of Theology: A Resource for the Worldwide Church* (Westmount, IL: Intervarsity Press, 2009), pp. 718–724; and on anti-Semitism, 'volk' and racism see Kevin P. Spicer, *Anti-Semitism, Christian Ambivalence and the Holocaust* (Bloomington, IN: Indiana University Press, 2007), pp. 287–291.

8   For the idea of racism being 'thought, speech,' 'action' and 'power,' rather than merely being prejudice or an acknowledgement of difference, see Fuller, *The United Independent*, passim.

9   See Goldenberg, *The Curse of Ham*, introduction; 'Maafa' is a Swahili word used to describe the destruction of African peoples and civilisations and their subsequent enslavement. It was first used in this way by Marimba Ani, *Let the Circle be Unbroken: The Implications of African Spirituality in the Diaspora* (New York: Nkonimfo Publications, 1988), passim.

10 Ottobah Cugoano, *Thoughts and Sentiments on the Evil and Wicked Traffic of the Slavery and Commerce of the Human Species ...* (London: T. Beckett, 1787), pp. 33–40; David Walker, *Walker's Appeal, in Four Articles: Together with a Preamble to the Colored Citizens of the World, but in Particular, and Very Expressly to Those of the United States of America. Written in Boston, in the State of Massachusetts, Sept. 28, 1829* (Boston, MA: David Walker, 1830), pp. 67–68.

11 Of course this desire did not begin in the early modern period and Anglo-Saxon writers and kings such as Alfred commissioned Anglo-Saxon versions of parts of the Bible, see Gerry Knowles, *Cultural History of the English Language* (London: Routledge, 2014), pp. 62–177.

12 The academics that have written about the development of the Bible in the fifteenth, sixteenth and early seventeenth centuries have detailed explanations for their erudition. Readers wishing to find out more may follow the notes or the bibliography in this book.

13 See Margaret Deanesly, *The Lollard Bible and Other Medieval Biblical Visions* (Cambridge: Cambridge University Press, 1920), pp. 231–310.

14 Archbishop Arundel, Letter to Pope Gregory XII, 1411/1412, quoted in Michael T. Schmidt, *Translating the Bible Literally: The History and Translation Methods of the King James Version, The New American Standard Bible and the English Standard Version* (Bloomington, IN: West Bow Press, 2016), p. 10; on Wycliffe also see Harry Freedman, *The Murderous History of Bible Translations: Power, Conflict and the Quest for Meaning* (London: Bloomsbury Publishing, 2016), pp. 79–86, 207–212.

15 John Wycliffe, Nicholas Hereford (tr.), *Wycliffe Bible*, 1382–1395, Genesis 9, v. 18–27; and in John Wycliffe, *The Dore of Holy Scripture* (London: John Gough, 1540), Genesis 9, v. 18–27.

16 For a cross-cultural, interfaith exposition on 'the Flood' see Florentino Garcia Martinez, Gerard P. Lettikhuizen (eds.), *Interpretations of the Flood* (Leiden/Boston, MA: Brill, 1998), passim.

17 Wycliffe, *Wycliffe Bible*, Genesis 7, v. 11–24, and 8, v. 5–17.

18 In other parts of the Bible he was described as an older son of Noah.

19 'Plain reading' means as 'a reasonable person' would read the text, rather than 'literal' which has its own theological meaning. Plain reading is used in the 'plain meaning rule' in statutory construction. See Sharon Hanson, *Legal Method, Skills and Reasoning* (London/New York: Routledge, 2009), pp. 87–227; To see it applied in theology see Thomas Kazen, *Scripture Interpretation, or Authority?: Motives and Arguments in Jesus' Halakic Conflicts* (Tubingen: Mohr Siebeck, 2013), pp. 102, 154, 290.

20 The difference between cursing and prophecy is separated by a thin line. Later in this book we examine this. Of course, Noah's curse also contained a prophecy.

21 Wycliffe, *The Dore of Holy Scripture*, 'Right with God' is a quotation from Romans 5, v. 1.

22 See below.

23 For more on this see Moses I. Finley, *Ancient Slavery and Modern Ideology* (London: Penguin, 1998), passim; Keith Bradley, Paul Cartledge (eds.), *The Cambridge World History of Slavery*, Volume 1: *The Ancient Medieval World* (Cambridge: Cambridge University Press, 2011), passim; William Philips, *Slavery from Roman Times to the Early Transatlantic Trade* (Manchester: Manchester University Press, 1985), passim.

24 Quotations from Wycliffe, *The Dore of Holy Scripture*, Genesis 9, v. 18–27.

25 Wycliffe, *Wycliffe Bible*, Genesis 9, v. 19–27; some modern authors have erroneously added the words 'slave' and 'slaves' in brackets into the text of this Bible, see John Wycliffe, John Purvey, Editor unknown, 'Wycliffe Bible,' *Bible Study Tools: Grow Deeper in the Word* (2018), www.biblestudytools.com/wyc/genesis/9.html, accessed 19/02/2018.

26 James Townley, *Illustrations of Biblical Literature, The History and Fate of the Sacred Writings, From The Earliest Period to the Present Century*, Volume 1 (London: Longman, Hurst, Rees, Orme and Brown, 1821), pp. 160–163.

27 Excellent books on this subject are: Jaroslav Pelikan, Valerie R. Hotchkiss, David Price (eds.), *The Reformation of the Bible: The Bible of the Reformation* (New Haven, CT: Yale University Press, 1996), pp. 23–63; David Daniell, *The Bible in English: Its History and Influence* (New Haven, CT: Yale University, 2003), pp. 19–95; Frederick Fyvie Bruce, *The History of the Bible in English* (Cambridge: James and Clarke, 2002), pp. 1–96.

28 Jerome, 'Latin Vulgate,' fourth century CE (2018), www.biblestudytools. com/vul/genesis/9.html, accessed 19/02/2018.

29 Attributed to William Tyndale, by John Foxe, *Actes and Monuments … Foxe's Book of Martyrs* (London: John Day, 1563), n.p. in John F. A. Sawyer, *The Blackwell Companion to the Bible and the Culture* (New York: John Wiley, 2012), p. 56; Eliakim Littell, Robert S. Little, *The Living Age*, Volume 105 (Philadelphia, PA: The Living Age Company, 1870), pp. 454–457; see Freedman, *The Murderous History of Bible Translations*, pp. 1, 99–119, 142–150.

30 'Everyman' is a metaphor for the 'common man' – he appears as a character in Author unknown, *The Somonyng of Everyman* (1518), see Geoffrey M. Cooper, Christopher Wortham, *The Summoning of Everyman* (Perth: University of Western Australia Press, 1980), passim; Patricia L. Carlin, *Shakespeare's Mortal Men: Overcoming Death, in History, Comedy, and Tragedy* (New York: P. Lang, 1993), pp. 21–25.

31 Attributed to William Tyndale, by John Foxe, *Actes and Monuments*, quoted in Littell, *The Living Age*, Volume 105, pp. 454–457.

32 On 'plain English' in the Bible see Daniell, *The Bible in English: Its History and Influence*, pp. 133–172; John Eadie, *The English Bible: An External and Critical History of the Various English Translations of the Scripture* (London: Macmillan and Company, 1876), pp. 107–142.

33 William Tyndale, *Tyndale Bible* (1525, 1536), www.biblestudytools.com/ tyn/genesis/9.html, accessed 21/02/2018, several versions of the Tyndale version were available in early modern England – they include those by Coverdale etc.; see Richard Taverner, *The Most Sacred Bible Whiche is*

the Holy Scripture, Conteyning the Old and Newe Testament, translated into English [by W. Tyndale and M. Coverdale], *and newly recognised …Richard Taverner* (London: John Byddell, John Barthlet, 1539), passim.

34 I acknowledge that several religious documents in their original form do make an ambiguous reference to 'skin,' for example in the *Sanhedrin Tractate* 108 b, which is part of the *Tanhuma* compiled between 200 CE–500 CE, it does say 'Ham was smitten in his skin.' But this is not explained, please see John T. Townsend, *Midrash Tanhuma: Genesis* (Jersey City, NJ: Ktav Publishing House, 1989), pp. 31–61; a different view is offered by David H. Aaron, 'Early Rabbinic Exegesis, on Noah's Son Ham and the So-Called Hamitic Myth,' *Journal of the American Academy of Religion* (1995), pp. 721–759, who suggests that 'blacks' are referenced in the early texts as objects of the Curse; but the following writers have a similar view as that quoted in this book: Benjamin Braude (as above); and Whitford, *The Curse of Ham in the Early Modern Era*, pp. 24–28. Whitford suggests that the word 'black' has been inserted to explain the word 'slave' by translators of certain Aramaic, Babylonian and Hebrew texts including the Talmud and Tanhuma.

35 *The Miles Coverdale Bible* (1535), Genesis 9, v. 20–27:

> Noe beganne to take hede vno ye tyllinge of the grounde, & planted a vyniarde. 21. And dranke of the wyne, and was dronken, and laye vncouered in his tente. 22. Now when Ha the father of Canaan sawe his fathers preuities, he tolde his two brethren with- out. 23. The toke Sem and Iaphet a mantell and put it vpo both their shulders, and wente backwarde, and couered their fathers secretes: & their faces were turned asyde, yt they shulde not se their fathers preuyties. 24. So whan Noe awaked from his wyne, and perceaued what his yonger sonne had done vnto him, 25. he sayde: Cursed be Canaan, and a seruaunt of seruauntes be he vnto his brethren. 26. He sayde morouer: Praysed be the LORDE God of Sem, and Canaan be his seruaunt. 27. God increase Iaphet, and let him dwell in the tentes of Sem, and Canaan be his seruaunt.

On these Bibles in general see Daniell, *The Bible in English*, pp. 133–172 (*Tyndale*), 173–197 (*Coverdale*), 190–197 (*Matthew's*), 198–220 (*Great Bible*), 291–319 (*Geneva*), 427–450 (*KJV*).

36 Authors including Lancelot Andrews, William Bedwell, Francis Burleigh, Richard Clarke (trs., eds.), *King James Version of the Bible* (London: Robert Baker, 1611), Genesis 9, v. 20–27. The work began in 1604 and was finished in 1611; quoted in 'Bible Study Tools,' www. biblestudytools.com/kjv/genesis/9.html.

37 This applies to most modern Bibles too. But this is beyond the scope of the analysis of this book.

38 The writers who believe in monogenesis are discussed throughout this book. Other thinkers at this time believed in polygenesis, and Jewish, Christian, Islamic and Animist scholars discussed this idea, see the poetry of Judah Ha-Levi, *Mi kamokha: She-nohagim Le-omro Ba-Shabat Sheli-fene Purim* (Mantua: publisher unknown, 1557), passim; Augustine of Hippo, R. W. Dyson (ed.), *Augustine: The City of God Against the Pagans* (Cambridge: Cambridge University Press, 1998), pp. 3–51; and the ninth-century work of Aḥmad ibn ʿAlī Ibn Waḥshīyah, *Ancient Alphabets and Hieroglyphic Characters Explained: With an Account of the Egyptian Priests, Their Classes, Initiation, and Sacrifices/ in the Arabic Language by Ahmad bin Abubekr bin Wahshih; and in English by Joseph Hammer* (London: Printed by W. Bulmer and Co. and G. and W. Nicol, 1806), Books 1–2.

39 Quoted in Purvey, Wycliffe, *Wycliffe Bible*, Genesis 10, v. 6–12, 'Bible Study Tools,' www.biblestudytools.com/wyc/genesis/10.html.

40 For more on these civilisations see Cheikh Anta Diop, *The African Origin of Civilization: Myth or Reality* (Paris: Presence Africaine, 1967, new edition, Chicago, IL: Chicago University Review Press, 1989), passim; Molefi Kete Asante, *The History of Africa: The Quest for Eternal Harmony* (New York: Routledge, 2012), pp. 15–39, 99–161; Frank M. Snowden, *Before Colour Prejudice: The Ancient View of Blacks* (Cambridge, MA: Harvard University Press, 1983), pp. 1–19; Basil Davidson, *African Civilization Revisited: From Antiquity to Modern Times* (Trenton, NJ: Africa World Press, 1991), passim; Basil Davidson, *Black Mother: A Study of the Precolonial Connection Between Africa and Europe* (London: Longman, 1970), passim; and Robin Walker, *When We Ruled* (London: Every Generation Media, 2005), passim.

41 See all texts cited in the previous note.

42 Stephen Howe is one of these writers in *Afrocentrism: Mythical Pasts and Imagined Homes*, pp. 1–16, 215–229; Others include: Lefkowitz, *Black Athena Revisited*, pp. 113–120; Lefkowitz, *Not Out of Africa*, passim; John Gunther, *Inside Africa* (London: Hamish Hamilton, 1955), pp. 21–25; Elliott Percival Skinner, *Peoples and Cultures of Africa: An Anthropological Reader* (Washington, DC: Natural History Press, 1972), pp. 61–63.

43 As the following authors do: Diop, *African Origin of Civilisation*, passim; John Archer, 'J. R. Archer's Presidential Address to the Inaugural Meeting of the African Progress Union, 1918,' *West Africa*, 2:101 (4 January 1919), pp. 840–842 and quoted in Fryer, *Staying Power*, pp. 410–416; Anthony Tony Browder, *Nile Valley Contributions to*

Civilisations (Washington, DC: Institute of Karmic Guidance, 1992), passim; Yosef Ben-Jochannan, *Africa: Mother of Western Civilisation* (Baltimore, MD: Black Classic Press, 1997), passim.

44 This includes: Ishakamusa Barashango, *God the Bible and the Black Man's Destiny* (Baltimore, MD: Afrikan World Books, 2002), passim; Yosef Ben-Jochannan, *African Origins of the Major Western Religions* (Baltimore, MD: Black Classic Press, 1991), passim; Ben-Jochannan, *The Need for a Black Bible* (Baltimore, MD: Black Classic Press, 1996), passim; Aylmer Von Fleischer, *Retake Your Fame: Black Contribution to World Civilisation*, Volume 1 (s.l.: Aylmer Von Fleischer, 2004), Chapter 6; and Asante; Browder; Diop; Sertima; Scobie, and similar concepts from others that may not call themselves African-centred.

45 Flavius Josephus, *The Antiquities of the Jews*, Book 1, Chapter 6, Section 2, (94 CE); quoted in the work of pioneering African-American historians such as: James W. C. Pennington, *A Textbook of the Origin and History, &c. &c. of the Colored People* (Hartford, CT: L. Skinner, 1841), n.p.; Drusilla Dunjee Houston, *Wonderful Ethiopians of the Ancient Cushite Empire: Origin of the Civilisation of the Cushites* (1926, new edition, New York: City University of New York Press, 2007), p. xviii.

46 For more on the Barmakids see Kevin van Bladel, 'The Bactrian Background of the Barmakids,' in A. Akasoy, C. Burnett, R. Yoeli-Tlalim, *Islam and Tibet: Interactions along the Musk Routes* (London: Ashgate, 2011), pp. 43–88.

47 Ibn Khallikan, *A Biographical Dictionary* [1211–1282] (London: Oriental Translation Fund of Great Britain and Ireland, 1871), pp. 344–346; the conflation of the African kingdom, Kush (Cush) with a son of Noah is discussed below.

48 For more on Annius see Anthony Grafton, Glen W. Most, Salvatore Settis, *The Classical Tradition* (Cambridge, MA/London: Belknap Press, 2010), pp. 46–47, 138, 339, 398, 445, 498, 866; Alfred Hiatt, *The Making of Medieval Forgeries: False Documents in Fifteenth-Century England* (London: British Library and University of Toronto Press, 2004), pp. 9–14; Anthony Grafton, *Defenders of the Text: The Traditions of Scholarship in an Age of Science, 1450–1800* (Cambridge/London: Harvard University Press, 1991), pp. 76–104; for more on the making of early modern forgeries see Anthony Grafton, *Forgers and Critics: Creativity and Duplicity in Western Scholarship* (Princeton, NJ/Oxford: Princeton University Press, 1990), passim.

49 Annius of Virterbo quoted in Whitford, *The Curse of Ham in the Early Modern Era*, p. 62.

50 Whitford, *The Curse of Ham in the Early Modern Era*, p. 59.

51 For a longer discussion on this 'conflation' see the next chapter and Whitford, *The Curse of Ham in the Early Modern Era*, p. 17.

52 See Goldenberg, *The Curse of Ham*, pp. 176–182; Goldenberg, *Black and Slave: The Origins and History of the Curse of Ham* (Berlin/Boston, MA: Walter de Gruyter, 2017), pp. 153–155, his appendices are also helpful, pp. 207–244.

53 See Walter Earl Stevens, *Berosus Chaldaeus: Counterfeit and Fictive Editors of the Early Sixteenth Century* (New York: Cornell University, 1979), pp. 1–25, 291–294.

54 Walter Raleigh repeats these stories in *The Historie of the VVorld. In Fiue Bookes ... By Sir Walter Ralegh, Knight* (London: Walter Stansby/Walter Burre, 1617), pp. 30–32, 35, 126–140; and Arthur Kelton advocates them in *A Chronicle with a Genealogie Declarying that the Britons and Welshmen Are Lindly Descended from Brute* (London: Richard Grafton, 1547), p. D1.

55 More on the Annian genealogy is explored later in this book.

56 Heinrich Cornelius Agrippa, *De Incertitudine and Vanitate Scientiarum and Artum* (Paris: Johannes Petrum, 1531), p. CXI, quoted in Whitford, *Curse of Ham in the Early Modern Era*, p. 72; another translation is C. M. Duan (ed.), Heinrich Agrippa, *Of the Vanitie and Uncertaintie of Artes and Sciences* (Northridge, CA: California State University, 1974), p. 273.

57 See Jan N. Bremmer, *Greek Religion and Culture: The Bible and the Ancient Near East* (Lieden/Boston, MA: Brill, 2002), pp. 57–73, 73–101; for how that conflation occurs with all protagonists see Joseph Campbell, *The Hero with a Thousand Faces* (Princeton, NJ: Princeton University Press, 1971), passim.

58 Guillaume Postel de Etienne, *Cosmographicae ...* (Basel: Ioaneem Oporinum, 1561), p. D3; also see Bernard Lewis, *Race and Slavery in the Middle East: An Historical Inquiry* (Oxford: Oxford University Press, 1990), pp. 55–59.

59 The word 'Ethiopian' was interchangeable with the words 'Blackamoore,' 'Moor' and later 'Negro'; to see how it was used in early modern England see Onyeka, 'What's in a Name?'; Onyeka, *Blackamoores*, pp. 41–90.

60 For a definition of the word Ethiopia see *The Oxford English Dictionary*, p. 423; *Oxford Dictionary of English*, p. 595; for more on what the word 'Ethiopian' meant in Tudor and Stuart England see Onyeka, *Blackamoores*, pp. 41–46; and Onyeka, 'What's in a Name,' pp. 34–39; on the Greek myth itself see Glyn Parry, 'Berosus and the Protestants: Reconstructing Protestant Myth,' *Huntingdon Library Quarterly*, 64:1/2 (2001), pp. 1–21.

61 William Shakespeare, *Anthony and Cleopatra*, Act I, Scene V, L. 29, 1606–1608; Proudfoot, *Shakespeare*, p. 128.

62 Jonson, *Masque of Blacknesse*, p. 4; also see Onyeka, *Blackamoores*, p. 46; Stephen Orgel (ed.), Ben Jonson, 'The Masque of Blackness, 1605,' in *Ben Jonson: Complete Masques* (New Haven, CT: Yale University Press, 1969), passim; Bernadette Andrea, 'Black Skin, The Queen's Masques: Africanist Ambivalence and Feminine Author(ity) in the Masques of *Blackness* and *Beauty.*' *English Literary Renaissance* 29:2 (1999), pp. 246–281; Rafael Velez Nunez, 'Beyond the Emblem: Alchemical Albedo in Ben Jonson's The Masque of Blackness,' *Sederi*, 8 (1997), pp. 257–263.

63 See Ronal Segal, *Islam's Black Slaves: A History of Africa's Other Black Diaspora* (London: Atlantic Books, 2001), passim; Goldenberg, *The Curse of Ham*, pp. 4–8, 107, 132, 133, 138; other authors offer different views, see Iyengar, *Shades of Difference*, pp. 7–13, 67, 76–78; for yet another perspective see George Junne, *The Black Eunuchs of the Ottoman Empire: Networks of Power in the Court of the Sultan* (London/New York: I.B. Tauris, 2016), passim.

64 See Onyeka, 'What's in a Name?'; and see Spade (tr. ed.), *Five Texts on the Mediaeval Problem of Universals*, passim; Rudi A. Te Veldi, *Participation and Substantiality in Thomas Aquinas* (Leiden: E. J. Brill, 1995), passim; humanism is a widely discussed issue and some writers, such as Paul Oskar Kristeller, suggest that the term should only apply to Renaissance scholars from Italy, see Kristeller, *The Classics and Renaissance Thought, etc.* (Cambridge, MA: Harvard University Press, 1955), introduction; other historians such as Joel L. Kraemer use the term more generally, see Jill Kraye (ed.), *The Cambridge Companion to Renaissance Humanism* (Cambridge: Cambridge University Press, 1996), pp. 74, 109, 249 (Colet), 247–250 (Grocyn), 137, 140, 247–262 (More).

65 Here the word 'empiricism' relates to empirical research based on experiment and observation, not the school of philosophy of the same name.

66 The idea of 'Greek culture' is really a contradiction, since there was never a unified Ancient Greek way. We are principally talking about the culture engendered from the schools of learning situated in Athens where Socrates etc. taught and studied. We should note that contrary to what was sometimes stated, women were admitted to some of these schools, as were people of African, Asian, etc. descent. And many Greek writers were vocal in stating that their learning originated from Kemet and elsewhere, see the third-century Diogenes Laertius, *Lives of the Eminent Philosophers* (London/Cambridge, MA: Harvard University Press, 1972) (Books 1–5), pp. 435, 443, (Books 6–10), p. 323.

67 See Frank Viola, George Barna, *Pagan Christianity? Exploring the Roots of Our Church Practices* (new edition, Carol Stream, IL: Tyndale House Publishers, 2008), pp. 1–9 (the Bible), 9–47 (the Church); Philippe Walter, *Christianity: The Origins of a Pagan Religion* (Rochester, VT: Inner Traditions, 2006), passim (how pagan festivals and places of worship became Christian ones); Ishakamusa Barashango, *African People and European Holidays: A Mental Genocide*, Books 1 and 2 (New York: Lushena Books, 2001), passim.

68 Goldenberg, *Black and Slave*, p. 23; Whitford, *The Curse of Ham in the Early Modern Era*, pp. 101–102.

69 See Whitford, *The Curse of Ham in the Early Modern Era*, p. 102.

70 The relevant sections of Best's words are not discussed sequentially as his comments are very similar to a stream of consciousness, *A True Discourse*, p. 29.

71 See Onyeka, *Blackamoores*, pp. 211–241; Onyeka, 'Port Towns, Diversity and Tudor England,' *Port Towns*, 22 July 2014, http://porttowns.port.ac.uk/port-towns-diversity-tudor-england-2/; Onyeka, 'The Missing Tudors'; other records confirming this are to be found in Habib, *Black Lives*, pp. 274–368.

72 Quotations from Best, *A True Discourse*, pp. 28–32.

73 A dramatic attempt at this 'washing' is in Jonson, *Character of Two Royall Masques*, pp. 3–5. For more on this see Onyeka, *Blackamoores*, pp. 44–46, 59, 66, 78(n), 113; A similar washing occurs where the Gypsies' complexions turn from 'Ethiop to whiteness' in Jonson's, *A Masque of the Metamorphos'd Gypsies*, 1621, including a collective folio of Jonson's various titles: *Horatius Flaccus: His Art of Poetry. Englished by B. J. With other workes of the Author ['Execration against Vulcan,' 'The Masque of the Gypsies,' and 'Epigrams,' etc.], etc.* (London: Richard Bishop for Andrew Cooke, 1640–1641)

74 Quotations are from Best, *A True Discourse*, p. 30.

75 Brant Berlin, Paul Kay, *Basic Color Terms: Their Universality and Evolution* (London: University of California Press, 1969), passim; and see Tawrin Baker, Sven Dupre et al. (eds.), *Early Modern Color Worlds* (Leiden/Boston, MA: Brill, 2016), passim; Carole Patricia Biggam, *The Semantics of Colour: A Historical Approach* (New York: Cambridge University Press, 2012), passim; Frances Cress Welsing, *The Isis (Yssis) Papers: The Keys to the Colors* (Chicago, IL: Third World Press, 1991), passim.

76 Best, *A True Discourse*, p. 31.

77 Ibid., p. 31.

78 Ibid., pp. 28–29.

79 Ibid., p. 28.

80   Ibid., p. 30.

81   Peter Braun, Manfred Weinberg, *Ethno/Graphie ... of Literatur und Anthropologie*, 17 (Tubingen: Narr, Francke, Attempto, Furlang, 2002), p. 374 ('nine ether hair'), sometimes erringly called: 'Afro-hair,' 'kinky,' 'curly,' etc.

82   Early modern evidence for such a presence can be found in: Conestaggio, *The Historie of the Uniting of the Kingdom of Portugal to the Crowne of Castill*, pp. 1, 5–7, 39; Abentarique, *The History of the Conquest of Spain by the Moors*, p. 36; Purchas, *Purchas His Pilgrimage*, pp. 193–195.

83   The phrase 'global African presence' was used by the following authors: Ivan Van Sertima (ed.), Edward Scobie, *A Global African Presence* (New York: A&B Books, 1994), passim; see Rogers, *World's Great Men of Colour*, pp. 1–7; Rogers, *Sex and Race*, Volume 1, pp. 151–160, 196–220; and Sertima (ed.), Scobie, *African Presence in Early Europe*, passim; Ivan Van Sertima, Runoko Rashidi (eds.), *The African Presence in Early Asia* (New Brunswick, NJ: Transaction Publishers, 1985), passim; Runoko Rashidi, *The Global African Community: The African Presence in Asia, Australia, and the South Pacific* (Washington, DC: Institute for Independent Education, 1995), passim; Runoko Rashidi, *African Star over Asia: The Black Presence in the East* (London: Books of Africa, 2012), passim; Walker, *When We Ruled*, passim.

84   Quotation from Best, *A True Discourse*, p. 28.

85   Native Americans are 'a member of any of the indigenous peoples of North and South America and the Caribbean Islands' (*Oxford Dictionary of English*, p. 1171).

86   See William Harrison, 'Description of England,' Volumes 2 and 3 (1577, 1584), in *Modern History Sourcebook*, www.fordham.edu/halsall/mod/1577harrison-england.html, accessed 10/09/2007; Stow, *The Annales of England*, p. 485; John Stow, Edmund Howes, *The Annales, or Generall Chronicle of England*, p. 485.

87   Quotations from Alden Vaughan, 'Sir Walter Raleigh's Indian Interpreters, 1584–1618.' *The William and Mary Quarterly* 59:2 (2002), pp. 341, 347; Sidney Lee, 'Caliban's Visits to England,' *Cornhill Magazine*, 34 (1913), pp. 333–345; James Laurence Bolton (ed.), *Alien Communities of London in the Fifteenth Centuries* (Stamford: Richard III and York History Trust with Paul Watkins, 1998), pp. 29, 42.

88   Best, *A True Discourse*, p. 30. There is of course an inherent contradiction in the way that Best uses the term 'original Man' to describe a person, family and group of people.

89   Best, *A True Discourse*, pp. 31–32.

90 See Joao de Barros (1496–1570), *Ásia de João de Barros: Dos Feitos Que os Portugueses Fizeram no Descobrimento e Conquista dos Mares e Terras do Oriente* (Lisbon: Imprensa Nacional-Casa da Moeda, 1988), passim.

91 Abba Bahrey, *History of the Galla* (1593), discussed in Mohammed Hassen, 'The Historian Abba Bahrey and the Importance of His "History of the Galla."' *Horn of Africa* 14:1–2 (1990/91), pp. 90–106; Mohammed Hassen, 'The Significance of Abba Bahrey in Oromo Studies: A Commentary on the Works of Abba Bahriy and Other Documents Concerning the Oromo, Getatchew Haile.' *Journal of Oromo Studies* 14:2 (July 2007), pp. 131–155; Mohammed Hassen, *The Oromo and the Christian Kingdom of Ethiopia 1300–1700* (Woodbridge: Boydell and Brewer, 2015), pp. 222–259.

92 Guildhall Record Office, St Olave, P69/OLA1/A/01/GL Ms 28867, p. 50.

93 See the records for these Africans in Onyeka, *Blackamoores*, pp. 249–260; Habib, *Black Lives*, pp. 274–368.

94 Quotation from Meredith Hanmer, *The Baptizing of a Turke A Sermon* … (London: Robert Walde-Grave, 1586), p. 5.

95 Mathew Paris in Henry Richards Luard (ed.), *Flores Historiarum*, Volume 3 (London: HMSO, 1890), p. 24: The idea that Saracens could be Africans is controversial but is supported by Maghan Keita, 'Saracens and Black Knights.' *Arthuriana* 16:4 (1 December 2006), pp. 65–77; John Dalberg Acton, George Walter Prothero, et al. *Cambridge Modern History*, Volume 1 (Cambridge: Cambridge University Press, 1912), pp. 9, 10, Volume 9 (1906), pp. 9, 349; Debra Higgs Strickland, *Saracens, Demons, and Jews: Making Monsters in Medieval Art* (Princeton, NJ: Princeton University Press, 2003), p. 169; Geraldus Cambrensis, Joseph Stevenson (tr.), *Concerning the Instruction of Prince* … (Felinfach: JMF Books, 1991), p. 59; Rebecca Martin, *Wild Men and Moors in the Castle of Love: The Castle-Siege Tapestries, in Nuremberg, Vienna, and Boston (German (Alsace) Weavers)* (Chapel Hill, NC: University of North California, 1983), p. 82; and John Skelton in Norman Verrle McCullough, *The Negro in English Literature* (Ilfracombe: H. Stockwell, 1962), p. 42.

96 Sue Anderson, 'Human Skeletal Remains from Wolsey Street, Ipswich, (IAS5003),' January 2009, Report unpublished, pp. 6, 25, 49–51 (contains DNA tests proving the Ipswich Man was an African); Neil Ferguson (dr.), Tania Lindon (pr.), *History Cold Case*, Episode 1, BBC2, 6 May 2010; and Adrian Bell, 'History Cold Case,' Email, sent 08/05/2010, 10/05/2010, accessed 10/05/2010, 12/05/2010, respectively.

97 Hanmer, *The Baptizing of a Turke*, p. D4.

98 Sacrament is a way of describing Christian rites or practices.

99 Hanmer, *The Baptizing of a Turke*, p. B4.

100 Isidore was Bishop of Seville in the sixth century and wrote a book called *Etymologiae*. It was popular in early modern Europe, where he talked about the 'Origins' of living things including peoples: Isidore, *Ethimologiarum Isidori Hispalensis Episcopi* ... (Strasburg: J. Mentelin, 1470); Stephen A. Barney, *The Etymologies of Isidore of Seville* (Cambridge: Cambridge University Press, 2006), passim.

101 Isidore, *Ethimologiarum Isidori Hispalensis Episcopi* ..., pp. 193–198. Although Isidore did mention Canaan, this appeared to be a minor aspect of his origin stories about Africans.

102 Ibid.

103 Hanmer, *The Baptizing of a Turke*, pp. 2–5.

104 Ibid., p. 2.

105 Ibid., p. E5.

106 Ibid., pp. 2–5.

107 Legat, *A Watch-worde for Warre*, p. xv.

108 Purchas, *Purchas His Pilgrimage*, p. 133; the more pertinent discussion on the relationships between Jewish people and Africans in early modern England is examined in Onyeka, *Blackamoores*, pp. 126–135.

109 Hanmer, *The Baptizing of a Turke*, pp. 2–5.

110 Ibid., p. 5.

111 On Hanmer's criminal activities and involvement with Drake see John Strype, *Annals of the Reformation and Establishment of Religion ... During the First Twelve Years of Elizabeth I's Happy Reign*, Volume 3 (London: John Wyatt, 1709), pp. 216–217; Weever, *Ancient Funeral Monuments*, p. 427; Henry Ellis, *The History and Antiquities of the Parish of Saint Leonard Shoreditch* ... (London: J. Nicholas, 1798), p. 24; Tittler, Jones, *Companion to Tudor Britain*, p. 420, Hanmer was 'a somewhat disreputable fellow.'

112 For a different perspective on Drake's activities see Onyeka, *Blackamoores*, pp. 6–7, 11, 25–26, 50–51, 137, 154–159, 160–161, 170, 176, 180–181, 212–221.

113 Hanmer, *The Baptizing of a Turke*, p. E4 (slavery).

114 Quotations from Weever, *Ancient Funeral Monuments*, p. 427; and Thomas Cromwell, *Walks through Islington; Comprising an Historical and Descriptive* ... (London: Sherwood Gilbert and Piper, 1835), pp. 78–79.

115 Strype, *Annals of the Reformation*, pp. 216–217.

116 Cromwell, *Walks through Islington*, pp. 78–79.

117 But without more evidence this is difficult to prove.

118 Ellis, *History and Antiquities*, p. 24.

119 Best, *A True Discourse,* pp. 28–32; these sorts of ideas are also in Philemon Holland, *The History of the World Commonly Called the Natural Historie of C Plinius Secondus, Translated by Philemon Holland* (London: Adam Philip, 1601), pp. 96, 146–147, 157; for the later application of these kinds of ideas see: Author unknown, *A Forensic Dispute on the Legality of Enslaving Africans Held at the Commencement in Cambridge New England, July 21, 1773*, pp. 5, 25–27, 39; Douglas Lorimer, *Colour, Class and the Victorians: English Attitudes to the Negro in the Mid-Nineteenth Century* (New York: Leicester University Press, 1978), pp. 10, 19–28, 131–161; Skinner, *Peoples and Cultures of Africa*, pp. 61–63; and Joseph Greenberg, *The Languages of Africa* (1963, 3rd edition, Bloomington, IN: Indiana University Press, 1970), pp. 24, 42, 45.

120 See Author unknown, 'Broughton, Hugh (BRTN569H),' A Cambridge Alumni Database, University of Cambridge, http://venn.lib.cam. ac.uk/cgi-bin/search-2016.pl?sur=&suro=w&fir=&firo=c&cit=&cit o=c&c=all&z=all&tex=BRTN569H&sye=&eye=&col=all&maxco max=50, accessed 23/02/2018; Hugh Broughton, *A Briefe Discourse of the Scriptures* (London: W. White, 1614), pp. 1–5, 63–66 (on Africans).

121 Ben Jonson, *The Alchemist. Catiline, His Conspiracy* (London: D. Midwinter, 1756), p. 49, 'And is gone mad with studying Broughton's works'; Erin Julian, Helen Ostovich (eds.), *The Alchemist: A Critical Reader* (London: Arden Shakespeare, 2013), pp. 134, 186–187, 195, 201, 210.

122 This last idea was taken up by François Bernier, 'A New Division of the Earth,' *Journal des Sçavans* (24 April 1684), in T. Bendyphe (tr.) 'Memoirs Read before the Anthropological Society of London,' Volume 1, 1863–1864, pp. 360–364.

123 Similar ideas are expressed by Thomas Peyton (1620) and Thomas Hall (1661), see Whitford, *The Curse of Ham in the Early Modern Era*, p. 85.

124 Broughton, *A Briefe Discourse of the Scriptures*, pp. 63–66.

125 See Mary Floyd-Wilson, *English Ethnicity and Race in Early Modern Drama* (Cambridge: Cambridge University Press, 2003), pp. 1–20, 23–67; Sara Read, Jennifer Evans (eds.), *Maladies and Medicine: Exploring Health and Healing, 1540-1740* (Barnsley: Pen and Sword, 2017), pp. 4–65; for a cross-cultural perspective on the theory of the humors see Noga Arikha, *Passion and Tempers: A History of the Humours* (New York: HarperCollins, 2002), passim.

126 On the significance of those characteristics for Africans see Raymond Scupin, Christopher R. De Corse, *Anthropology: A Global Perspective* (1995, new edition, London: Prentice Hall, 1998), p. 574; Rebecca F. Kennedy, C. Sydnor Roy, *Race and Ethnicity in the Classical World: An Anthology of Primary Sources in Translation* (Indianapolis, IN/

Cambridge: Hackett Publishing, 2013), pp. 35–65; Nicolas Bancel, Thomas David, Dominic Thomas (eds.), *The Invention of Race: Scientific and Popular Representations* (London: Routledge, 2004), pp. 1–33.

127   Broughton, *A Briefe Discourse*, pp. 63–66.

128   Thomas Hall, *An Exposition By Way of Supplement, On the Fourth, Fifth, Sixth, Seventh, Eighth and Ninth Chapters of the Prophecy of Amos ... Many Polemical Points Debated ...* (London: Henry Mortlock, 1661), pp. 539–541, in Whitford, *The Curse of Ham in the Early Modern Era*, p. 85.

129   Isaac Bassie, *The Deed Man's Real Speech* (London: James Collins, 1673), p. 18.

130   Quotation from William Shakespeare, *Anthony and Cleopatra* (1603–1623), Act II, Scene VI, L. 67–68, in Proudfoot, *Shakespeare*, p. 133.

131   Sometimes it is difficult to know who is quoting who, for example, Abraham Hartwell's translation of Odoardo Lopez' work by the Italian Phlilpo Pigafetta, *A Report of the Kingdom of Congo, A Region of Africa ...* (London: John Wolfe, 1597), p. 1, 'That the blackecolour which is in the skinnes of the Ethiopians and Negroes &c. proceedeth not from the Sunne.'

132   Purchas, *Purchas His Pilgrimage*, pp. 38–39.

133   Ibid., pp. 38–41; other Englishmen for similar reasons may make reference to Ham's descendants being African, or the lineal or genealogical descent of kings in Africa. This included the Englishman Thomas Knight's translation of Honorious Augustodensis' work. Other English translators are discussed in Whitford's *The Curse of Ham in the Early Modern Era*, pp. 116–118.

134   Eden, *Decades of the Newe World West India*, introduction.

135   Ibid., p. 187.

136   On 'Libya' see Diop, *The African Origin of Civilization*, pp. 1–5, 56–57, 64 65, 68 70, 72–73, 93–94, 214–216.

137   On 'Ghana' see M. Angulu Onwuejeogwu, Bana Okpu, Chris Ebighgbo, *African Civilizations: Origin, Growth, and Development* (Lagos: UTO Publications, 2000), p. 232; David C. Conrad, *Empires of West Africa: Ghana, Mali and Songhay* (New York: Facts on File, 2005), pp. 17–33; Chancellor Williams, *The Destruction of Black Civilisation: Great Issues of a Race from 4500 B.C. to 2000 A.D.* (New York: Third World Press, 1987), pp. 195–219; Walker, *When We Ruled*, pp. 359–367.

138   The origins of these places and people are discussed in Josephus, *Jewish Antiquities*, I, vi, 2, (94 CE), interpreted in John Mclintock, *Cyclopaedia of Biblical, Theological and Ecclesiastical Literature: H, I, J* (New York: Harper & Brothers, 1872), pp. 34–43.

139 On 'Troglodytes' see Gustav Nachtigal, A. G. B. Fisher (trs.), *Sahara and Sudan: Tripoli and Fezzan; Tibesti or Tu*, Volume 1 (London: C. Hurst and Company, 1879), pp. 381–383; others such as Herodotus and the Medieval English writer Ranulphus Higden repeated the idea that the Garamantes hunted the Troglodytes, see Higden in Churchill Babington (ed.), John Trevisa (tr.), *Polychronicon: Together with the English Translations of John Trevisa ...* (London: Longman, 1865), p. 159. Eden also included areas in Asia as part of Ham's domain, such as 'Cappadocia' in modern day Turkey. For more on this civilisation see Daniela Dueck, Hugh Lindsay, Sarah Pothecary, *Strabo's Cultural Geography: The Making of a Kolossourgia* (Cambridge/New York: Cambridge University Press, 2005), pp. 200–216.

140 George Owen Harry, *The Genealogy of the High and Mighty Monarch James ... King of Great Brittayne, ... With His Lineall Descent from Noah by Divers Direct Lynes to Brutus ... the Worthy Descent of His Majesties Ancestour Owen Tudyr ...* (London: S. Stafford, 1604), pp. 1–3.

141 See Rachel Bowlby, *Freudian Mythologies: Greek Tragedy and Modern Identities* (Oxford: Oxford University Press, 2007), pp. 18–21, 162–163; and Leon Burnett, Sanja Bahun, *Myth, Literature, and the Unconscious* (London: Karnac Books, 2014), pp. 50–76.

142 Edward Leigh, *Critica Sacra ...* (London: A. Miller, R. Daniel, for T. Underhill, 1650), p. 76; for more on Leigh see Whitford, *The Curse of Ham in the Early Modern Era*, p. 100.

143 Many have written on this subject, but see Nahile Jules Some, *The Re-Invention of Africa: The Dilemma of Literature Produced by Africans in French Context* (Berkeley, CA/Los Angeles, CA: University of California Press, 2005), pp. 4–7; of course there are many other etymological origins suggested for the word 'Africa' including that it comes from the Afer people, or the Phoenician word: 'Afar' meaning 'dust,' or that it means to separate, or from the Latin word 'Aprica': 'sunny' etc.

144 Leo Africanus, *A Geographical Historie of Africa, Written in Arabicke and Italian ... by Iohn Leo a More ...* (London: John Pory, 1600), p. 6.

145 Ibid., pp. 39–41.

Four

1 Robert Boyle, *Experiments and Considerations Touching Colours* (London: Henry Herringman, 1664), p. 44.

2 Browne, *Pseudodoxia Epidemica*, p. 332.

3 Other views on this can be found in Matthieu Chapman, *Anti-Black Racism in Early Modern English Drama: The Other 'Other'*

(New York/Abingdon: Taylor & Francis, 2016), passim; Vie Kobina Odonkor, *Race and Blackness in Early Modern England: A Study of Shakespeare's Titus Andronicus, The Merchant of Venice, Othello and the Tempest* (Gainesville, FL: Florida State University, 2002), passim; Jean E. Feerick, *Strangers in Blood: Relocating Race in the Renaissance* (Toronto/Buffalo, NY/London: University of Toronto Press, 2010), passim, the notes in this book contain a list of further reading; and Kaufmann, *Black Tudors*, passim; A contrasting perspective is offered in Loomba, Burton, *Race in Early Modern England*, passim; and the very interesting book by Ivan Hannaford, *Race: The History of an Idea in the West* (Baltimore, MD: Johns Hopkins University Press, 1996), pp. 1–186; Onyeka, *Blackamoores*, pp. 297–341.

4   The idea of 'painting' the Moor, 'blackface' or 'counterfeiting' the Moor is part of an English tradition of making oneself Black, see Andrea Ria Stevens, *Inventions of the Skin: The Painted Body in Early English Drama 1400–1672* (Edinburgh: Edinburgh University Press, 2013), passim.

5   Purchas, *Purchas His Pilgrimages* (1613), pp. 5, 15, 21; and quotations from Elizabeth Story Donno (ed.), Richard Madox, *An Elizabethan in 1582: The Diary of Richard Madox, Fellow of All Saints* (London: Hakluyt Society, 1976), pp. 18, 49, 173, 193. Donno calls Madox 'the most educated' and 'intelligent person' on the journey and implies his observations are rational and astute; a similar view was advocated in Purchas, *Purchas his Pilgrimages*, pp. 538, 541, 582–585; and commented on in B. J. Sokol, *Shakespeare and Tolerance* (Cambridge: Cambridge University Press, 2008), pp. 10, 21.

6   William Shakespeare, *Richard III* (London: Andrew Wise, 1597), C3. In this case the curse came true. But Buckingham may also be dismissing Queen Margaret's curse because of gender bias; this is discussed by Jennifer C. Vaught (ed.), *Masculinity and Emotion in Early Modern English Literature* (London: Ashgate, 2008), pp. 73–88 (the rhetoric of words and gender inequality), 88–116 (women cursing men and the effect); and in Kirilka Stavreva, *Words Like Daggers: Violent Female Speech in Early Modern England* (Lincoln, NE: University of Nebraska Press, 2015), pp. 1–17, 45–71.

7   Quotations from *Oxford Dictionary of English* (2nd edition, Oxford: Oxford University Press, 2003), p. 426.

8   Marcus Harmes, Victoria Bladen (eds.), *Supernatural and Secular Power in Early Modern England* (Farnham: Ashgate, 2015), pp. 41–81 (on witches), 100, 111, 188 (on curses); it may depend if the curse is uttered by a man or a woman. In early modern England, men may be given more 'allowance' to curse, see Shokhan Rasool Ahmed, *Magic*

and Gender in Early Modern England (Bloomington, IN: Author House, 2014), passim.

9 Margaret's curses do become prophecy, see Shakespeare, *Richard III*, C3 (quotation).

10 'Skyclad': meaning naked; to compound Noah's sin, pagan witches were often thought to 'curse' while 'intoxicated' and skyclad, just as Noah was doing, see Justine Glass, *The Witchcraft: The Sixth Sense and Us* (London: Neville Spearman, 1969), pp. 15, 101; Frank Donovan, *Never on a Broomstick* (New York: Bell Publishing, 1971), p. 117.

11 William Strachey (1612), '[Native Americans are a] vagabond race of Cham,' in *The Historie of Travaile into Virginia Britannia: Expressing the Cosmographie and Commodities of the Country, Togither with the Manners Customes of the People* ... (London: Hakluyt Society, 1849), p. 47; and Nicholas Guyatt, *Providence and the Invention of the United States, 1607–1806* (Cambridge: Cambridge University Press, 2006), pp. 37–39; Stephen R. Haynes, *Noah's Curse: The Biblical Justification of American Slavery* (New York: Oxford University Press, 2002), pp. 143–145.

12 The detail of how and why these people were thought and written about as being cursed in early modern England is complex, but important evidence can be found in: Thomas Rogers (ed.), Scheltco Geveren, *Of the End of This World, and Second Coming of Christ* ... (London: Henrie Middleton, 1583), passim (on foreigners, Catholics and other Europeans including kings); Hanmer, *The Baptizing of a Turke*, passim (Muslims, Catholics); on Elizabeth I being cursed see Pope Pius V, 'Regnans in Excelsis,' Papal Bull 1570 in John Strype, *Annals of the Reformation and Establishment of Religion, and Other Various Occurrences* ... (1709–1725, new edition, Oxford: Clarendon Press, 1824), pp. 23–24: 'the bull of pope Pius V against Queen Elizabeth ... putting her under a curse, and ... those that should obey her to be involved under the said curse'; and Pope Sixtus Papal Bull 1588. In 1597 the Pope read curses against Elizabeth; on women, some thought they were cursed for 'Eve's sin' and menstruation was the punishment, see Sara Read, *Menstruation and the Female Body in Early Modern England* (New York: Palgrave Macmillan, 2003), pp. 32–38; and Jan Baptiste van Helmont, John Chandler (tr.), *Van Helmont's Worke's Containing His Most Excellent Philosophy, Physick, Chirurgery, Anatomy* ... (London: Lodowick Lloyd, 1664), pp. 648, 743.

13 Clement of Rome, *Recognitos Divi Clementis* (Basel: Bebel, 1536), p. 65.

14 Jean de Cartigny, William Goodyear (tr.), *The Voyage of the Wandering Knight* (London: Thomas East, 1581), p. 7.

15 For more on these legends see Bowlby, *Freudian Mythologies*, pp. 18–21, 162–163; and Burnett, Bahun, *Myth, Literature, and the Unconscious*, pp. 50–76.

16 Gervase Markham (ed.), Juliana Berners, *The Gentlemans Academie, or the Booke of S. Albans; Containing Three Most Exact and Excellent Bookes: The First of Hawking, the Second of all the Proper Terms of Hunting and the Last of Armorie: All Compiled by Juliana Barnes in the Yere from the Incarnation of Christ 1486: And Now Reduced into a Better Method by G. M. (i.e. Gervase Markham.) … (by Richard Farmer)* (London: Humfrey Lownes, 1595), pp. 43–44; some authors dispute the importance of Berners and suggest she was more of a translator and editor, see Joseph Haslewood (ed.), Juliana Berners, *The Book Containing the Treatises of Hawking; Hunting; Coat-Armour; Fishing; and Blasing of Arms. As printed at Westminster, by Wynkyn de Worde, … Book of St Albans …* (London: Harding and White, 1810–1811), introduction.

17 Markham, Berners, *Book of St Albans*, pp. 43–44; some early modernists believed that all the Canaanites died in the flood, see William Mckee Evans, 'From the Land of Canaan to the Land of Guinea: The Strange Odyssey of the Sons of Ham.' *American Historical Association* 85:1 (1980), pp. 15–43.

18 See Haslewood, Berners, *Book of St Albans*, introduction; George West Van Siclen, *An American Edition of the Treatyse of Fysshynge wyth an Angle from the Boke of St. Albans … attributed to Dame Juliana Berners. Edited by G. W. Van Siclen* (New York: J. L. Black, 1875), introduction; William Van Wyck (ed.), *A Treatise on Fishing with a Hook Attributed to Dame Juliana Berners … Rendered into Modern English by William Van Wyck* (New York: Van Rees Press, 1933), introduction.

19 Gyles Godet, *A Brief Abstract of the Genealogy and Race of All the Kings of England …* (London: Gyles Godet, 1560–1562), p. 7.

20 The Curse of Ham idea was also used to support the oppression of the 'churls' or poor and justify the feudal system, see Paul Freedman, *Images of the Medieval Peasant* (Stanford, CA: Stanford University Press, 1999), pp. 86–104.

21 Markham, Berners, *Booke of St Albans*, pp. 43–44 (the 'curse of Ham' is linked to the 'curse of Caine').

22 Ibid., pp. 43–44; yet another view is offered by John Mandeville, a fourteenth-century English traveller and explorer, *Voiage and Travayle of Syr John Maundeville Knight* (London: Thomas East, 1568), p. k4, he says 'then Cham took the best part Eastwards, that is called Asia. Sem took Affricke and Japeth took Europe.'

23 Markham, Berners, *Book of St Albans*, p. 44.

24 Quotations from John Jackson, *The Pedigree and Peregrination of Israel Being an Abridgement of the Histories of the Creation of Adam, Cain & Abel, Noah, etc. With Meditations and Prayers upon Each Historie* (London: M. Simmons, 1649), pp. 20, 21; the idea of the 'vagabond race of Cham' was also used in relation to Native Americans, see Strachey (1612), *The Historie of Travaile into Virginia*, p. 47.

25 Aaron Thompson (tr.), *British History, Translated into English from the Latin* of *Jeffrey of Monmouth* … (1136, new edition, London: J. Boyer, 1718), pp. 34–36 (Albion), 246; the Scots were sometimes described as having a different lineage: 'The Scots a people mixed of the Scithian and Spanish blood,' see William Harrison in Furnivall, Norden et al. (eds.), *Harrison's Description of England in Shakespeare's Youth* …, Volumes 2 and 3, pp. 13–14.

26 Arthur Kelton, *A Chronicle with a Genealogie Declarying That the Britons and Welshmen Are Lindly Descended from Brute* (London: Richard Grafton, 1547), p. D1.

27 William Harrison in Furnivall, Norden et al. (eds.), *Harrison's Description of England in Shakespeare's Youth* …, Volumes 2 and 3, pp. 2–5; also see Thompson (tr.), *British History … Jeffrey of Monmouth*, pp. 34–36 (Albion), 246 (Stonehenge built with stone from Africa), 362, 363, 365 (Africans that shaped England); John Hardying (1378–1465) wrote a very similar version of history in *The Chronicle of John Hardyng, Containing an Account of Public Transactions from the Earliest Period of English History … Together with the Continuation of Richard Grafton [1572] … Preface and Index by Henry Ellis*, Volume 1 (New York: Ames Press, 1974), pp. 362–365: 'Gurmonde King of Afficans conquered Brytane and do parted it in seven kingdoms to Saxons and English … King of Affricanes was a pagan'; also quoted in Guasco, *Slaves and Englishmen*, p. 19; Paulina Kewes, Ian W. Archer, Felicity Heal (eds.), *Oxford Handbook of Holinshed's Chronicles* (Oxford: Oxford University Press, 2013), p. 162.

28 Martin Luther, *Deutsch Catechismus* (Wittenberg: George Rhaw, 1531), p. 29.

29 Pseduo-Epicurean ideals are often paraphrased with the saying, 'eat, drink and be merry for tomorrow we die.' But this phrase is actually a conflation of two biblical ones in Ecclesiastes 8: 15 and Isaiah 22: 13; Pseudo-Epicureanism differed from Epicureanism (proper) that believed in 'pleasure' but pursued it with modesty and not hedonism. Pseudo-Epicureanists, however, believed in the pursuit of pleasure at all costs. For a general discussion on these matters see Terrence Irwin, *The Development of Ethics: From Socrates to the Reformation*, Volume 1 (New York: Oxford University Press, 2007), pp. 260–283.

30 On Henry's character see Milo Keynes, 'The Personality and Health of King Henry VIII (1491–1571).' *Journal of Medical Biology* 13:1 (1 August 2005), pp. 174–183.

31 Godet, *Genealogy and Race of All the Kings of England*, p. 7.

32 On the Greek deities mentioned see Gaius Plinius Secundus (Pliny), *Naturalis Historie* (Paris: Reginaldi Chalderi, 1516), p. 47.

33 George Owen Harry, *The Genealogy of the High and Mighty Monarch James ... King of Great Brittayne, ... With His Lineall Descent from Noah by Divers Direct Lynes to Brutus ... the Worthy Descent of His Majesties Ancestour Owen Tudyr ...* (London: S. Stafford, 1604), pp. 1–5.

34 The quotation is from Mandeville, *Voiage and Travayle* (1568), p. k4; but Mandeville believed that Ham was in the East so the extended quotation was: 'then Cham took the best part Eastwards, that is called Asia. Sem took Affricke and Japeth took Europe, Cham was the mightiest of his brethren.'

35 On this genealogy see Richard Lynche, *An Historical Treatise of the Travels of Noah into Europe ...* (London: Adam Islip, 1602), passim (this lineage also included the kings of Troy); on the Annian genealogy and Hieronymus Gebweiler see Whitford, *The Curse of Ham in the Early Modern Era*, pp. 67–68.

36 'Genesis' is called 'The Book of Moses' in Thomas Matthew's (John Rodgers') (ed. tr.) *Matthews Bible: The Byble Whych Is All the Holy Scripture: in Whych Are Contayned the Old and Newe Testament, Truelye and Purely Translated into Englishe by Thomas Matthewe* (London: Tyndale, 1537), p. iii. (woodcut images of Ham etc.); and images of a white Ham are in Martin Luther's *Deutsch Catechismus*, p. 29.

37 For a longer discussion on this 'conflation' see Whitford, *The Curse of Ham in the Early Modern Era*, pp. 17–34.

38 In Robert Redman, *Here Begynneth the Boke Called the Pype, or Tonne, of the Lyfe of Perfection. The Reason or Cause Wherof Dothe Playnely Appere in the Processe. (A Worke or Boke of ... Saynt Bernarde, Nnamed by ye Title Thus. De Precepto et Dispensatione. That is to Saye, of Commaundement and Dispensacion ... Translate and Tourned into Englyshe by ... Rycharde Whytforde.),* [In a binding of contemporary brown calf, with the Arms of Henry VIII stamped on the upper cover, and those of Katherine of Aragon on the lower] (London: Robert Redman, 1532), p. ciiii.

39 Luther, *Deutsch Catechismus*, p. 29 (wood cut).

40 Ibid.

41 Quotations from ibid., p. 31.

42 Quotations from Frances Howgill, *Caines Bloudy Race Known by Their Fruits. Or, a True Declaration of the Innocent Sufferings of*

the Servants of the Living God [i.e. the Quakers] ... *in the City of Westchester, etc.* (London: Thomas Simmons, 1657), n.p.

43 Ibid.; David Jenner, *Cain's Mark and Murder. K. Charles the I. His Martyrdom. Delivered in a Sermon* (London: John Williams, 1681), p. 5.

44 Jenner, *Cain's Mark and Murder*, p. 5.

45 Ibid., p. 10. For more on those that executed Charles I see Charles Spencer, *Killers of the King: The Men Who Dared to Execute Charles I* (London/New York: Bloomsbury, 2014), passim.

46 Jenner, *Cain's Mark and Murder*, p. 10.

47 Another group of English authors that believed this 'service' or 'slavery' was purely cultural, to do with Hebrew and or ancient biblical practices see Roger Edgeworth, *Sermons Very Fruitfull, Godly, and Learned, Preached and Sette Foorth by Maister Roger Edgeworth, Doctoure of Diuinitie, Canon of the Cathedrall Churches of Sarisburie, Welles and Bristow, Residentiary in the Cathedrall Churche of Welles, and Chauncellour of the Same Churche: with a Repertorie or Table, Directinge to many Notable Matters Expressed in the Same Sermons* (London: Robert Caly, 1557), passim; and Hugh Latimer, *27 Sermons Preached by ... Maister Hugh Latimer, as Well Such as in Tymes Past Haue Bene Printed, as Certayne Other ... Neuer Yet Set Forth in Print ... 9. Sermons Vpon Certayne Gospels and Epistles* (London: John Day, 1562), p. 115.

48 John Bale, *Illustrium Maioris Britanniae Scriptorum* (Ipswich: Ioannem Ouerton, 1548), p. B6; and is discussed in Parry, 'Berosus and the Protestants,' pp. 1–21.

49 Edmund Bonner, *A Profitable and Necessarye Doctryne, with Certain Homilies ... Edmund Byshop of London, for the Instruction and Information of the People Beynge Within His Diocese of London* (London: J. Cawoode, 1555), p. 1.

50 Wolfgang Musculus, *Mosis Genesim Plenissimi Commentarii* (Basel: Iannis Heruggii, 1565), p. 250; Whitford, *The Curse of Ham in the Early Modern Era*, p. 77.

51 The works of Thomas More include: William Rastell (ed.), Thomas More, *The Works of Sir Thomas More Knyght ... The First Boke* (London: John Cawod, Richard Tottell, 1528, 1557), passim; Thomas More, John Holt, *Lac Puero M Holti Mylke for Chyldren, (A Latin Grammar, with Two Epigrams)* (London: Wynkyn de Worde, 1508?), passim; Alvaro De Silva (ed.), Thomas More, *The Last Letters of Thomas More* (Grand Rapids, MI/Cambridge: W.B. Eerdmans, 2000), passim; on the influence of books such as *Utopia* see Anthony Pagden, *The Languages of Political Theory in Early Modern Europe* (Cambridge: Cambridge University Press, 1987), pp. 123–157; the author acknowledges that *Utopia* only

became popular in England after More's death; Thomas More was made a Patron Saint of Statesmen and Politicians on 31 October 2000 by Pope Paul II, see John Paul, *Apostolic Letter, Issued Motu Proprio, Proclaiming Saint Thomas More Patron of Politicians and Statesmen* (Vatican: Libreria Editrice Vaticana, 2000), http://w2.vatican.va/content/john-paul-ii/en/motu_proprio/documents/hf_jp-ii_motu-proprio_20001031_thomas-more.html.

52 The author was one of the first to discuss this work on early modern ethnology in Onyeka, *Blackamoores*, pp. 53–54.

53 Not to be confused with 'necromancers,' in the context he appears to be referring to Animism – not merely 'the Black arts' as we may assume, see Rastell (ed.), More, *The Works of Sir Thomas More*, p. 120.

54 Marion Leathers Kuntz (tr., ed.), Jean Bodin, *Colloquium of the Seven about Secrets of the Sublime* (Princeton, NJ/London: Princeton University Press, 1975), pp. xv–xxviii, xlvii–lxvi (family of man), 144, 145, 146, 147, 153, 162 (harmony of music, food and man is an ideal), 470, 471 (persecution of Moors of Spain morally wrong); by contrast one of Bodin's other major works expresses religious intolerance of witchcraft: *De la Demonomanie des Sorciers …* (Paris: Du Puys, 1580), passim.

55 A dramatic representation of their views may be seen in the speeches of Aaron 'the Moor' in William Shakespeare, 'Titus Andronicus,' (1588–1593), in Proudfoot, Kastan (eds.), *Arden Shakespeare*, p. 42, L. 100–105, 'Coal-Black is better than another hue/ In that it scorns to bear another hue/ For all the water in the ocean/ Can never turn the swan's black legs to white'; and Niger's speech in Ben Jonson's *The Character of Two Royall Masques*, pp. 3–5:

> Yet, since the fabulous voices of some few/ Poor brain-sick men, styled poets here with you/ Have, with such envy of their graces, sung/ The painted beauties other empires sprung/ Letting their loose and winged fictions fly/ To infect all climates, yea, our [Black] purity.

The Moorish King's speeches in Thomas Middleton's pageant, *The Triumphs of Truth …* (London: Nicholas Okes, 1613), pp. 1, 21, 22, 23: 'Is it at me as my complexion draw …/ [Have they not seen] A king so blacke before.'

56 Hiob Ludolf used the term 'Indian' to refer to those people that bordered the Indian Ocean including Africans in East Africa, see Hiob Ludolf that quoted the Ethiopian Abba Gorgoryos (1595–1658) in *A New History of Ethiopia … Vulgarly, Though Erroneously Called the Empire of Prester John …* (London: Samuel Smith, 1684), pp. 8–10; the term 'Inde' is

discussed in more detail in the following: Sidney Lee, 'Caliban's Visits to England,' *Cornhill Magazine*, 34 (1913), pp. 333–345; Bolton (ed.), *Alien Communities of London in the Fifteenth Centuries*, pp. 29, 42; and *The Oxford English Dictionary*, pp. 815, 880, 1171; it is also used in the word 'Indian' and 'infidel' and can suggest otherness or simply being a non-Christian. The term was generic but More's focus appeared to be on people 'of colour' and not those who have a different religion or culture.

57 Rastell (ed.), More, *The First Boke*, pp. 125–126.

58 Ibid.

59 Ibid., p. 127.

60 Elizabeth Francis Rogers (ed.), Thomas More, *The Correspondence of Sir Thomas More* (Princeton, NJ: Princeton University Press, 1947), p. 4; Onyeka, *Blackamoores*, pp. 114–117, 242–264; Sherwood, 'Blacks in Elizabethan England,' pp. 40–42; and Habib, *Black Lives*, pp. 274–294.

61 David Northrup, *Africa's Discovery of Europe: 1450–1850* (New York/Oxford: Oxford University Press, 2013), passim.

62 Origen, 'The Homilies of Origen,' repeated in Iyengar, *Shades of Difference*, pp. 19, 48, 67, 92–93; also see Gay Byron, *Symbolic Blackness and Ethnic Difference in Early Christian Literature* (London: Routledge, 2003), pp. 73–74.

63 Rastell (ed.), More, *The First Boke*, p. 125.

64 Heliotropism is an idea that the sun is the cause of Africans' blackness, see Siobhan Collins, Louise Denmead, ' "There Is All Africa [...] Within Us": Language, Generation and Alchemy in Browne's Explication of Blackness,' in Kathryn Murphy, Richard Todd (eds.), *'A Man Very Well Studyed': New Contexts for Thomas Browne* (Leiden/Boston, MA: Brill, 2008), pp. 127–146. For a more detailed discussion on heliotropism see Iyengar, *Shades of Difference*, pp. 6–8, 84–85.

65 Rastell (ed.), More, *The First Boke*, p. 125.

66 Ibid., pp. 126–127.

67 Francis Bacon, 'Experiment Solitary Touching the Coloration of Black and Tawny Moors,' *Novum Organum* (1620), in James Spedding (ed.), *The Works of Francis Bacon Collected and Edited by James Spedding ...* (London: Longman and Co., 1857), p. 473.

68 The 'Bacon Method' is discussed in Michel Malherbe, Markku Peltonen (ed.), *The Cambridge Companion to Bacon* (Cambridge: Cambridge University Press, 1996), pp. 75–99.

69 Bacon, *Novum Organam*, p. 473.

70 Interestingly, Hiob Ludolf quoted the Ethiopian Abba Gorgoryos (1595–1658) and others that claimed the River Niger was a tributary of the River Nile and both were Black in origin and colour, see Ludolf, *A New History of Ethiopia*, pp. 4, 33, 40, 41.

71 On this African presence see London, GL Ms 9243–9245 (St Botolph without Aldgate), GL Ms 4310, GL Ms 9222; Author unknown, *St Martin in the Fields Parish Register*, Volume 1 (London: publisher unknown, 27 September 1571), p. 116; Plymouth and West Devon Record Office, Plymouth, St Andrews/MF1–4; Devon Record Office, East Allington/20/08/1577 PR; and Northampton Records Office, Northampton, Microfiche 120, pp. 1–3; Onyeka, *Blackamoores*, pp. 152–194.

72 See Deborah Gabriel, *Layers of Blackness: Colourism in the African Diaspora* (London: Imani Media, 2007), passim; Kathy Russell, Midge Wilson, *The Colour Complex: The Politics of Skin Colour among African Americans* (Waterlooville: Anchor Books, 1992), passim; for definitions of 'dark-skinned' see Asante, Mazama, *Encyclopedia of Black Studies*, p. 370.

73 On the textures of African people's hair see: Andrew Boorde, *Introduction to the Book of Knowledge ...* (London: William Copeland, 1550), pp. 88–89; George *Best, A True Discourse ...* (London: H. Bynyman, 1578), pp. 28–32; John Minsheu, *A Dictionarie in Spanish and English ...* (London: E. Bollifant, 1599), p. 72; Blount (tr.), Conestaggio, *The Historie of the Uniting of the Kingdom of Portugal to the Crowne of Castill*, pp. 1, 5, 7, 39; and Pory (tr.), Africanus, *A Geographical Historie of Africa*, p. 6; Braun, Weinberg, *Ethno/Graphie*, p. 374 ('nine ether hair').

74 On 'alchemical' transformations please see Rafael Velez Nunez, 'Beyond the Emblem: Alchemical Albedo in Ben Jonson's The Masque of Blackness.' *Sederi* 8 (1997), pp. 257–263; for a fictionalised dramatisation of this alchemical transformation see Onyeka, *Blackamoores*, pp. xxv–xxvi, 44–46, 59, 66, 78(n63), 113.

75 Bacon, *Novum Organum*, p. 473.

76 Ibid., p. 473.

77 The term 'only skin deep' is often used to suggest that colour complexion is superficial, as regards biological and/or genetic matters, but not necessarily when it comes to social and political issues etc., see Cedric Herring, Verna Keith, Hayword Derrick Horton, *Skin Deep: How Race and Complexion Matter in the 'Colour-Blind' Era* (Champaign, IL: University of Illinois Press, 2004), passim; and see Nina G. Jablonski, *Living Color: The Biological and Social Meaning of Skin Color* (Berkeley, CA/London/Los Angeles, CA: University of California Press, 2012), passim.

78 For more on these writers see Bertrand Russell, *History of Western Philosophy* (London: George Allen Unwin, 1945), introduction; and Robert Audi (ed.), *The Cambridge Dictionary of Western Philosophy* (Cambridge: Paw Prints, 2008), introduction.

79 Bacon, *Novum Organum*, p. 70.

80 For more on Scaliger and Viterbo see Anthony Grafton, Ann Blair (eds.), *The Transmission of Culture in Early Modern Europe* (Philadelphia, PA: University of Pennsylvania Press, 2004), pp. 1–8, 8–39; and Anthony Grafton, *What Was History? The Art of History in Early Modern Europe* (Cambridge: Cambridge University Press, 2012), pp. 245–246.

81 See Floyd-Wilson, *English Ethnicity and Race*, pp. 1–20, 23–67; Read, Evans (eds.), *Maladies and Medicine*, pp. 4–65; for a cross-cultural perspective on the theory of the humors see Arikha, *Passion and Tempers*, passim.

82 Francis Bacon, *Essays or Counsels, Civil & Moral, of Sir Francis Bacon, Lord Verulam … Whereunto Is Added the Wisdom of the Ancients … Of the Colours of Good and Evil* (1625, London: H. Herringman, 1696), p. 3.

83 Biological determinism is a widely discussed issue, see Richard Lewontin, Steven Rose, Leon J. Kamin, *Not in Our Genes: Biology, Ideology, and Human Nature* (Chicago, IL: Haymarket Books, 2017), passim; Ann Arbor Science for the People Collective, *Biology as a Social Weapon/The Ann Arbor Science for the People Editorial Collective* (Minneapolis, MN: Burgess, 1977), passim; Chris Willmott, *Biological Determinism, Free Will and Moral Responsibility: Insights from Genetics and Neuroscience* (New York: Springer, 2016), pp. 19–37; W. Carson Byrd, Matthew W. Hughey, 'Biological Determinism and Racial Essentialism: The Ideological Double Helix of Racial Inequality.' *Annals of the American Academy of Political and Social Science* 661:1 (10 August 2015), pp. 8–22.

84 Aristotle, *Politics*, Book VII, Chapter 13, quoted in Arthur Stephen McGrade, John Kilcullen (eds., trs.), *Texts in the History of Political Thought: William of Ockham, A Letter to the Friars Minor and Other Writings* (Cambridge: Cambridge University Press, 1995), p. 150; and discussed in Stefano Fogelberg Rota, Andreas Hellerstedt, *Shaping Heroic Virtue: Studies in the Art and Politics of Supereminence in Europe and Scandinavia* (Leiden/Boston, MA: Brill, 2015), pp. 20–21(n); there is an acknowledgement that in other works Aristotle stated opposing theories.

85 On the divine right of kings see: James I, *The True Lawe of Free Monarchies: or, the Reciprock and Mutuall Dutie Betwixt a Free King, and His Natural Subiectes* (Edinburgh: Robert Waldegrave, 1598), passim; James I speech to Houses of Parliament, Whitehall, London, 21 March 1610, reported in Joseph Robson Tanner, *Constitutional Documents of the Reign of James I A.D. 1603–1624* (Cambridge: Cambridge University Press, 1960), p. 15; Robert Filmer, *The Necessity of the Absolute Power of All Kings: And in Particular of the King of England*

(1648, London: W. H. & T. F., 1680), passim; John Neville Figgs, *The Theory of the Divine Right of Kings: Prince Consort Dissertation, 1892* (Cambridge: University of Cambridge, 1892), passim.

86   For example on colour, Aristotle's writings questioned why 'the seede of a man is white, and the seede of a woman red?' His answer was:

> it is white in man, by reason of his great heate, and because it is digested better, and made white in the stones, the flesh of which is white, as the flesh of the pappes. But the seede of a woman is red, because it is the superfluitie of the second digestion, which is done in the liuer, which is red. Orels we may say, that it is because the flowers is corrupt indigested bloud, and therefore it hath the colour of bloud.

Aristotle, *In the Problemes of Aristotle with Other Philosophers and Phisitions. Wherein Are Contayned Diuers Questions, with Their Answers, Touching the Estate of Mans Bodie* (London: Arn Hatfield, 1607), D. 4.

87   Albertus Magnus was a thirteenth-century Bavarian bishop who wrote on the classics, for a discussion on his work see Jean Paul Tilmann, *An Appraisal of the Geographical Works of Albertus Magnus and His Contributions to Geographical Thought* (Detroit, MI: University of Michigan, 1971), pp. 101–108; for speculation on his ethnicity see Bayo Akerele, *Black Restoration Is a Black Responsibility: Nigeria and the Black Leadership Imperative* (Benin City: University of Benin, 2000), p. 32.

88   Bacon, *Wisdom of the Ancients*, n.p.

89   Thomas Underdowne (tr.), *An Æthiopian Historie, Written in Greeke by Heliodorus: very Wittie and Pleasaunt, Englished by Thomas Underdoune. With the Argumente of Euery Booke, Sette before the Whole Woorke* (London: Henry Wykes, 1569), passim; Iyengar, *Shades of Difference*, p. 21.

90   Augustine of Hippo, *City of God*; quoted in Lewis Lewkenor, Ferdinand Walker, Antonio de Torquemada, *The Spanish Mandeuile of Miracles. Or The Garden of Curious Flowers VVherin are Handled Sundry Points of Humanity, Philosophy, Diuinitie, and Geography, Beautified with Many Strange and Pleasant Histories. First written in Spanish, by Anthonio De Torquemeda, and Out of that Tongue Translated into English* (London: James Roberts, 1600), n.p.

91   See Onyeka, *Blackamoores*, pp. 59–60.

92   For more on chromatics please see the excellent book by John Gage, *Color and Meaning: Art, Science and Symbolism* (Berkeley, CA: University of California Press, 1994), pp. 7–67, 67–90, 261–270; and John Gage, *Colour and Culture: Practice and Meaning from Antiquity to Abstraction* (Berkeley, CA: University of California Press, 1999),

pp. 29–39, 91–129, 213–247. Of course the point raised here about Browne is debatable and others would claim that later writers such as François Bernier (1620–1688) were more influential.

93   The term 'political correctness' was actually used in an ironic way by those classified as 'liberals' or the 'new left' etc. The general public feels it is a way of censoring or limiting racist, sexist, homophobic, etc. speech, words, images etc. It has now become a tool that the 'right' use to criticise the 'left,' see Geoffrey Hughes, *Political Correctness: A History of Semantics and Culture* (London: John Wiley and Sons, 2011), passim; John K. Wilson, *The Myth of Political Correctness: The Conservative Attack on Higher Education* (Durham, NC: Duke University Press, 1995), passim.

94   Often this is attributed to François Bernier (1622–1688), for more on his work see François Bernier, 'A New Division of the Earth,' *Journal des Sçavans* (24 April 1684), in T. Bendyphe (tr.) 'Memoirs Read before the Anthropological Society of London,' Volume 1 (1863–1864), pp. 360–364.

95   Browne, *Pseudodoxia Epidemica*, p. 322.

96   Ibid., p. 322.

97   The ramifications of these different terms are discussed by the author in earlier work, see Onyeka, *Blackamoores*, pp. 41–106; Onyeka, 'What's in a Name?,' pp. 34–39; and for a different view on 'race' in early modern England see Loomba, Burton, *Race in Early Modern England*, passim.

98   Browne, *Pseudodoxia Epidemica*, pp. 323–324.

99   Ibid., p. 324.

100   Ibid.; similar ideas are also quoted in Greek classical legends and alluded to by Leo Aficanus.

101   Browne, *Pseudodoxia Epidemica*, pp. 323–324.

102   Ibid., p. 324.

103   Ibid., pp. 324–325.

104   Juan Huarte, *Examin de Ingenious Para les Sciencias* (1588), p. 250, quoted in Schorsch, *Swimming the Christian Atlantic*, p. 361. Huarte was actually born in Navarre on the border of Spain and France.

105   Henry Anthony Jetto, 21 March 1596, Baptism, Worcestershire Archives, Worcestershire, *Holt Parish Register*, ref. 985, p. 19; his will is at 'Will of Henrie Jetto' Will number 102, dated and signed on 20 September 1626, but executed 13 September 1638, Worcestershire Archives, Worcester; see Onyeka, *Blackamoores*, pp. 239–241.

106   Worcestershire Archives and Archaeology Service, Worcester, *Holt Parish Register*, ref. 985, p. 19. Henrie's baptism, thereafter the same register 1598–1640, with other descendants noted during that period

and after. Significantly, a possible modern day descendant of Henrie Jetto, Grata Jeter Clarke, suggests a different origin for the family name, see *The Jeter Mosaic: Seven Centuries in the History of a Family* (Mount Pleasant, SC: Arcadia-Clarke, 1987), pp. 8–57, 739 (definitions of the word 'Jetto'), 761 (origins of the 'first' Jetto), 772 (Jetto's family).

107 More details can be found on this family in Onyeka, *Blackamoores*, pp. 239–241, 259–260, 262–264.

108 Ibid.

109 On racial distinctiveness see William Wright, *Black History and Black Identity: A Call for a New Historiography* (Westport, CT: Greenwood Publishing, 2002), pp. 99–101.

110 This is a well documented subject, see books such as David Dabydeen, Paul Edwards (eds.), *Black Writers in Britain 1760–1890* (Edinburgh: Edinburgh University, 1991), passim; Paul Edwards, James Walvin, 'Africans in Britain, 1500–1800,' in *The African Diaspora: Interpretive Essays* (Cambridge, MA: Harvard University Press, 1976), pp. 173–204; Faiza Ghazala, Greater London Council Ethnic Minorities Unit, *A History of the Black Presence in London* (London: Greater London Council, 1986), pp. 7–8; Hall, *Things of Darkness*, p. 13; Folarin Shyllon, *Black People in Britain 1555–1883* (Oxford: Oxford University Press, 1977), preface, pp. 1–10; James Walvin, *Black and White: The Negro in English Society, 1555–1945* (London: Allen Lane, 1973), pp. 1–31; Walvin, *Black Ivory*, preface; Charles Malcolm Macinnes, *England and Slavery* (London: Arrowsmith, 1934), pp. 107–139; Gretchen Holbrook Gerzina, *Black London: Life before Emancipation* (New Brunswick, NJ: Rutgers University, 1997), p. 5; Kathy (Kathleen) Chater, *Untold Histories: Black People in England and Wales during the Period of the British Slave Trade, c. 1660–1807* (Manchester: Manchester University Press, 2008), pp. 23–30; and Rogers, *Nature Knows No Colour-Line*, p. 156 quotes 'Anglicanus,' *Gentleman's Magazine* 34 (October 1764), pp. 493, 495.

111 Guildhall Record Office, London, GL Ms 9222/1, Parish register, p. 560, 'Anne Vause a Black-more wife to Anthonie Vause, Trompetter of the said Country,' burial 24 April 1618.

112 For a discussion on this see Onyeka, *Blackamoores*, pp. 230–231.

113 'Salomon Cowrdrer of Poplar' was also a sailor, who 'came out of the East Indies,' which may mean the term 'niger' was used in this case to refer to a dark-skinned 'Black person' that was not directly from Africa. A similar view is shared by Miranda Kaufmann in 'Africans in Early Modern London,' www.mirandakaufmann.com/lmaafricans. html, accessed 02/04/2018. However, the term could also refer to

someone of African descent that lived in Asia; or the term 'East Indies' was a reference to another region altogether such as the eastern side of the Caribbean op. 'West Indies.'

114 Guildhall Record Office London, GL Ms 9245, p. 37.

115 Ibid., GL Ms 9245 p. 23.

116 Ibid., GL Ms 9245 p. 53.

117 See Onyeka, *Blackamoores*, pp. 226-231, 249-260; Habib, *Black Lives*, pp. 274-294; Sherwood, 'Blacks in Elizabethan England,' pp. 40-42.

118 Edward Lopez was a Portuguese explorer who travelled to Angola in 1578. The accounts of his voyage are included in John Green, Astley Thomas (eds.), *A New General Collection of Voyages and Travels ... in Europe, Asia, Africa and America ... Also the Manners and Customs of the Several Inhabitants ...: Consisting of the Most Esteemed Relations, which Have Been Hitherto Published in Any Language ...*, Volume 3 (The Hague: Library of Netherlands, 1746), pp. 132-137; there was also an Andrew Battell of Leigh who lived in Angola as a slave in the sixteenth century, see Onyeka, *Blackamoores*, pp. 213-214; Andrew Battell, *The Strange Adventures of Andrew Battell of Leigh, in Angola and Adjoining Regions* (London: Hakluyt Society, 1901), pp. 110, 136.

119 Browne, *Pseudodoxia Epidemica*, pp. 324-325.

120 Ibid., p. 328.

121 Ibid., p. 329. Browne also wrote about how dark-skinned Africans did not live in North Africa. Of course that was incorrect.

122 Ibid., p. 329. A similar sentiment is shared in Abraham Harwtell's translation of Odoardo Lopez' work, by the Italian Phlilpo Pigafetta, *A Report of the Kingdom of Congo, A Region of Africa ...* (London: John Wolfe, 1597), n.p.:

> But because neither any ancient Writer before this age, nor he himselfe, hath euer been able to declare the true cause of these colours in humane bodies, very honestly and modestly he leaueth it undecided, and referreth it to some secret of Nature, which hitherto hath been knowne to God alone, and neuer as yet reuealled to man.

123 Browne, *Pseudodoxia Epidemica*, p. 329.

124 Ibid., p. 329.

125 Ibid., p. 330.

126 Ibid., p. 331.

127 Ibid., p. 330.

128 Quotations, ibid., pp. 325-331.

129 Ibid., p. 331.

130 See Williams, *The Destruction of Black Civilisation*, passim; Naim Akbar, *Chains and Images of Psychological Slavery* (Jersey City, NJ: New Mind Productions, 1984), pp. 1–8; and Naim Akbar, *Breaking the Chains of Psychological Slavery* (Jersey City, NJ: Mind Productions and Associates, 1996), pp. 1–8, 27.

131 Browne, *Pseudodoxia Epidemica*, p. 332.

132 Quotations from ibid., p. 333. This idea was repeated in poetry and prose, as an aside or a central theme, by many early modernists discussed in this book and in Onyeka, *Blackamoores*. For example, by William Davenant, as an aside in his poem, *Gondibert: An Heroick Poem* ... (London: Thomas Newcomb for John Holden, 1651), n.p. 'Black beauty (which black Meroens had prais'd/ Above their own) gravely adorn'd each part/ In Stone, from Nyle's head Quarries, slowly rais'd,/ And slowlyer polish'd by Numidi an Art .../ Here all the Ornament is rev'rend black.'

133 Browne, *Pseudodoxia Epidemica*, p. 332.

134 Ibid., pp. 332–333.

135 Juliana Berners (1395) in Elizabeth Spearing (ed.), *Revelations of Divine Love* (London: Penguin, 1998), p. 54; The term 'comely' was often used to complement the 'simple perfect blackness,' as echoed in early modern Bibles in the *Song of Solomon*, 'though art' or 'I am Black but comely,' etc. See Iyengar, *Shades of Difference*, pp. 44–49, 51, 58, 61, 62–63, 'The Anglican Church is both black and comely,' pp. 65–68.

136 The author is aware that this is an extremely important issue; some of these matters are discussed in more detail below and in Onyeka, *Blackamoores*, pp. 67–70; readers may also wish to examine the work of Joan E. Taylor, *What Did Jesus Look Like?* (London: T&T Clarke, 2018), passim; William Mosley, *What Color Was Jesus?* (Chicago, IL: African American Images, 1987), passim; Edward J. Blum, Paul Harvey, *The Color of Christ: The Son of God and the Saga of Race in America* (Chapel Hill, NC: University of North Carolina Press, 2012), passim; and the work of Ishakamusa Barashango; but ultimately the wider issues related to this matter require a more detailed exposition.

137 Browne, *Pseudodoxia Epidemica*, pp. 335–338.

138 Ibid., pp. 335–338.

139 Melanin has been widely discussed and debated, see Timothy Owens Moore, *The Science of Melanin* (Redan, GA: Zamani Press, 2004), passim; Samuel M. Peck, *Pigment (Melanin): Studies of the Human Skin After Application of Thorium X with Special Reference to the Origin and Function of Dendritic Cells* (Chicago, IL: Medical Association, 1930), passim; Dr Sebi argues that it is not melanin but carbon, 'Dr Sebi What Is Carbon, Melanin and Protein?' *YouTube*, published 26/07/2016, www.youtube.com/watch?v=YL7dlpIauEE, accessed 02/04/2018.

140 Browne, *Pseudodoxia Epidemica*, p. 334.

141 There were of course other early modern English writers that discussed ethnology, one of them was John Bulwer. He stated he did not know what the origin of blackness was, but nevertheless described Africans using derogatory terms, see John Bulwer, *Anthropometamorphosis: Man Transform'd; or, the Artificial Changeling. Historically Presented, in the Mad and Cruel Gallantry, Foolish Bravery, Ridiculous Beauty, Filthy Finenesse, and Loathsome Lovelinesse of Most Nations, Fashioning & Altering Their Bodies from the Mould Intended by Nature. With a Vindication of the Regular Beauty and Honesty of Nature. And an Appendix of the Pedigree of the English Gallant* (London: William Hunt, 1654), pp. A3–A4. However, his prime purpose seemed to have been to advocate the virtue of the 'English gallant' over 'other nations'; for a different view see David M. Goldenberg, *The Origin and History of the Curse of Ham* (Boston, MA/Berlin: Walter de Gruyter, 2017), pp. 130–131; Iyengar, *Shades of Difference*, pp. 134, 207–208.

142 Robert Runia has a different view to that expressed in this chapter, that Boyle's comments show the beginning of a racialised discourse which gives birth to scientific racism, in 'Great Heads, Great Minds and the Genesis of Scientific Racism.' *Journal for Early Modern Cultural Studies* 15:2 (Spring 2015), pp. 112–118.

143 See Cristina Malcolmson, Henry Turner, *Studies of Skin Colour in the Early Royal Society: Boyle, Cavendish, Swift* (London: Ashgate, 2013), passim; and see Patricia Sloane (ed.), *Primary Sources: Selected Writings on Colour from Aristotle to Albers* (New York: Design Press, 1991), pp. 4–5 (Leonardo Da Vinci), 10–11 (Boyle); and William R. Newman, Lawrence M. Principe, *Alchemy Tried in the Fire: Starkey, Boyle, and the Fate of Helmontian Chymistry* (Chicago, IL: Chicago University Press, 2005), passim, this book also includes the work of George Starkey, a colonial Bermudian born of English descent, that had lived in New England. His books on nature and science include *The Marrow of Alchemy* (1654), *The Reformed Commonwealth of Bees* (1655), *The Dignity of Kingship Asserted* (1655), *Three Tracts of the Great Medicine of Philosophers for Humane and Metalline Bodies* (London: T. Sowle, 1694), passim.

144 Robert Boyle, *Experiments and Considerations Touching Colours* (London: Henry Herringman, 1664), p. 27.

145 Ibid., p. 29.

146 Ibid., p. 33.

147 Ibid., p. 34.

148 Ibid., pp. 41–42, Boyle suggests 'a solution of silver will dye hair' a 'black colour.'

149 Ibid., p. 42.

150 Ibid., p. 42.

151 Ibid., p. 44.

152 Ibid., p. 46.

153 Ibid., p. 46.

154 The phrase 'here amongst us' was used by Laura Hunt Yunglbut, *Strangers Settled Here Amongst Us: Policies, Perceptions and the Presence of Aliens in Elizabethan England* (London/New York: Routledge, 1994), passim.

155 Boyle, *Experiments and Considerations*, p. 45.

156 See Howard Marchitello, *Narrative and Meaning in Early Modern England: Browne's Skull and Other Histories* (Cambridge/New York: Cambridge University Press, 1997), pp. 124–189; Silvia De Renzi (ed.), *Pathology in Practice: Diseases and Dissections in Early Modern Europe* (London: Routledge, 2017), passim; Jonathan Sawday, *The Body Emblazoned: Dissection and the Human Body in Renaissance Culture* (London: Routledge, 2005), passim.

157 Boyle also wrote, in *Experiments and Considerations*, p. 46: 'on the other hand, white people removing to very hot climates, have their skins … tho' neither they nor their children are observ'd, even in the country or negroes, to descend to a true black.' But he acknowledged that it was possible for white people to have Black children and Africans to have white children. Boyle, as with Browne, stated that the original man was white, but did not rule Africans out of inclusion in the family of Adam, simply because they were Black.

Five

1 *The Returns of the Constables of Brickendon*, 26 July 1631, DP/48/1/1/, Herts Record Office, Thomas Inverness, Ruple Fearye, *The Returns of the Constables of the Hamlet of Brickenden of the Objectives and Churchwardens of the Parishe of All Saints in Hertford Whose Names Are Subject …*, Volume 1 (unpublished), p. B3.

2 The term 'folk devil' was coined by Stanley Cohen, in, *Folk Devils and Moral Panics* (St Albans: Paladin, 1973), passim; the idea of 'moral panics' was discussed in detail by authors such as Stuart Hall in C. Critcher, T. Jefferson (eds.), *Policing the Crisis: Mugging, the State and Law and Order* (London: Macmillan, 1978), passim.

3 On the issue of intertextualism see Nora Shuart-Faris, David Bloome, *Uses of Intertextuality in Classroom and Educational Research* (Connecticut: Information Age, 2004), pp. 3–17, 353–373.

4 The fascination with Othello is a constant feature with academics, see Piedra, 'In Search of the Black Stud,' pp. 22–44; Habib, *Shakespeare and Race*, pp. 35, 49, 74; Matar, *Islam in Britain,* pp. 50–70; Fiedler, *The Stranger in Shakespeare*, pp. 139–199; Hall, *Things of Darkness*, p. 211; Hendricks, 'Surveying "Race" in Shakespeare,' pp. 1–23; Kirkpatrick Hunter, 'Othello and Colour Prejudice,' p. 153; Braude, 'The Sons of Noah and the Construction of Ethnic and Geographical Identities in the Medieval and Early Modern Periods,' pp. 103–142; Macdonald, 'Black Ram, White Ewe,' pp. 188–207. Other authors including Jonathan Burton, Ania Loomba and Patricia Parker are listed in the Selected Bibliography; the author acknowledges his own fascination, see Onyeka, *Young Othello: The Tragedy of the White Swan* (London: Narrative Eye, 2016/2017), passim.

5 Kenneth Little, *Negroes in Britain* (London: Routledge and Kegan Paul, 1947), p. 166; however, Little's book provides excellent information on the African presence in South Wales during the nineteenth and twentieth centuries.

6 Fryer, *Staying Power*, pp. 1–14, 113–133, 146, 191–236; the quotation is from Scott, *History of the Moorish Empire in Europe*, p. 355.

7 On the importance of Fryer's work see the following: James Walvin in Peter Fryer, *Rhythms of Resistance: African Musical Heritage in Brazil* (London: Pluto, 2000), p. 2; Marika Sherwood, 'Britain, Slavery and the Trade in Enslaved Africans.' *History in Focus* 12 (spring 2007), www.history.ac.uk/ihr/Focus/Slavery/articles/sherwood.html, accessed 12/03/2008; Gemma Romain, *Connecting Histories: A Comparative Exploration of African-Caribbean and Jewish History and Memory in Modern Britain* (London: Keagan Paul, 2006), pp. 84, 204–207; Qualifications and Curriculum Authority (QCA) Website, 'Innovating with History,' www.qca.org.uk/history/innovating/history_matters/worked_for_me/ks3/cameo9.htm, accessed 07/18/2008.

8 Matar, *Islam in Britain*, p. 2.

9 The term 'sub-Sahara Africa' and 'sub-Saharan African' have been used by the United Nations and a range of academic and non-academic writers since the 1950s. For recent commentaries on this please see Charles Agyemang, 'Negro, Black African, African Caribbean, African American or What? Labelling African Origin People in the 21st Century.' *Journal of Epidemiology and Community Health* 59:12 (2 September 2005), pp. 1014–1018; Faith Karimi, 'Group: Use of "Sub Saharan Africa" Disparaging,' *CNN*, 20 September 2010, http://edition.cnn.com/2010/WORLD/africa/09/20/sub.saharan.africa/index.html; Chika Onyeani, 'Contemptuousness of Sub-Saharan Africa,' *Worldpress.org*, 16 July 2009,

http://worldpress.org/Africa/3382.cfm; Peter J. Aspinall, *The Africa Diaspora Population in Britain: Migrant Identities and Experiences* (New York: Palgrave Macmillan, 2016), pp. 84–102.

10 Hall, *Things of Darkness*, p. 211.

11 Habib, *Black Lives*, pp. 1–69; Ungerer, *The Mediterranean Apprenticeship of British Slavery*, pp. 1–62.

12 On racism in the twentieth and twentieth-first centuries one may consult this diverse range of authors: Arthur Schomburg in Benjamin P. Bowser, Louis Kushnick, Paul Grant (eds.), *Against the Odds: Scholars Who Challenged Racism in the Twentieth Century* (Amherst, MA: University of Massachusetts Press, 2002), passim; Fuller, *The United Independent*, passim; Haki R. Madhubuti, *Enemies: The Clash of Races* (Chicago, IL: Third World Press, 1978), passim; Painter, *The History of White People*, pp. 59–91, 190–212, 256–278, 311–327, 343–374; Haki R. Madhubuti, *Black Men: Obsolete, Single, Dangerous? Afrikan American Families in Transition: Essays in Discovery, Solution and Hope* (Chicago, IL: Third World Press, 2000), passim. Of course some English early modernists may have perceived Africans as a threat, but the contention is that these people would have been far fewer in number than is often portrayed by modern historians.

13 To reiterate: the enslavement of African people was not a 'trade' in the strictest sense of the word, and therefore it did not have any 'byproducts.'

14 Considerable confusion has unfortunately been propagated on this matter, some of it has roots in academia, other sources are more nebulous. For example, there is a suggestion that two letters written in 1596, and a 1601 Proclamation, did legalise the enslavement of Africans in Tudor England. These issues have been analysed at length in Onyeka, *Blackamoores*, pp. 1–40, 211–238.

15 A similar view is expressed by Kwame Anthony Appiah, Henry Louis Gates, *Africana: The Encyclopedia of the African and African American Experience* (Oxford: Oxford University Press, 2005), preface and introduction.

16 Maria's records are in Wiltshire and Swindon Records Office, Wiltshire Family History Society, *Calne Parish Register, 1538–1602*, Volume 1 (London: A. Webb, 1944), n.p.; Wiltshire and Swindon Records Office, *Calne Parish Register*, ref. 2083/1, n.p.

17 Jules Janick, *Horticultural Reviews*, Volume 44 (London: John Wiley and Sons, 2011), pp. 23–88.

18 In Onyeka, *Blackamoores*, pp. 46, 211; the name of the town is spelt how it is in her record: Colne. In modern English the name is spelt with an 'a.'

19 There was more than one record for Maria Mandula where she was described in this way, see Wiltshire and Swindon Records Office, *Calne Parish Register*, n.p., 10 December 1585, burial, etc.

20 For more on the terms used to refer to Africans at this time see Onyeka, 'What's in a name?,' pp. 34–39; Onyeka, *Blackamoores*, pp. 41–90; the word 'Ethiopian' was interchangeable with the words 'Blackamoore,' 'Moor' and later 'Negro.'

21 Ibid.; For a definition of the word 'Ethiopia' see *The Oxford English Dictionary*, p. 423; *Oxford Dictionary of English*, p. 595; for more on the Greek myth itself see Parry, 'Berosus and the Protestants,' pp. 1–21.

22 Isidore, *Ethimologiarum Isidori Hispalensis Episcopi*, pp. 190–193; Barney, *The Etymologies of Isidore of Seville*, n.p.; this view was also articulated by Iyengar in *Shades of Difference*, pp. 29, 34, 248(n).

23 See Matteo Salvadore, *The African Prester John and the Birth of Ethiopian–European Relations, 1402–1555* (London: Routledge, 2016), passim.

24 Letter signed by King Henry IV to 'Prester John King of Abyssinia,' 20 October 1422, see Northrup, *Africa's Discovery of Europe*, p. 65; see Richard Pankhurst's book, *Historic Images of Ethiopia* (Addis Ababa: Shama Books, 2005), pp. 55–57. Pankhurst has English translations of various letters written to Prester John and others attributed to him.

25 Prester John appears constantly in early modern literature, see William Lithgow, *A Most Delectable, and True Discourse, of an Admired Painefull Peregrination ...* (London: Nicholas Okes, 1614), pp. S2, S3; and Hartwell (tr.), Lopez, Pigafetta, *A Report of the Kingdom of Congo, A Region of Africa*, pp. 580–581.

26 Prester John also appears in Richard Eden's *Decades of the Newe World West India*, pp. 356, 357; and Francisco Alvares, *Ho Preste Joam das Indias Verdadera das Informacam das Terras do Preste Joam Agora Nouamete Impresso, etc.* (Lisbon: L. Rodriguez, 1540), passim.

27 Anthony Gilby, *The Psamles of David, Truly Opened and Explained by Paraphasis ... Set Foorth in Latin by ... Theodore Besa, Faithfully Translated into English, by Anthonie Gilbie, and by Him Newlie Purged from Sundrie Faultes Escaped in the First Print, etc.* (London: Henrie Denham, 1581), pp. 99–100.

28 Ibid.; Jacob Joradens, *Moses and His Ethiopian Wife*, Rubens House Antwerp, oil on canvas, 106.5 × 80 cm, 1650.

29 Gilby, *The Psamles of David*, pp. 102–107.

30 Ibid., pp. 91, 99, 100 (the phrase is repeated many times). See Onyeka, *Blackamoores*, pp. 66–72, 86–90(n); see David Bindman, Henry Louis Gates, Frank M. Snowden, *The Image of the Black in*

Western Art, Volumes I–IV (New York: Harvard University Press, 2010–2014).

31 Gilby, *The Psamles of David*, pp. 92, 102–103.

32 Ibid., p. 103.

33 Ibid., p. 95; and in Isidore, *Ethimologiarum Isidori Hispalensis*, p. 28.

34 Gilby, *The Psamles of David*, p. 93.

35 Thomas Rogers (d. 1616) was a chaplain to Richard Bancroft Archbishop of Canterbury and the 'chief overseer' of the *King James Version* of the Bible, see Thomas Jones, *A Catalogue of the Collection of Tracts For and Against Popery* … (Manchester: Chetham Society, 1865), p. 7; Thomas Rogers also wrote, *The English Creed, Wherin Is Contained in Tables an Exposition on the Articles Which Every Man Is Subscribe To* (London: publisher unknown, 1579), passim; and Thomas Rogers, *A Philosophicall Discourse, Entituled the Anatomie of the Minde. Newlie Made* (London: A. Maunsell, 1576), passim.

36 Thomas Rogers (ed.), Scheltco Geveren, *Of the End of This World, and Second Coming of Christ* … (London: Henrie Middleton, 1583), p. 4:

> The chaste daughter of Sion and beloved spouse of Jesus Christ … I am not ignorant the entirely beloved spouse of Christ, thous hast been plagued now a long time for the lack of thy kinde and loving husband: which notwithstanding thou are blacke and browne, by reason of the extreme heate of the Sunne, the light of God the father, to which (as yet) thou canst not approach, yet only with all his heart embraceth thee as his friend, for fairness. For thy blackness by his holy sprite he hath turned to beautiful-nesse and thy unseeming spottes of Sinne by his precious blood are no white scene.

Also, see Onyeka, *Blackamoores*, pp. 66–72, 86–90(n), for a longer discussion on this and the question of blackness and whiteness representing sin.

37 The last quotation is from Rogers (ed.), Scheltco Geveren, *Of the End of This World*, p. 5.

38 Similar sentiments about the 'Bride of Christ' are quoted by many early modern writers such as James Thomas (tr.), Antonio Brucioli, *A Commentary upon the Canticle of Canticles, Written First in Italian by Antonio Brucioli, and Now Translated into English by Th. Iames Fellow* … (London: Printed by R. F[ield] for Tho. Man, 1598), p. 76. Some commentaries focus on the virtues of blackness, others, such as Thomas and Brucioli, concentrate on the relative juxtaposition of 'seeming' fair and 'being' Black. More early modernists are quoted in Iyengar, *Shades of Difference*, p. 19 (quotation).

39 Origen, 'The Homilies of Origen,' repeated in Iyengar, *Shades of Difference*, pp. 19, 48, 67, 92–93.

40 Quotations from Origen in Iyengar, *Shades of Difference*, pp. 92–93.

41 Richard Barnfield, *The Affectionate Shepheard. Containing the Complaint of Daphnis for the Loue of Ganymede* (London: For John Danter [Thomas Newman], 1594), pp. 1–18.

42 This idea of the virtue of blackness being not able to blush is a recurring theme in early modern literature, see the speeches of Aaron in William Shakespeare, 'Titus Andronicus,' (1588–1593), in Proudfoot, Kastan (eds.), *Arden Shakespeare*, p. 42, L. 100–105.

43 Barnfield, *The Affectionate Shepheard*, pp. 1–18.

44 Quotations, ibid.; similar ideas are expressed by Iyengar, *Shades of Difference*, pp. 58–61; for this reason she states that Protestants wear black not 'gay' or 'gawdy colours,' pp. 60–61.

45 Barnfield, *The Affectionate Shepheard*, pp. 1–18.

46 Johanna Joaneson's record are at (GL Ms 4107/2 p. 34); for more on Lady Mary Wroth see Noami J. Miller, *Changing the Subject: Mary Wroth and Figurations of Gender in Early Modern England* (Lexington, KY: The University Press of Kentucky, 1960), passim; Josephine A. Roberts, *The Poems of Lady Mary Wroth* (Baton Rouge, LA: Louisiana State University Press, 1983), passim; Paul Salzman, 'Contemporary References in Wroth's Urania,' *The Review of English Studies*, New Series, 29:114 (May 1978), pp. 178–180; Gary Waller, *The Sidney Family Romance: Mary Wroth, William Herbert, and the Early Modern Construction of Gender* (Detroit, MI: Wayne State University Press, 1993), passim; Bernadette Andrea, 'Pamphilia's Cabinet: Gendered Authorship and Empire in Lady Mary Wroth's Urania,' *English Literary History*, 68:2 (2001), pp. 335–358.

47 Jonson, *The Character of Two Royall Masques*, pp. 2–4; Andrea, 'Black Skin, The Queen's Masques, …' pp. 246–281.

48 Samuel Daniel, *The True Discription of a Royall Masque. Presented at Hampton Court, Upon Sunday Night, being the Eight of Ianuary. 1604. And Personated by the Queenes Most Excellent Majestie, Attended by Eleuen Ladies of Honour* (London: Edward Allde, 1604), Daniel wrote a negative view on the 'blackening.'

49 It is a modern facetious phrase developed in Ebonics, and related to sexual preference, but it has come to have a wider meaning, see Charles Clay Doyle, Wolfgang Mieder, *The Dictionary of Modern Proverbs* (New Haven, CT: Yale University Press, 2012), p. 22.

50 This sonnet was part of the series: Mary Wroth, *Pamphilia to Amphilanthus* (1621), it can be found with a bibliography including

commentaries at *Renascence Editions*, www.luminarium.org/renascence-editions/mary.html, accessed 05/05/2018.

51 John Churton Collins (ed.), Edward Herbert, *The Poems of Lord Herbert of Cherbury* (1665, 2nd edition, London: Chatto and Windus, 1881), pp. 6, 58, 59.

52 Ibid.

53 Ibid.; this idea is strongly supported by Iyengar, *Shades of Difference*, p. 75.

54 Arthur Dent, *The Plaine Mans Path-Way to Heauen. Wherein Euery Man May Clearly See, Whether He Shall Be Saued or Damned. Set Forth Dialogue Wise, for the Better Understanding of the Simple* (London: Robert Dexter, 1601), p. 139, 'no more than a Black-moore can change his skinne, or a Leopard his spots.'

55 On the idea of 'washing the Ethiop white' see Floyd-Wilson, *English Ethnicity and Race in Early Modern Drama*, pp. 111–130; on a metaphorical washing please see Thomas Calvert, *The Blessed Jew of Marocco; or, a Blackmoor Made White. Being a Demonstration of the True Messias Out of the Law and Prophets, by Rabbi Samuel a Jew, Turned Christian; Written First in the Arabick, After Translated into Latin, and Now Englished. To Which Are Annexed a Diatriba of the Jews' Sins, and Their Miserie All over the World. Annotations to the Book, with Large Digressions, Discovering Jewish Blindnesse …* (York: T. Broad, 1648), passim.

56 *Oxford Dictionary of English*, p. 1247 (quotations on otherness); on strangeness and otherness see Loomba, Burton, *Race in Early Modern England*, preface, introduction; and Bennett, Grossberg, Morris (eds.), *New Keywords*, pp. 249–250; and the word 'stranger' see *Oxford Dictionary of English*, p. 1746; Faggett, *Black and Other Minorities in Shakespeare's England*, pp. 1–6, 25; and Ian Smith, *Race and Rhetoric in the Renaissance: Barbarian Errors* (Basingstoke: Palgrave Macmillan, 2009), pp. 23–43, 46–62, 121.

57 The meaning of 'domiciled' is '[treating] the country … as their permanent home, or [having a] substantial connection with [it]'; the meaning of 'denizen' is an 'inhabitant of, or an alien admitted into the country that now has rights'; 'a native is one who is a citizen by birth or naturalisation,' *Oxford Dictionary of English*, pp. 464, 515, 1171; for more on these terms and others see Luu, *Immigrants and the Industries of London, 1500–1700*, pp. 42–144; and Faggett, *Black and Other Minorities*, pp. 1–6.

58 John Stow, *A Summary of the Chronicles of England, Abridged and Continued unto 1598* (1565, new edition, London: R. Bardocke, 1598), pp. 768–769; Jessica Browner, 'The Wrong Side of the River: London's Disreputable Southbank in the Sixteenth and Seventeenth Century,' *Essays in History*, 36 (1994), http://etext.virginia.edu/

journals/EH/EH36/EH36.html, accessed 12/06/2007; Susan Styles, *The Poor Law* (London: Macmillan Education, 1985), preface. For different explanations of who is a 'stranger' see *Oxford Dictionary of English*, p. 1746; Faggett, *Black and Other Minorities*, pp. 1–6, 25; and Smith, *Race and Rhetoric in the Renaissance*, pp. 23–43, 46–62, 121.

59 Stow, *A Summary of the Chronicles of England*, pp. 768–769 (stranger riots); and Andrew Spicer in Nigel Goose, Lieun Luu (eds.) *Immigrants in Tudor and Early Stuart England* (Eastbourne: Sussex Academic Press, 2005), p. 92; similar views are expressed by Faggett, *Black and Other Minorities*, p. 6; and Smith, *Race and Rhetoric in the Renaissance*, pp. 10–12.

60 The 'strange woman['s]' records are to be found in Cornwall Record Office, Old County Hall, Truro, Cornwall, TR1 3AY, Registers of Bodmin, ref Mf 12 FP 13/1/11, *Burials 1558–1757*, 12 April 1606; the 'Irish child,' Wiltshire Family History Society, *Malmesbury Abbey Parish Registers … 1591–1837, Burials* (2011), 22 April 1591, p. 4.

61 Other evidence on community and belonging are offered by Naomi Tadmor, *The Social Universe of the English Bible: Scripture, Society, and Culture in Early Modern England* (New York: Cambridge University Press, 2010), pp. 1–23, 82–119.

62 This is in regard to the tort of negligence, see James Gordley, *The Development of Liability Between Neighbours* (Cambridge/London: Cambridge University Press, 2014), pp. 36–61.

63 Authors various, *King James Version of the Bible*, 1611, Luke 1: 65. This quotation and interpretation, amongst others, are offered by the social historian Keith Wrightson in Norman Jones, Daniel Woolf (eds.), *Local Identities in Late Medieval and Early Modern England* (New York: Palgrave Macmillan, 2007), p. 23. There are at least seventeen direct references to being a good neighbour in the KJV, in addition to many parables including that of the 'Good Samaritan.'

64 Jones, Woolf, *Local Identities*, p. 23, this book is a very good introduction to these concepts as they explore different ideas of local and national neighbourliness in Tudor and early Stuart societies.

65 The idea that societal life can be divided between public and private spheres is discussed widely by social historians and others. For an analysis of the private sphere in Tudor society see Lena Cowen Orlin, *Locating Privacy in Tudor London* (Oxford: Oxford University Press, 2007), pp. 1–15; Conal Condren, 'Public, Private, and the Idea of the "Public Sphere" in Early-Modern England,' *Intellectual History Review*, 19:1 (2009), pp. 15–28; Paula Backsneider (ed.),

The Intersections of the Public and Private Spheres in Early Modern England (London: Frank Cass, 1996), pp. 1–22, 175–199.

66 William Keeling, *Liturgiae Britannicae, Or, The Several Editions of The Book of Common Prayer of the Church of England: From Its Compilation to the Last Revision* (London: William Pickering, 1549, 1552, 1604, 1842, 1851), pp. 280–281.

67 Ibid.

68 Quotations from the US Declaration and the American Constitution, and matters related are discussed by George William Van Cleve, *A Slaveholder's Union: Slavery, Politics, and the Constitution in the Early American Republic* (Chicago, IL: University of Chicago Press, 2010), pp. 101–185; David Waldstreicher, *Slavery's Constitution from Revolution to Ratification* (New York: Hill and Wang, 2009), pp. 57–153; John P. Kaminski, *A Necessary Evil?: Slavery and the Debate over the Constitution* (Madison, WI: Madison House: 1995), pp. 41–67, 243–279.

69 Precatory words are non-binding in law; inchoate rights are incomplete.

70 Some of the American founding fathers embraced abolitionist causes in later life, but had, or continued to own, enslaved Africans. This included John Jay and James Madison. As for Alexander Hamilton he did not own enslaved people directly, but he bought them for others. And his mother and other members of his family also owned Africans. Only John Adams remained consistently opposed to the enslavement of Africans; see Allan Mclane Hamilton, *The Intimate Life of Alexander Hamilton: Based Chiefly upon Original Family Letters and Other Documents, Many of Which Have Never Been Published* (New York: Charles Scribner's Sons, 1910), pp. 268–270; Richard B. Morris, *Seven Who Shaped Our Destiny: The Founding Fathers As Revolutionaries* (New York: Harper & Row, 1973), passim.

71 John Hooper, *A Godly Confession and Protestacion of the Christian Fayth … Wherin Is Declared What a Christian Manne Is Bound to Beleve of God, Hys King, His Neighbour, and Hymselfe* (London: J. Daye, 1551), n.p.

72 Markham (ed.), Berners, *Book of St Albans*, pp. 1–42, on Africans see pp. 43–44; Mulcaster, *Positions Which Are Necessarie for the Training Up of Children*, n.p.; Broughton, *A Briefe Discourse of the Scriptures*, pp. 63–66. The author acknowledges that Broughton also articulates some ideas about Africans that contradict each other and contain negative connotations.

73 For a similar view see Ian Green, *Humanism and Protestantism in Early Modern English Education* (London: Routledge, 2016), pp. 146–152.

74 The term 'intersectionality' was first used by Kimberle Crenshaw in 'Mapping the Margins: Intersectionality, Identity Politics, and Violence against Women of Color,' *Stanford Law Review*, 43:6 (July 1991),

pp. 1241–1299. It is a widely discussed matter, some of the key texts on this subject are Kimberle Crenshaw, *Critical Race Theory: The Key Writings That Formed the Movement* (New York: New Press, 1995), pp. 336–384, 440–449; and by the same author, *On Intersectionality: The Essential Writings of Kimberle Crenshaw* (New York/Jackson, TN: New Press, 2012), pp. 1–52.

75 Hertfordshire Records Office, Barley, Herts, DP48/1/1, p. 139. It may be '6 July,' the record is not clear.

76 Contrary to urban fiction, popularised in the book and series *Roots* by Alex Haley, the name 'Toby' is not just a European name that comes from Biblical, Greek and Hebrew origins, see Alex Haley, *Roots* (Garden City, NY: Doubleday, 1976), passim; in fact, the name spelt 'Tobi' is popular in several languages including Yoruba (West Africa) and means 'God is good'; there is also an island called 'Tobi' in Micronesia and the people speak Tobian, see Mike Hollywood, *Papa Mike's Palau Islands Handbook* (Bloomington, IN: iUniverse, 2006), pp. 118–121; it is difficult to say whether the origin for 'Tobye['s]' name was European, African or from elsewhere.

77 G. L. Registers of St Olave Hart Street, GL Ms 9223, p. 121.

78 William Harrison, in Furnivall, Norden et al. (eds.), *Harrison's Description of England in Shakespeare's Youth ...*, Volumes 2 and 3, p. 34.

79 Thomas Fuller, *The Histories of the Worthies of England* (1662, new edition, London: F. C. and J. Rivington, 1811), p. 50.

80 More on this can be found in Onyeka, *Blackamoores*, pp. 133–135, 213.

81 Mary Fillis' records are at Guildhall Record Office, *St Botolph Without Aldgate Memorandum Daybook*, Volume 6 (London, 1596–1597), pp. 257–258, P69/BOT2/ A101/Ms 9234/6 and GL Ms 9234/6.

82 For more on the Moriscos, the Inquisition and the Morisco Revolt see Blount (tr.), Conestaggio, *The Historie of the Uniting of the Kingdom of Portugal to the Crowne of Castill*, pp. 5–7; Limborch, *The History of the Inquisition*, pp. 129–132; Lane-Poole, *Story of the Moors in Spain*, p. 270; Bourke, *A Concise History of the Moors in Spain*, p. xviii; Lloyd, *The Spanish Inquisition*, pp. 44–46, 54, 105.

83 Hugh Chisholm, *The Encyclopaedia Britannica: A Dictionary of Arts, Sciences, Literature and General Information* (Cambridge: Cambridge University Press, 1911), p. 339; and Jose Hinojosa Montalvo, *Jews of the Kingdom of Valencia: From Persecution to Expulsion, 1391–1492* (Jerusalem: Magnes Press, 1993), p. 205 (Moorish needle-makers).

84 Of course Mary could have been trafficked or smuggled to England, but there is little evidence to support this.

85 Mary Fillis' records: G. L. *St Botolph Without Aldgate Memorandum Daybook*, Volume 6, pp. 257–258.

86 Ibid.

87 On Millicent Porter see Habib, *Black Lives*, pp. 91–92, 142–143, 241–242, 325.

88 Quotations from Mary Fillis' record, Guildhall Record Office, *St Botolph Memorandum Daybook*, pp. 257–258, and GL Ms 9234/6.

89 See Onyeka, *Blackamoores*, pp. 135–136, 211–221; similar perspectives on this matter are offered in BBC, 'Britain's First Black Community in Elizabethan London,' *BBC News Magazine*, www.bbc.co.uk/news/maga zine-18903391, accessed 20/07/2012; Rebecca Dobbs (pr.) Michael Wood (presenter), *The Great British Story*, Episode 5, BBC 2, 20/07/2012.

90 Purchas, *Pvrchas His Pilgrimages* (1613), p. 546.

91 Quotations are from Grace's records at the Devon Record Office, Devon, Hatherleigh 05/13/1604 PR1; Hatherleigh 08/10/1606 PR1; Hatherleigh 12/23/1607 PR1; Hatherleigh 05/08/1611 PR1; Hatherleigh 06/06/1613 PR1; on this subject, Faggett suggests the same in *Black and Other Minorities in Shakespeare's England*, pp. 49–50.

92 At this time in England, these terms were not automatically used in a derogatory way. The author discusses this matter in some detail in Onyeka, 'What's in a Name?,' pp. 34–39.

93 For more on the term 'Negro' see McCullough, *The Negro in English Literature*, pp. 23–47, 143–144; Richard B. Moore, *The Name 'Negro': Its Origin and Evil Use* (Baltimore, MD: Black Presence, 1960), pp. 16–18.

94 Race laws were created in France in 1685 called 'Code Noir' and they were enforced in their colonies. Similar laws were created in the USA during the eighteenth and nineteenth centuries and were also known as 'Black Codes' or 'Black laws,' see Juang, Morrissette (eds.), *Africa and the Americas*, pp. 277–279; Rodriguez (ed.), *Slavery in the United States*, Volume 2, pp. 7, 13, 230–231, 541–543; Asante, Mazama, *Encyclopedia of Black Studies*, pp. 188–189.

95 Quotations are from Grace's family's records at the Devon Record Office, Devon, Hatherleigh 05/13/1604 PR1; Hatherleigh 10/08/1606 PR1; Hatherleigh 23/12/1607 PR1; Hatherleigh 08/05/1611 PR1; Hatherleigh 06/06/1613 PR1.

96 A similar view on the status of single mothers and women in general in early modern England is offered by Leonidas Rosser, *Baptism: Its Nature, Obligation, Mode, Subjects and Benefits* (Philadelphia, PA: publisher unknown, 1854), pp. 19–23, 30–33, 379–386; Gowing, 'Giving Birth at the Magistrates Gate,' pp. 137–150; and Jeannie Dalporto (ed.), *Women in Service in Early Modern England* (Aldershot: Ashgate, 2008), pp. 1–22.

97 From Grace's family's records, Devon Record Office, Devon, Hatherleigh 05/13/1604 PR1; Hatherleigh 10/08/1606 PR1; etc.

98 bell hooks, *Ain't I a Woman: Black Women and Feminism* (New York: Routledge, 2004), pp. 9–16.

99 On how women were treated as slaves on plantations and in the house see Gwendolyn Midlo Hall, *Social Control in Slave Plantation Societies* (London: Johns Hopkins Press, 1971), pp. 2, 9–13; Thomas Durant, David Knottnerus, *Plantation Society and Race Relations: The Origins of Inequality* (Westport, CT/London: Praeger, 1999), pp. 48, 131, 140, 156–157; George Monger, *Marriage Customs of the World: From Henna to Honeymoons* (Santa Barbara, CA: ABC-CLIO, 2004), p. 173; George Bourne, *Slavery Illustrated in Its Effects on Women and Domestic Society* (Boston, MA: Issac Knapp, 1837), pp. 7, 33–45, 64, 101, 111, 124, 127; and Higginbotham, *In the Matter of Colour*, pp. 3–143.

100 There is of course another possibility regarding Grace's status and this is that she may have been a prostitute, courtesan or a 'Blackbird.' The term 'Blackbird' was later used to describe women of African descent who were prostitutes or courtesans in Georgian Britain, in Duncan Salkeld, 'Black Luce and the "Curtizans" of Shakespeare's London,' *Signature*, 2 (Chichester: University of Chichester, Winter 2000), pp. 1–10; Kathy (Kathleen) Chater, however, has a contrary view about 'Blackbirds' in *Untold Histories*, pp. 41–50. Nevertheless, this seems unlikely as Grace was able to get church baptisms for both of her children, which would be less likely if she was a 'Blackbird.'

101 Guildhall Record Office, London, GL Ms 28867, baptism, 26 January 1616; and GL Ms 28867, Parish register, p. 72, 'Mark Antonio, a negro Christian,' burial 28 January 1616.

102 Ibid.

103 The will of Henrie Anthonie Jetto, 20 September 1626, *Holt Parish Registers*, Worcestershire Archives and Archaeology Service, Butts, Worcester, WR1 3PB: see Onyeka, *Blackamoores*, p. 204.

104 The will of 'Persida Jetto widow,' July 1640, Will Probate Records 186–223, *Holt Parish Registers*: This is not the only document where Jetto is referred to as a 'yeoman,' see Onyeka, *Blackamoores*, pp. 239–241.

105 Quotations from Thomas Fuller, *The Holy State. The Profane State* (London: Roger Daniel for John William, 1642), pp. 119–123; the quote of 'forty shillings' is from *Oxford Dictionary of English*, p. 2043; even as early as Geoffrey Chaucer's time, a yeoman was considered a stalwart member of society, see Chaucer, *The Canterbury Tales* (London: Cassell Petter and Galpin, 1386, 1486), n.p.

106 In this sense the title 'yeoman' seems to be describing 'a commoner who cultivates his own land.' There is evidence in Jetto and Persida's

wills to confirm this. It may be possible that the term referred to Jetto being 'in royal service' or 'one part of a yeomanry force,' but there is no evidence to support this; the quotation is from Fuller, *The Holy State*, p. 120.

107   '20 shillings' or 'bobs' would be approximately £270–£290 in 2018 terms. This was not an inconsiderable amount, see Maggie Pierce Secara, 'Money and Coinage: The Basics,' *Life in Elizabethan England*, published 28/03/2008, www.elizabethan.org/compendium/6.html, accessed 03/08/2018.

108   These are the words of Henrie Anthonie Jetto in his will, written in his own hand and signed as proof of his undertakings; it is included as a primary document in Onyeka, *Blackamoores*, p. 204.

109   This included: 'Thomas Jetter buried' in Holt on 15 May 1717, *Holt Parish Registers*, ref. 985, Worcestershire Archives.

110   Private conversations between the author and members of the Bluck family, but see Onyeka, *Blackamoores*, pp. 239–241.

111   Ibid.

112   These variations in Ackame's name seemed to reflect attempts by Englishmen to pronounce and then write a name with West or Central African origins. And not the result of early modernists lacking a standardised vernacular. But without more evidence this is difficult to prove.

113   Henry Capell, Hertfordshire Records Office, *East Hertfordshire Munster Book*, HHLS 6990, p. 15. The muster books were written by the Capells and included all able-bodied people ready for war.

114   Herts. Records Office, Parish Records, Brickendon, p. 19, DP/48/1/1.

115   Ibid., p. 69.

116   Ibid., p. 7, DP/48/1/1-3, the marriage record is almost indecipherable but mentions the words 'a Blackemoore.'

117   Ibid., p. 29.

118   Ibid., p. 30.

119   DP/48/1/1/, Herts Record Office, Inverness, Fearye, *The Returns of the Constables of the Hamlet of Brickenden*, Volume 1, p. B3.

120   Herts Record Office, Parish Records, DP/48/1/1-3, p. 8.

121   This is discussed in more detail in Onyeka, *Blackamoores*, pp. 152–194.

122   For more on the Dassells see ibid., pp. 176–177; and National Archives, Kew, London, HCA 24/39/49–51; but Gustav Ungerer says these Africans were slaves in 'The Presence of Africans in Elizabethan England and the Performance of *Titus Andronicus* at Burley-on-the-Hill, 1595/96,' pp. 19–56.

123 G. L. St Mildred Poultry, GL Ms 4429/1, Parish register, 'John Jaquoah, a king's sonne in Guinnye,' baptised 1 January 1610/11, London Metropolitan Archives.

124 Onyeka, *Blackamoores*, pp. 170–181.

125 This also includes Walter Annerby: 'the son of Nosser [a noble next to the King] Annerby [was] borne in the kingdom of Dungala [Dungal in Kaabu, Guinea Bissau, West Africa], was baptized upon the third day of February being Shrove Sundaie, in the Eight year King James, anno, [1610/11],' All Hallows, Tottenham: London Metropolitan Archives, London, LMA DRO/015/A/01/001.

126 Northrup, *Africa's Discovery of Europe*, pp. 1–15.

127 The references for the records that contain these Africans are to be found throughout this book and in the Selected Bibliography.

128 See previous note.

129 Onyeka, *Blackamoores*, pp. xxii, xx, xxvi–xxvii, 8, 15, 59, 65, 131–132, 134, 154, 211, 219, 221, 231.

130 Ibid., East Smithfield, pp. 72, 109, 133, 154, 219; St Olave Hart Street, pp. 8, 44, 51, 65, 127, 211; Stepney, pp. 62, 128, 231; other parts of London, pp. 47–48, 114–115, 132–135, 178–179; Plymouth (St Andrews), pp. xxii, xiv, xxii, xxvi, 8, 15, 17–18, 27–28, 42, 59, 72, 108, 111, 113, 117, 136, 156, 158–159, 211, 227–228, 230, 240.

131 The *Moderate Intelligencer* has been described as a periodical dedicated to promoting the puritan cause and that of the army, hence the reference in the article to 'Mars': the God of War.

132 John Dillingham, John Lilburne (eds.), *Moderate Intelligencer: Impartially Communicating Martiall Affairs to the Kingdom of England* VII, 10–17 April 1645 (London: Richard White, 1645), p. 53. This same article from the *Intelligencer* was quoted in Habib, *Black Lives*, pp. 162–168, 351–352, but with a very different interpretation; another rival periodical started by Lilburne, Richard Overton, Edward Sexby and John Wildman was called the *Moderate* and it supported the Levellers, see Joad Raymond, *The Invention of the Newspaper: English Newsbooks, 1641–1649* (Oxford/ New York: Clarendon Press, 2005), pp. 30–31, 39–41, 64–66; Will Slauter, 'Book Review: An Anatomy of an English Radical Newspaper,' *Cambridge Scholars Publishing*, posted 19/03/2018, https://cambridgescholarsblog. wordpress.com/2018/03/19/book-review-an-anatomy-of-an-english-radical-newspaper/, accessed 20/04/2018.

133 The full quotation reveals that there had been a shift in some Englishmen's ideas on this: Thomas Rymer in *A Short View of Tragedy: The Critical Works of Thomas Rymer 1692–1693* (London: Yale University Press, 1956), pp. 82–176:

> The Character of that State is to employ strangers in their Wars; but shall a Poet thence fancy that they will set a Negro to be their General; or trust *a Moor* to defend them against the Turk? With us a Black-amoor might rise to be a Trumpeter; but Shakespeare would not have him less than a Lieutenant-General. With us a Moor might marry some little drab, or Small-coal Wench: Shakespeare, would provide him the Daughter and Heir of some great Lord, or Privy-Councellor: And all the Town should reckon it a very suitable match.

Rymer was actually comparing his own view as a late-seventeenth-century/eighteenth-century Englishman with that of Shakespeare. Rymer's words should not be taken as symptomatic of Shakespeare's England because he was not living there. But his quotation was included here to show that Africans in England continued to have relationships with white English people, long after the middle of the seventeenth century. For other views on this see Celia R. Daileader, *Racism, Misogyny, and the Othello Myth: Inter-racial Couples from Shakespeare to Spike Lee* (Cambridge: Cambridge University Press, 2005), pp. 46–47.

134 Evidence is to be found throughout this book and in Guildhall Record Office, London: GL Ms 9243–9245, GL Ms 4310, GL Ms 9222; Author unknown, *St Martin in the Fields Parish Register*, Volume 1 (London: publisher unknown, 27 September 1571), p. 116; Plymouth and West Devon Record Office, Plymouth, St Andrews/MF1-4; Devon Record Office, East Allington/20/08/1577 PR; and Northampton Records Office, Northampton, Microfiche 120, pp. 1–3.

135 John Stow, *A Survey of London* ... (1598, London: Whittaker, 1603, 1842), pp. 30, 38, 54, 207 (the stranger riots also took place on 'Evil May Day').

136 Henry Machyn in John Gough Nicols (ed.), *The Diary of Henry Machyn Citizen and Merchant Taylor of London* (London: Camden Society, 1848), pp. 20, 33 (quotation), 89. Machyn may be referring to people of African descent here, rather than just simply Morris dancing, but without more evidence this is difficult to confirm; on the 'Lords of Misrule' and Morris dancing see Forrest, 'Morris and Matachin,' p. 19; and Cutting, *History and the Morris Dance*, pp. 18, 19, 20, 169.

137 The Minister was a leading writer on topical issues. He had also been a fervent opponent to Catholicism and a supporter of James I, see John Rhodes, *The Countrie Mans Comfort. Or Religious Recreations Fitte for All Well Disposed Persons* ... (1588, London: M. D. Dawson, 1637), n.p.

138 John Wilmot, 'A Ramble in St James Park,' poem, 1672 circa, in David M. Vieth (ed.), John Wilmot, *The Complete Poems of John Wilmot* (London: Yale University Press, 2002), pp. 40, 187(n); there were brothels in

Lincoln's Inn Fields see Author unknown, *Wonderful Strange News from Wood Street Counter* (1642), quoted in John Adlard (ed.), *Restoration Bawdy: Poems, Songs and Jests on the Subject of Sensual Love* (London: Taylor & Francis, 2003), p. 12; according to Fergus Linnane, 'officers of the parish' took bribes from pimps and prostitutes to ignore the activities there, in *London: The Wicked City; A Thousand Years of Prostitution and Vices* (London: Robson, 2007), pp. 75, 167, 174, 189.

139 The exact intent of the ordinances are disputed, some suggest their purpose was to outlaw Christmas, etc., other academics suggest to control. It is certain that the ordinances were flouted and this forced the hand of the government – in June 1647 festivals such as Christmas were restricted further, see Samuel Rawson Gardiner, *The Constitutional Documents of the Puritan Revolution, 1625–1660* (London: Clarendon Press, 1906, 1979), pp. 99–103; Glyn Hughes, *The Lost Feast of Christmas* (London: Lulu.Com, 2016), pp. 9–14.

140 It is the largest public square in London, see Nicholas Pevsner, *London: The Cities of London and Westminster*, Volume 1 (London: Penguin, 1973), pp. 58, 367.

141 For more on Marranos that lived in early modern England and Iberia see Charles Meyers, 'Elizabethan "Marranos" Unmasked.' *The Journal of the Jewish Museum of Australia* 97:3 (1997), pp. 14–15; David Katz, *Jews in the History of England, 1485–1850* (1994, new edition, Oxford: Oxford University Press, 1997), pp. 1–107; and C. J. Sisson, 'A Colony of Jews in Shakespeare's London.' *Essays and Studies* 23 (1938), pp. 38–51; Susan Adams et al., 'The Genetic Legacy of Religious Diversity and Intolerance: Paternal Lineages of Christians, Jews, and Muslims in the Iberian Peninsula.' *The American Journal of Human Genetics* 83:6 (4 December 2008), pp. 725–736; Ian Davidson Kalmar, 'Moorish Style: Orientalism, the Jews, and Synagogue Architecture.' *Jewish Social Studies History Culture and Society* 7:3 (spring/summer 2001), pp. 68–100; and Yeshiva University Museum, *The Sephardic Journey 1492–1992* (New York: Yeshiva University Museum, 1992), p. 291.

142 For more on the Portuguese ambassador see evidence in Habib, *Black Lives*, pp. 162(n), 163(n); the Anglo-Portuguese Alliance is one of the longest in history, if one excludes the period when Spain ruled Portugal and when the Portuguese nobility were exiled in England and elsewhere, see L. M. E. Shaw, *The Anglo-Portuguese Alliance and the English Merchants in Portugal, 1654–1810* (Abingdon/New York/Oxford: Routledge, 2017), introduction.

143 Gay men would frequent the public toilets in Lincoln's Inn Fields, see Kate Chedgzoy, Emma Francis, Murray Pratt, *In a Queer Place: Sexuality and Belonging in British and European Contexts* (Aldershot: Ashgate, 2002),

p. 156; this tradition continued into the eighteenth century, see Rictor Norton, *Mother Clap's Molly House: The Gay Subculture in England 1700–1830* (Los Angeles, CA: University of California Press, 2008), p. 71; Nell Gwyn also lived there and it was close to theatrical performances and other entertainments, see Arthur Holton Marks, *Historical Notes on Lincoln's Inn Fields* (London: Hertford Record Co., 1922), p. 69.

144 To be more precise: 'a low frequency-high arousal ritual,' see Harvey Whitehouse, *Modes of Religiosity: A Cognitive Theory of Religious Transmission* (Walnut Creek, CA/London: Alta Mira Press, 2004), pp. 84, 141–147, 159–162.

145 This definition of 'mis-memory' is included in Siobhan Kattago, *The Ashgate Research Companion to Memory Studies* (London/New York: Routledge, 2015), pp. 179–181 (quotation on p. 179); William D. Phillips, *Slavery in Medieval and Early Modern Iberia*, pp. 18–163.

Conclusion

1 St Augustine's Church, St John Hackney Record Office, 18 May 1630, LMA P79/JN 1/021, Hackney Museum, London; also quoted in Benjamin Clarke FLS, *Glimpses of Ancient Hackney and Stoke Newington: Being a Reprint of a Series of Articles Appearing in the Hackney Mercury, from April 23rd, 1892, to November 25th, 1893. With an Appendix Dealing with the Conversion of a Portion of Hackney Churchyards into Open Space* (London: Hackney Mercury Offices, 1893), p. 286; and Habib, *Black Lives*, p. 347.

2 Onyeka, *Blackamoores*, pp. 249–264.

3 For more on this see David Goldenberg, 'Reading Rabbinic Literature: It's Not All Black and White (A Response to Jonathan Schorsch),' www.sas.upenn.edu/~dmg2/Reading%20Rabbinic%20Literature%20%28Response%20to%20Jonathan%20Schorsch%29.pdf, accessed 22/02/2016; David Goldenberg, 'The Development of the Idea of Race: Classical Paradigms and Medieval Elaborations' (Review Essay), *International Journal of the Classical Tradition* 5 (1999), pp. 561–570; David Goldenberg, 'The Curse of Ham: A Case of Rabbinic Racism?,' in Jack Salzman, Cornel West (eds.), *Struggles in the Promised Land* (New York/Oxford: Oxford University Press, 1997), pp. 21–51; David Goldenberg, 'Rabbinic Knowledge of Black Africa: (Sifre Deut. 320).' *Jewish Studies Quarterly* 5 (1998), pp. 318–328; David Goldenberg, 'What Did Ham Do to Noah?,' in Gunter Stemberger, Mauro Perani (eds.), *'The Words of a Wise Man's Mouth Are Gracious' (Qoh 10,12)* (Berlin: Walter de Gruyter, 2005), pp. 257–265; David Goldenberg, 'It Is Permitted to Marry a Kushite.' *Association for Jewish Studies Review*

37 (2013), pp. 29–49; Braude, 'The Sons of Noah and the Construction of Ethnic and Geographical Identities in the Medieval and Early Modern Periods,' pp. 103–142.

4   Thomas Eliot, *The Dictionary of Syr Thomas Eliot Knyght* (London: for Thomas Berthelet, T. Eliot, 1538), pp. 1, 3 (contains letter to Lord Cromwell), ref. BLL01001064307, British Library, London.

5   William Salesbury, *A Dictionary in English and Welshe* (London: Richard Crowley, 1547), p. 3; Andrew Boorde, *The First Boke of the Introduction of Knowledge. The Whych Doth Teach a Man to Speake and Parte of All Maner of Languages and to Know the Vsage and Fashion of all Maner of Countries … with Woodcuts* [images] (London: William Copeland, 1550), pp. 88–89. He even mentions that sometimes they 'be slaves,' but again not that they were cursed; Boorde's work is discussed in more detail in *Blackamoores*, pp. 42–45, 56, 57.

6   John Withal, *Short Dictionary* (London: to Robert Dudley, publisher unknown, 1581), p. 32.

7   John Minsheu, *A Dictionarie in Spanish and English* (London: E. Bollifant, 1599), p. 172.

8   Ludolf (tr.), Gorgoryos, *A New History of Ethiopia*, preface, p. 13; and in Northrup, *Africa's Discovery of Europe*, p. 31.

9   Elizabeth Story Donno (ed.), *Richard Madox. An Elizabethan in 1582: The Diary of Richard Madox, Fellow of All Saints* (London: Hakluyt Society, 1976), pp. 18, 49, 173, 193.

10   Pliny the Elder, *Begin. Caius Plynius Marco suo Salutem. [Fol. 3:] Caii Plynii Secundi Naturalis Historiae Liber. I. End. [Colophon:] Caii Plynii Secundi Naturalis Historiae Libri Tricesimiseptimi et Ultimi Finis, etc.* (Venetiis: Nicolaum Jenson, 1472), passim; also see Barnabe Rich, *The Famous Hystory of Herodotus* (London: Thomas Marshe, 1584), p. 96.

11   Holland, *The History of the World Commonly Called the Natural Historie of C Plinius Secondus*, pp. 96, 146–147, 157.

12   Quotation comes from Thomas Middleton's pageant, *The Triumphs of Truth* (London: Nicholas Okes, 1613), p. 23, it is the name of the fictional ship on which the king and queen of the Moors arrived in England.

13   My view on this has not been advanced without considerable research, some of the artists that reveal this tradition are: Artist unknown, *Adoration of the Magi*, c. 1400, Troyes, France; Joos Van Cleve, *Adoration of the Magi*, 1526–1528, Antwerp, oil on oak panel, 251 × 185 cm, Gemäldegalerie, Dresden (Cleve has a series of paintings with Balthazar in them. He has the white hair of an older man but a youthful expression, this may be to do with the age of the model. In those paintings, Balthazar is wearing the most ornate early modern attire that the author has seen); Hans Memling, *Triptych of Jans Floreins, Central Panel with Adoration*

of the Magi, 1479, 95 × 271 cm, ref. P 001557, Museo del Prado, Madrid (this painting was used on the front cover of Onyeka, *Blackamoores*, all editions); Artist unknown, *Altarpiece with Adoration of the Magi*, c. 1475, Hammarby Kyrka, Södermanland, Sweden; Geertgen tot Sint Jans, *Adoration of the Magi*, two versions both 1480–1485, oil on panel, 111 × 69 cm, no ref., National Gallery, Prague; Workshop of Master of the Lubin Poland Figures, *Adoration of the Magi*, 1492–1493, Muzeum Narodowe we Wrocławiu, Wrocław; Georges Trubert, *The Adoration of the Magi*, 1480–1490, France, tempera colours, gold leaf, gold and silver paint, and ink on parchment, ref. MS. 48 fol. 59, J. Paul Getty Museum, Los Angeles, CA; Hans Baldung Grien, *Adoration of the Magi*, 1507, oil on wood, Staatliche Museum, Berlin, Saint Maurice the Theban (African) knight is also depicted; Gerard David, *The Adoration of the Magi*, c. 1490, Netherlands, Alte Pinakothek, Munich; Hieronymus Bosch, *The Epiphany or the Adoration of the Magi*, 1510, oil on wood panel, 38 × 72 cm, by 138 × 34 cm, ref. 21032, Museo Nacional del Prado, Madrid; Artist unknown, *Adoration of the Magi*, part of the Rood Screen Panel, c. 1520, England, oil and gilt on oak, ref. W.54-1928, Victoria and Albert Museum, London; Fray Juan Maino Bautista, *The Adoration of the Magi*, 1612–1614, oil on canvas, 315 × 174.5 cm, ref. P000886, Museo Del Prado, Madrid; these images and others can be seen in Bindman, Gates, Snowden, *The Image of the Black in Western Art*, Volumes I–IV; Vincent Boele, Ernest Schreuder, Elmer Kolfin (eds.), *Black Is Beautiful: Rubens to Dumas* (Amsterdam: Die Nieuwe Kerk, 2008), pp. 15, 20, 24, 37, 39, 59, 61, 69, 74, 93, 96 etc.; Onyeka, *Blackamoores*, pp. 101, 102, 198, 199.

14   It was not until the twentieth century that Christianity became dominant in the continent of Africa – it expanded from 9 million followers in 1910, to over 516 million at the beginning of the twenty-first century. These dates and figures are from the Pew Foundation, 'Global Christianity: A Report on the Size and Distribution of the World's Christian Population,' 19 December 2011, Pew Research Centre, www.pewforum.org/2011/12/19/global-christianity-exec, accessed 21/02/2016, pp. 8–16, 53–57, 71–79, 87–95, 111; they are quoted in several scholarly books and articles including Luca Mavelli (ed.), *Towards a Postsecular International Politics: New Forms of Community, Identity and Power* (New York: Palgrave Macmillan, 2014), p. 117; and Stephen Hopgood, *The Endtimes of Human Rights* (Ithaca, NY: Cornell University Press, 2013), p. 154.

15   On this see Adrian Hastings (ed.), *A World History of Christianity* (Cambridge/Grand Rapids, MI: Williams B. Eerdmans Publishing, 1999), introduction; Rodney Stark, *The Triumph of Christianity: How the Jesus Movement Became the World's Largest Religion* (New York: HarperCollins, 2011), introduction, pp. 1, 9, 22; Dyron B. Daughrity, *The Changing World of Christianity: The Global*

History of a Borderless Religion (Bern: Peter Lang, 2010), pp. 1–21; Alvin J. Schmidt, *How Christianity Changed the World* (New York: HarperCollins, 2009), introduction.

16   There is a difference of opinion as to whether Catalina de Motril was the same person referred to in early modern records as Catalina de Cardones; in Onyeka, *Blackamoores*, both Catalinas are described as one person, pp. 117–118, 230, 231; but the author Lauren Johnson makes a distinction and claims they are two different people, 'A Life of Catalina, Katherine of Aragon's Moorish Servant,' *English Historical Fiction Authors*, 21 March 2015, https://englishhistoryauthors.blog spot.com/2015/03/a-life-of-catalina-katherine-of-aragons.html, accessed 09/06/2018; Kaufmann now seems to concur, personal email 'Catalina,' 08/06/2018; the author is still not sure, but acknowledges the arguments.

17   For different views on Blanke see Miranda Kaufmann in *Black Tudors*; and Michael Ohajuru's *The John Blanke Project*, www.johnblanke. com/, accessed 12/03/2016; as well as David Olusoga, *Black and British: A Forgotten History*, BBC TV series, 21 November – 17 December 2016. The TV series and the plaque to John Blanke are discussed in this article: Jasper Rees, 'Black and British: A Forgotten History Revealed a Fascinating Side of Our Past – Review,' *The Telegraph*, 9 November 2016, www.telegraph.co.uk/tv/2016/11/09/black-and-british-a-forgotten-history-revealed-a-fascinating-sid/, accessed 12/03/2016.

18   Plymouth and West Devon Record Office, St Andrews/December 10/1583/MF1-4.

19   Fortunatus' records are in City of Westminster Archives Centre, London, 1601/2 January/21/St Clements Dane/ Volume1Burials/ MF 1; and Hertfordshire Archives and Local Studies, Cheshunt, 1570/16April/ [D/P29/13/5].

20   Elizabeth I's 'little blackmore['s]' presence is quoted in two warrants issued 14 April 1574, B. L. Egerton 2806; and on 13 April 1575, in Janet Arnold, *Queen Elizabeth's Wardrobe Unlocked ...* (Leeds: Maney, 1988), p. 106.

21   Quotation contains the paraphrased words of Elizabeth I by Thomas Sherley, 29 November 1600, see Casper Van Senden, Thomas Sherley, 'Cecil Papers Petition, Merchant of Lubeck to the Queen,' 29 November 1600, *Calendar of the Manuscripts of the Most Honourable the Marquess of Salisbury*, Volume 10 (London: Historical Manuscripts Commission, 1883–1976), p. 431; it is discussed more in Onyeka, *Blackamoores*, pp. 10–15, 22–27, 289–291.

22   Reported in Luther Porter Jackson, *Journal of Negro History*, 9:1 (January 1924), p. 15.

23   English Ambassador, Collegio Secreta Esposizioni, Rome, 'Calendar of State Papers: Venice 23 August 1609,' *British History Online*, www.

british-history.ac.uk/cal-state-papers/venice/vol11/pp309-325, created University of London 2017, accessed 28/04/2018.

24   Anne Boleyn was born in 1501, Henry VIII in 1491. Henry would have been 10 years old when she was conceived, making him an unlikely father.

25   Hakluyt, *The Principal Navigations*, Volume 6, p. 137 (Moroccan ambassadors); William Percy, Mathew Dimmock, *William Percy's Mahomet and His Heaven: A Critical Edition* (Aldershot: Ashgate, 2006), pp. 6–11 (Moroccan ambassadors); Matar, *Islam in Britain*, p. 2; Matar, *Turks, Moors and Englishmen in the Age of Discovery*, pp. 21, 64; and Stubbs, *The Discoverie of a Gaping Gulf* (1579), pp. 4, 32, 35, 42 (on Moors and a Moorish marriage).

26   Stubbs, *The Discoverie of a Gaping Gulf*, pp. 4, 32, 35, 42 (nevertheless, Stubbs makes the qualification that England should not make the mistake of Spain, where the 'Turke and his Saracens [a term that can include Africans] … [made] war within the Nation').

27   On morganatic unions please see Rosser, *Baptism: Its Nature, Obligation, Mode, Subjects and Benefits*, pp. 19–23, 30–33, 379–386; Gowing, 'Giving Birth at the Magistrates Gate,' pp. 137–150; and Dalporto, *Women in Service in Early Modern England*, introduction.

28   Plymouth and West Devon Record Office, St Andrews/May 2/1593/ MF1-4, St Andrews/April 14/1594/MF1-4.

29   Bristol City Archives, Bristol Record Office, Bristol, P/ST PJR/1/1/CMB 1576–1621, n.p.; on the influence and power of Thomas Smythe see Foss, *Biographia Juridica*, p. 617; Maine Historical Society, *Collections of the Maine Historical Society*, Volume 18, pp. 34–36; and Brenner, *Merchants and Revolution*, pp. 96–100, 109, 154, 216, 223, 433, 434, 526, 529.

30   St Philip and Jacob, Bristol, 14 December 1603, P/ST PJR/1/1/CMB 1576–1621, Bristol City Archives; it is now possible to reassess an earlier view that it was Thomas Smythe that was the 'Blackamoore' – the author had not seen until recently the connections to the previous entry, nor the significance of the African boy in the painting of the Smythe family. The boy depicted could potentially be a descendant of Joane (Blackamore) and Thomas Smythe, this is despite the modern title attributed to the picture, see Gilbert Jackson, *Daughter of Florence Poulett and Thomas Smyth of Ashton Court with Her Black Page*, 1621–1640, oil on canvas, 66 × 58.5 cm, Red Lodge Museum, Bristol.

31   Some academics may now say that the idea of 'race' is a socially constructed concept. Perhaps it is more accurate to say how we perceive and group somatic and other differences: both phenotype and genotype are guided by societal concerns. However, in the past in pursuance of justifying colonialism, slavery, racism, etc. this 'science' was believed and purported to be 'exact.' The writers on this, and on 'immutable characteristics,' 'Manifest Destiny' and so on, are daedalian but a useful book to read is Kevin Reilly,

Stephen Kaufman, *Racism: A Global Reader* (Armonk, NY: M. E. Sharpe, 2003), pp. 13–27, 52–58, 195–206; on the effect of the 'Science of Racism' see Sandra Greene, *West African Narratives of Slavery: Texts from Late Nineteenth- and Early Twentieth-Century Ghana* (Bloomington, IN: Indiana University Press, 2011), pp. 13–27, 52–58; the phrase 'Maafa' means disaster. It was used by Marimba Ani, in *Let the Circle Be Unbroken: The Implications of African Spirituality in the Diaspora* (New York: Nkonimfo Publications, 1998), passim.

32   Aurelia Martín Casares, *Juan Latino: Talento y Destino* (Granada: Univesidad de Granada, 2016), passim; Elizabeth R. Wright, *The Epic of Juan Latino: Dilemmas of Race and Religion in Renaissance Spain* (Toronto: University of Toronto Press, 2016), passim.

33   See Diego Ortiz de Zunga (1677) in Andrew Spicer, Jane L. Stevens Crawshaw (eds.), *The Place of the Social Margins 1350–1750* (London: Routledge, 2016), pp. 123–124; and in Carmen Fraccia, 'The Place of African Slaves in Early Modern Spain,' in Spicer, Cranshaw (eds.), *The Place of the Social Margins*, pp. 158–181.

34   Higiemonte was depicted in the work of Joachim von Sandrart, *L'Academia Todesca Della Architectura, Scultura e Pittura: Oder Teutsche Academie Der Edlen Bau-, Bild- und Mahlerey-Künste Portrait of Higiemonte From Teutsche Academie* (Nuremberg: publisher unknown, 1675, 1683), n.p., illustrations by Richard Collin (1626–1698), Hieronymus Cock (1580–1570) and Joannes Meyssens (1612–1670).

35   Diego Rodriguez de Velazquez, *Juan De Pareja*, 1649–1650, oil on canvas, 81.3 × 69.9 cm, ref. 1971.86, Metropolitan Museum of Art, New York; Pareja's work included *Portrait of Agustín Moreto*, 1648–1653, oil on canvas, Lazaro Galdiano Foundation, Madrid.

36   On his status see Madlyn M. Kaur, *Velazquez: The Art of Painting* (London: HarperCollins, 1976), p. 110; Agnes Lugo-Ortiz, *Slave Portraiture in the Ancient World* (Cambridge/London: Cambridge University Press, 2013), pp. 147–169.

37   Ludolf, *A New History of Ethiopia*, p. 13; and in Northrup, *Africa's Discovery of Europe*, p. 31.

38   Ludolf, *A New History of Ethiopia*, p. 72.

39   Some dispute whether Africanus was of African descent; more on his views on blackness and alchemy can be found in Francis C. R. Thee, *Julius Africanus and the Early Christian View of Magic* (Tubingen: J. C. B. Mohr, 1984), passim.

40   Abba Mikael, *Book of Wise Philosophers*, in Maurice Muhatia Makumba, *An Introduction to African Philosophy: Past and Present* (Nairobi: Paulines Publications Africa, 2007), pp. 84–85, 201; Valentin-Yves Mudimbe, *The Invention of Africa: Gnosis, Philosophy and the Order of Knowledge* (Bloomington, IN: Indiana University Press, 1988), p. 201.

41   Claude Sumner, *The Rationalism of Zera Yacob/by Ayelè Teklehaymanot and, The Monastery of Dabra Libanos/by Abba Ayele Teklehaymanot* (Addis Abba: Capuchin Franciscan Institute of Philosophy and Theology, 2000), passim; Kwasi Wiredu, *A Companion to African Philosophy* (Malden, MA/ Oxford: John Wiley and Sons, 2008), pp. 172–184.

42   Similar perspectives are offered by Northrup, *Africa's Discovery of Europe*, pp. 8, 12; but not by Nabil Matar, 'The First Turks and Moors in England,' in Randolph Vigne, Charles Littleton (eds.), *From Strangers to Citizens: The Integration of Immigrant Communities in Britain, Ireland, and Colonial America, 1550–1750* (Eastbourne: Sussex Academic Press, 2001), pp. 261, 262; on religious diversity in West Africa in particular see John Hunwick, *Timbuktu and the Songhay Empire: Al Sadis Tarikh Al-Sudan Down to 1613 and Other Contemporary Documents* (Leiden: Brill, 1999), pp. 281, 282; Edith Bruder, *The Black Jews of Africa: History, Religion, Identity* (New York/Oxford: Oxford University Press, 2008), pp. 7, 51–59, 97–132; and Zoltán Szombathy (ed. and tr.), *The History of Bidyini and Kaabu* ... (Piliscsaba: Avicenna Institute of Middle Eastern Studies, 2007), p. 61.

43   Michael Comerford, *Collections Relating to the Dioceses of Kildare and Leighlin*, Volume 2 (Dublin: James Duffy and Sons, 1883), p. 180; *The Irish Digest*, Volume 69 (Dublin: Irish Digest, 1960), p. 62.

Appendix 1

1   Rastell (ed.), More, *The Works of Sir Thomas More Knyght ... The First Boke*, pp. 125–127.

2   Browne, *Pseudodoxia Epidemica*, pp. 322–338.

Appendix 2

1   Francis Charles Hingeston (ed.), *Royal and Historical Letters During the Reign of Henry IV King of England and France and Lord of Ireland* (London: Longman Green Longman and Roberts, 1860), pp. 419–422; and Northrup, *Africa's Discovery of Europe*, p. 65.

Postscript

1   The rest of Martin Luther King's speech, 1967, quoted in Herbert Robinson Marbury, *Pillars of Cloud and Fire: The Politics of Exodus in African American Biblical Interpretation* (New York: New York University Press, 2015), p. 228.

Selected Bibliography

Where the author has completed more than one work, those works are listed with the most significant first.

Adoration of the Magi
(Below is a redacted bibliography related to artists that have depicted the Adoration of the Magi.)

Artist unknown. *Altarpiece with Adoration of the Magi*, c. 1475. @ Hammarby Kyrka, Södermanland, Sweden.

Artist unknown. *Adoration of the Magi*. c. 15th century. Parchment codex, 35.5 cm × 25.5 cm. France. @ Bibliothèque Sainte-Geneviève, Paris.

Artist unknown. *Adoration of the Magi*. c. 1520. Part of the Rood Screen Panel, oil and gilt on oak. England. ref. W.54-1928 @ Victoria and Albert Museum, London.

Bautista, Fray Juan Maino. *The Adoration of the Magi*. 1612–1614. Oil on canvas, 315.0 cm × 174.5 cm. ref. P000886 @ Museo del Prado, Madrid.

Bindman, David. Henry Louis Gates. Frank M. Snowden. *The Image of the Black in Western Art*, Volumes I–IV. New York: Harvard University Press, 2010–2014.

Boele, Vincent. Ernest Schreuder. Elmer Kolfin (eds.). *Black Is Beautiful: Rubens to Dumas*. Amsterdam: Die Nieuwe Kerk, 2008.

Bosch, Hieronymus. *The Epiphany or the Adoration of the Magi*. 1510. Oil on wood panel, 38 cm × 72 cm, by 138 cm × 34 cm. ref. 21032 @ Museo Nacional del Prado, Madrid.

Botticini, Rafaelo. *Adoration of the Magi*. c. 1490. Tempera on wood, 79 cm. Italy. @ The Art Institute of Chicago, Chicago.

Coecke, Pieter van Aeslt. *The Adoration of the Magi*. 1502–1550. Oil on panel, 109.8 cm × 72.8 cm. Brussels. @ Christie's New York. Fine Art Storage Services, Brooklyn, NY.

Collectar Saint-Lo Rouen. *Adoration of the Magi*. c. 1400s. fol. 13v. Illuminated manuscript, 24 cm × 18 cm. @ Paris, Bibliothèque Sainte-Geneviève, Paris.

David, Gerard. *The Adoration of the Magi*. c. 1490. Netherlands. @ Alte Pinakothek, Munich.

Durer, Albrect. *Adoration of the Magi*. 1504.99 cm × 113.50 cm. Florence. @ Galleria Piazzale Degli Uffizi, Florence.

Geertgen, tot Sint Jans. *Adoration of the Magi*. 1480–1485. Two versions, both oil on panel, 111 cm × 69 cm. @ National Gallery Prague.

———. *Adoration of the Magi*. c. 1480. Oil on panel. Netherlands. @ Rijksmuseum, Amsterdam.

Grien, Hans Baldung. *Adoration of the Magi*. 1507. Oil on wood @ Staatliche Museum, Berggruen Museum, Berlin. Saint Maurice the Theban (African) knight is also depicted.

Memling, Hans. *Triptych of Jans Floreins, Central Panel with Adoration of the Magi*. 1479.95 cm × 271.00 cm. ref. P 001557 @ Museo del Prado, Madrid. Front cover of Onyeka, *Blackamoores*, all editions.

Onyeka. *Africans in Tudor England, Their Presence, Status and Origins*. 2013, new edition, London: Narrative Eye, 2014. pp. 101, 102, 198, 199.

Poyer, Jean. *The Hours of Henry VIII*. c. 1490. Illuminated manuscript, 25.6 cm × 18.0 cm. @ The Morgan Library and Museum, New York.

Trubert, Georges. *The Adoration of the Magi*. 1480–1490. Tempera colors, gold leaf, gold and silver paint, and ink on parchment. France. ref. MS. 48 fol. 59 @ J. Paul Getty Museum, Los Angeles.

———. *The Adoration of the Magi*. c. 1480. Tempera colours, gold leaf, gold and silver paint, and ink on parchment, 11.4 cm × 8.6 cm. France. ref. MS 48 fol. 59 @ J. Paul Getty Museum, Los Angeles.

Van Cleve, Joos. *Adoration of the Magi*. 1526–1528. Oil on oak panel, 251 cm × 185 cm. Antwerp. @ Gemäldegalerie, Dresden.

Velazquez, Diego. *Adoración de los Reyes*. 1619. Oil on canvas. @ Museo del Prado, Madrid.

Workshop of Hieronymus Bosch. *Adoration of the Magi*. 1468–1560. Oil, tempera and gold on panel, 71.1 cm × 56.5 cm.

Workshop of Master of the Lubin Poland, Figures. *Adoration of the Magi*. 1492–1493. @ Muzeum Narodowe we Wrocławiu, Wrocław.

Zeitblom, Bartholome. *Adoration of the Magi*. c. 1490–1505. Oil on wood with fabric ground, 158.5 cm × 103.8 cm. @ Museum der Bildenden Künste, Leipzig.

General Bibliography

Aaron, David H. 'Early Rabbinic Exegesis, on Noah's Son Ham and the So-Called Hamitic Myth.' *Journal of the American Academy of Religion* 63:4, 1995, pp. 721–759.

Abanime, Emeka. 'Elizabeth I and Negroes.' *Cahiers Elizabethans* 19, 19 April 1981, p. 2.

Abentarique, Tarif. *The History of the Conquest of Spain by the Moors. Together with the Life of the Most Illustrious Monarch Menesh Almanzar and of the Several Revolutions of the Mighty Empire of the Caliphs and of the African Kingdoms ... Now Made English.* London: Fleach, sold by T. Fox, 1687.

Abudacnus, Josephus. *The True History of the Jacobites of Egypt, Lybia, Nubia, &c: Their Origine, Religion, Ceremonies, Laws, and Customs, Whereby You May See How They Differ from the Jacobites of Great Britain.* London: Printed for Eliphal Jaye ... and published by R. Baldwin ..., 1692.

Adams, Laurie. *The Methodologies of Art: An Introduction.* New York: Icon Editions, 1996.

Adams, Simon (ed.). *Household Accounts and Disbursement Books of Robert Dudley, Earl of Leicester.* London: Cambridge University Press, 1995.

Adams, Susan et al. 'The Genetic Legacy of Religious Diversity and Intolerance ... Christians, Jews, and Muslims in the Iberian Peninsula.' *The American Journal of Human Genetics* 83:6, 4 December 2008, pp. 725–736.

Adi, Hakim. 'Black People in Britain,' in Douglas Hamilton. Robert J. Blyth (eds.). *Representing Slavery.* London: Lund Humphries, 2007, pp. 92–102.

Africanus, Leo. *A Geographical Historie of Africa, Written in Arabicke and Italian ... by Iohn Leo a More ...* London: John Pory, 1600.

Agbetu, Toyin. 'Professor Hakim Adi Joins UK List of Academic Giants.' *Ligali, Human Rights, Natural Justice,* 5 January 2015.

Agrippa, Henrich Cornelius. *De Incertitudine and Vanitate Scientiarum and Artum.* Paris: Johannes Petrum, 1531.

Agrippa, Henrich Cornelius. C. M. Duan (ed.). *Of the Vanitie and Uncertaintie of Artes and Sciences.* Northridge, CA: California State University, 1974.

Agyemang, Charles. 'Negro, Black African, African Caribbean, African American or What? Labelling African Origin People in the 21st Century.' *Journal of Epidemiology and Community Health* 59:12, 2 September 2005, pp. 1014–1018.

Ahmed, Shokhan Rasool. *Magic and Gender in Early Modern England.* Bloomington, IN: Author House, 2014.

Akbar, Naim. *Chains and Images of Psychological Slavery.* Jersey City, NJ: New Mind Productions, 1984.

———. *Breaking the Chains of Psychological Slavery.* Jersey City, NJ: Mind Productions and Associates, 1996.

Akerele, Bayo. *Black Restoration Is a Black Responsibility: Nigeria and the Black Leadership Imperative.* Benin City: University of Benin, 2000.

Alford, Stephen. 'Urban Safe Houses for the Unfree in Medieval England: A Reconsideration.' *Slavery and Abolition* 32:3, September 2011, pp. 363–375.

Ali, Ahmed. Ibrahim Ali. *The Black Celts: An Ancient African Civilisation in Ireland and Britain.* Cardiff: Punite Publications, 1992.

Ali, Duse Mohamed. 'Leaves from an Active Life.' *The Comet*, 1937–1938.

Alvares, Francisco. *Ho Preste Joam das Indias Verdadera das Informacam das Terras do Preste Joam Agora Nouamete Impresso, etc.* Lisbon: L. Rodriguez, 1540.

Anderson, Gary. *Fundamentals of Educational Research*. London: Taylor & Francis, 2005.

Anderson, Sue. 'Human Skeletal Remains from Wolsey Street, Ipswich (IAS5003).' January 2009, Report unpublished.

Andrea, Bernadette. 'Black Skin, The Queen's Masques: Africanist Ambivalence and Feminine Author(ity) in the Masques of *Blackness* and *Beauty*.' *English Literary Renaissance* 29:2, 1999, pp. 246–281.

———. 'Pamphilia's Cabinet: Gender Authorship and Empire in Lady Mary Wroth's *Urania*.' *English Literary History* 68:2, 2001, pp. 335–358.

Andrews, Kehinde. 'The Black Studies Movement in Britain: Addressing the Crisis in British Academia and Social Life,' in *Aiming Higher: Race, Inequality and Diversity in the Academy*. London: Runnymede Trust, 2015.

———. 'At Last the UK Has a Black Studies University Course: It's Long Overdue.' *Guardian*, 20 May 2016. www.theguardian.com/comment isfree/2016/may/20/black-studies-university-course-long-overdue, accessed 06/09/16.

Andrews, Kenneth R. *Trade, Plunder and Settlement: Maritime Enterprise and the Genesis of the British Empire, 1480–1630*. Cambridge: Cambridge University Press, 1984.

Anger, Jane. 'Her Protection for Women' (1589), in Randall Martin (ed.). *Women Writers in Renaissance England: An Annotated Anthology*. London: Routledge, 2014, pp. 80–97.

Ani, Marimba. *Let the Circle be Unbroken: The Implications of African Spirituality in the Diaspora*. New York: Nkonimfo Publications, 1988.

Ann Arbor Science for the People Collective. *Biology As a Social Weapon*. Minneapolis, MN: Burgess Pub. Co., 1977.

Anthiaume, Albert-Marie-Ferdinand. 'Un pilote et cartographe havrais au XVIe siècle: Guillaume Le Testu.' *Bulletin de Géographie Historique et Descriptive* 1–2, 1911, pp. 135–202.

Antunes, Catia. 'Early Modern Ports 1500–1750.' *European History Online*, 3 December 2010. http://ieg-ego.eu/en/threads/crossroads/ courts-and-cities/catia-antunes-early-modern-ports-1500-1750, accessed 01/02/18.

Appiah, Kwame Anthony. Henry Louis Gates. *Africana: The Encyclopedia of the African and African American Experience*. Oxford: Oxford University Press, 2005.

Archer, John. Peter Fryer (ed.). 'J. R. Archer's Presidential Address to the Inaugural Meeting of the African Progress Union, 1918.' *West Africa* II, 101, 4 January 1919, pp. 840–842, quoted in Peter Fryer. *Staying Power: The History of Black People in Britain since 1504*. 1984, reprint, London: Pluto Press, 1989, pp. 410–416.

Arikha, Noga. *Passion and Tempers: A History of the Humours*. New York: HarperCollins, 2002.

Aristotle. *In the Problemes of Aristotle with Other Philosophers and Phisitions. Wherein Are Contayned Diuers Questions, with Their Answers, Touching the Estate of Mans Bodie*. London: Arn Hatfield, 1607.

———. *Politics*. Book VII, Chapter 13, in Arthur Stephen McGrade. John Kilcullen (eds., trs.). *Texts in the History of Political Thought, William of Ockham. A Letter to the Friars Minor and Other Writings*. Cambridge: Cambridge University Press, 1995.

Arnold, Janet. *Queen Elizabeth's Wardrobe Unlocked*. Leeds: Maney, 1988.

Artist unknown. *Abd el-Ouahed Ben Messaoud Ben Mohammed Anoun, Moorish Ambassador to Queen Elizabeth I*. c. 1600. Oil on oak panel, 114.5 cm × 79.0 cm. Tate Britain, London. From the University of Birmingham, The Barber Institute of Fine Arts, Birmingham, ref: A0427.

Arundel, Archbishop. Letter to Pope Gregory XII. 1411/1412, in Michael T. Schmidt. *Translating the Bible Literally: The History and Translation Methods of the King James Version, the New American Standard Bible and the English Standard Version*. Bloomington, IN: West Bow Press, 2016, p. 10.

Asante, Molefi K. *Contemporary Black Thought: Alternative Analyses in Social and Behavioral Science*. New York: Sage, 1980.

———. *The Afrocentric Idea*. 1987, new edition, Philadelphia, PA: Temple University Press, 1998.

———. *The Painful Demise of Eurocentrism: An Afrocentric Response to Critics*. Trenton, NJ: Africa World Press, 1999.

———. *Afrocentricity: The Theory of Social Change*. 1998, new edition, Trenton, NJ: African American Images/Africa World Press, 2003.

———. *An Afrocentric Manifesto: Toward an African Renaissance*. Cambridge: Polity Press, 2007.

———. *The History of Africa: The Quest for Eternal Harmony*. New York: Routledge, 2012.

———. 'Afrocentricity: Imagination and Action.' *Dissenting Knowledges Pamphlet Series* 12, Multiversity and Citizens, Los Angeles, CA: UCLA, 2013, n.p.

Asante, Molefi K. Ama Mazama (eds.). *The Encyclopedia of Black Studies*. 2004, new edition, London: Sage, 2005.

Ashcroft, Bill. Gareth Griffiths. Helen Tiffin (eds.). *The Post Colonial Studies Reader*. London/New York: Taylor & Francis, 2006.

Aspinall, Peter J. *The Africa Diaspora Population in Britain: Migrant Identities and Experiences*. New York: Palgrave Macmillan, 2016.

Audi, Robert (ed.). *The Cambridge Dictionary of Western Philosophy*. Cambridge: Paw Prints, 2008.

Aughterson, Kate. *Renaissance Woman: A Sourcebook: Constructions of Femininity in England*. London: Routledge, 2003.

Augustine of Hippo. *City of God*, in Lewis Lewkenor. Ferdinand Walker. Antonio de Torquemada. *The Spanish Mandeuile of Miracles. Or The Garden of Curious Flowers VVherin Are Handled Sundry Points of Humanity, Philosophy, Diuinitie, and Geography, Beautified with Many Strange and Pleasant Histories. First Written in Spanish, by Anthonio De Torquemeda, and Out of That Tongue Translated into English*. London: James Roberts, 1600. n.p.

———. R. W. Dyson (ed.). *Augustine: The City of God Against the Pagans*. Cambridge: Cambridge University Press, 1998.

Author unknown. *A Forensic Dispute on the Legality of Enslaving Africans Held ... in Cambridge New England July 21, 1773*. Boston, MA: Thomas Leverett, 1773.

Author unknown. 'Broughton, Hugh (BRTN569H).' A Cambridge Alumni Database. University of Cambridge. http://venn.lib.cam.ac.uk/cgi-bin/search-2016.pl?sur=&suro=w&fir=&firo=c&cit=&cito=c&c=all&z=all&tex=BRTN569H&sye=&eye=&col=all&maxcomax=50, accessed 23/02/18.

Author unknown. 'Guide to Our Sources.' *Devon Record Office*. www.devon.gov.uk/bishops_transcripts.htm, accessed 04/01/16.

Author unknown. 'Order of 1563,' National Archives, *Parish Records*. 'A provincial constitution of Canterbury,' 25 October 1597 but approved in 1598. National Archives, *Parish Records*.

Author unknown. *St Martin in the Fields Parish Register*, Volume 1. London: publisher unknown, 27 September 1571, p. 116.

Author unknown. 'Straight of Gibraltar – Map & Description.' *World Atlas*, www.worldatlas.com/aatlas/infopage/gibraltar.htm, accessed 12/25/16.

Author unknown. *The Somonyng of Everyman* (1518), in Geoffrey M. Cooper. Christopher Wortham. *The Summoning of Everyman*. Perth: University of Western Australia Press, 1980.

Authors various. 'A Brief, Listing a Series of Complaints against [Richard] Carmarden of London, Surveyor of the Customs to Queen Elizabeth, and the Damage Caused by His Misbehavior to Shipping, Trade, and Receipt of Customs.' (16th century). ref. Hench # 5a.7 (6435-a), Folder 2 : 13. Charlottesville, VA: University of Virginia Library, Special Collections Library, Charlottesville, VA, Medieval and European Manuscripts.

Authors various. *Articles of Peace, Commerce, & Alliance, Between the Crowns of Great Britain and Spain Concluded in a Treaty at Madrid the 13/23 Day of May, In the Year of Our Lord God, 1667/ Translated out of Latin. Treaties, etc*. London: publisher unknown, 1667.

Authors various. *Congressional Record: Proceedings and Debates of the Congress*, Volume 110, Part 10. Washington, DC: US Government Printing Office, 1964.

Authors various. Letter signed by Queen Elizabeth. National Archives, Kew, London, PC 2/21, f. 306, 18 July 1596.

Authors various. Proclamation c. January 1601. National Archives, Kew, London, *Tudor Royal Proclamations*, 1601/804.5–805.

Authors various. St Augustine's Church. St John Hackney Record Office. 18 May 1630. ref. LMA P79/JN 1/021, Hackney Museum, London.

Authors various. *The Articles of the Treaty of Peace, Signed and Sealed at Munster, in Westphalia, 24 of October, 1648 ... As also the Treaty of Peace between France and Spain, Concluded at Nimmeguen, the 17 of September, 1678*. London: W. Onley, 1697.

Authors various. *The [Great] Bible in Englyshe of the Largest and Greatest Volume ... According to the Translation Apoynted by the Queen Maiesties Iniunctions to Be Read in Churches with in Her Maiesties Realme ... At the Coste and Charges of Richard Carmarden*. Rouen: C. Hamillon, 1566.

Authors various. *The Irish Digest* 69. Dublin: Irish Digest, 1960, p. 62.

Authors various. Warrants issued 14 April 1574, B.L. Egerton 2806. 13 April 1575, in Janet Arnold. *Queen Elizabeth's Wardrobe Unlocked*. Leeds: Maney, 1988, p. 106.

Authors various. *Wonderful Strange News from Wood Street Counter* (1642), in John Adlard (ed.). *Restoration Bawdy: Poems, Songs and Jests on the Subject of Sensual Love*. London: Taylor & Francis, 2003.

Authors various including Lancelot Andrews. William Bedwell. Francis Burleigh. Richard Clarke (trs. eds.). *King James Version of the Bible*. London: Robert Baker, 1611.

Authors various including Thomas Sherley. Casper Van Senden. Letter to Lord Mayors signed by Queen Elizabeth. National Archives, Kew, London, PC 2/21, f. 304, 11 July 1596.

Bacharach, Jere L. Josef W. Meri (eds.). *Medieval Islamic Civilization: An Encyclopedia*, Volume 2. New York/London: Routledge, 2006.

Backscheider, Paula (ed.). *The Intersections of the Public and Private Spheres in Early Modern England*. London: Frank Cass, 1996.

Bacon, Francis. *The Two Bookes of Francis Bacon of the Proficience and Advancement of Leaning, Divine Humane*. London: Henrie Tomes, 1605.

———. 'Experiment Solitary Touching the Coloration of Black and Tawny Moors,' in *Novum Organum* (1620), in James Spedding (ed.). *The Works of Francis Bacon Collected and Edited by James Spedding ...* London: Longman and Co, 1857.

———. *Essays or Counsels, Civil & Moral, of Sir Francis Bacon, Lord Verulam ... Whereunto Is Added the Wisdom of the Ancients ... Of the Colours of Good and Evil*. 1625, London: H. Herringman, 1696.

Bacon, Roger. *Opus Majus* (1267). *Summa Grammatica* (1240–1250), in Roger Bacon. Thomas S. Maloney (ed.). *On Signs (Opus Maius, Part 3, Chapter 2)*. Toronto: Pontifical Institute of Mediaeval Studies, 2013.

———. David Lindberg (ed.) *Roger Bacon and the Origins of Perspectiva in the Middle Ages: A Critical Edition and English Translation of Bacon's Perspectiva with Introduction and Notes*. Oxford: Clarendon Press, 1996.

Bahrey, Abba. *History of the Galla* (1593), in Mohammed Assen. 'The Historian Abba Bahrey and the Importance of His "History of the Galla".' *Horn of Africa* 14:1&2, 1990/91, pp. 90–106.

Baker, David B. *The Oxford Handbook of the History of Psychology: Global Perspectives*. Oxford: Oxford University Press, 2012.

Baker, David J. Willy Maley (eds.). *British Identities and English Renaissance Literature*. London: Cambridge University Press, 2002.

Baker, John. *The Oxford History of the Laws of England*, Volume 6: 1483–1558. Oxford: Oxford University Press, 2003.

———. 'Human Rights and the Rule of Law in Renaissance England.' *Northwestern Journal of International Human Rights* 2, spring 2004, www.law.northwestern.edu/journals/jihr/v2/3/, accessed 10/01/13.

Baker, Robert. *Travails in Guinea/Robert Baker's 'Brefe Discourse'* (1568), in Richard Hakluyt (ed.). *The Principal Navigations*. London: Hakluyt's Collection, 1598, pp. 7–8, 27.

Baker, Tawrin. Sven Dupre et al. (eds.). *Early Modern Color Worlds*. Leiden/Boston, MA: Brill, 2016.

Bale, John. *Illustrium Maioris Britanniae Scriptorum*. Ipswich: Ioannem Ouerton, 1548.

Bancel, Nicolas. Thomas David. Dominic Thomas (eds.). *The Invention of Race: Scientific and Popular Representations ...* London: Routledge, 2004.

Bandinel, James. *Some Account of the Trade in Slaves from Africa: As Connected with Europe*. London: Longman Brown, 1842.

Bannerman, William Bruce (ed.). *Registers of St Olave Hart Street, London, 1563–1700*. London: Harleian Society, 1916.

Barashango, Ishakamusa. *African People and European Holidays: A Mental Genocide*, Books 1 and 2. New York: Lushena Books, 2001.

———. *God the Bible and the Black Man's Destiny*. Baltimore, MD: Afrikan World Books, 2002.

Barber, Jill. 'African Caribbean People in Herts (1570–1840).' *Herts Memories*, www.hertsmemories.org.uk/page_id__174.aspx?path=0p34p138p3p101p, 16/07/09, accessed 18/02/10.

Barker, John R. *Race*. Dallas: Ostara Publications, 2016.

Barker, Simon. Hilary Hinds (eds.). *Routledge Anthology of Renaissance Drama*, http://cw.routledge.com/textbooks/0415187346/companion-text/pdf/masqueofblackness2.pdf, accessed 02/08/15.

Barlet, Olivier. *Contemporary African Cinema*. East Lansing, MI: Michigan State University Press, 2016.

Barney, Stephen A. *The Etymologies of Isidore of Seville*. Cambridge: Cambridge University Press, 2006.

Barnfield, Richard. *The Affectionate Shepheard. Containing the Complaint of Daphnis for the Loue of Ganymede*. London: For John Danter [Thomas Newman], 1594.

Barros, Joao de. *Ásia de João de Barros: Dos feitos que os Portugueses Fizeram no Descobrimento e Conquista dos Mares e Terras do Oriente*. Lisbon: Imprensa Nacional-Casa da Moeda, 1988.

Bartels, Emily Carroll. *Spectacles of Strangeness: Imperialism, Alienation, and Marlowe*. Philadelphia, PA: University of Pennsylvania Press, 1993.

———. 'Too Many Blackamoors: Deportation, Discrimination and Elizabeth I.' *Studies in English Literature* 46:2, spring 2006, pp. 305-322.

Barthelemy, Anthony Gerard. *Black Face, Maligned Race: The Representation of Blacks in English Drama from Shakespeare to Southerne*. London: Louisiana State University Press, 1987.

Bassie, Isaac. *The Deed Man's Real Speech*. London: James Collins, 1673.

Battell, Andrew. *The Strange Adventures of Andrew Battell of Leigh, in Angola and Adjoining Regions*. London: Hakluyt Society, 1901.

Bauer, Susan Wise. *The History of the Renaissance World: From the Rediscovery of Aristotle to the Conquest of Constantinople*. New York: W. W. Norton & Company, 2013.

BBC. 'History Suspended at University,' 13 January 2006. http://news.bbc.co.uk/1/hi/education/4609170.stm, accessed 07/01/16.

———. 'Britain's First Black Community in Elizabethan London.' *BBC News Magazine*. www.bbc.co.uk/news/magazine-18903391, accessed 20/07/12. Rebecca Dobbs (pr.). Michael Wood (presenter). 'The Great British Story,' Episode 5, BBC 2, 20/07/12.

Beckett, John. *City Status in the British Isles 1803-2002*. Aldershot: Ashgate, 2005.

Begg, Ean. *The Cult of the Black Virgin*. London: Arkana, 1985.

Bell, Adrian. 'History Cold Case.' Personal email, sent 08/05/10, 10/05/10, accessed 10/05/10, 12/05/10.

Belton, Brian. *Questioning Gypsy Identity: Ethnic Narratives in Britain and America*. Walnut Creek, CA: Alta Mira Press, 2005.

BeMiller, James N. Roy L. Whistler (eds.). *Starch: Chemistry and Technology*. Orlando, FL: Academic Press, 1984.

Ben-Jochannan, Yosef. *Cultural Genocide in the Black and African Studies Curriculum*. New York: ECA Associates, 1972.

———. *African Origins of the Major Western Religions*. Baltimore, MD: Black Classic Press, 1991.

———. *The Need for a Black Bible*. Baltimore, MD: Black Classic Press, 1996.

———. *Africa: Mother of Western Civilisation*. Baltimore, MD: Black Classic Press, 1997.

Bennett, Tony. Lawrence Grossberg. Meaghan Morris (ed.). *New Keywords: A Revised Vocabulary of Culture and Society*. Oxford: Blackwell, 2005.

Benson, Robert L. Giles Constable, Carol D. Lanham (eds.). *Renaissance and Renewal in the Twelfth Century*. Cambridge, MA: Harvard University Press, 1982.

Benton, Lauren. *Law and Colonial Cultures: Legal Regimes in World History, 1400-1900*. Cambridge: Cambridge University Press, 2002.

Berkley, George. John Hill (ed.). *The Naval History of Britain: From the Earliest Periods of Which There Are Accounts in History*. London: T. Osborne and J. Shipton, 1756.

Berlin, Brant. Paul Kay. *Basic Color Terms: Their Universality and Evolution*. London: University of California Press, 1969.

Bernal, Martin. *Black Athena: The Afroasiatic Roots of Classical Civilisation*. 3 Volumes. London/New Brunswick, NJ: Fee Association Books/ Rutgers University, 1987–2006.

Berners, Juliana. Gervase Markham (ed.). *The Gentlemans Academie, or the Booke of S. Albans: Containing Three Most Exact and Excellent Bookes: The First of Hawking, the Second of All the Proper Terms of Hunting and the Last of Armorie: All Compiled by Juliana Barnes in the Yere from the Incarnation of Christ 1486: And Now Reduced into a Better Method by G. M. (i.e. Gervase Markham.) ... (by Richard Farmer)*. London: Humfrey Lownes, 1595.

———. Elizabeth Spearing (ed.). *Revelations of Divine Love*. 1395, London: Penguin, 1998.

Bernier, François. 'A New Division of the Earth,' *Journal des Sçavans* (24 April 1684), in T. Bendyphe (tr.). *Memoirs Read before the Anthropological Society of London*, Volume 1. 1863–1864, pp. 360–64.

Berniker, Eli. David E. McNabb. 'Dialectical Inquiry: A Structured Qualitative Research Method.' *The Qualitative Report* 11:4, 2006, pp. 642–664.

Best, George. *A True Discourse of the Late Voyages of Discovery, for the Finding of a Passage to Cathya, by the Northwest, under the Conduct of Martin Frobisher ...* London: H. Bynyman, 1578.

Biggam, Carole Patricia. *The Semantics of Colour: A Historical Approach*. New York: Cambridge University Press, 2012.

Bindman, David. Henry Louis Gates. Frank M. Snowden. *The Image of the Black in Western Art*, Volumes I–IV. New York: Harvard University Press, 2010–2014.

Bisson, Douglas. *The Merchant Adventurers of England: The Company and the Crown, 1474–1564*. London: Associated University Press, 1993.

Black British Academics. 'Staff and Students of Colour Speak Out on Racism in Academia.' *Black British Academics Phd Network*, 17 October 2015. http://phdnetwork.blackbritishacademics.co.uk/2015/10/17/staff-and-stu dents-of-colour-speak-out-on-racism-in-academia/, accessed 07/01/16.

Blackburn, Robin. *The Making of New World Slavery: From the Baroque to the Modern, 1492–1800*. London: Verso Books, 1998.

Blackstone, William. *Commentaries on the Laws of England*, Volume 1. London: William Walker, 1826.

Blount, Edward (tr.). Ieronimo Conestaggio. *The Historie of the Uniting of the Kingdom of Portugal to the Crowne of Castill ...* London: A. Hatfield for E. Blount, 1600.

Blum, Edward J. Paul Harvey. *The Color of Christ: The Son of God and the Saga of Race in America*. Chapel Hill, NC: University of North Carolina Press, 2012.

Bodin, Jean. *Methodus ad Facilem Historiarum Cognitionem*. Paris: Apud M. Iuuenem, 1566.

———. *De la Demonomanie des Sorciers* ... Paris: Du Puys, 1580.

———. Marion Leathers. Daniels Kuntz (trs., eds.). *Colloquium of the Seven about Secrets of the Sublime*. Princeton, NJ/London: Princeton University Press, 1975.

Bolton, James Laurence (ed.). *Alien Communities of London in the Fifteenth Centuries*. Stamford: Richard III and York History Trust with Paul Watkins, 1998.

Bonner, Edmund. *A Profitable and Necessarye Doctryne, with Certain Homilies ... Edmund Byshop of London, for the Instruction and Information of the People Beynge within His Diocese of London*. London: J. Cawoode, 1555.

Boorde, Andrew. *The First Boke of the Introduction of Knowledge. The Whych Doth Teach a Man to Speake and Parte of All Maner of Languages and to Know the Usage and Fashion of All Maner of Countries ... with Woodcuts* [images]. London: William Copeland, 1550.

Bourke, Thomas. *A Concise History of the Moors in Spain from the Invasion of That Kingdom to Their Final Expulsion from It*. London: Rivington Hatchard, 1811.

Bourne, George. *Slavery Illustrated in Its Effects on Women and Domestic Society*. Boston, MA: Issac Knapp, 1837.

Bovill, E. W. *The Golden Trade of the Moors*. London: Oxford University Press, 1958.

Bowlby, Rachel. *Freudian Mythologies: Greek Tragedy and Modern Identities*. Oxford: Oxford University Press, 2007.

Bowyer, William. John Nichols. *Literary Anecdotes of the Eighteenth Century*, Volumes 1–3. London: Nichols and Son Company, 1812.

Boyce, Michael. 'The Uncomfortable Racism of C. S. Lewis.' *Geekdom House*. https://geekdomhouse.com/the-uncomfortable-racism-of-c-s-lewis/, accessed 28/01/18.

Boyer, Allen. *Sir Edward Coke and the Elizabethan Age*. London: Stanford University Press, 2003.

Boyle, Robert. *Experiments and Considerations Touching Colours*. London. Henry Herringman, 1664.

Brabant, Margaret. *Politics, Gender, and Genre: The Political Thought of Christine de Pizan*. Boulder, CO: Westview Press, 1992.

Bradley, Keith. Paul Cartledge (eds.). *The Cambridge World History of Slavery*, Volume 1: The Ancient Medieval World. Cambridge: Cambridge University Press, 2011.

Bradshaw, Benjamin. Peter Roberts (eds.). *British Consciousness and Identity: The Making of Britain, 1533–1707*. Cambridge: Cambridge University Press, 1998.

Braude, Benjamin. 'The Sons of Noah and the Construction of Ethnic and Geographical Identities in the Medieval and Early Modern Periods.' *William and Mary Quarterly* 65, January 1997, pp. 103–142.

Braun, Peter. Manfred Weinberg. *Ethno/Graphie ... of Literatur und Anthropologie*, 17. Tubingen: Narr, Francke, Attempto, Furlang, 2002.

Bremmer, Jan N. *Greek Religion and Culture: The Bible and the Ancient Near East*. Lieden/Boston, MA: Brill, 2002.

Brenner, Robert. *Merchants and Revolution: Commercial Change, Political Conflict, and London ...* London: Verso, 2003.

Bressey, Caroline. Gemma Romain. The Equiano Centre, University College London. www.ucl.ac.uk/equianocentre/Paul_Goodwin.html, accessed 05/01/16.

Breverton, Terry. *Owen Tudor, Founding Father of the Tudor Dynasty*. Amberley: Amberley Publishing, 2017.

Brewster, David. *Brewer's Dictionary of Phrase and Fable ...* London: H. Altemus, 1870.

Briffault, Robert. *The Troubadours*. Bloomington, IN: Indiana University Press, 1965.

Brigden, Susan. *New Worlds, Lost Worlds: The Rule of the Tudors, 1485–1603*. London: Allen Lane, 2000.

Bristol Record Office. Bristol. ref. P/ST PJR/1/1/CMB 1576–1621, n.p.

———. St Philip and Jacob. Bristol. 14 December 1603. ref. P/ST PJR/1/1/CMB 1576–1621.

The British Archaeological Society Association and Royal Archaeological Institute of Great Britain and Ireland. *Archaeological Journal* 69. London: Royal Archaeological Institute, 1912, p. 485.

Bromley, John. *The Armorial Bearings of the Guilds of London: A Record of the Heraldry of the Surviving Companies with Historical Notes*. London: F. Warne, 1960.

Broomhall, Susan. Stephanie Tarbin. *Women, Identities and Communities in Early Modern Europe*. Aldershot: Ashgate, 2008.

Broughton, Hugh. *A Concent of Scripture*. London: G. Simson and W. White, 1588. Jodocus Hondius, (date unknown) Map, p. 5, leaves of plates, map; 22 cm. ref. R.B.R. fol. 343 B875co 1590.

———. *A Briefe Discourse of the Scriptures*. London: W. White, 1614.

Browder, Anthony T. *Nile Valley Contributions to Civilisations*. Washington, DC: Institute of Karmic Guidance, 1992.

Brown, Sarah Annes. Robert I. Lublin (eds.). *Reinventing the Renaissance: Shakespeare and His Contemporaries in Adaptation and Performance*. New York: Springer, 2013.

Brown, W. *Tolerance and/or Equality? 'The Jewish Question' and the 'Woman Question.'* Urbana, IL: University of Illinois Press, 2004.

Browne, Thomas. *Pseudodoxia Epidemica: or, Enquiries into Very Many Received Tenents and Commonly Presumed Truths*. London: Edward Dod, 1646.

Browner, Jessica. 'The Wrong Side of the River: London's Disreputable Southbank in the Sixteenth and Seventeenth Century.' *Essays in History* 36, 1994. http://etext.virginia.edu/journals/EH/EH36/EH36.html, accessed 12/06/07.

Bruce, Frederick Fyvie. *The History of the Bible in English*. Cambridge: James and Clarke, 2002.

Bruder, Edith. *The Black Jews of Africa: History, Religion, Identity*. New York/Oxford: Oxford University Press, 2008.

Bulwer, John. *Anthropometamorphosis: Man Transform'd; or, the Artificial Changeling. Historically Presented, in the Mad and Cruel Gallantry, Foolish Bravery, Ridiculous Beauty, Filthy Finenesse, and Loathsome Lovelinesse of Most Nations, Fashioning & Altering Their Bodies from the Mould Intended by Nature. With a Vindication of the Regular Beauty and Honesty of Nature. And an Appendix of the Pedigree of the English Gallant*. London: William Hunt, 1654.

Burger, Thomas. Frederick Lawrence (eds. trs.). *The Structural Transformation of the Public Sphere: An Inquiry into a Category of Bourgeois Society*. Cambridge, MA: The MIT Press, 1989.

Burnett, Leon. Sanja Bahun. *Myth Literature and the Unconscious*. London: Karnac Books, 2014.

Burrell, John. *The Divine Right of Kings Proved from the Principles of the Church of England, in a Sermon Preached …* London: John Hayes, 1683.

Burton, Jonathan. Ania Loomba. *Race in Early Modern England: A Documentary Companion*. New York: Springer, 2007.

Bury, John Bagnall. *The Cambridge Medieval History*, Volume 2. London: The University Press, 1964.

Bush, Lester E. *Neither White Nor Black: Mormon Scholars Confront the Race Issue in a Universal Church*. Salt Lake City, UT: Signature Books, 1984.

Butts v Penny, (1677), 2 Levinz, p. 20, in Colin Bobb-Semple. *English Common Law, African Enslavement and Human Rights*. Charleston, SC: CreateSpace, 2012, pp. 19–20.

Byrd, W. Carson. Matthew W. Hughey. 'Biological Determinism and Racial Essentialism: The Ideological Double Helix of Racial Inequality.' *Annals of the American Academy of Political and Social Science* 661:1, 10 August 2015, pp. 8–22.

Byron, Gay. *Symbolic Blackness and Ethnic Difference in Early Christian Literature*. London: Routledge, 2003.

Caballero, Ernesto Gimenez. *Genio de Espano …* Madrid: Ediciones Jerarquía, 1938, in Nil Santianez (ed.). *Topographies of Fascism: Habitus, Space, and Writing in Twentieth Century Spain*. Toronto: University of Toronto Press, 2013, p. 76.

Calvert, Thomas. *The Blessed Jew of Marocco; or, a Blackmoor Made White. Being a Demonstration of the True Messias out of the Law and Prophets, by Rabbi Samuel a Jew, Turned Christian; Written First in the Arabick, After Translated into Latin, and Now Englished. To Which Are Annexed a Diatriba of the Jews' Sins, and Their Miserie All Over the World. Annotations to the Book, with Large Digressions, Discovering Jewish Blindnesse …* York: T. Broad, 1648.

Cambrensis, Geraldus. Joseph Stevenson (tr.). *Concerning the Instruction of Prince* ... Felinfach: JMF Books, 1991.

Campbell, Joseph. *The Hero with a Thousand Faces*. Princeton, NJ: Princeton University Press, 1971.

Campbell, Kenneth L. *Western Civilisation: A Global and Comparative Approach: Since 1600*, Volume 2. London: Routledge, 2015.

Cannon, John. *The Oxford Companion to British History*. Oxford: Oxford University Press, 2002.

Canova-Green, Marie-Claude. Ralph Richard (ed.). 'Burlesque Ballet, a Ballad and a Banquet in Ben Jonson's The Gypsies Metamorphos'd (1621).' *Dance Research*. Edinburgh: Edinburgh University Press, 2007. *Oxford Index* http://oxfordindex.oup.com/view/10.3366/edinburgh/9780748635849.003.0006, accessed 29/08/15.

Careri, John Francis (Giovanni) Gemelli. *A Collection of Voyages Travel, Some Now First Printed from Original Manuscripts, Others Now First Published in English*. London: Henry Lintot, John Osborn, 1744-1746.

———. *A Voyage Round the World in Six Parts* (1728), in Lewis Hanke. *The Spanish Struggle for Justice in the Conquest of America*. Philadelphia, PA: University of Pennsylvania Press, 1949, p. 148.

Carew, George. Thomas Stafford (ed.). *Pacata Hibernia. Ireland Appeased and Reduced. Or, an Historie of the Late Warres of Ireland, Especially within the Province of Mounster vnder the Government of Sir G. Carew ... Illustrated with Seventeene Severall Mappes* ... London: Aug. Mathewes for Robert Milbourne, 1633.

———. *The Survey of Cornwall. And an Epistle Concerning the Excellencies of the English Tongue. Now First Published from the Manuscript* ... *[Written in 1602 and 1605 Respectively]*. London: Samuel Chapman, 1723.

———. *Letters from George Lord Carew to Sir Thomas Roe, Ambassador to the Court of the Great Mogul 1615-1617*. London: Camden Society, 1860.

Carlin, Patricia L. *Shakespeare's Mortal Men: Overcoming Death, in History, Comedy, and Tragedy*. New York: P. Lang, 1993.

Carlyle, Thomas. 'Occasional Discourse on the Negro Question.' *Fraser's Magazine for Town and Country* 40, 1849, pp. 670-679.

Cartigny, Jean de. William Goodyear (tr.). *The Voyage of the Wandering Knight*. London: Thomas East, 1581.

Cartwright: In the Matter of. 11 Elizabeth, 2 Rushworth's College (1569), p. 468.

Casares, Aurelia Martín. *Juan Latino: Talento y Destino*. Granada: Universidad de Granada, 2016.

Cawston, George. Augustus Henry Keane. *Early Chartered Companies, A.D. 1296-1858*. Manchester: Ayer Publishing, 1968.

Chandler, Wayne. Ivan Van Sertima (ed.). *African Presence in Early Europe*. Piscataway, NJ: Transaction Publishers, 1985, pp. 144-176.

Chambers, Robert. William Chambers. *Chambers Miscellany of Useful and Entertaining Tracts*. Edinburgh: William and Robert Chambers, 1846.

Chapman, Matthieu. *Anti-Black Racism in Early Modern English Drama: The Other 'Other.'* New York/Abingdon: Taylor & Francis, 2016.

Chater, Kathy (Kathleen). *Untold Histories: Black People in England and Wales During the Period of the British Slave Trade, c. 1660–1807.* Manchester: Manchester University Press, 2008.

Chaucer, Geoffrey. *The Canterbury Tales of Chaucer* ... 1386. London: Cassell Petter and Galpin, 1400, 1486.

Chedgzoy, Kate. Emma Francis. Murray Pratt. *In a Queer Place: Sexuality and Belonging in British and European Contexts.* Aldershot: Ashgate, 2002.

Chisholm, Hugh. *The Encyclopaedia Britannica: A Dictionary of Arts, Sciences, Literature and General Information.* Cambridge: Cambridge University Press, 1911.

Churchward, Albert. *The Signs and Symbols of Primordial Man ... The Evolution of Religious Doctrines from the Eschatology of the Ancient Egyptians* ... London: E.P. Dutton and Co., 1910.

Cipolla, Carlo M. *The Economic Decline of Empire.* London: Routledge, 2013.

Cirencester, Richard. John Allen Giles (tr. ed.). *The Chronicle of Richard of Devizes Concerning the Deeds of Richard the First, King of England: Also Richard of Cirencester's Description of Britain.* London: James Bohn, 1841.

City of Westminster Archives Centre, London. 1601/2 January/21/St Clements Dane/volume1Burials/MF 1; 1660 October/4/St Pauls/Volume1Burials/MF1, p. 236.

Clarke, Benjamin. *Glimpses of Ancient Hackney and Stoke Newington: Being a Reprint of a Series of Articles Appearing in the Hackney Mercury, from April 23rd, 1892, to November 25th, 1893. With an Appendix Dealing with the Conversion of a Portion of Hackney Churchyards into Open Space.* London: Hackney Mercury Offices, 1893.

Clarke, Grata Jeter. *The Jeter Mosaic: Seven Centuries in the History of a Family.* Mount Pleasant, SC: Arcadia-Clarke, 1987.

Clarkson, Thomas. *Thoughts upon Slavery.* London: Joseph Crukshank, 1778.

Clement of Rome. *Recognitos Divi Clementis.* Basel: Bebel, 1526, 1536.

Coffin, Cyril. 'Aliens in Dorset 1525.' *The Dorset Page.* www.thedorsetpage.com/history/Aliens/Aliens.htm, posted 2000, accessed 02/01/07.

Cohen, Anthony P. *The Symbolic Construction of Community.* Chichester: Ellis Horwood, 1985.

Cohen, Stanley. *Folk Devils and Moral Panics.* St Albans: Paladin, 1973.

Coke, Edward. *Semayne's Case.* 1 January 1604, 5 Coke Rep. 91.

———. *The Lord Coke His Speech and Charge. With a Discouerie of the Abuses and Corruption of Officers* ... London: Nathaniell Butter, 1607.

Collins, Edward Herbert. John Churton (ed.). *The Poems of Lord Herbert of Cherbury.* 1665, 2nd edition, London: Chatto and Windus, 1881.

Collins, Siobhan. Louise Denmead. '"There Is All Africa [...] within Us": Language, Generation and Alchemy in Browne's Explication of

Blackness,' in Kathryn Murphy. Richard Todd (eds.). '*A Man Very Well Studyed': New Contexts for Thomas Browne*. Leiden/Boston, MA: Brill, 2008, pp. 127–146.

Comerford, Michael. *Collections Relating to the Dioceses of Kildare and Leighlin*, Volume 2. Dublin: James Duffy and Sons, 1883.

Condren, Conal. 'Public, Private, and the Idea of the "Public Sphere" in Early-Modern England.' *Intellectual History Review* 19:1, 2009, pp. 15–28.

Conestaggio, Ieronimo. *The Historie of the Uniting of the Kingdom of Portugal to the Crowne of Castill …* London: A. Hatfield for E. Blount, 1600.

Conrad, David C. *Empires of West Africa: Ghana, Mali and Songhay*. New York: Facts on File, 2005.

Conway, Alison Margaret. *The Protestant Whore: Courtesan Narrative and Religious Controversy in England, 1680–1750*. Toronto: University of Toronto Press, 2010.

Coote, Stephen. *Drake: The Life and Legend of an Elizabethan Hero*. London/New York: Simon and Schuster, 2003.

Copher, Charles B. Gayraud S. Wilmore (eds.). *African American Religious Studies: An Interdisciplinary Anthology*. Ann Arbor, MI: Duke University Press, 1989.

Corbett, Julian Stafford. *Drake and the Tudor Navy: With a History of the Rise of England as a Maritime Power*. London: Longman Green, 1898.

Cormack, Margaret Jean (ed.). Giovanna Fiume. *Saints and Their Cults in the Ancient World*. Columbia, SC: University of South Carolina Press, 2007.

Cornwall Record Office. Old County Hall, Truro, Cornwall, TR1 3AY, Registers of Bodmin, ref. Mf 12 FP 13/1/11, *Burials 1558–1757*, 12 December 1563; 12 April 1606.

Courtauld, George. *The Pocket Book of Patriotism*. Halstead: Halstead Books, 2004.

———. *Pocket Book of Patriots: 100 British Heroes*. London: Random House, 2010.

Crawford, Patricia. *Exploring Women's Past: Essays in Social History*. Carlton: Sisters Publishing, 1983.

———. 'Public Duty, Conscience and Women in Early Modern England,' in John Morrill. Paul Slack et al. (eds.). *Public Duty, and Private Conscience in Seventeenth-Century England: Essays Presented to G.E. Aylmer*. Oxford: Clarendon Press, 1993, pp. 201–234.

Crenshaw, Kimberle. 'Mapping the Margins: Intersectionality, Identity Politics, and Violence against Women of Color.' *Stanford Law Review* 43:6, July 1991, pp. 1241–1299.

———. *Critical Race Theory: The Key Writings That Formed the Movement*. New York: New Press, 1995.

———. *On Intersectionality: The Essential Writings of Kimberle Crenshaw*. New York/Jackson, MS: New Press, 2012.

Cressy, David. *Society and Culture in Early Modern England*. London: Ashgate, 2003.

———. *Literacy and the Social Order: Reading and Writing in Tudor and Stuart England*. Cambridge: Cambridge University Press, 2006.

Croft, Pauline. 'English Commerce with Spain and the Armada War, 1558–1603,' in Simon Lester Adams. M. J. Rodriguez-Salgado (eds.). *England, Spain and the Gran Armada, 1585–1604: Essays from the Anglo-Spanish Conferences*. 1988, new edition, Edinburgh: Rowman and Littlefield, 1991, pp. 236–263.

———. 'Trading with the Enemy, 1585–1604.' *Historical Journal* 32, June 1989, pp. 281–302.

Cromwell, Thomas. *Walks through Islington; Comprising an Historical and Descriptive …* London: Sherwood Gilbert and Piper, 1835.

Cromwell, Thomas et al. 'Supplication against the Ordinaries.' A petition passed by the House of Commons in 1532, in Geoffrey Rudolph Elton (ed.). *Studies in Tudor and Stuart Politics and Government: Papers and Reviews*. 1973, new edition, Cambridge: Cambridge University Press, 2003.

———. 'Order for Keeping Parish Registers,' on 29 September 1538, in 'Parish Records: 1538, 1563 and 1598.' National Archives, *Parish Records*, accessed 12/08/08.

Cuddon, John Anthony. *Dictionary of Literary Terms and Literary Theory*. Oxford: Wiley Blackwell, 2013.

Cugoano, Ottobah. *Thoughts and Sentiments on the Evil and Wicked Traffic of the Slavery and Commerce of the Human Species …* London: T. Beckett, 1787.

Curio, Caelius Augustinus. *A Notable History of the Saracens …* London: William How and Abraham Veale, 1575.

Cutting, John. *History and the Morris Dance: A Look at Morris Dancing from the Earliest Days until 1850*. Alton: Dance Books, 2005.

Dabydeen, David. Paul Edwards (eds.). *Black Writers in Britain 1760–1890*. Edinburgh: Edinburgh University Press, 1991.

Dabydeen, David. James Gilmore (eds.). *The Oxford Companion to Black British History*. Oxford: Oxford University Press, 2007.

Dadson, Trevor J. *Los Moriscos de Villarrubia de los Ojos (siglos XV–XVIII). Historia de una Minoría Asimilada, Expulsada y Reintegrada*. Tiempo emulado. Historia de América y España. Madrid: Iberoamericana, 2007.

———. *Tolerance and Coexistence in Early Modern Spain: Old Christians and Moriscos in the Campo de Calatrava*. Rochester: Tamesis, 2014.

Dagbovie, Pero Gaglo. *The Early Black History Movement: Carter G. Woodson, and Lorenzo Johnston Greene*. Urbana, IL: University of Illinois Press, 2007.

Daileader, Celia R. *Racism, Misogyny, and the Othello Myth: Inter-racial Couples from Shakespeare to Spike Lee*. Cambridge: Cambridge University Press, 2005.

Dalberg-Acton, Baron John Emerich Edward David, George Walter Prothero, et al. *Cambridge Modern History*, Volume 1. Cambridge: Cambridge University Press, 1912.

Dalporto, Jeannie (ed.). *Women in Service in Early Modern England*. Aldershot: Ashgate, 2008.

Dandelet, Thomas James. John A. Marino (eds.). *Spain in Italy: Politics, Society, and Religion 1500–1700*. Leiden/Boston, MA: Brill, 2007.

Daniel, Samuel. *The True Discription of a Royall Masque. Presented at Hampton Court, upon Sunday Night, being the Eight of Ianuary. 1604. And Personated by the Queenes Most Excellent Majestie, Attended by Eleuen Ladies of Honour*. London: Edward Allde, 1604.

Daniell, David. *The Bible in English: Its History and Influence*. New Haven, CT: Yale University Press, 2003.

Das, Veena. 'Collective Violence and the Shifting Categories of Communal Riots, Ethnic Cleasening and Genocide,' in Dan Stone (ed.). *The Historiography of Genocide*. New York: Springer, 2008, pp. 93–127.

Daughrity, Dyron B. *The Changing World of Christianity: The Global History of a Borderless Religion*. Bern: Peter Lang, 2010.

Davenant, William. *Gondibert: An Heroick Poem …* London: Thomas Newcomb for John Holden, 1651.

Davenport, Charles Benedict. *Heredity in Relation to Genetics*. New York: H. Holt, 1911.

Davidson, Basil. *Black Mother: A Study of the Precolonial Connection between Africa and Europe*. London: Longman, 1970.

———. *African Civilization Revisited: From Antiquity to Modern Times*. Trenton, NJ: Africa World Press, 1991.

Davies, Robert Rees. *The First English Empire: Power and Identities in the British Isles 1093–1343*. Oxford: Oxford University Press, 2000.

Day, Rosemary O. *The Professions in Early Modern England, 1450–1800: Servants of the Commonweal*. Harlow: Longman, 2000.

De Azeved, Pedro (ed.). *Archivo Historico Portuguez*. Madrid: Libano da Silva, 1903.

De Pareja, Juan. *Portrait of Agustín Moreto*. 1648–1653. Oil on canvas. Lazaro Galdiano Foundation, Madrid.

De Pizan, Christine. Bryan Anslay (tr.). *Begin. Here Begynneth the Boke of the Cyte of Ladyes, the Which Boke Is Deyded in to iij Partes. End …* London: H. Pepwell, 1521.

De Renzi, Silvia (ed.). *Pathology in Practice: Diseases and Dissections in Early Modern Europe*. London: Routledge, 2017.

De Ugalde, Fray Francisco. 1520. In Jean-Benoit Nadeau. Julie Barlow. *The Story of Spanish*. Oxford/London: Oxford University Press, 2013, p. 172.

De Velazquez, Diego Rodriguez. *Juan De Pareja*. 1649–1650. Oil on canvas, 81.3 cm × 69.9 cm. ref. 1971.86. Metropolitan Museum of Art, New York.

De Zunga, Diego Ortiz. 1677. In Andrew Spicer. Jane L. Stevens Crawshaw (eds.). *The Place of the Social Margins 1350–1750*. London: Routledge, 2016.

Deanesly, Margaret. *The Lollard Bible and Other Medieval Biblical Visions*. Cambridge: Cambridge University Press, 1920.

Dekker, Thomas. *Lanthorne and Candlelight. Or the Bell-Mans Second Nights Walke. In Which He Brings to Light, a Broode of More Strange Villanies, Than Ever Were till This Yeare Discovered*. London: Iohn Busbie, 1608.

Deloach, Ronald J. *Living without a Name: A View through Black Eyes*. Pittsburgh, PA: Dorrance Publishing, 2009.

Demers, Patricia. *Women's Writing in English: Early Modern England*. Toronto: University of Toronto Press, 2005.

Dent, Arthur. *The Plaine Mans Path-Way to Heauen. Wherein Euery Man May Clearly See, Whether He Shall Be Saued or Damned. Set Forth Dialogue Wise, for the Better Understanding of the Simple*. London: Robert Dexter, 1601.

Devon Record Office (DRO), Great Moor House, Bittern Road, Sowton, Exeter, Devon, EX2 7NY: East Allington/20/08/1577 PR.

Devon Record Office (DRO), Devon, Hatherleigh 13/05/1604 PR1, Hatherleigh 10/08/1606 PR1, Hatherleigh 23/12/1607 PR1, Hatherleigh 08/05/1611 PR1, Hatherleigh 06/06/1613 PR1.

Diawara, Manthia. *In Search of Africa*. New York: Harvard University Press, 2009.

Dillingham, John. John Lilburne (eds.). *Moderate Intelligencer: Impartially Communicating Martiall Affairs to the Kingdom of England VII. 10–17 April 1645*. London: Richard White, 1645, p. 53.

Diop, Cheikh Anta. *The African Origin of Civilisation: Myth or Reality*. Paris: Presence Africaine, 1967, new edition, Chicago, IL: Chicago University Review Press, 1989.

Donno, Elizabeth Story (ed.). Richard Madox. *An Elizabethan in 1582: The Diary of Richard Madox, Fellow of All Saints*. London: Hakluyt Society, 1976.

Donovan, Frank. *Never on a Broomstick*. New York: Bell Publishing Company, 1971.

Doran, Robert M. (ed.). Bernard Lonergan. *Method in Theology*. Toronto: University of Toronto Press, 2017.

Doward, Jamie. 'Middlesex University Cuts Spark International Protests from Philosophers.' *The Guardian*, 9 May 2010. www.theguardian.com/world/2010/may/09/middlesex-university-cuts-protest-philosophers.

Dowling, James. Archer Ryland. *Reports of Cases Argued and Determined in the Court of Kings Bench*. London: S. Sweet, R. Pheney, A. Maxwell, 1822.

Doyle, Charles Clay. Wolfgang Mieder. *The Dictionary of Modern Proverbs*. New Haven, CT: Yale University Press, 2012.

Drake, Francis. *Sir Francis Drake Revived Calling Upon the Dull or Effeminate Age to Follow His Noble Steps for Gold and Silver*. 1621, revised edition, London: Nicolas, Bourne, 1628.

Drake, Francis. William Davenant. *The History of Sir Francis Drake, Expressed by Instrumentall and Vocal Musick* ... London: Henry Herringman, 1659.

Dresser, Madge. *Slavery Obscured: The Social History of the Slave Trade in an English Provincial Port*. 2001, new edition, Bristol: Redcliff Press, 2007.

Drew-Bear, Annette. *Painted Faces on the Renaissance Stage: The Moral Significance of Face-Painting Conventions*. Lewisburg, PA/London: Bucknell University Press, 1994.

Drout, Michael D. C. (ed.). Brain Rosebury. 'Race in Tolkien Films.' *J.R.R. Tolkien Encyclopedia: Scholarship and Critcial Assessment*. Abingdon: Taylor & Francis, 2007.

Dueck, Daniela. Hugh Lindsay. Sarah Pothecary. *Strabo's Cultural Geography: The Making of a Kolossourgia*. Cambridge/New York: Cambridge University Press, 2005.

Duffield, Ian. *Duse Mohamed Ali and the Development of Pan-Africanism 1866–1945*. PhD thesis. Edinburgh: Edinburgh University, unpublished, 1971.

Duffield, Mark. Vernon Hewitt. *Empire, Development and Colonialism: The Past in the Present*. Woodbridge: Boydell and Brewer, 2013.

Dunbavin, Paul. *Picts and Ancient Britons: An Exploration of Pictish Origins*. London: Third Millennium Publishing, 1998.

Durant, Thomas. David Knottnerus. *Plantation Society and Race Relations: The Origins of Inequality*. Westport, CT/London: Prager, 1999.

Dworkin, Ronald. *Taking Rights Seriously*. New York: Harvard University Press, 1977.

Dyrness, William A. (ed.). *Global Dictionary of Theology: A Resource for the Worldwide Church*. Westmount, IL: Intervarsity Press, 2009.

Dyson, Humfrey (collator). *A Book Containing All Such Proclamations as Were Published by the Reigine of the Late Queen Elizabeth 1559–1602*. London: Bonham Norton and John Bull, 1618.

Eadie, John. *The English Bible: An External and Critical History of the Various English Translations of the Scripture*. London: Macmillan and Company, 1876.

Ealden, Mary. 'Lecture at NPG Blackamoores.' Email sent to Narrative Eye 06/07/14, accessed 07/07/14.

Eastwood, Jonathan. *The Bible Word-Book: A Glossary of Old English Bible Words*. London/Cambridge: Macmillan and Co, 1866.

Eden, Richard. *The Decades of the Newe World or West India* ... London: William Powell, 1555.

Edgeworth, Roger. *Sermons Very Fruitfull, Godly, and Learned, Preached and Sette Foorth by Maister Roger Edgeworth, Doctoure of Diuinitie, Canon of the Cathedrall Churches of Sarisburie, Welles and Bristow, Residentiary in the Cathedrall Churche of Welles, and Chauncellour of the*

Same Churche: With a Repertorie or Table, Directinge to Many Notable Matters Expressed in the Same Sermons. London: Robert Caly, 1557.

Edwards, Geoffrey Paul. *Early African Presence in the British Isles, an Inaugural Lecture* ... Edinburgh: Centre of African Studies, Edinburgh University, 1990.

Edwards, Paul. James Walvin. 'Africans in Britain, 1500–1800,' in *The African Diaspora: Interpretive Essays*. Cambridge, MA: Harvard University Press, 1976, pp. 173–204.

Eliot, Thomas. *The Dictionary of Syr Thomas Eliot Knyght*. London: for Thomas Cromwell, T. Eliot, 1538.

Elliott, John Huxtable. *Empires of the Atlantic World: Britain and Spain in America, 1492–1830*. New Haven, CT: Yale University Press, 2007.

Ellis, Henry. *The History and Antiquities of the Parish of Saint Leonard Shoreditch* ... London: J. Nicholas, 1798.

Else, Holly. 'Black PhD Students Are Pioneers in Their Subjects, Says Professor.' *Times Higher Education*, 26 February 2015. www.timeshighereducation.com/news/black-phd-students-are-pioneers-in-their-subjects-says-professor/2018715.article.

Elton, Geoffrey Ruddolph. *The Tudor Constitution: Documents and Commentary*. 1960, Cambridge/London: Cambridge University Press, 1982.

English Ambassador. Collegio Secreta Esposizioni. Rome. 'Calendar of State Papers: Venice 23 August 1609.' *British History Online*. www.british-history.ac.uk/cal-state-papers/venice/vol11/pp309-325, published University of London 2017, accessed 28/04/2018.

Estienne, Henri. *The Stage of Popish Toyes: Conteining Both Tragicall and Comicall Partes* ... London: Henry Binneman, 1581.

Etchells, Guy. 'Timeline of Events Concerning the Keeping of Records Pre 1812.' *Genealogy Roots Web*. http://freepages.genealogy.rootsweb.ances try.com/~framland/acts/pre1812.htm, accessed 12/12/05.

Evans, William Mckee. 'From the Land of Canaan to the Land of Guinea: The Strange Odyssey of the Sons of Ham.' *American Historical Review* 85, February 1980, pp. 15–43.

Exquemelin, Alexandre Olivier. *Bucaniers of America: or, a True Account of the Most Remarkable Assaults Committed of Late Years Upon the Coasts of the West-Indies, by the Bucaniers of Jamaica and Tortuga, Both English and French. Wherein Are Contained More Especially, the Unparallel'd Exploits of Sir Henry Morgan, Our English Jamaican Hero, Who Sack'd Puerto Velo, Burnt Panama, &c. Written Originally in Dutch by John Esquemeling, One of the Bucaniers, Who Was Present at Those Tragedies; and Thence Translated into Spanish by Alonso de Bonne-Maison, Doctor of Physick, and Practitioner at Amsterdam. Now Faithfully Rendred into English*. London: William Crooke, 1684.

Fage, John Donnelly. Roland Anthony Oliver. Richard Gray (eds.). *The Cambridge History of Africa* ..., Volume 5. Cambridge: Cambridge University Press, 1976.

Faggett, Harry Lee. *Black and Other Minorities in Shakespeare's England.* Prairie View, TX: Prairie View Press, 1971.

Feerick, Jean E. *Strangers in Blood: Relocating Race in the Renaissance.* Toronto/Buffalo, NY/London: University of Toronto Press, 2010.

Ferguson, Neil (dr.). Tania Lindon (pr.). *History Cold Case*, Episode 1, BBC2, 6 May 2010.

Ferme, Mariane Conchita. *'Hammocks Belong to Men, Stools to Women': Constructing and Contesting Gender Domains in a Mende Village (Sierra Leone, West Africa)*, Volume 1. Chicago, IL: University of Chicago, 1992.

Fiedler, Leslie A. *The Stranger in Shakespeare.* New York: Stein and Day, 1972.

Figgs, John Neville. *The Theory of the Divine Right of Kings. Prince Consort Dissertation, 1892.* Cambridge: University of Cambridge, 1892, London: Creative Media Partners, 2015.

Filmer, Robert. *The Necessity of the Absolute Power of All Kings: And in Particular of the King of England* 1648, London: W. H. & T. F., 1680.

Finley, Moses I. *Ancient Slavery and Modern Ideology.* London: Penguin, 1998.

Fleischer, Aylmer Von. *Retake Your Fame: Black Contribution to World Civilisation*, Volume 1. s.l.: Aylmer Von Fleischer, 2004.

Fleming, Patricia. 'The Politics of Marriage Among Non-Catholic European Royalty.' *Current Anthropology* 14:3, pp. 231–249.

Floyd-Wilson, Mary. *English Ethnicity and Race in Early Modern Drama.* Cambridge: Cambridge University Press, 2003.

Flynn, Patrick T. Jena-Marie Kauth. John Kevin Doyle et al. (eds.). *Substance, Judgement, and Evaluation: Seeking the Worth of a Liberal Arts, Core Texts Education.* Lanham, MD: University Press of America, 2010.

Forest, John. *'Morris and Matachin': A Study in Contemporary Choreography.* London: English Folk Dance and Song Society, 1984.

Forhan, Kate Langdon. *The Political Theory of Christine Pizan.* London: Routledge, 2017.

Foss, Edward. *Biographia Juridica, a Biographical Dictionary of the Judges of England: From the Conquest to the Present Time ...* New edition, New Jersey: Law Book Exchange, 1999.

Fracchia, Carmen. 'The Place of African Slaves in Early Modern Spain,' in Andrew Spicer. Jane L. Stevens Crawshaw (eds.). *The Place of the Social Margins, 1350–1750.* New York: Routledge, 2017, pp. 117–135.

Franklin, James. *The Science of Conjecture: Evidence and Probability before Pascal.* Baltimore, MD: Johns Hopkins University Press, 2015.

Fraser, Peter. 'Slaves or Free People: The Status of Africans in England 1550-1750,' in Randolph Vigne. Charles Littleton (eds.). *From Strangers to Citizens: The Integration of Immigrant Communities in Britain, Ireland, and Colonial America, 1550–1750.* Eastbourne: Sussex Academic Press, 2001, pp. 254–260.

Freedman, Harry. *The Murderous History of Bible Translations: Power, Conflict and the Quest for Meaning*. London: Bloomsbury, 2016.

Freedman, Paul. *Images of the Medieval Peasant*. Stanford, CA: Stanford University Press, 1999.

Fryer, Peter. *Staying Power: The History of Black People in Britain since 1504*. 1984, reprint, London: Pluto Press, 1989.

Fuchs, Barbara. 'A Mirror Across the Water: Mimetic Racism, Hybridity, and Cultural Survival,' in Paul Beidler. Gary Taylor (eds.). *Writing Race Across the Atlantic World*. New York: Palgrave Macmillan, 2005, pp. 9–26.

———. *Exotic Nation: Maurophilia and the Construction of Early Modern Spain*. Philadelphia, PA: University of Pennsylvania Press, 2008.

Fuller, Neely. *The United Independent Compensatory Code/System/ Concept/a Textbook/Work Book for Thought, Speech and/or Action for Victims of Racism (White Supremacy)*. s.l.: Neely Fuller, 1957–1980.

Fuller, Thomas. *The Holy State. The Profane State*. London: Roger Daniel for John William, 1642.

———. *The Histories of the Worthies of England*. 1662, new edition, London: F. C. and J. Rivington, 1811.

Gabriel, Deborah. *Layers of Blackness: Colourism in the African Diaspora*. London: Imani Media, 2007.

———. 'Race, Racism and Resistance in British Academia,' in *A Critical Study of (Trans) National Racism: Interdependence of Racist Phenomenon and Resistance Forms*. Berlin: Springer, 2015.

Gage, John. *Color and Meaning: Art, Science and Symbolism*. Berkeley, CA: University of California Press, 1994.

———. *Colour and Culture: Practice and Meaning from Antiquity to Abstraction*. Berkeley, CA: University of California Press, 1999.

Galque, Andrés Sánchez. *Los Tres Mulatos de Esmeraldas* (Portrait of Don Francisco de a Robe and Sons Don Pzzas and Don Domingo). 1599. Oil on canvas. Madrid.

Camboa, Pedro Sarmiento de Nuna da Silva. *New Light on Drake: A Collection of Documents Relating to His Voyage of Circumnavigation, 1577–1580*. London: Hakluyt Society, 1968.

Gardiner, Samuel Rawson. *The Constitutional Documents of the Puritan Revolution, 1625–1660*. London: Clarendon Press, 1906, 1979.

Garraghan, Gilbert J. *A Guide to Historical Method*. New York: Fordham University Press, 1946.

Gautruche, Pierre. *The Poetical Histories Being a Complete Collection of All the Stories Necessary for a Perfect Understanding of the Greek and Latine Poets and Other Ancient Authors Written Originally in French, by the Learned Jesuite. P. Galtruchius. Now Englisht and Enricht with Observations Concerning the Gods Worshipped by Our Ancestors in This Island by the Phoenicians, and Syrians in Asia with Many Useful Notes and Occasional Proverbs Gathered Out of the Best Authors. Unto Which Are Added Two Treatises. One of the Curiosities of Old Rome, and of the Difficult Names Relating to the Affairs of That City. The Other Containing the Most Remarkable Hieroglyphicks of Ægypt. By Marius d'Assigny, B.D.* London: B. Griffin, 1602–1681.

George, Hereford Brooke. Arthur Sidgwick. *Poems of England.* London: Macmillan, 1896.

Gerard, Albert (ed.). *European-Language Writing in Sub-Saharan Africa*, Volume 1. Budapest: Akademiai Kiado, 1986.

Gerzina, Gretchen Holbrook. *Black London: Life Before Emancipation.* New Brunswick, NJ: Rutgers University Press, 1997.

Ghazala, Faiza. Greater London Council Ethnic Minorities Unit. *A History of the Black Presence in London.* London: Greater London Council, 1986.

Gilby, Anthony. *The Psamles of David, Truly Opened and Explained by Paraphasis ... Set Foorth in Latin by ... Theodore Besa, Faithfully Translated into English, by Anthonie Gilbie, and by Him Newlie Purged from Sundrie Faultes Escaped in the First Print, etc.* London: Henrie Denham, 1581.

Gill, Anton. Nick Barratt. *Who Do You Think You Are?: Trace Your Family History Back to the Tudors.* London: HarperCollins, 2006.

Gilroy, Paul. *There Ain't No Black in the Union Jack: The Cultural Politics of Race and Nation.* London: Hutchinson, 1987.

———. *Modernity and Double Consciousness.* London: Verso, 1993.

———. *After Empire: Multiculture or Postcolonial Melancholia.* London: Routledge, 2004.

Glass, Justine. *The Witchcraft: The Sixth Sense and Us.* London: Neville Spearman, 1969.

Glasser, Jack. *Suspect Race: Causes and Consequences of Racial Profiling.* Oxford/London: Oxford University Press, 2014.

Godet, Gyles. *A Brief Abstract of the Genealogy and Race of All the Kings of England ...* London: Gyles Godet, 1560–1562.

Goldenberg, David M. 'The Curse of Ham: A Case of Rabbinic Racism?' in Jack Salzman. Cornel West (eds.). *Struggles in the Promised Land: Toward a History of Black-Jewish Relations.* New York: Oxford University Press, 1997, pp. 21–51.

———. 'Rabbinic Knowledge of Black Africa (Sifre Deut. 320).' *Jewish Studies Quarterly* 5, 1998, pp. 318–328.

———. 'The Development of the Idea of Race: Classical Paradigms and Medieval Elaborations' (Review Essay). *International Journal of the Classical Tradition* 5, 1999, pp. 561–570.

———. *The Curse of Ham: Race and Slavery in Early Judaism, Christianity, and Islam.* Princeton, NJ: University Press, 2003.

———. 'What Did Ham Do to Noah?' in Gunter Stemberger. Mauro Perani (eds.). *'The Words of a Wise Man's Mouth Are Gracious' (Qoh 10,12).* Berlin: Walter de Gruyter, 2005, pp. 257–265.

———. *The Curse of Ham: Race and Slavery in Early Judaism, Christianity, and Islam.* Princeton, NJ: Princeton University Press, 2009.

————. 'It Is Permitted to Marry a Kushite.' *Association for Jewish Studies Review* 37, 2013, pp. 29–49.

————. *Black and Slave: The Origins and History of the Curse of Ham.* Berlin/Boston, MA: Walter de Gruyter, 2017.

————. 'Reading Rabbinic Literature: It's Not All Black and White. (A Response to Jonathan Schorsch).' www.sas.upenn.edu/~dmg2/ Reading%20Rabbinic%20Literature%20%28Response%20to%20 Jonathan%20Schorsch%29.pdf, accessed 22/02/16.

Goodwin, George. *Fatal Rivalry, Flodden 1513: Henry VIII, James IV and the Battle for Renaissance Britain.* New York: Hachette, 2013.

Gordley, James. *The Development of Liability Between Neighbours.* Cambridge/London: Cambridge University Press, 2014.

Gosse, Philip. *Hawkins Scourge of Spain.* New York: Harper and Brothers, 1930.

Gottschalk, Louis. *Understanding History: A Primer of Historical Method.* New York: Alfred A. Knopf: 1950.

Gowing, Laura. 'Giving Birth at the Magistrates Gate: Single Mothers in the Early Modern City,' in Susan Broomhall. Stephanie Tarbin (eds.). *Women, Identities and Communities in Early Modern Europe.* Aldershot: Ashgate, 2008, pp. 137–150.

Grafton, Anthony. *Forgers and Critics: Creativity and Duplicity in Western Scholarship.* Princeton, NJ/Oxford: Princeton University Press, 1990.

————. *Defenders of the Text: The Traditions of Scholarship in an Age of Science, 1450–1800.* Cambridge, MA/London: Harvard University Press, 1991.

————. *What Was History? The Art of History in Early Modern Europe.* Cambridge: Cambridge University Press, 2012.

Grafton, Anthony. Ann Blair (eds.). *The Transmission of Culture in Early Modern Europe.* 1990, new edition, Philadelphia, PA: University of Pennsylvania Press, 2004.

Grafton, Anthony. Glen W. Most. Salvatore Settis. *The Classical Tradition.* Cambridge, MA/London: Belknap, 2010.

Graham, Roderick et al. (dr.). *Elizabeth R*, BBC2, 17 February 1971.

Gransden, Antonia. *Historical Writing in England, c. 550–1307.* 1970, new edition, London: Routledge, 1996.

Green, Ian. *Humanism and Protestantism in Early Modern English Education.* London: Routledge, 2016.

Green, John. Ashley Thomas (eds.). *A New General Collection of Voyages and Travels … in Europe, Asia, Africa and America …* London: Thomas Astley, 1745.

Greenberg, Joseph. *The Languages of Africa.* 1963, 3rd edition, Bloomington, IN/The Hague: Indiana University Press/Mouton & Co., 1970.

Greenblatt, Stephen. *Learning to Curse: Essays in Early Modern Culture.* New York/Abingdon: Routledge, 2012.

Greene, Robert. *The Honorable Histoire of Frier Bacon, and Frier Bongay.* London: Edward White, 1594.

———. *The Estate of English Fugitives Under the King of Spain and His Ministers*. London: John Drawater, 1595.

Greene, Sandra. *West African Narratives of Slavery: Texts from Late Nineteenth- and Early Twentieth-Century Ghana*. Bloomington, IN: Indiana University Press, 2011.

Griffiths, Paul. 'Secrecy and Authority in Sixteenth and Seventeenth Century London.' *Historical Journal* 40:4, 1997, pp. 925–951.

Grove, Jack. 'Black Scholars Still Experience Racism on Campus.' *Times Higher Education Supplement*, 20 March 2014. www.timeshighereducation.com/news/black-scholars-still-experience-racism-on-campus/2012154.article, accessed 07/01/16.

Guasco, Michael. '"Free from the Tyrannous Spanyard?" Englishmen and Africans in Spain's Atlantic World,' *Slavery and Abolition: A Journal of Comparative Studies* 29:1, 2008, pp. 1–22.

———. *Ideas of Race*. Oxford Bibliographies Online Research Guides. Oxford: Oxford University Press, 2010.

———. *Origins of Slavery*. Oxford Bibliographies Online Research Guides. Oxford: Oxford University Press, 2010.

———. *Abolition of Slavery*. Oxford Bibliographies Online Research Guides. Oxford: Oxford University Press, 2010.

———. *Slaves and Englishmen: Human Bondage in the Early Modern Atlantic World*. The Early Modern Americas. Philadelphia, PA: University of Pennsylvania Press, 2014.

Guibbory, A. *'The Jewish Question' and 'The Woman Question' in Samson Agonistes: Gender, Religion, and Nation*. Cambridge: Cambridge University Press, 2004.

Guildhall Record Office, London. GL Ms 28867, GL Ms 4429/1, GL Ms 4448, GL Ms 9243–9245, GL Ms 4310, GL Ms 9222, GL Ms 9222/1, GL Ms 9245.

———. 'Black and Asian People Discovered in Records Held by the Manuscripts Section.' *Manuscripts Section*, Aldermanbury, London.

———. *St Botolph Without Aldgate Memorandum Daybook*, Volume 6. London: Parish of St Botolph without Aldgate, 1596–1597, pp. 257–258, ref. P69/BOT2/ A101/Ms 9234/6 and GL Ms 9234/6.

———. 'Dederi' or 'John Jaquoah.' G.L. St Mildred Poultry, GL Ms 4429/1. London, Parish register, baptised 1 January 1610/11.

Gunn, Geoffrey C. *First Globalization: The Eurasian Exchange, 1500–1800*. Lanham, MD: Rowman and Littlefield, 2003.

Gunther, John. *Inside Africa*. London: Hamish Hamilton, 1955.

Gurr, Nadine. Benjamin Cole. *The New Face of Terrorism: Threats from Weapons of Mass Destruction*. London: I.B. Tauris, 2000.

Guyatt, Nicholas. *Providence and the Invention of the United States, 1607–1806*. Cambridge: Cambridge University Press, 2006.

Gyford, Phil (ed.). Samuel Pepys. 'The Diary of Samuel Pepys, Daily Entries from the 17th Century London Diary.' www.pepysdiary.com/diary/1669/02/23/, accessed 18/01/18.

Gypsy Lore Society. *Journal of the Gypsy Lore Society* 2:2, 1891, pp. 34–37.

Ha-Levi, Judah. *Mi kamokha: She-nohagim Le-omro Ba-Shabat Sheli-fene Purim*. Mantua: publisher unknown, 1557.

Habib, Imtiaz. *Shakespeare and Race: Postcolonial Praxis in the Early Modern Period*. Lanham, MD: University Press of America, 1999.

———. *Black Lives in the English Archives, 1500–1677: Imprints of the Invisible*. London: Ashgate, 2008.

Hakluyt, Richard (ed.). *The Principal Navigations ...* London: Hakluyt's Collection, 1598.

Haley, Alex. *Roots*. Garden City, NY: Doubleday, 1976.

Hall, Gwendolyn Midlo. *Social Control in Slave Plantation Societies: A Comparison of St. Domingue and Cuba*. London: Johns Hopkins University Press, 1971.

Hall, Kim. *Things of Darkness: Economies of Race and Gender in Early Modern England*. 1995, 2nd edition, Ithaca, NY: Cornell University Press, 1996.

Hall, Stuart. (ed.). *Representations: Cultural Representations and Signifying Practices*. London: Sage, 1997.

Hall, Stuart. C. Critcher. T. Jefferson (eds.). *Policing the Crisis: Mugging, the State and Law and Order*. London: Macmillan. 1978.

Hall, Stuart. Dorothy Hobson. Andrew Lowe. Paul WIllis. (eds.). *Culture, Media, Language: Working Papers in Cultural Studies, 1972–1979*. London: Routledge, 2003.

Hall, Stuart. David Morley. Kuan-Hsing Chen (eds.). *Stuart Hall: Critical Dialogues in Cultural Studies*. London: Routledge, 1996.

Hall, Thomas. *An Exposition by Way of Supplement, on the Fourth, Fifth, Sixth, Seventh, Eighth and Ninth Chapters of the Prophecy of Amos ... Many Polemical Points Debated ...* London: Henry Mortlock, 1661.

Hamilton, Allan Mclane. *The Intimate Life of Alexander Hamilton: Based Chiefly upon Original Family Letters and Other Documents, Many of Which Have Never Been Published*. New York: Charles Scribner's Sons, 1910.

Hancock, Ian. 'The Struggle for the Control of Identity.' *Perspectives*. www.osi.hu/rpp/perspectives1f.htm, accessed 06/07/07.

Hanmer, Meredith. *The Baptizing of a Turke. A Sermon ...* London: Robert Walde-Grave, 1586.

Hannaford, Ivan. *Race: The History of an Idea in the West*. Baltimore, MD: Johns Hopkins University Press, 1996.

Hanson, Sharon. *Legal Method, Skills and Reasoning*. London/New York: Routledge, 2009.

Hardying, John. *The Chronicle of John Hardyng, Containing an Account of Public Transactions from the Earliest Period of English History ... Together with the Continuation of Richard Grafton [1572] ... Preface and Index by Henry Ellis*, Volume 1. New York: Ames Press, 1974.

Harman, Thomas. *A Caveat or Warning for Common Cursetors, Vulgarly Called Vagabonds ...* 1566. London: Henry Middleton, new edition, 1573.

Harmes, Marcus. Victoria Bladen (eds.). *Supernatural and Secular Power in Early Modern England*. Farnham: Ashgate, 2015.

Harrison, William. 'Description of England,' Volumes 2 and 3 (1577, 1584), in *Modern History Sourcebook*. www.fordham.edu/halsall/mod/1577harrison-england.html, accessed 10/09/07.

Harrison, William. Frederick James Furnivall, John Norden et al. (eds.). *Harrison's Description of England in Shakespeare's Youth* ..., Volumes 2 and 3. 1577, 1584, 1877, new edition, London: New Shakespeare Society, 1878.

Harry, George Owen. *The Genealogy of the High and Mighty Monarch James ... King of Great Brittayne, ... With His Lineall Descent from Noah by Divers Direct Lynes to Brutus ... the Worthy Descent of His Majesties Ancestour Owen Tudyr ...* London: S. Stafford, 1604.

Hart, Christopher. *Doing a Literature Search: A Comprehensive Guide for the Social Sciences*. London: Sage, 2001.

Hart, Herbert Lionel Adolphus. *The Concept of Law*. Oxford: Clarendon Press, 1961.

Hartwell, Abraham (tr.). Odoardo Lopez. Phlilpo Pigafetta. *A Report of the Kingdom of Congo, a Region of Africa ...* London: John Wolfe, 1597.

Haskins, Charles Homer. *The Renaissance of the Twelfth Century*. Cambridge, MA: Harvard University Press, 1927.

Haslewood, Joseph ... *Book of St Albans* ... London: Harding and White, 1810–1811.

Hassen, Mohammed. 'The Significance of Abba Bahrey in Oromo Studies: A Commentary on the Works of Abba Bahriy and Other Documents Concerning the Oromo, Getatchew Haile.' *Journal of Oromo Studies* 14:2, July 2007, pp. 131–155.

———. *The Oromo and the Christian Kingdom of Ethiopia 1300–1700*. Woodbridge: Boydell and Brewer, 2015.

Hastings, Adrian (ed.). *A World History of Christianity*. Cambridge/Grand Rapids, MI: Williams B. Eerdmans, 1999.

Hawkins, John. *A True Declaration of the Troublesome Voyage of Mr John Hawkins to the Parties of Guyana and the West Indies, in the Yeares of Our Lord in 1567 and 1568*. London: Thomas Purfoot, 1569.

Haynes, Stephen R. *Noah's Curse: The Biblical Justification of American Slavery*. New York: Oxford University Press, 2002.

Heinze, Rudolph W. *The Proclamations of the Tudor Kings*. Cambridge: Cambridge University Press, 1976.

Hendricks, Margo. 'Surveying Race in Shakespeare,' in Catherine M. S. Alexander. Stanley Wells (eds.). *Shakespeare and Race*. Cambridge: Cambridge University Press, 2000, pp. 1–22.

Hendricks, Margo. Patricia Parker (eds.). *Women, 'Race' and Writing in the Early Modern Period*. New York: Routledge, 1994.

Henry IV. Signed letter to 'Prester John King of Abyssinia.' 20 October 1422, in David Northrup. *Africa's Discovery of Europe: 1450–1850*. New York/Oxford: Oxford University Press, 2002, p. 65.

Herbert, Edward (Cherbuy). John Churton Collins (ed.). *The Poems of Lord Herbert of Cherbury*. 1665, 2nd edition, London: Chatto and Windus, 1881.

Herring, Cedric.Verna Keith. Hayword Derrick Horton. *Skin Deep: How Race and Complexion Matter in the 'Colour-Blind' Era*. Champaign, IL: University of Illinois Press, 2004.

Hertfordshire Records Office. Hertfordshire Archives and Local Studies, Cheshunt. 1570/16April/ [D/P29/13/5], 'Fortunatus' record. www. hertsmemories.org.uk/content/herts-history/people/african-caribbean-people-in-herts-before-1830/fortunatus.

———. Barley, Herts, ref. DP48/1/1, p. 139.

———. Brickendon, Herts. ref. DP/48/1/1-3, p. 7.

———. Brickendon, Herts, Thomas Inverness, Ruple Fearye, *The Returns of the Constables of the Hamlet of Brickenden of the Objectives and Churchwardens of the Parishe of All Saints in Hertford Whose Names Are Subject ...*, Volume 1. (Unpublished), ref. DP/48/1/1/, p. B3.

———. East Herts, Herts, Henry Capell, *East Hertfordshire Munster Book*, ref. HHLS 6990, p. 15.

Hiatt, Alfred. *The Making of Medieval Forgeries: False Documents in Fifteenth-Century England*. London: British Library and University of Toronto Press, 2004.

Higden, Ranulphus. Churchill Babington (ed.). John Trevisa (tr.). *Polychronicon: Together with the English Translations of John Trevisa ...* London: Longman, 1865.

Higginbotham, Alyoisus Leon. *In the Matter of Colour: Race and the American Legal Process: The Colonial Period*. Oxford: Oxford University Press, 1980.

Higgins, Godfrey. *Anacalypsis, An Attempt to Draw Aside the Veil of the Saitic Isis: or, an Inquiry into the Origin of Languages, Nations, and Religions*. 1883, 1878, new edition, London: TGS Publishing, 1927.

Hill, Peter. *A History of Hostelries in Northamptonshire*. Amberley: Amberley Publishing, 2010.

Hill, R. A. *Black Zionism: Marcus Garvey and the Jewish Question*. Columbia, MI: University of Missouri Press, 1998.

Hingeston, Francis Charles (ed.). *Royal and Historical Letters During the Reign of Henry IV King of England and France and Lord of Ireland*. London: Longman Green Longman and Roberts, 1860.

Hipshon, David. *Richard III and the Death of Chivalry*. Stroud: History Press, 2009.

Hirschfeld, Fritz. *George Washington and Slavery: A Documentary Portrayal*. Columbia, MI/London: University of Missouri Press, 1997.

Hirst, Michael et al. *The Tudors*. Showtime/Reveille/Working Title. 2007.

Holbrook, Peter. *Literature and Degree in Renaissance England: Nashe, Bourgeois Tragedy, Shakespeare*. Newark, DE: University of Delaware Press, 1994.

Holinshed, Raphael. *The Late Volume of Chronicles England, Scotland and Ireland with Their Descriptions*. London: J. Harrison, 1587.

Holland, Philemon. *The History of the World Commonly Called the Natural Historie of C Plinius Secondus, Translated by Philemon Holland*. London: Adam Philip, 1601.

Hollywood, Mike. *Papa Mike's Palau Islands Handbook*. Bloomington, IN: iUniverse, 2006.

Holyoak, Keith J. Robert G. Morison. *The Cambridge Handbook of Thinking and Reasoning*. New York: Cambridge University Press, 2005.

Hondius, Jodocus. *Typus Totius Orbis Terrarum in quo & Christiani Militis Certamen Super Terram*, in *Pietatis Studiosi Gratiam, Graphicè Designatur à Iud. Hondio Caelatore*. Amsterdam: I Hondius, 1596.

hooks, bell. *Ain't I a Woman: Black Women and Feminism*. Boston, MA: South End Press, 1981.

Hooper, John. *A Godly Confession and Protestacion of the Christian Fayth ... Wherin Is Declared What a Christian Manne Is Bound to Beleve of God, Hys King, His Neighbour, and Hymselfe*. London: J. Daye, 1551.

Hopgood, Stephen. *The Endtimes of Human Rights*. Ithaca, NY: Cornell University Press, 2013.

Horning, Audrey. *Ireland in the Virginian Sea: Colonialism in the British Atlantic*. Chapel Hill, NC: University of North Carolina Press, 2013.

Hornsby, Stephen. Michael Hermann. *British Atlantic, American Frontier: Spaces of Power in Early Modern British America*. Lebanon, NH: University Press of New England, 2005.

Hoskins, William George. *Local History in England*. Harlow: Longman, 1984.

Houston, Drusilla Dunjee. *Wonderful Ethiopians of the Ancient Cushite Empire: Origin of the Civilisation of the Cushites*. 1926, new edition, New York: City University of New York Press, 2007.

Howe, Stephen. *Afrocentrism: Mythical Pasts and Imagined Homes*. 1998, new edition, London: Verso, 1999.

Howell, Martha. Walter Prevenier. *From Reliable Sources: An Introduction to Historical Methods*. Ithaca, NY: Cornell University Press, 2001.

Howgill, Frances. *Caines Bloudy Race Known by Their Fruits. Or, a True Declaration of the Innocent Sufferings of the Servants of the Living God* [i.e. the Quakers] ... *in the City of Westchester*, etc. London: Thomas Simmons, 1657.

Huarte, Juan. *Examin de Ingenious Para les Sciencias*. (1588), in Jonathan Schorsch. *Swimming the Christian Atlantic: Judeoconversos, Afroiberians, and Amerindians in the Seventeenth Century*. Leiden/Boston, MA/Biggleswade: Brill, 2009, p. 361.

Hudson, Rykesha. 'Onyeka Rewriting Black History.' *Voice Newspaper*, 30 April–6 May 2015. www.voice-online.co.uk/article/book-reveals-africans-lived-tudor-england, accessed 07/01/16.

Hughes, Geoffrey. *Political Correctness: A History of Semantics and Culture*. London: John Wiley and Sons, 2011.

Hughes, Glyn. *The Lost Feast of Christmas*. London: Lulu.Com, 2016.

Hull, Gloria T. Patricia Bell Scott. Barbara Smith (eds.). *All the Women Are White, All the Blacks Are Men, But Some of Us Are Brave: Black Women's Studies*. New York: Feminist Press at City University of New York, 1993.

Human Rights Watch. *Racist Violence in the UK*. New York: Human Rights Watch, 1997.

Hunter, George Kirkpatrick. 'Othello and Colour Prejudice.' *Proceedings of the British Academy* 53, 1967, p. 153.

Hunwick, John. *Timbuktu and the Songhay Empire: Al Sadis Tarikh Al-Sudan down to 1613 and Other Contemporary Documents*. Leiden: Brill, 1999.

Ibekwe, Chinweizu. *The West and the Rest of Us: White Predators, Black Slavers, and the African Elite*. New York: Vintage Books, 1975.

———. *Towards the Decolonization of African Literature*, Volume 1. Enugu: Fourth Dimension Publishers, 1980.

———. *Anatomy of Female Power: A Masculinist Dissection of Matriarchy*. Lagos: Pero, 1990.

Ingram, Kevin (ed.). Francisco Marquez Villanueva. 'On the Concept of Mudejarism,' in *The Conversos and Moriscos in Late Medieval Spain and Beyond*, Volume 1: Departures and Change. Leiden/Boston, MA: Brill, 2009, pp. 23–51.

Irving, Washington. *Life of George Washington*. London: Henry G. Bohn, 1855–1857.

Irwin, Terrence. *The Development of Ethics: From Socrates to the Reformation*, Volume 1. New York: Oxford University Press, 2007.

Isaacs, Jeremy. *The World at War*, 'The Making of the World at War.' TV Series, Thames Television, 1973–1974.

Isidore. *Ethimologiarum Isidori Hispalensis Episcopi* ... Strasburg: J. Mentelin, 1470.

Iyengar, Sujata. *Shades of Difference: Mythologies of Skin Colour in Early Modern England*. Philadelphia, PA: University of Pennsylvania Press, 2008.

Jablonski, Nina G. *Living Color: The Biological and Social Meaning of Skin Color*. Berkeley, CA/London/Los Angeles, CA: University of California Press, 2012.

Jackson, Gilbert. *Daughter of Florence Poulett and Thomas Smyth of Ashton Court with Her Black Page*. 1621–1640. Oil on canvas, 66 cm × 58.5 cm. Bristol Red Lodge Museum.

Jackson, John. *The Pedigree and Peregrination of Israel Being an Abridgement of the Histories of the Creation of Adam, Cain & Abel, Noah, etc. With Meditations and Prayers upon Each Historie*. London: M. Simmons, 1649.

Jackson, John G. Willis Nathaniel Huggins. *An Introduction to African Civilisation*. New York: Avon House, 1937.

Jackson, John P. (jr.). Nadine M. Weidman. *Race, Racism and Science: Social Impact and Interaction*. Santa Barbara, CA: ABC CLIO, 2004.

Jackson, Luther Porter. *Journal of Negro History* 9:1, January 1924, p. 15.

James, C. L. R. *The Black Jacobins: Toussaint L'Ouverture and the San Domingo Revolution*. London: Alison and Busby, 1980.

James I. *The True Lawe of Free Monarchies: or, the Reciprock and Mutuall Dutie Betwixt a Free King, and His Natural Subiectes*. Edinburgh: Robert Waldegraue, 1598.

James I. Speech to Houses of Parliament, Whitehall, London, 21 March 1610, in Joseph Robson Tanner (ed.). *Constitutional Documents of the Reign of James I A.D. 1603–1624*. Cambridge: Cambridge University Press, 1960, p. 15.

Jannick, Jules. *Horticultural Reviews*, Volume 44. London: John Wiley and Sons, 2011, pp. 23–88.

Jarrott, Charles et al. *Anne of the Thousand Days*. Universal Pictures, 1969.

Jefferson, Thomas. John Adams. Benjamin Franklin. *In Congress, July 4, 1776. A Declaration by the Representatives of the United States of America, In General Congress Assembled*. London: publisher unknown, 1776.

Jenkins, Howard Malcolm. 'The Family of William Penn.' *The Pennsylvania Magazine of History and Biography* 20:1, The Historical Society of Pennsylvania, 1896, pp. 1–29.

Jenner, David. *Cain's Mark and Murder. K. Charles the I. His Martyrdom. Delivered in a Sermon*. London: John Williams, 1681.

Jerome. 'Latin Vulgate.' 4th century CE (2018). www.biblestudytools.com/vul/genesis/9.html, accessed 19/02/18.

Jetto, Henrie. 'Will of Henrie Jetto.' Will number 102, dated and signed on 20 September 1626, but executed 13 September 1638, Worcestershire Archives, Worcester.

Jobson, Richard. *The Golden Trade: Or, a Discovery of the River Gambia, and the Golden Trade of the Aethiopians. Also, the Commerce with a Great Blacke Merchant, Buckor Sano, and His Report of the Houses Covered with Golde, and Other Strange Observations for the Good of Our Owne Countrey; Set Down as They Were Collected in Travelling, Part of the Yeares, 1620 and 1621*. London: Nicholas Oke, 1623.

Joekes, Susan. *Women in Pastoral Societies in East and West Africa*. London/Edinburgh: International Institute for Environment and Development, 1991.

Jones, Ann Rosalind. Peter Stallybrass. *Renaissance Clothing and the Materials of Memory*. Cambridge: Cambridge University Press, 2000.

Jones, Gareth Steadman. 'The Pathology of English History.' *New Left Review* 46, 1967, pp. 29–43.

Jones, Inigo. *Masquer a Daughter of Niger*. Watercolour, in Collections of the Duke of Devonshire, Bakewell, Derbyshire, Reference Catalogue 1. Stephen Orgel (ed.). *The Theatre of the Stuart Court. Including the Complete Designs for Productions at Court, for the Most Part in the Collection of the Duke of Devonshire, Together with Their Texts and Historical Documentation*. London/Berkeley, CA: University of California Press, 1973.

Jones, Thomas. *A Catalogue of the Collection of Tracts For and Against Popery* ... Manchester: Chetham Society, 1865.

Jonson, Ben. *The Character of Two Royall Masques, the One of Blacknesse. The Other of Beautie Personated by the Most Magnificent of Queenes Anne Queene of Great Britain, with Her Honourable Ladys 1605 and 1608 at Whitehall.* London: Thomas Thorp, 1605.

———. *Hymenæi: or the Solemnities of Masque, and Barriers* ... *Performed* ... *at Court* ... *to the* ... *Celebrating of the Marriage-Union, betweene Robert, Earle of Essex, and the Lady Frances, Second Daughter to* ... *the* ... *Earle of Suffolke.* London: V. Sims for T. Thorpe, 1606.

———. *Volpone or the Fox* ... 1606, new edition, London: T. Thorpe, 1607.

Jonson, Ben. *A Masque of the Metamorphos'd Gypsies*, 1621, inc. collective folio of Ben Jonson's work various titles: *Horatius Flaccus: His Art of Poetry. Englished by B.J. With Other Workes of the Author ["Execration against Vulcan," "The Masque of the Gypsies," and "Epigrams," etc.], etc.* London: Richard Bishop for Andrew Cooke, 1640–1641.

———. *The Alchemist. Catiline, His Conspiracy.* London: D. Midwinter, 1756.

———. Stephen Orgel (ed.). 'The Masque of Blackness, 1605,' in *Ben Jonson: Complete Masques.* New Haven, CT: Yale University Press, 1969.

———. William Gifford (ed.). *The Works of Ben Jonson with Notes, Critical and Explanatory and a Biographical Memoir Part Three.* Whitefish, MT: Kessinger Publishing, 2004.

Joradens, Jacob. *Moses and His Ethiopian Wife.* 1650. Oil on canvas, 106.5 cm × 80.0 cm. Rubens House, Antwerp.

Jordan, Anne Marie. 'Image of Empire: Slaves in the Lisbon Household and Court of Catherine of Austria,' in T. F. Earle and K. J. P. Lowe (eds.). *Black Africans in Renaissance Europe.* Cambridge: Cambridge University Press, 2005, pp. 155–181.

Jordan, Constance. *Shakespeare's Monarchies: Ruler and Subject in the Romances.* Ithaca, NY: Cornell University Press, 1999.

Jordan, Winthrop D. *White Over Black: American Attitudes Toward the Negro, 1550–1812.* Chapel Hill, NC: University of North Carolina Press, 1968.

Josephus, Flavius. *The Antiquities of the Jews.* Book I, Chapter 6, Section II (94 CE), in James W. C. Pennington. *A Textbook of the Origin and History, &c. &c. of the Colored People.* Hartford: L. Skinner, 1841.

Jowitt, Claire. Daniel Carey. *Richard Hakluyt and Travel Writing in Early Modern Europe.* London: Ashgate, 2012.

Juang, Richard. Noelle Morrissette (eds.). *Africa and the Americas: Culture, Politics, and History: A Multidisciplinary Encyclopedia.* Santa Barbara, CA/Oxford: ABC-CLIO, 2008.

Julian, Erin. Helen Ostovich (eds.). *The Alchemist: A Critical Reader.* London: Arden Shakespeare, 2013.

Junne, George. *The Black Eunuchs of the Ottoman Empire: Networks of Power in the Court of the Sultan.* London/New York: I.B. Tauris, 2016.

Kalmar, Ian Davidson. 'Moorish Style: Orientalism, the Jews, and Synagogue Architecture.' *Jewish Social Studies: History, Culture and Society* 7:3, spring/summer 2001, pp. 68–100.

Kamen, Henry. *The Spanish Inquisition: A Historical Revision*. New Haven, CT: Yale University Press, 1998.

Kaminski, John P. *A Necessary Evil?: Slavery and the Debate over the Constitution*. Madison, WI: Madison House: 1995.

Kantorowicz, Ernst H. *The King's Two Bodies: A Study in Medieval Political Ideology*. New York: Princeton University Press, 2016.

Kapur, Shekhar et al. *Elizabeth*. Polygram, 1998.

——— et al. *Elizabeth: The Golden Age*. Universal Studios, 2007.

Karenga, Maulana. *Introduction to Black Studies*. Los Angeles, CA: University of Sankore Press, 1982.

Karimi, Faith. 'Group: Use of "Sub Saharan Africa" Disparaging.' *CNN*, 20 September 2010. http://edition.cnn.com/2010/WORLD/africa/09/20/sub.saharan.africa/index.html.

Kattago, Siobhan. *The Ashgate Research Companion to Memory Studies*. London/New York: Routledge, 2015.

Katz, David. *Jews in the History of England, 1485–1850*. 1994, new edition, Oxford: Oxford University Press, 1997.

Katzer, Jeffrey. Kenneth H. Cook. *Evaluating Information: A Guide for Users of Social Science Research*. Boston, MA: McGraw Hill Humanities, 1994.

Kaufmann, Miranda. 'Caspar Van Senden, Sir Thomas Sherley and the "Blackamoor" Project.' *Historical Research* 81:212, May 2008, pp. 366–371.

———. 'Sir Pedro Negro: What Colour Was His Skin?' *Oxford Journals, Notes and Queries* 55:2, 2008, pp. 142–146.

———. Personal emails sent to Onyeka, 27 February – 15 March 2015.

———. blog @ www.mirandakaufmann.com/, accessed 27/12/15.

———. '"Making a Beast with Two Backs": Interracial Relationships in Early Modern England.' *Literature Compass* 12:1, January 2015, pp. 22–37. Published online at Wiley Online Library 08/01/15, http://onlinelibrary.wiley.com/doi/10.1111/lic3.12200/full, accessed 05/01/16.

———. *The Black Tudors*. London: Oneworld, 2017.

———. 'Africans in Early Modern London.' www.mirandakaufmann.com/lmaafricans.html, accessed 02/04/18.

Kaur, Madlyn M. *Velazquez: The Art of Painting*. London: HarperCollins, 1976.

Kaze, Thomas. *Scripture Interpretation, or Authority?: Motives and Arguments in Jesus' Halakic Conflicts*. Tubingen: Mohr Siebeck, 2013.

Keeling, William. *Liturgiae Britannicae, Or, The Several Editions of The Book of Common Prayer of the Church of England: From Its Compilation to the Last Revision*. London: William Pickering, 1549, 1552, 1604, 1842, 1851.

Keita, Maghan. *Race and the Writing of History: Riddling the Sphinx*. London: Oxford University Press, 2000.

———. 'Saracens and Black Knights.' *Arthuriana* 16:4, 1 December 2006, pp. 65–77.

———. 'Race: What The Bookstore Hid,' in Celia Chazelle et al. (eds.). *Why the Middle Ages Matter: Mediveal Light on Modern Injustice*. London: Routledge, 2012, pp. 130–141.

Kelsey, Harry. *Philip of Spain, King of England: The Forgotten Sovereign*. London: I.B. Tauris, 2012.

Kelton, Arthur. *A Chronicle with a Genealogie Declarying That the Britons and Welshmen Are Lindly Descended from Brute*. London: Richard Grafton, 1547.

Kennedy, Rebecca F. C. Sydnor Roy. *Race and Ethnicity in the Classical World: An Anthology of Primary Sources in Translation*. Indianapolis, IN/Cambridge: Hackett Publishing, 2013.

Kerr, Robert (ed.). *A General History Collection of Voyages and Travels, Arranged in Systematic Order: Forming a Complete History of the Origin and Progress of Navigation, Discovery, and Commerce, by Sea and Land, from the Earliest Ages to the Present Time*, Volume 7. Edinburgh: W. Blackwood and Sons, 1824.

Kewes, Paulina. Ian W. Archer. Felicity Heal (eds.). *Oxford Handbook of Holinshed's Chronicles*. Oxford: Oxford University Press, 2013.

Keys, David. 'Details of Horrific First Voyages in Transatlantic Slave Trade.' *The Independent*. 17 August 2018. www.msn.com/en-gb/news/world/details-of-horrific-first-voyages-in-transatlantic-slave-trade-revealed/ar-BBM2ycN?li=BBoPWjQ&ocid=mailsignout, accessed 17/08/18.

Keynes, Milo. 'The Personality and Health of King Henry VIII (1491–1571).' *Journal of Medical Biology* 13:1, 1 August 2005, pp. 174–183.

Khallikan, Ibn. *A Biographical Dictionary* [1211–1282]. London: Oriental Translation Fund of Great Britain and Ireland, 1871.

Khan, Razib. 'Inbreeding and the Downfall of the Spanish Hapsburgs.' *Discover: Science of the Curious*. 14 April 2017. http://blogs.discovermagazine.com/gnxp/2009/04/inbreeding-the-downfall of the-spanish-hapsburgs/#.WnC9XXzLgdU, accessed 30/01/18.

Killingray, David. *Africans in Britain*. London: Taylor & Francis, 1994.

Kilson, Martin L. Robert L. Rotberg (eds.). *The African Diaspora: Interpretive Essays*. Cambridge, MA: Harvard University Press, 1976.

King, Martin Luther. Speech (1967), in Herbert Robinson Marbury. *Pillars of Cloud and Fire: The Politics of Exodus in African American Biblical Interpretation*. New York: New York University Press, 2015, p. 228. This section of the speech can be seen at Martin Luther King, 'Somebody Told a Lie – MLK That's Never Quoted.' www.youtube.com/watch?v=UGtjAaJeUWY, published 9 June 2011, accessed 12/02/18.

Kipling, Rudyard. 'The Whiteman's Burden' (1899), in Winthorp D. Jordan, *The Whiteman's Burden: Historical Origins of Racism in the United States*. Oxford: Oxford University Press, 1974, pp. 26–65.

Kirby, Michael. *Judicial Activism, Authority, Principle and Policy in the Judicial Method*. London: Sweet and Maxwell, 2004.

Kirk, Richard. Ernest Kirk (eds.). *Returns of Aliens Dwelling in the City and Suburbs of London from the Reign of Henry VIII. To That of James I*, Volume 4, Quarto Series 10. London: Huguenot Society of London, 1900–1908.

Kitto, John Vivian. 'St Martin-in-the-Fields: The Accounts of the Church Wardens, 1525–1603.' *British History Online*, 1901, pp. 457–475. www.british-history.ac.uk/report.aspx?compid=81909, accessed 25/10/08.

Knight, Charles. *The English Encyclopaedia*. London: Bradbury Evans, 1868.

Knowles, Gerry. *Cultural History of the English Language*. London: Routledge, 2014.

Knox, John. *The First Blast of the Trumpet: Against the Monstrous Regimen of Women*. Edinburgh: Andrew Steuart, 1571.

Kohn, Hans. Craig J. Calhoun. *The Idea of Nationalism: A Study in Its Origins and Background*. New York: Macmillan, 1944.

Kolchin, Peter Robert. *First Freedom: The Responses of Alabama's Blacks to Emancipation and Reconstruction*. Westport, CT: Greenwood Press, 1972.

———. *Unfree Labor: American Slavery and Russian Serfdom*. Cambridge, MA: The Belknap Press, Harvard University, 1987.

Korda, Alexander. *The Private Life of Henry VIII*. United Artists, 1933.

Kraye, Jill (ed.). *The Cambridge Companion to Renaissance Humanism*. Cambridge: Cambridge University Press, 1996.

Kristeller, Paul Oskar. *The Classics and Renaissance Thought, etc.* Cambridge, MA: Harvard University Press, 1955.

Kulka, Otto Duv. 'The Jewish Question' in German Speaking Countries, 1848–1914: A Bibliography*. New York/London: Garland Publishing, 1994.

Lacey, Robert. *Aristocrats*. London: Hutchinson, 1983.

Laertius, Diogenes. *Lives of the Eminent Philosophers*. London/Cambridge, MA: Harvard University Press, 1972.

Lalwan, Rory (ed.). *Sources for Black and Asian History at the City of Westminster Archives …* London: Westminster City Archives, 2005.

Lane-Poole, Stanley. *Story of the Moors in Spain*. London: G. P. Putnam and Sons, 1886.

Lang, Richard (ed.). *Two Tudor Subsidy Assessment Rolls*. London: The London Record Society Publications, 1993.

Latimer, Hugh. *27 Sermons Preached by … Maister Hugh Latimer, as Well Such as in Tymes Past Haue Bene Printed, as Certayne Other … Neuer Yet Set Forth in Print … 9. Sermons Vpon Certayne Gospels and Epistles*. London: John Day, 1562.

Law, Robin (ed.). Great Britain Record Office. *Correspondence from the Royal African Company Factories at Offra and Whyda on the Slave*

Coast of West Africa in the Public Record Office 1678-1693. Edinburgh: Centre of African Studies, Edinburgh University, 1990.

Lawrence, Jerome. Robert Edwin Lee. *Inherit the Wind*. 1955, new edition, New York: Dramatists Play, 2000.

Le Hardy, William (ed.). 'Sessions of the Peace and Gaol Delivery A.D. 1613, Sessions Roll,' in *County of Middlesex, Calendar to the Sessions Records, New Series, 1612-1614*, Volume 1. London: Clerk of the Peace, 1935, pp. 117-154.

Le Testu, Guillaume. *Cosmographie Universelle Selon les Navigateurs, Tant Anciens Que Modernes*. 1555, Vincennes: Bibliothèque du Service Historique de l'Armée de Terre, DLZ 14.

Lee, Maurice (ed.). *Dudley Carleton to John Chamberlain 1603-1624. Jacobean Letters*. New Brunswick, NJ: Rutgers University Press, 1972.

Lee, Sidney. 'Caliban's Visits to England.' *Cornhill Magazine* 34, 1913, pp. 333-345.

Levin, Carole. *The Reign of Elizabeth I*. Basingstoke: Palgrave Macmillan, 2001.

Lefkowitz, Mary. *Black Athena Revisited*. Chapel Hill, NC: University of North Carolina Press, 1996.

———. *Not Out of Africa: How Afrocentrism Became an Excuse to Teach Myth as History*. New York: Basic Books, 1996.

Legat, John. *A Watch-worde for Warre Not so New as Necessary ... Against the Spaniard*. London: Printer to the University of Cambridge, 1596.

Leigh, Edward. *Critica Sacra ...* London: A. Miller, R. Daniel, for T. Underhill, 1650.

Lemon, Rebecca. *Treason by Words: Literature, Law and Rebellion in Shakespeare's England*. Ithaca, NY: Cornell University Press, 2005.

Levine, Michael. *African American and Civil Rights: From 1619 to the Present*. Phoenix, AZ: Oryx, 1996.

Lew, Bernard. *Race and Slavery in the Middle East: An Historical Inquiry*. Oxford: Oxford University Press, 1990.

Lewalski, Barbara. 'Lucy, Countess of Bedford: Images of a Jacobean Courtier and Patroness,' in Kevin Sharpe. Steven N. Zwicker (eds.). *Politics of Discourse*. Berkeley, CA: University of California Press, 1987.

Lewis, C. S. *Chronicles of Narnia. The Horse and His Boy*. London: Geoffrey Bles, 1954.

Lewontin, Richard. Steven Rose. Leon J. Kamin. *Not in Our Genes: Biology, Ideology, and Human Nature*. Chicago, IL: Haymarket Books, 2017.

Limborch, Philippus. *The History of the Inquisition*. London: Samuel Handler, 1731.

Linebaugh, Peter. Marcus Rediker. *The Many Headed Hydra: Sailors, Slaves, Commoners and the Hidden History of the Revolutionary Atlantic*. Boston, MA: Beacon Press, 2000.

Lingelbach, William Ezra. *The Merchant Adventurers of England: Their Laws and Ordinances with Other Documents*. New York: B. Franklin, 1971.

Linnane, Fergus. *London: The Wicked City; A Thousand Years of Prostitution and Vices*. London: Robson, 2007.

Lithgow, William. *A Most Delectable, and True Discourse, of an Admired Painefull Peregrination* ... London: Nicholas Okes, 1614.

Littell, Eliakim. Robert S. Little. *The Living Age*, Volume 105. Philadelphia, PA: The Living Age Company, 1870.

Little, Kenneth. *Negroes in Britain*. London: Routledge, Kegan Paul, 1947.

Lloyd, Janet. *The Spanish Inquisition: A History*. London/New Haven, CT: Yale University Press, 2006.

Lockyer, Roger. *Tudor and Stuart Britain, 1485–1714*. New York: Pearson Education, 2005.

Lomas, Sophie Crawford (ed.). Edward Stafford. *Calendar of State Papers, Foreign Series*, Volume 21. London: Her Majesty's Stationery, 1927, p. 73.

London Metropolitan Archives, Registers of St Dunstan, and All Saints Church, Stepney, ref. LMA P93/DUN/255.

———. All Hallows, Tottenham, London, ref. LMA DRO/015 /A/01/001.

Long, Edward. *The London Chronicle*, Article in edition XXIII: 2537, 13–16 March 1773, p. 250.

Loomba, Ania. Jonathan Burton (eds.). *Race in Early Modern England: A Documentary Companion*. London: Palgrave Macmillan, 2007.

Loomie, Albert. 'Religion and Elizabethan Commerce with Spain.' *The Catholic Historical Review* 50, April 1964, pp. 27–51.

Lopez, Edward. in John Green. Astley Thomas (eds.). *A New General Collection of Voyages and Travels* ... *in Europe, Asia, Africa and America* ... *Also the Manners and Customs of the Several Inhabitants* ...: *Consisting of the Most Esteemed Relations, Which Have Been Hitherto Published in Any Language* ..., Volume 3. The Hague: Library of Netherlands, 1746, pp. 132–137.

Lorimer, Douglas. *Colour, Class and the Victorians: English Attitudes to the Negro in the Mid-Nineteenth Century*. New York: Leicester University Press, 1978.

Lover, James Frances. *The Master of Novices: An Historical Synopsis and a Commentary*. Whitefish, MT: Literary Licensing, 2013.

Lowe, Kate. Thomas Earle (eds.). *Black Africans in Renaissance Europe*. Cambridge: Cambridge University Press, 2005.

Lower, Mark Anthony. *English Surnames: Essays on Family Nomenclature*. London: John Russel Smith, 1842.

Lowles, Nick. *White Riot: The Violent Story of Combat 18*. Wrea Green: Milo Books, 2003.

Ludolf, Hiob. Abba Gorgoryos. *A New History of Ethiopia* ... *Vulgarly, Though Erroneously Called the Empire of Prester John* ... London: Samuel Smith, 1684.

Lugo-Ortiz, Agnes. *Slave Portraiture in the Ancient World*. Cambridge/London: Cambridge University Press, 2013.

Lukacs, George. Edith Bone (trs.). *Studies in European Realism*. London: The Merlin Press, 1972.

Lukacs, George. John Mander. Necke Mander (trs.). *The Meaning of Contemporary Realism*. London: Merlin Press, 1963.

Luther, Martin. *Deutsch Catechismus*. Wittenberg: George Rhaw, 1531.

Luu, Lien. *Immigrants and the Industries of London, 1500–1700*. Aldershot: Ashgate, 2005.

Lynche, Richard. *An Historical Treatise of the Travels of Noah into Europe* ... London: Adam Islip, 1602.

Mabillon, Jean. *De Re Diplomatica*. Paris: publisher unknown, 1681.

Macdonald, Joyce Green. 'Black Ram, White Ewe: Shakespeare, Race and Women,' in Dympna Callaghan (ed.). *A Feminist Companion to Shakespeare*. Oxford: Wiley Blackwell, 2001, pp. 206–225.

Machyn, Henry. John Gough Nicols (ed.). *The Diary of Henry Machyn Citizen and Merchant Taylor of London*. London: Camden Society, 1848.

Macinnes, Charles Malcolm. *England and Slavery*. London: Arrowsmith, 1934.

MacKeith, Lucy. *Local Black History: A Beginning in Devon*. London: Archives and Museum of Black Heritage, 2003.

Mackensie, Eneas. 'Incorporated Companies: Merchant Adventurers: Historical Account of Newcastle-upon-Tyne: Including the Borough of Gateshead, 1827.' *British History Online*, pp. 662–670, www.british-history.ac.uk/report.aspx?compid=43401, accessed 18/01/08.

Mackinnion, Gillies. *Gunpowder Treason and Plot*. BBC 2, 14 April 2004.

Maclean, John (ed.). David Watkin Waters. *The Art of Navigation in England in Elizabethan and Early Stuart Times*. London: Hollis and Carter, 1958.

MacPeek, James Andrew Scarborough. *The Black Book of Knaves and Unthrifts*. Storrs, CT: University of Connecticut, 1969.

MacRitchie, David. *Ancient and Modern Britons: A Retrospect*. 2 Volumes. 1884, 3rd edition, 1985, reprint, Los Angeles, CA: Preston, 1986.

———. *Scottish Gypsies Under the Stewarts*. Edinburgh: D. Douglas, 1894.

Maddern, Philippa. '"In Myn Own House": The Troubled Connections Between Servant Marriages, Late Medieval English Households Communities and Early Modern Historiography,' in Stephanie Tarbin. Susan Broomhall (eds.). *Women, Identities and Communities in Early Modern Europe*. Aldershot: Ashgate, 2008, pp. 45–60.

Madhubuti, Haki R. *Enemies: The Clash of Races*. Chicago, IL: Third World Press, 1978.

———. *Black Men: Obsolete, Single, Dangerous?: Afrikan American Families in Transition: Essays in Discovery, Solution and Hope*. Chicago, IL: Third World Press, 2000.

Maerlant, Jacob Van. *Charlemagne Killing a Moorish Leader*. Image on vellum, 32 cm × 233 cm, in *Spiegel Historiael*. West Flanders: publisher unknown, 1325–1355, n.p.

Maguire, Richard C. 'Presenting the History of Africans in Provincial Britain: Norfolk as a Case Study.' *The Journal of the Historical Association History* 19:338, December 2014, pp. 819–838.

Maine Historical Society. *Collections of the Maine Historical Society*, Volume 18. Portland, OR: Maine Historical Society, 1831, pp. 34–36.

Malcolmson, Cristina. Henry Turner. *Studies of Skin Colour in the Early Royal Society: Boyle, Cavendish, Swift*. London: Ashgate, 2013.

Malherbe, Michel. Markku Peltonen (ed.). *The Cambridge Companion to Bacon*. Cambridge: Cambridge University Press, 1996.

Maloney, William James. *The Medical Lives of History's Famous People*. New York: Bentham Science Publishers, 2014.

Mancall, Peter C. Carole Shammas (eds.). *Governing the Sea in the Early Modern Era: Essays in Honor of Robert C. Ritchie*. San Marino, CA: Huntington Library, 2015.

Mandeville, John. *Voiage and Travayle of Syr John Maundeville Knight*. London: Thomas East, 1568.

Marchitello, Howard. *Narrative and Meaning in Early Modern England: Browne's Skull and Other Histories*. Cambridge/New York: Cambridge University Press, 1997.

Markham, Gervase. *The Gentlemans Academie, or the Booke of S. Albans; Containing Three Most Exact and Excellent Bookes: The First of Hawking, the Second of All the Proper Terms of Hunting and the Last of Armorie: All Compiled by Juliana Barnes in the Yere from the Incarnation of Christ 1486: And Now Reduced into a Better Method by G. M. (i.e. Gervase Markham.) ... (by Richard Farmer)*. London: Humfrey Lownes, 1595.

Marks, Arthur Holton. *Historical Notes on Lincoln's Inn Fields*. London: Hertford Record Co., 1922.

Marlowe, Christopher. *Tamburlaine the Great*. London: Marlowe, 1592.

———. *The Tragedy of Dido Queen of Carthage*. London: Thomas Nash, 1594.

———. *The Famous Tragedy of the Jew of Malta* ... London: Nicholas Vavasour, 1633.

———. Fredson Bowers (ed.). *The Complete Works of Christopher Marlowe*. Cambridge: Cambridge University Press, 1973.

Marrapodi, Michele (ed.). *Shakespeare and the Italian Renaissance: Appropriation, Transformation, Opposition*. London: Routledge, 2015.

Marsh-Caldwell, Anne. *The Song of Roland, as Chanted Before the Battle of Hastings, by the Minstrel Taillefer*. London: Hurst and Blackett, 1854.

Martin, Rebecca. *Wild Men and Moors in the Castle of Love: The Castle-Siege Tapestries, in Nuremberg, Vienna, and Boston (German (Alsace) Weavers)*. Chapel Hill, NC: University of North California, 1983.

Martin, Samuel. *An Essay Upon Plantership, Humbly Inscribed to His Excellency George Thomas Esq; Chief Governor of the Leeward Islands*. London: T. Cadell, 1765, 1773. Quoted in *London Chronicle*, XXIII: 2537, 13–16 March 1773, p. 250.

Martinot, Steve. *The Rule of Racialization: Class, Identity and Governance*. Philadelphia, PA: Temple University Press, 2003.

Martone, Erica. *Encyclopedia of Blacks in European History and Culture: A–J, K–Z*. Santa Barbara, CA: Greenwood Press, 2008–2009.

Massey, Gerald. *Ancient Egypt the Light of the World, Containing an Attempt to Recover and Reconstitute the Lost Origines of the Myths and Mysteries … with Egypt for the Mouthpiece and Africa as the Birthplace*, Volume 1: *Egyptian Origines in the British Isles*. 1881, republished, London: Secaucus University Books, 1974.

Matar, Nabil. *Islam in Britain, 1558–1685*. New York: Cambridge University Press, 1998.

———. *Turks Moors and Englishmen in the Age of Discovery*. New York: Columbia University Press, 2000.

Matito, Domínguez. María Luisa Lobato (eds.). Trevor J. Dadson. 'Un Ricote Verdadero: El Licenciado Alonso Herrador de Villarrubia de los Ojos del Guadiana – Morisco Que Vuelve.' *Memoria de la Palabra: Actas del VI Congreso de la Asociación Internacional Siglo de Oro*, Burgos-La Rioja 15–19 de julio 2002/coord. por Francisco. Volume 1, 2004 (2007), pp. 601–612.

Matoesian, Gregory M. *Law and the Language of Identity: Discourse in the William Kennedy Smith Rape Trial*. Oxford/New York: Oxford University Press, 2001.

Matthew, Thomas. John Rodgers (eds. trs.). *Matthews Bible: The Byble Whych Is All the Holy Scripture: In Whych Are Contayned the Old and Newe Testament, Truelye and Purely Translated into Englishe by Thomas Matthewe*. London: Tyndale, 1537.

Mavelli, Luca (ed.). *Towards a Postsecular International Politics: New Forms of Community, Identity and Power*. New York: Palgrave Macmillan, 2014.

Mayall, David. *Gypsy Identities, 1500–2000: From Egipcyans and Moon-men to the Ethnic Romany*. London: Routledge, 2004.

McClure, Alexander. *The Translators Revived: A Biographical Memoir of the Authors of the English Version of the Holy Bible*. 1853. Mobile, AL: R. E. Publications, republished by the Marantha Bible Society, 1984.

McCullagh, Christopher Behan. *Justifying Historical Descriptions*. London/Cambridge: Cambridge University Press, 1984.

McCullough, David. *1776*. New York: Simon and Schuster, 2005.

McCullough, Norman Verrle. *The Negro in English Literature*. Ilfracombe: A. Stockwell, 1962.

Mckee, Alexander. *The Queen's Corsair: Drake's Journey of Circumnavigation, 1577–1580*. London: Souvenir Press, 1978.

Mckee, Sally (ed.). *Crossing Boundaries: Issues of Cultural and Individual Identity in the Middle Ages and the Renaissance*. Turnhout: Brepols, 1999.

Mclintock, John. *Cyclopaedia of Biblical, Theological and Ecclesiastical Literature: H, I, J*. New York: Harper & Brothers, 1872.

Meeres, Frank. *Strangers: A History of Norwich's Incomers*. Norwich: Norwich Heritage Economic and Regeneration Trust, 2012.

Memling, Hans. *Triptych of Jan Floreins*. 1425/40–1494. Central panel with *Adoration of the Magi*. Memling Museum, Bruges.

Merriam, George Spring. *The Negro and the Nation: A History of American Slavery and Enfranchisement*. New York: Haskell House, 1970.

Merrim, Stephanie. *Early Modern Women's Writing and Sor Juana Ines de la Cruz*. Nashville, TN: Vanderbilt University Press, 1999.

Meyers, Charles. 'Elizabethan "Marranos" Unmasked.' *The Journal of the Jewish Museum of Australia* 97:3, 1997, pp. 14–15.

Middleton, Thomas. *The Triumphs of Truth* ... London: Nicholas Okes, 1613.

Mikael, Abba. in Maurice Muhatia Makumba. *An Introduction to African Philosophy: Past and Present*. Nairobi: Paulines Publications Africa, 2007, pp. 84–85.

Miller, Naomi J. *Changing the Subject: Mary Wroth and Figurations of Gender in Early Modern England*. Lexington, KY: University Press of Kentucky, 1960.

Miller, W. E. 'Negroes in Elizabethan London.' *Notes and Queries* 8, 4 April 1961, p. 138.

Mills, John Stuart. 'The Negro Question.' *Fraser's Magazine for Town and Country* 41, 1850, pp. 25–31.

———. *System of Logic Ratiocinative and Inductive Being a Connected View of the Principles of Evidence and the Methods of Scientific Investigation*. Whitefish, MT: Kessinger Publications, 2004.

Milton, John. John S. B. Dolle et al. (eds). *Paradise Lost: A Poem in Twelve Books*. 1st edition 1667, London: S. Simmons, 1674.

Minsheu, John. *A Dictionarie in Spanish and English*. London: E. Bollifant, 1599.

Mondiwa, Rowena. *Media Diversified*. http://mediadiversified.org/2014/02/12/its-time-to-talk-about-black-tudors/, accessed 01/01/16.

Monger, George. *Marriage Customs of the World: From Henna to Honeymoons*. Santa Barbara, CA: ABC CLIO, 2004.

Montagu, Ashley (ed.). *UNESCO Statement on Race: An Annotated Elaboration and Exposition of the Four Statements on Race Issued by the United Nations Educational, Scientific, and Cultural Organization*. 3rd edition, New York: Oxford University Press, 1972.

———. *Man's Most Dangerous Myth: The Fallacy of Race*. Redditch: Read Books, 2013.

Montalvo, Jose Hinojosa. *Jews of the Kingdom of Valencia: From Persecution to Expulsion, 1391–1492*. Jerusalem: Magnes Press, 1993.

Moore, Richard B. *The Name 'Negro': Its Origin and Evil Use*. Baltimore, MD: Black Presence, 1960.

Moore, Timothy Owens. *The Science of Melanin*. Redan, GA: Zamani Press, 2004.

Morant, Philip. *The History and Antiquities of Colchester in the County of Essex*. Colchester: J. Fenno, 1789.

More, Thomas. Alvaro De Silva (ed.). *The Last Letters of Thomas More*. Grand Rapids, MI/Cambridge: W.B. Eerdmans, 2000.

More, Thomas. John Holt. *Lac Puero M Holti Mylke for Chyldren, (A Latin Grammar, with Two Epigrams)*. London: Wynkyn de Worde, 1508.

More, Thomas. William Rastell (ed.). *The Works of Sir Thomas More Knyght ... The First Boke*. London: John Cawod, Richard Tottell, 1528, 1557.

Morgan, Kenneth. *Slavery, Atlantic Trade and the British Economy, 1660–1800*. Cambridge: Cambridge University Press, 2000.

Morgan, Philip D. 'Maritime Slavery.' *Slavery and Abolition* 31:3, 2010, pp. 311–326.

———. *Maritime Slavery*. London: Routledge, 2012.

Morgan, T. J. Prys Morgan. *Welsh Surnames*. Cardiff: University of Wales Press, 1985.

Morris, Richard B. *Seven Who Shaped Our Destiny: The Founding Fathers as Revolutionaries*. New York: Harper & Row, 1973.

Mosely, William. *What Color Was Jesus?* Chicago, IL: African American Images, 1987.

Mott, Adrian Spear. Richard Hakluyt. *Hakluyt's Voyages*. Boston, MA: Houghton Miflin, 1929.

Mudimbe, Valentin-Yves. *The Invention of Africa: Gnosis, Philosophy and the Order or Knowledge*. Bloomington, IN: Indiana University Press, 1988.

Mulcaster, Richard. *Positions Wherein Those Primitive Circumstances Be Examined, Which Are Necessarie for the Training Up of Children, Either for Skill in Their Booke, or Health in Their Bodie ...* London: T. Vautrollier, 1581.

Musculus, Wolfgang. *Mosis Genesim Plenissimi Commentarii*. Basel: Iannis Heruggii, 1565.

Nachtigal, Gustav. A. G. B. Fisher (trs.). *Sahara and Sudan: Tripoli and Fezzan; Tibesti or Tu*, Volume 1. London: C. Hurst and Company, 1879.

Nama, Adilifu. *Race on the QT: Blackness and the Films of Quentin Tarantino*. Austin, TX: University of Texas, 2015.

Narrative Eye. www.narrative-eye.org.uk/petition.html, accessed 12/12/15.

———. 'Inclusive Curriculum' petition kick-started by *Blackamoores*, www.ipetitions.com/petition/inclusivecurriculum/, accessed 01/01/16.

———. www.narrative-eye.org.uk/index.html, accessed 01/01/16.

National Archives, Kew, London. *Early Chancery Proceedings* (ECP), C1/148/67.

———. *Exchequer Accounts*, 417 (6) folio 50 RO in Letters and Papers Henry VIII 1.1.505# 1025.

———. John Hawkins. *Letter to Queen Elizabeth*. 16 September 1567. SP 12/44, f. 16 16/9/1567.

———. *High Courts of Admiralty (HCA), Reports*, 1547, ref. 24/39/49–51.

———. *High Courts of Admiralty (HCA), Reports*, 1592, ref. 24/39/49–51.

———. *Lay Subsidy Records, Returns for the City of London in 1292–1392* … ref. PRO E179/144/2 and E179/144/3.

———. Prerogative Court of Canterbury, Prob 11/492, Poley Quire Numbers: 1–44. dated 19 February 1707.

———. 'A Provincial Constitution of Canterbury.' 25 October 1597 but approved in 1598. National Archives, *Parish Records*. www.nation alarchives.gov.uk/familyhistory/guide/people/parish.htm, accessed 19/06/07.

Newman, William R. Lawrence M. Principe. *Alchemy Tried in the Fire: Starkey, Boyle, and the Fate of Helmontian Chymistry*. Chicago, IL: Chicago University Press, 2005.

Nerhot, Patrick. *Law, Interpretation and Reality: Essays in Epistemology, Hermeneutics and Jurisprudence*. Berlin: Springer Science and Business Media, 2013.

Netzloff, Mark. '"Counterfeit Egyptians" and Imagined Borders: Jonson's "The Gypsies Metamorphosed".' *ELH*, *Johns Hopkins University* 68:4, winter 2001, pp. 763–793. https://muse.jhu.edu/login?auth=0&type=summary&url=/journals/elh/v068/68.4netzloff.html, accessed 29/08/15.

Norden, John. *Speculum Britanniæ. The First Parte. An Historicall and Chorographicall Discription of Middlesex. Therein Are … Sett Downe, the Names of the Cyties … Parishes, etc.* London: John Norden, 1593.

———. *A Chorographicall Discription of the Severall Shires and Islands of Middlesex, Essex, Surrey, Sussex, Hamshire, Weighte, Garnesey & Jarsey. Performed by the Traveyle and View of John Norden. [With His Dedication to Queen Elizabeth, an Address to the Lords of the Privy Council, and Maps of Essex and Hampshire]*. London: John Norden, 1595.

Norman, Zachary. 'Group Lobbies Michael Gove to Include Black Tudors in the National Curriculum.' *Guardian*. www.guardian-series.co.uk/news/wfnews/10800194Group_lobbies_Michael_Gove_to_include_black_Tudors_in_national_curriculum/, accessed 25/12/15.

Northampton Records Office. Northampton, Microfiche 120, pp. 1–3.

Northrup, David. *Africa's Discovery of Europe: 1450–1850*. New York/Oxford: Oxford University Press, 2013.

Norton, Rictor. *Mother Clap's Molly House: The Gay Subculture in England 1700–1830*. Los Angeles, CA: University of California, 2008.

Nicolas, Nicholas Harris. Edward Tyrrell (eds.). *A Chronicle of London, from 1089 to 1483: Written in the Fifteenth Century, and for the First Time Printed from Mss. in the British Museum: To Which Are Added Numerous Contemporary Illustrations, Consisting of Royal Letters, Poems, and Other Articles …* London: Longman, Rees, Brown Orme and Green, 1823.

Nicols, Philip. *Sir Francis Drake Revived*. 1882, new edition, Whitefish, MT: Kessinger Publishing, 2004.

Nicholson, Edward Williams Byron. *Keltic Researches: Studies in the History and Distribution of the Ancient Goidelic Language and Peoples*. Oxford: Oxford University Press, 1904.

Niebrzydowski, Sue. 'The Sultana and Her Sisters: Black Women in the British Isles, before 1530.' *Women's History Review* 10:2, 2001, pp. 187–210.

Northampton Records Office, Wootton Hall Park, Northampton, NN4 8BQ: Northampton, Microfiche 120, pp. 1–3.

Nunez, Rafael Velez. 'Beyond the Emblem: Alchemical Albedo in Ben Jonson's The Masque of Blackness.' *Sederi* 8, 1997, pp. 257–263.

Obano, Rex. *The Moors of England*. London: unpublished, 2015.

———. *The Moors of England*. www.alfredfagonaward.co.uk/2015-awards/, accessed 05/01/16.

Oberg, Michael Leroy (ed.). *Samuel Wiseman's Book of Record: The Official Account of Bacon's Rebellion in Virginia, 1676–1677*. New York/Oxford: Lexington Books, 2005.

Odhiambo, Nicholas Oyugi. *Ham's Sin and Noah's Curse and Blessed Utterances: A Critique of Current Views*. Bloomington, IN: Author House, 2014.

Odonkor, Vie Kobina. *Race and Blackness in Early Modern England: A Study of Shakespeare's Titus Andronicus, The Merchant of Venice, Othello and the Tempest*. Gainesville, FL: Florida State University, 2002.

O'Hara, Diana. *Courtship and Constraint: Rethinking the Making of Marriage in Tudor England*. Manchester: Manchester University Press, 2002.

Ohajuru, Michael. *The John Blanke Project*. www.johnblanke.com/, accessed 12/03/16.

Okely, Judith. *The Traveller-Gypsies*. Cambridge: Cambridge University Press, 1983.

Ollman, Bertell. *Dialectical Investigations*. London: Routledge, 1993.

Olsen, Kirstin. *Daily Life in 18th-Century England*. Oxford: Greenwood Publishing, 1999.

Olusoga, David. *Black and British: A Forgotten History*. BBC TV series, 17 December – 5 December 2016.

Onyeani, Chika. 'Contemptuousness of Sub-Saharan Africa.' *Worldpress.org*. 16 July 2009. http://worldpress.org/Africa/3382.cfm.

Onyeka. 'Arcane Etymology of the Blackamoore,' in Hakim Adi (ed.). *Black British History: New Perspectives*. London: Zed Books, 2019.

Onyeka. 'The Missing Tudors: Black People in Sixteenth-Century England.' *BBC History Magazine* 13:7, July 2012, pp. 32–33.

———. 'What's in a Name?' *History Today* 62:10, October 2012, pp. 34–39.

———. *Blackamoores: Africans in Tudor England, Their Presence, Status and Origins*. 2013, new edition, London: Narrative Eye, 2014.

———. 'The Black Equestrians: Africans in Georgian Britain.' *History Today* 64:7, July 2014. www.historytoday.com/onyeka/black-equestrians#sthash. E8iWMY82.dpuf.

———. 'The Missing Pages of England's History.' *Culture Pulse*, July 2014, p. 33. https://issuu.com/culturepulse/docs/july_2014_issue_25, accessed 29/07/14.

———. 'Africans in Tudor England.' *Historical Honey*, 25 August 2014, http://historicalhoney.com/africans-in-tudor-england/.

———. 'Artisans, Servants, Musicians and Kings: Africans in Tudor England,' in *Commonwealth Year Book*. Commonwealth Secretariat, Commonwealth of Nations, 2015, pp. 75–76.

———. *London's Lost Graveyard: The Crossrail Discovery.* Dir. Kenny Scott, True North. Channel 4, Sunday 19 July 2015.

———. *Young Othello: The Tragedy of the White Swan.* London: Narrative Eye, 2016/2017.

———. 'Holy Trumpets, John Blanke the Black Trumpeter.' *Black History Magazine*, November 2017.

———. 'Port Towns, Diversity and Tudor England,' *Port Towns.* http://porttowns.port.ac.uk/port-towns-diversity-tudor-england-2/.

Onwuejeogwu, M. Angulu. Bana Okpu. Chris Ebighgbo. *African Civilizations: Origin, Growth, and Development.* Lagos: UTO Publications, 2000.

Origen. 'The Homilies of Origen,' in Sujata Iyengar. *Shades of Difference: Mythologies of Skin Colour in Early Modern England.* Philadelphia, PA: University of Pennsylvania Press, 2013.

Orlin, Lena Cowen. *Locating Privacy in Tudor London.* Oxford: Oxford University Press, 2007.

Owens, Sarah E. Jane E. Mangan (eds.). *Women of the Iberian Atlantic.* Baton Rouge, LA: Louisiana State University Press, 2012.

Oxford Dictionary of English. 2nd edition, Oxford: Oxford University Press, 2003.

The Oxford English Dictionary. London: Oxford University Press, 1998.

Padmore, George. 'The Negro Question,' in *The Life and Struggles of Negro Toilers.* London: International Trade Union Committee of Negro Workers …, 1931.

Pagden, Anthony. *The Languages of Political Theory in Early Modern Europe.* Cambridge: Cambridge University Press, 1987.

Painter, Nell Irvin. *The History of White People.* New York: W. W. Norton and Company, 2010.

Painter, William. *The Palace of Pleasure. Beautified, Adorned and Well Furnished, with Pleasaunt Histories and Excellent Nouelles, Selected Out of Diuers.* London: Henry Denham, 1566.

Palmer, James. 'Ghosts of Crossrail.' *Sunday Times Magazine*, 12 August 2015, p. 43.

Pankhania, Josna. *Liberating the National History Curriculum.* London: Falmer Press, 1994.

Pankhurst, Richard. *Historic Images of Ethiopia*. Addis Ababa: Shama Books, 2005.

Paris, Mathew. Henry Richards Luard (ed.). *Flores Historiarum*, Volume 3. London: HMSO, 1890.

Parker, Geoffrey. *The Army of Flanders and the Spanish Road, 1567–1659*. London: Cambridge University Press, 1972.

———. *The Grand Strategy of Philip II*. New Haven, CT: Yale University Press, 2000.

———. *Imprudent King: A New Life of Philip II*. New Haven, CT: Yale University Press, 2014.

Parry, Glyn. 'Berosus and the Protestants: Reconstructing Protestant Myth.' *Huntingdon Library Quarterly* 64:1/2, 2001, pp. 1–21.

Paul, Kathleen. *Whitewashing Britain: Race and Citizenship in the Postwar Era*. Ithaca, NY/London: Cornell University Press, 1997.

Peck, Samuel M. *Pigment (Melanin): Studies of the Human Skin After Application of Thorium X with Special Reference to the Origin and Function of Dendritic Cells*. Chicago, IL: Medical Association, 1930.

Pelikan, Jaroslav. Valerie R. Hotchkiss. David Price (eds.). *The Reformation of the Bible: The Bible of the Reformation*. New Haven, CT: Yale University Press, 1996.

Penn, William. Robert Venables. *A Great ... Victory Obtained by the English Forces, Under the Command of General Penn and Gen. Venables against the French and Others, in the West Indies ...* London: publisher unknown, 1655.

Peralba, Małgorzata Oleszkiewicz. *The Black Madonna in Latin America and Europe: Tradition and Transformation*. Albuquerque, NM: University of New Mexico Press, 2007.

People's Book Prize. www.peoplesbookprize.com/book.php?id=1107, accessed 01/01/15.

Percy, William. Mathew Dimmock. *William Percy's Mahomet and His Heaven: A Critical Edition*. Aldershot: Ashgate, 2006.

Percyvall, Richard. *A Dictionarie in Spanish and English, First Published by R. Percivale Now Enlarged by J. Minsheu. Hereunto Is Annexed in Ample English Dictionarie with the Spanish Words Adjoined*. London: E. Bollifant, 1599.

Pevsner, Nicholas. *London: The Cities of London and Westminster*, Volume 1. London: Penguin, 1973.

Pew Foundation. 'Global Christianity: A Report on the Size and Distribution of the World's Christian Population.' *Pew Research Centre*, 19 December 2011. www.pewforum.org/2011/12/19/global-christianity-exec, accessed 21/02/16.

Phillips, Joshua. *English Fictions of Communal Identity, 1485–1603*. Farnham: Ashgate, 2003.

Phillips, Ulrich Bonnell. *American Negro Slavery: A Survey of the Supply, Employment and Control of Negro Labor as Determined by the Plantation Regime*. New York/London: D. Appleton and Co, 1918.

Phillips, William D. *Slavery from Roman Times to the Early Transatlantic Trade*. Manchester: Manchester University Press, 1985.

———. *Slavery in Medieval and Early Modern Iberia*. The Middle Ages Series. Philadelphia, PA: University of Pennsylvania Press, 2013.

Piedra, Jose. 'In Search of the Black Stud,' in Louise Fradenburg. Carla Freccero (eds.). *Premodern Sexualities*. New York: Routledge, 1996, pp. 22–44.

(Pliny) Gaius Plinius Secundus. *Naturalis Historie*. Paris: Reginaldi Chalderi, 1516.

Pliny the Elder Plynii Secundi. *Naturalis Historiae Liber*. Venetiis: Nicolaum Jenson, 1472.

Plowden, Edmund. *Law Report*, 1571, from a legal case 1550, in Ernst H. Kantorowicz, *The King's Two Bodies: A Study in Medieval Political Ideology*. New York: Princeton University Press, 2016, p. 7.

Plymouth and West Devon Record Office, Plymouth, St Andrews/MF1–4.

Pollock, Griselda (ed.). *Psychoanalysis and the Image*. Oxford: Blackwell Press, 2006.

Pope Pius V. 'Regnans in Excelsis.' Papal Bull 1570, in John Strype. *Annals of the Reformation and Establishment of Religion, and Other Various Occurrences* ... 1709–1725, new edition, Oxford: Clarendon Press, 1824.

Pope John Paul II. *Apostolic Letter, Issued Motu Proprio, Proclaiming Saint Thomas More Patron of Politician and Statesmen*. 31 October 2000. Vaticana: Libreria Editrice Vaticana, 2000. http://w2.vatican.va/content/john-paul-ii/en/motu_proprio/documents/hf_jp-ii_motu-proprio_20001031_thomas-more.html.

Porta, Giambattista Della. *Magiae Naturalis* ... Antverpiae: Ex officina C. Plantini, 1564.

Pory, John (tr.). Leo Africanus. *A Geographical Historie of Africa, Written in Arabicke and Italian* ... *by Iohn Leo a More* ... London: John Pory, 1600.

Postel, Guillaume de Etienne. *Cosmographicae* ... Basel: Ioaneem Oporinum, 1561.

Powers, James F. *A Society Organized for War: The Iberian Municipal Militias in the Central Middle Ages, 1000–1284*. Berkeley, CA: University of California Press, 1987.

Prak, Maarten Roy (ed.). *Craft Guilds in the Early Modern Low Countries: Work, Power and Representation*. Aldershot: Ashgate, 2006.

Preston, Paul. *The Spanish Holocaust: Inquisition and Extermination in Twentieth-Century Spain*. London: Harper Press, 2012.

Price, Richard (ed.). *Maroon Societies: Rebel Slave Communities in the Americas*. New York: Anchor Books, 1973.

Purchas, Samuel. *Purchas His Pilgrimage; or Relations of the World and the Religions Observed in All Ages and Places Discovered from the Creation unto the Present* ... London: William Stansby for Henrie Fetherstone, 1613.

Purfoot, Thomas. *The Historical Discourse of Muley Hamet's Refining the Three Kingdoms, of Moruecos Fes and Sus. The Religion and Policies of the More or Barbarian* ... London: Clement Knight, 1609.

Purvey, John. John Wycliffe. Terrence B. Noble (ed.). *Wycliffe Bible* (1388). Genesis 10, v. 6–12. 'Bible Study Tools.' 2001. www.biblestudytools.com/wyc/genesis/10.html, accessed 12/03/15.

Qualifications and Curriculum Authority (QCA). 'Innovating with History.' www.qca.org.uk/history/innovating/history_matters/worked_for_me/ks3/cameo9.htm, accessed 18/07/08.

Quilligan, Maureen. *The Allegory of Female Authority: Christine de Pizan's Cité Des Dames.* Ithaca, NY: Cornell University Press, 1991.

Rabil, Albert (ed.). Henricus Cornelius Agrippa. *Declamation on the Nobility and Preeminence of the Female Sex.* Chicago, IL: University of Chicago Press, 1996.

Raleigh, Walter. *The Historie of the VVorld. In Fiue Bookes ... By Sir Walter Ralegh, Knight.* London: Walter Stansby/Walter Burre, 1617.

Ramondo, Francesco. *Ideal of the Courtly Gentleman in Spanish Literature, Its Ascent and Decline.* Bloomington, IN: Trafford Publishing, 2013.

Rashidi, Runoko. *The Global African Community: The African Presence in Asia, Australia, and the South Pacific.* Washington, DC: Institute for Independent Education, 1995.

———. *African Star Over Asia: The Black Presence in the East.* London: Books of Africa, 2012.

Rawlings, Helen. *The Debate on the Decline of Spain.* Manchester: Manchester University Press, 2012.

Raymond, Joad. *The Invention of the Newspaper: English Newsbooks, 1641–1649.* Oxford/New York: Clarendon Press, 2005.

Read, Sara. *Menstruation and the Female Body in Early Modern England.* New York: Palgrave Macmillan, 2003.

Read, Sara. Jennifer Evans (eds.). *Maladies and Medicine: Exploring Health and Healing, 1540–1740.* Barnsley: Pen and Sword, 2017.

Redman, Robert. *Here Begynneth the Boke Called the Pype, or Tonne, of the Lyfe of Perfection. The Reason or Cause Wherof Dothe Playnely Appere in the Processe. (A Worke or Boke of ... Saynt Bernarde, Named by ye Title Thus. De Precepto et Dispensatione. That Is to Saye, of Commaundement and Dispensacion ... Translate and Tourned into Englyshe by ... Rycharde Whytforde.),* [In a binding of contemporary brown calf, with the Arms of Henry VIII stamped on the upper cover, and those of Katherine of Aragon on the lower]. London: Robert Redman, 1532.

Rees, Jasper. 'Black and British: A Forgotten History Revealed a Fascinating Side of Our Past – Review.' *The Telegraph,* 9 November 2016. www.telegraph.co.uk/tv/2016/11/09/black-and-british-a-forgotten-history-revealed-a-fascinating-sid/, accessed 12/03/16.

Reese, Max Meredith. *The Cease of Majesty: A Study of Shakespeare's History Plays.* London: Richard Arnold Publishers, 1961.

Reiss, Tom. *The Black Count: Glory Revolution, Betrayal and the Real Count of Monte Cristo.* London: Harvill Secker, 2012.

Rhodes, John. *The Countrie Mans Comfort. Or Religious Recreations Fitte for All Well Disposed Persons* ... 1588. London: M. D. Dawson, 1637.

Rich, Barnabe. *The Famous Hystory of Herodotus.* London: Thomas Marshe, 1584.

Richardson, Jonathan. *An Essay on the Whole Art of Criticism as It Relates to Painting ... An Argument in Behalf of the Science of a Connoisseur ...* London: W. Churchill, 1719.

Ritchie, Jane. Jane Lewis. Carol McNaughton Nicholls et al. (eds.). *Qualitative Research Practice: A Guide for Social Science Students and Researchers.* New York/London: Sage, 2013.

Roberts, Gareth (writer). Charles Palmer (director). 'The Shakespeare Code.' *Dr Who Series.* BBC, 7 April 2007.

Roberts, Josephine A. *The Poems of Lady Mary Wroth.* Baton Rouge, LA: Louisiana State University Press, 1983.

Robinson, Allan Richard. Paola Malanotte-Rizzoli. *Ocean Processes in Climate Dynamics: Global and Mediterranean Examples.* New York: Springer, 1994.

Rodney, Walter. *How Europe Underdeveloped Africa.* Washington, DC: Howard University Press, 1974.

Rodriguez, Junius (ed.). *Slavery in the United States: A Social, Political, and Historical Encyclopedia,* Volume 2. Santa Barbara, CA/Oxford: ABC-CLIO, 2007.

Roe, Thomas. *An Account of the Embassy of Sir Thomas Roe to the Great Mogul ... Collected from His Own Journal,* 23 March 1616, in John Harris (ed.). *Navigantium Atque Itinerantium Bibliotheca ...,* Volume 1. London: Bennet, 1705–1764, pp. 150, 445.

Rogers, Elizabeth Francis (ed.). Thomas More. *The Correspondence of Sir Thomas More.* Princeton, NJ: Princeton University Press, 1947.

Rogers, Joel Augustus. *Nature Knows No Colour-Line,* p. 156 quotes, 'Anglicanus.' *Gentleman's Magazine* 34, October 1764, pp. 493, 495.

———. *World's Great Men of Colour,* Volumes 1 and 2. 1931, new edition, New York: Touchstone Books, 1995.

———. *Sex and Race, Negro Caucasian Mixing in All Ages and All Lands,* Volumes 1–4. 1942, 9th edition, New York: Rogers, 1967.

———. *Nature Knows No Colour-Line.* St Petersburg, FL: Helga Rogers, 1952.

Rogers, Thomas. *A Philosophicall Discourse, Entituled The Anatomie of the Minde. Newlie made.* London: A. Maunsell, 1576.

———. *The English Creed, Wherin Is Contained in Tables an Exposition on the Articles Which Every Man Is Subscribe To.* London: publisher unknown, 1579.

Rogers, Thomas (ed.). Scheltco Geveren. *Of the End of This World, and Second Coming of Christ ...* London: Henrie Middleton, 1583.

Rolls, Albert. *The Theory of the King's Two Bodies in the Age of Shakespeare.* Lewiston, NY: Edwin Mellon Press, 2000.

Romain, Gemma. *Connecting Histories: A Comparative Exploration of African-Caribbean and Jewish History and Memory in Modern Britain*. London: Kegan Paul, 2006.

———. *Black British History*. London: Birkbeck University, Faculty of Continuing Education, 2007–2008. www.bbk.ac.uk/ce/history/documents/FFHI232UACB_003.pdf, accessed 05/11/08.

Ross, Alf. *On Law and Justice*. Clark: The Lawbook Exchange, 1959.

Rosser, Leonidas. *Baptism: Its Nature, Obligation, Mode, Subjects and Benefits*. Philadelphia, PA: Leonidas Rosser, 1854.

Rota, Stefano Fogelberg. Andreas Hellerstedt. *Shaping Heroic Virtue: Studies in the Art and Politics of Supereminence in Europe and Scandinavia*. Leiden/Boston, MA: Brill, 2015.

Rowe, Margery M. (ed.). Devon and Cornwall Record Society. *Tudor Exeter Tax Assessments 1489–1595: Including the Military Survey 1522*. Torquay: The Devonshire Press, 1977.

Ruddock, Alwyn. *Italian Merchants and Shipping in Southampton 1270–1600*. Southampton: University College, 1951.

Runia, Robert. 'Great Heads, Great Minds and the Genesis of Scientific Racism.' *Journal for Early Modern Cultural Studies* 15:2, spring 2015, pp. 112–118.

Russell, Bertrand. *History of Western Philosophy*. London: George Allen Unwin, 1945.

Rymer, Thomas. Curt Zimansky (ed.). *A Short View of Tragedy: The Critical Works of Thomas Rymer 1692–1693*. London: Yale University Press, 1956.

Salesbury, William. *A Dictionary in English and Welshe*. London: Richard Crowley, 1547.

Salisbury Cathedral Records Office. 'Mathias the Morian.' Wiltshire and Swindon History Centre, Wiltshire, Register 1, X3/84/1.

Salkeld, Duncan. 'Black Luce and the "Curtizans" of Shakespeare's London.' *Signature* 2. Chichester: University of Chichester, winter 2000, pp. 1–10.

Salman, Redcliffe N. *The History and Social Influence of the Potato*. Cambridge: Cambridge University Press, 1985.

Salvadore, Matteo. *The African Prester John and the Birth of Ethiopian–European Relations, 1402–1555*. London: Routledge, 2016.

Salzman, Paul. 'Contemporary References in Wroth's *Urania*.' *The Review of English Studies* New Series, 29:114, May 1978, pp. 178–180.

Sampson, Mike. 'Friends of Devon Archives, the Black Connection.' *Friends of Devon Newsletter* 25, May 2000, pp. 12–15.

———. 'Black Burials and Deaths 16th century' (email). Devon Record Office, Devon. 16 April 2006.

Sarisky, Darren. *Theology, History, and Biblical Interpretation: Modern Readings*. London: Bloomsbury, 2015.

Sawday, Jonathan. *The Body Emblazoned: Dissection and the Human Body in Renaissance Culture*. London: Routledge, 2005.

Sawyer, John F. A. *The Blackwell Companion to the Bible and Culture*. New York: John Wiley, 2012.

Scarsi, Selene. *Translating Women in Early Modern England: Gender in the Elizabethan Versions of Boirado, Ariosto and Tasso*. Farnham: Ashgate, 2001.

Schama, Simon et al. *A History of Britain*. 2 Entertain Video, 2000–2002.

Schleiner, Louise. *Tudor and Stuart Women Writers*. Bloomington, IN: Indiana University Press, 1994.

Schmidt, Alvin J. *How Christianity Changed the World*. New York: HarperCollins, 2009.

Schoenbaum, Simon (Samuel). *William Shakespeare: A Compact Documentary Life*. Oxford: Clarendon Press, 1977.

———. *Shakespeare's Lives*. London: Clarendon, 1991.

Schomburg, Arthur. Benjamin P. Bowser. Louis Kushnick. Paul Grant (eds.). *Against the Odds: Scholars Who Challenged Racism in the Twentieth Century*. Amherst, MA: University of Massachusetts Press, 2002.

Schorsch, Jonathan. *Jews and Blacks in the Early Modern World*. Cambridge: Cambridge University Press, 2004.

———. *Swimming the Christian Atlantic: Judeoconversos, Afroiberians, and Amerindians in the Seventeenth Century*. Leiden/Boston, MA/Biggleswade: Brill Extenza Turpin, 2008.

Schwyzer, Philip. *Literature, Nationalism, and Memory in Early Modern England and Wales*. Cambridge: Cambridge University Press, 2004.

Scobie, Edward. *Black Britannia: A History of Blacks in Britain*. Chicago, IL: Johnson Publishing Company, 1972.

———. 'The Moors and Portugal's Global Expansion.' *Department of Black Studies Pamphlet*. New York: City College, City University of New York, 1996.

Scobie, Edward, Ivan Van Sertima (ed.). *Journal of African Civilizations*. New Brunswick, NJ: Rutgers University Press, 1985.

———. Ivan Van Sertima (ed.). *A Global African Presence*. New York: A&B Books, 1994.

Scott, Samuel Parsons. *History of the Moorish Empire in Europe*. 1904, new edition, New York/Philadelphia, PA/London: Lippincott, 1994.

Scottish Local History Forum. www.slhf.org/member-event/blackamoores-scottish-national-gallery, accessed 01/01/16.

Scupin, Raymond. Christopher R. De Corse. *Anthropology: A Global Perspective*. 1995, new edition, London: Prentice Hall, 1998.

Sebi. 'Dr Sebi What Is Carbon, Melanin and Protein?' *YouTube*, published 26 July 2016. www.youtube.com/watch?v=YL7dlpIauEE, accessed 02/04/18.

Secara, Maggie Pierce. 'Money and Coinage: The Basics.' *Life in Elizabethan England*, 28 March 2008. www.elizabethan.org/compendium/6.html, accessed 03/08/18.

Segal, Ronal. *Islam's Black Slaves: A History of Africa's Other Black Diaspora*. London: Atlantic Books, 2001.

Selincourt, Aubrey de (tr.). Herodotus. *The Histories*. 1954, new edition, London: Penguin, 1974.

Senden, Casper Van. Thomas Sherley. 'Petitions to Robert Cecil,' 1600, *Calendar of the Manuscripts of the Most Honourable the Marquess of Salisbury*. London: Historical Manuscripts Commission, 1883-1976, Volume 10, p. 431, Volume 14, pp. 143, 144, 154.

Sertima, Ivan Van. *Black Women in Antiquity*. New York: Transaction Publishers, 1984.

Sertima, Ivan Van. Runoko Rashidi (eds.). *The African Presence in Early Asia*. New Brunswick, NJ: Transaction Publishers, 1985.

Sertima, Ivan Van (ed.). Edward Scobie. *African Presence in Early Europe*. New Brunswick, NJ: Transaction Publishers, 1985.

Sertima, Ivan Van (ed.). Edward Scobie. 'The African Presence in Early Europe.' *African Presence in Early Europe*. New Brunswick, NJ: Transaction Publishers, 1985.

Shafer, Robert Jones (ed.). *A Guide to Historical Method*. Homewood, IL: The Dorsey Press, 1969, 1974.

Shakespeare, William. *Richard III*. London: Andrew Wise, 1597.

———. *Titus Andronicus*, in Richard Proudfoot and David Kastan (eds.). *The Arden Shakespeare Complete Works*, revised edition, Walton on Thames: Thomas Nelson and Sons, 1998.

———. *Othello. The Merchant of Venice. Romeo and Juliet. Macbeth*. Proudfoot et al. (eds.). *The Arden Shakespeare*.

———. *As You Like it*. Proudfoot et al. (eds.). *The Arden Shakespeare*.

———. *Anthony and Cleopatra*. Proudfoot et al. (eds.). *The Arden Shakespeare*.

Shantz, Jeff. *Racism and Borders: Representation, Repression, Resistance*. New York: Algora Publishing, 2010.

Sharpe, James. *Early Modern England: A Social History, 1550–1760*. London: Bloomsbury Academic, 1997.

Shaw, L. M. E. *The Anglo-Portuguese Alliance and the English Merchants in Portugal, 1654–1810*. Abingdon/New York/Oxford: Routledge, 2017.

Sherwood, Marika. 'Blacks in Elizabethan England.' *History Today* 53:10, 2003, pp. 40–42.

———. 'Britain, Slavery and the Trade in Enslaved Africans.' *History in Focus* 12, Spring 2007. www.history.ac.uk/ihr/Focus/Slavery/articles/sherwood.html, accessed 03/12/08.

———. 'In This Curriculum, I Don't Exist.' The Institute of Historical Research, University of London School of Advanced Study. www.history.ac.uk/resources/history-in-british-education/first-conference/sherwood-paper, accessed 27/07/11.

Shinn, Abigail. Mathew Dimmock. Andrew Hadfield. *The Ashgate Research Companion to Popular Culture in Early Modern England*. Farnham: Ashgate, 2014.

Shore, Laurence. 'The Enduring Power of Racism: A Reconsideration of Winthrop Jordan's White Over Black.' *History and Theory* 44:2, 2005, pp. 195–226.

Shortt, Adam. Arthur G. Doughty (eds.). *Canada and Its Provinces: A History of the Canadian People and Their Institutions*. Toronto/ Edinburgh: Publishers Association of Canada, 1913.

Shuart-Faris, Nora. David Bloome (eds.). *Uses of Intertextuality in Classroom and Educational Research*. Connecticut: Information Age, 2004.

Shyllon, Folarin. *Black People in Britain 1553–1833*. Oxford: Oxford University Press, 1977.

Silk, Jeannie. *At Home in the Law: How the Domestic Violence Revolution Is Transforming Privacy*. New Haven, CT: Yale University Press, 2009.

Silver, George. *Paradoxes of Defence*. London: Edward Blount, 1599.

Sisson, C. J. 'A Colony of Jews in Shakespeare's London.' *Essays and Studies* 23, 1938, pp. 38–51.

Skelton, John. McCullough Norman Verrle. *The Negro in English Literature*. Ilfracombe: A. Stockwell, 1962.

Skinner, Elliott Percival. *Peoples and Cultures of Africa: An Anthropological Reader*. Washington, DC: Natural History Press, 1972.

Skutsch, Carl. *Encyclopedia of the World's Minorities*. London: Routledge, 2013.

Slack, Paul. *Poverty and Policy in Tudor and Stuart England*. London: Longman, 1988.

Slauter, Will. 'Book Review: An Anatomy of an English Radical Newspaper.' *Cambridge Scholars Publishing*, 19 March 2018. https:// cambridgescholarsblog.wordpress.com/2018/03/19/book-review-an-anatomy-of-an-english-radical-newspaper/, accessed 20/04/18.

Sloane, Patricia (ed.). *Primary Sources: Selected Writings on Colour from Aristotle to Albers*. New York: Design Press, 1991.

Smith, Ian. *Race and Rhetoric in the Renaissance: Barbarian Errors*. Basingstoke: Palgrave Macmillan, 2009.

Snowden, Frank M. *Before Colour Prejudice: The Ancient View of Blacks*. Cambridge, MA: Harvard University Press, 1983.

Sokol, B. J. *Shakespeare and Tolerance*. Cambridge: Cambridge University Press, 2008.

Some, Nahile Jules. *The Re-Invention of Africa: The Dilemma of Literature Produced by Africans in French Context*. Berkeley/Los Angeles, CA: University of California, 2005.

Somer, Paul Van. *Anne of Denmark*. 1617. The Royal Collection, London. See Onyeka, *Blackamoores*, p. 201, figure 27.

Somersett's Case: R. v. Knowles, ex parte Somersett, 20 State Tr. (1772), p. 1.

Soyer, Francois. *Ambiguous Gender in Early Modern Spain and Portugal: Inquisitors, Doctors and Transgression of Gender Norms*. Medieval and Early Modern Iberian World. Leiden/Boston, MA: Brill, 2012.

———. *The Persecution of the Jews and Muslims of Portugal: King Manuel I and the End of Religious Tolerance (1496–7) Medieval Mediterranean*. Leiden/Boston, MA: Brill, 2012.

————. *Popularizing Anti-Semitism in Early Modern Spain and Its Empire.* Medieval and Early Modern Iberian World. Leiden/Boston, MA: Brill, 2014.

Spade, Paul Vincent (tr. ed.). *Five Texts on the Mediaeval Problem of Universals: Porphyry, Boethius, Abelard, Duns Scotus, Ockham/ Translated and Edited by Paul Vincent Spade.* Indianapolis, IN: Hackett, 1994.

Spencer, Charles. *Killers of the King: The Men Who Dared to Execute Charles I.* London/New York: Bloomsbury, 2014.

Spicer, Andrew. in Nigel Goose. Lieun Luu (eds.). *Immigrants in Tudor and Early Stuart England.* Eastbourne: Sussex Academic Press, 2005.

Spicer, Kevin P. *Anti-Semitism, Christian Ambivalence and the Holocaust.* Bloomington, IN: Indiana University Press, 2007.

Spivak, Gayatri Chakravorty. 'Can the Subaltern Speak?' in Cary Nelson. Lawrence Grossberg (eds.). *Marxism and the Interpretation of Culture.* Urbana, IL: University of Illinois Press, 1988, pp. 271–313.

————. *Ethics, Subalternity and the Critique of Postcolonial Reason.* Cambridge: Polity, 2007.

St Michael Paternoster Church, Vintry Ward, London, ref. Vintry Ward MF 0574365.

Stafford, Edward. *Letter to Francis Walsingham, Secretaries of State; State Papers Foreign.* France (June–December 1586), 20 August 1586. National Archives, Kew, ref. SP 78/16, f. 90–91.

Stark, Rodney. *The Triumph of Christianity: How the Jesus Movement Became the World's Largest Religion.* New York: HarperCollins, 2011.

Starkey, George (ed. trs.). *The Marrow of Alchemy* (1654); *The Reformed Commonwealth of Bees* (1655); *The Dignity of Kingship Asserted* (1655); in *Three Tracts of the Great Medicine of Philosophers for Humane and Metalline Bodies ...* London: T. Sowle, 1694.

Stavreva, Kirilka. *Words Like Daggers: Violent Female Speech in Early Modern England.* Lincoln, NE: University of Nebraska Press, 2015.

Steinmetz, David C. *The Bible in the Sixteenth Century.* Durham, NC: Duke University Press, 1996.

Stephens, William Brewer. *Sources for English Local History.* Cambridge: Cambridge University Press, 1981.

Stevens, Andrea Ria. *Inventions of the Skin: The Painted Body in Early English Drama 1400–1672.* Edinburgh: Edinburgh University Press, 2013.

————. 'Mastering Masques of Blackness: Jonson's Masque of Blackness, The Windsor Text of The Gypsies Metamorphosed, and Brome's The English Moor.' Academia. www.academia.edu/7685991/ Mastering_Masques_of_Blackness_Jonsons_Masque_of_Blackness_ The_Windsor_text_of_The_Gypsies_Metamorphosed_and_ Bromes_The_English_Moor, accessed 28/08/15.

Stevens, Walter Earl. *Berosus Chaldaeus: Counterfeit and Fictive Editors of the Early Sixteenth Century.* Ithaca, NY: Cornell University Press, 1979.

Stone, Lawrence. 'Social Mobility in England 1500–1700.' *Past and Present* 33, April 1966, pp. 16–17.

Stow, John. *The Annales of England, Faithfully Collected Out of the Most Autenticall Authors, Records ... untill ... 1592.* London: R. Newbery, 1592.

———. *A Summary of the Chronicles of England, Abridged and Continued unto 1598.* 1565, new edition, London: R. Bardocke, 1598.

———. Edmund Howes. *The Annales, or Generall Chronicle of England, Begun First by Maister Iohn Stow, and After Him Continued ... vnto the Ende of This Present Yeere 1614, by E. Howes.* London: Thomas Dawson for Thomas Adams, 1615.

Strachey, William (1612). *The Historie of Travaile into Virginia Britannia: Expressing the Cosmographie and Commodities of the Country, Togither with the Manners Customes of the People ...* London: Hakluyt Society, 1849.

Stradling, Richard Anthony. *Europe and the Decline of Spain: A Study of the Spanish System, 1580–1720.* London: Allen & Unwin, 1981.

Strickland, Debra Higgs. *Saracens, Demons, and Jews: Making Monsters in Medieval Art.* Princeton, NJ: Princeton University Press, 2003.

Strype, John. *Annals of the Reformation and Establishment of Religion, and Other Various Occurrences ... 1709–1725,* new edition, Oxford: Clarendon Press, 1824.

Stubbs, John. *The Discoverie of a Gaping Gulf Whereinto England Is Like to Be Swallowed by an Other French Marriage, if the Lord Forbid not the Banes, by Letting Her Maiestie See the Sin and Punishment Thereof.* London: H. Singleton, 1579.

Styles, Susan. *The Poor Law.* London: Macmillan Education, 1985.

Sugden, John. *Sir Francis Drake.* London: Random House, 2006.

Sumner, Claude. *The Rationalism of Zera Yacob/by Ayelè Teklehaymanot and, The Monastery of Dabra Libanos/by Abba Ayele Teklehaymanot.* Addis Abba: Capuchin Franciscan Institute of Philosophy and Theology, 2000.

Sundkler, Bengt G. M. *Bantu Prophets in South Africa.* London: Lutterworth Press, 1948.

Szombathy, Zoltán (ed. and tr.). *The History of Bidyini and Kaabu ...* Piliscsaba: Avicenna Institute of Middle Eastern Studies, 2007.

Tadmor, Naomi. *The Social Universe of the English Bible: Scripture, Society, and Culture in Early Modern England.* New York/Cambridge: Cambridge University Press, 2010.

Taine, Hippolyte Adolphe. Henri Van Laun (trs.). *History of English Literature.* 1864, 2nd edition, Edinburgh: Edmonston and Douglas, 1872.

Taney, Roger B. (Chief Justice). *Dred Scott Case, Scott v Sandford.* United States Supreme Court (1857), 60 U.S. 393.

Taverner, Richard. *The Most Sacred Bible Whiche Is the Holy Scripture, Conteyning the Old and Newe Testament, Translated into English* [by W. Tyndale and M. Coverdale], *and Newly Recognised ... Richard Taverner.* London: John Byddell, John Barthlet, 1539.

Taylor, Joan E. *What Did Jesus Look Like?* London: T&T Clarke, 2018.

Te Veldi, Rudi A. *Participation and Substantiality in Thomas Aquinas.* Leiden: Brill, 1995.

Thee, Francis C. R. *Julius Africanus and the Early Christian View of Magic.* Tubingen: J. C. B. Mohr, 1984.

Thomas, Dylan. 'Do Not Go Gentle into That Good Night' (1947), in Marguerite Caetani (ed.). *Botteghe Oscure.* Roma: Marguerite Caetani, 1951.

Thomas, James (tr.). Antonio Brucioli. *A Commentary upon the Canticle of Canticles, Written First in Italian by Antonio Brucioli, and Now Translated into English by Th. Iames Fellow ...* London: Printed by R. F[ield] for Tho. Man, 1598.

Thomas, Melita. 'Scandalous Tudor Weddings: 7 Tudor Women That Married for Love.' *History Extra.* www.historyextra.com/feature/tudors/scandalous-tudor-weddings-7-women-who-braved-royal-wrath-marrying-love, accessed 21/01/18.

Thompson, Aaron (tr.). *British History, Translated into English from the Latin of Jeffrey of Monmouth ...* London: J. Boyer, 1718.

Tierney, Sean. 'Quentin Tarantino in Black and White,' in Michael G. Lacey. Kent A. Ono (eds.). *Critical Rhetorics of Race.* New York: New York University Press, 2011, pp. 81–97.

Tilmann, Jean Paul. *An Appraisal of the Geographical Works of Albertus Magnus and His Contributions to Geographical Thought.* Detroit, MI: University of Michigan, 1971.

Tittler, Robert. Norman L. Jones. *Companion to Tudor Britain.* London: John Wiley & Sons, 2008.

Tolkien, J. R. R. *The Lord of the Rings: The Return of the King.* London: George Allen and Unwin, 1954, new edition, London: HarperCollins, 1997.

Tomaini, Thea. *The Corpse as Text: Disinterment and Antiquarian Enquiry, 1700–1900.* Martlesham: Boydell and Brewer, 2017.

Townley, James. *Illustrations of Biblical Literature, The History and Fate of the Sacred Writings, from the Earliest Period to the Present Century,* Volume 1. London. Longman, Hurst, Rees, Orme and Brown, 1821.

Townsend, John T. *Midrash Tanhuma: Genesis.* Jersey City, NJ: Ktav Publishing House, 1989.

Townsend, Meredith. Richard Holt Hutton (eds.). *The Spectator,* 27 September 1884, p. 21. http://archive.spectator.co.uk/article/27th-september-1884/21/ancient-and-modern-britons.

Tracy, James D. *The Founding of the Dutch Republic: War, Finance, and Politics in Holland 1572–1588.* Oxford: Oxford University Press, 2008.

Tracy, Joseph. *Colonization and Missions: An Historical Examination of the State of Society ...* Boston, MA: Massachusetts Colonization Society, 1846.

Turpin-Petrosino, Carolyn. *Understanding Hate Crime: Acts, Motives, Offenders, Victims and Justice.* London: Routledge, 2015.

Tyndale, William. *Tyndale Bible* (1525, 1536). www.biblestudytools.com/tyn/genesis/9.html, accessed 21/02/18.

Tyndale, William. John Foxe. *Actes and Monuments ... Foxe's Book of Martyrs*. London: John Day, 1563.

Underdowne, Thomas (tr.). *An Æthiopian Historie, Written in Greeke by Heliodorus: Very Wittie and Pleasaunt, Englished by Thomas Underdoune. With the Argumente of Euery Booke, Sette before the Whole Woorke*. London: Henry Wykes, 1569.

Ungerer, Gustav. 'Recovering a Black African's Voice in an English Lawsuit,' in *Medieval and Renaissance Drama in England*. Madison, WI: Fairleigh Dickinson University Press, 2004, pp. 255–271.

———. *The Mediterranean Apprenticeship of British Slavery*. Madrid: Verbum Editorial, 2008.

———. 'The Presence of Africans in Elizabethan England and the Performance of *Titus Andronicus*, at Burley-on-the-Hill, 1595–96.' *Medieval Renaissance Drama in England Annual* 21, 2008, pp. 19–56.

Ungewitter, Franz Heinrich. *Europe, Past and Present: A Comprehensive Manual of European Geography ...* New York: Putnam, 1850.

University of Wisconsin. 'Casselman Archive of Islamic and Mudejar Architecture in Spain.' *Digital Collections University of Wisconsin-Madson Libraries*. https://uwdc.library.wisc.edu/collections/arts/casselmanimage/, accessed 28/01/18.

Unwin, Rayner. *The Defeat of John Hawkins*. London: Allen Unwin, 1961.

Urban, Sylvanus (ed.). 'An Account of the Several Orders of Knighthood ...' in *Gentleman's Magazine*. London: Edward Cave, 1753, pp. 613–614.

Valls, Andrew. *Race and Racism in Modern Philosophy*. Ithaca, NY: Cornell University Press, 2005.

Van Bladel, Kevin. 'The Bactrian Background of the Barmakids,' in A. Akasoy. C. Burnett. R. Yoeli-Tlalim (eds.). *Islam and Tibet: Interactions Along the Musk Routes*. London: Ashgate, 2011.

Van Cleve, George William. *A Slaveholder's Union: Slavery, Politics, and the Constitution in the Early American Republic*. Chicago, IL: University of Chicago Press, 2010.

Van Helmont, Jan Baptiste. John Chandler (tr.). *Van Helmont's Worke's Containing His Most Excellent Philosophy, Physick, Chirurgery, Anatomy ...* London: Lodowick Lloyd, 1664.

Van Siclen, George West. *An American Edition of The Treatyse of Fysshynge wyth an Angle from the Boke of St. Albans ... Attributed to Dame Juliana Berners. Edited by G. W. Van Siclen*. New York: J. L. Black, 1875.

Van Wyck, William (ed.). *A Treatise on Fishing with a Hook Attributed to Dame Juliana Berners ... Rendered into Modern English by William Van Wyck*. New York: Van Rees Press, 1933.

Vaughan, Alden. 'Sir Walter Raleigh's Indian Interpreters, 1584–1618.' *The William and Mary Quarterly* 59:2, 2002, pp. 341–376.

Vaughan, Virginia Mason. *Performing Blackness on English Stages, 1500–1800*. Cambridge: Cambridge University Press, 2005.

Vaught, Jennifer C. (ed.). *Masculinity and Emotion in Early Modern English Literature*. London: Ashgate, 2008.

Vieyra, Antonio. Jacinto Dias do Canto (eds.). *A Dictionary of the Portuguese and English Languages, in Two Parts ...* 1773, 2nd edition, London: J. Collingwood, 1827.

Viola, Frank. George Barna. *Pagan Christianity? Exploring the Roots of Our Church Practices*. New edition, Carol Stream, IL: Tyndale House Publishers, 2008.

Vitkus, Daniel. *Turning Turk: English Theatre and the Multicultural Mediterranean, 1570-1630*. New York: Palgrave Macmillan, 2003.

Von Sandrart, Joachim. *L'Academia Todesca Della Architectura, Scultura e Pittura: Oder Teutsche Academie Der Edlen Bau-, Bild- und Mahlerey-Künste Portrait of Higiemonte From Teutsche Academie*. Nuremberg: publisher unknown, 1675, 1683.

Waḥshīyah, Aḥmad ibn ʿAlī Ibn. *Ancient Alphabets and Hieroglyphic Characters Explained: With an Account of the Egyptian Priests, Their Classes, Initiation, and Sacrifices/in the Arabic Language by Ahmad bin Abubekr bin Wahshih; and in English by Joseph Hammer*. London: W. Bulmer and Co. and G. and W. Nicol, 1806, Books 1–2.

Waldstreicher, David. *Slavery's Constitution: From Revolution to Ratification*. New York: Hill and Wang, 2009.

Walker, David. *Walker's Appeal, in Four Articles: Together with a Preamble to the Colored Citizens of the World, but in Particular, and Very Expressly to Those of the United States of America. Written in Boston, in the State of Massachusetts, Sept. 28, 1829*. Boston, MA: David Walker, 1830.

Walker, Robin. *When We Ruled: The Ancient and Medieval History of Black Civilisations*. London: Every Generation Media Group, 2005, 2006.

Walker, Sue Sheridan. *Wife and Widow in Medieval England*. Ann Arbor, MI: University of Michigan Press, 1993.

Wall, Alison. *Power and Protest in England, 1525-1640*. London: Bloomsbury Academic, 2002.

Wallace, William Ross. 'What Rules the World' (1865), in *New 5 & 10 Cent Store, Musical Hand-Bill: The Hand That Rocks the World, Poetry by William Ross Wallace*. Toronto: Imrie & Graham, c. 1865.

Waller, Gary. *The Sidney Family Romance: Mary Wroth, William Herbert, and the Early Modern Construction of Gender*. Detroit, MI: Wayne State University Press, 1993.

Walter, Philippe. *Christianity: The Origins of a Pagan Religion*. Rochester, VT: Inner Traditions, 2006.

Walvin, James. *Black and White: The Negro in English Society, 1555-1945*. London: Allen Lane and the Penguin Press, 1973.

———. *Black Ivory: A History of British Slavery*. London: HarperCollins, 1992, 2001.

Walvin, James. Peter Fryer (ed.). *Rhythms of Resistance: African Musical Heritage in Brazil*. London: Pluto Press, 2000.

Wardhaugh, Julia. *Sub City, Young People, Homelessness and Crime*. 1999, new edition, London: Taylor & Francis, 2017.

Wariboko, Nimi. *Methods of Ethical Analysis: Between Theology, History and Literature*. Eugene, OR: Wipf Stock Publishers, 2013.

Warmington, Paul. *Black British Intellectuals and Education: Multiculturalism's Hidden Histories*. London: Routledge, 2014.

Webb, Eugene J. et al. *Unobtrusive Measures: Nonreactive Research in the Social Sciences*. Chicago, IL: Rand McNally, 1996.

Weever, John. *Ancient Funeral Monuments Within the United Monarchie of Great Britain … Intermixed and Illustrated with Variety of Historical Observations …* London: Thomas Harper, 1631.

Welsing, Frances Cress. *The Isis (Yssis) Papers: The Keys to the Colors*. Chicago, IL: Third World Press, 1991.

Wernham, Richard (ed.). Public Record Office. *List and Analysis of State Papers, Foreign Series: January to December 1595*. London: Her Majesty's Stationery Office, 1964.

Wertis, Richard (trs.). 'On Diplomatics,' in Peter Gay. Victor G. Wexler (eds.). *Historians at Work*, Volume 2: *Villa to Gibbon*. New York: Harper & Row, 1972, pp. 161–198.

Wheat, David. 'Mediterranean Slavery, New World Transformations: Galley Slaves in the Spanish Caribbean, 1578–1635.' *Slavery & Abolition* 31:3, 2010, pp. 327–344.

———. 'Garcia Mendes Castelo Branco, Fidalgo de Angola y Mercader de Esclavos en Veracruz y el Caribe a Principios del Siglo XVII,' in María Elisa Velázquez (ed.). *Debates Históricos Contemporáneos: Africanos y Afrodescendientes en México y Centroamérica*. Mexico City, DF: INAH, CEMCA, UNAM-CIALC, IRD, 2011, pp. 85–107.

———. 'The First Great Waves: African Provenance Zones for the Transatlantic Slave Trade to Cartagena de Indias, 1570–1640.' *The Journal of African History* 52:1, 2011, pp. 1–22.

———. 'The Spanish Caribbean in the Colonial Period,' in Ben Vinson (ed.). *Oxford Bibliographies in Latin American Studies*. New York: Oxford University Press, 2012.

———. *Atlantic Africa and the Spanish Caribbean, 1570–1640*. Chapel Hill, NC: University of North Carolina Press, 2016.

Wheat, David. David Borucki. David Eltis (eds.). 'Atlantic History and the Slave Trade to Spanish America.' *The American Historical Review* 120:2, 2015, pp. 433–461.

Wheat, David. Carl Wise. 'African Laborers for a New Empire: Iberia, Slavery, and the Atlantic World.' 2014. *Lowcountry Digital Library* (College of Charleston). http://ldhi.library.cofc.edu/exhibits/show/african_laborers_for_a_new_emp, accessed 02/01/16.

Whitehouse, Harvey. *Modes of Religiosity: A Cognitive Theory of Religious Transmission*. Walnut Creek, CA/London: Alta Mira Press, 2004.

Whitfield, Peter. *Sir Francis Drake*. New York: New York University Press, 2004.

Whitford, David M. *The Curse of Ham in the Early Modern Era: The Bible and the Justifications for Slavery*. Farnham: Ashgate, 2009.

Wilkinson, Aaron B. *Blurring the Lines of Race and Freedom: Mulattoes in English Colonial North America and the Early United States Republic.* Unpublished, Berkeley, CA: University of California, 2013.

Williams, Chancellor. *The Destruction of Black Civilisation: Great Issues of a Race from 4500 BC to 2000 AD.* 3rd edition, Chicago, IL: Third World Press, 1987.

Williams, Eric. *Capitalism and Slavery.* Richmond, NC: University of North Carolina Press, 1944.

Williams, Michael Warren. *The African American Encyclopedia,* Volume 2. New York/London: Marshall Cavendish, 1993.

Williams, Wesley. '"Anyone Who Says That the Prophet Is Black Should Be Killed": The De Arabization of Islam and the Transfiguration of Muhammad Is Islamic Tradition.' Academia. www.academia. edu/5259303/_Anyone_who_says_that_the_Prophet_is_black_should_be_killed_The_De-Arabization_of_Islam_and_the_Transfiguration_of_Muhammad_in_Islamic_Tradition.

Wilmot, John. 'A Ramble in St James Park.' (c. 1672), in David M. Vieth (ed.). *The Complete Poems of John Wilmot.* London: Yale University Press, 2002.

Willmott, Chris. *Biological Determinism, Free Will and Moral Responsibility: Insights from Genetics and Neuroscience.* New York: Springer, 2016.

Wilson, John K. *The Myth of Political Correctness: The Conservative Attack on Higher Education.* Durham, NC: Duke University Press, 1995.

Wilson, Kathleen. *The Island Race: Englishness, Empire and Gender in the Eighteenth Century.* London: Routledge, 2014.

Wiltshire and Swindon Records Office. *Salisbury St Thomas Parish Register.* no ref. 26 January 1653, n.p. and *Salisbury St Thomas Parish Registers and Bishop's Transcripts 1530–1837, Burials.* Devizes: Wiltshire Family History Society, new edition 2011, p. 67.

———. Wiltshire Family History Society. *Calne Parish Register, 1538–1602,* Volume 1. London, A. Webb, 1944, n.p. ref. 2083/1, n.p.

Wiredu, Kwasi. *A Companion to African Philosophy.* Malden, MA/Oxford: John Wiley and Sons, 2008.

Withal, John. *Short Dictionary …* London: publisher unknown, 1581.

Wolfflin, Heinrich. *Principles of Art History: The Problem of the Development of Style in Later Art.* New York: Dover Publications, 1915.

Worcestershire Archives. Worcestershire Archives and Archaeology Service, Butts, Worcester, Holt register. 'Henry Anthony Jetto.' 21 March 1596, Baptism, Holt Parish Register, ref. 985, p. 19.

———. Holt Parish Registers, 15 May 1717, ref. 985.

Wright, Bruce. *Black Robes, White Justice: Why Our Legal System Does Not Work for Blacks.* Secaucus, NJ: Lyle Stuart, 1987.

Wright, Elizabeth R. *The Epic of Juan Latino: Dilemmas of Race and Religion in Renaissance Spain.* Toronto: University of Toronto Press, 2016.

Wright, Stephanie Hodgson. *Women's Writing of the Early Modern Period, 1588–1688: An Anthology*. Edinburgh: Edinburgh University Press, 2002.

Wright, William. *Black History and Black Identity: A Call for a New Historiography*. Westport, CT: Greenwood Publishing, 2002.

Wrightson, Keith. In Norman Jones. Daniel Woolf (eds.). *Local Identities in Late Medieval and Early Modern England*. New York: Palgrave Macmillan, 2007.

Wroth, Mary. *Pamphilia to Amphilanthus* (1621). *Renascence Editions*. www.luminarium.org/renascence-editions/mary.html, accessed 05/05/18.

Wycliffe, John. Nicholas Hereford (tr.). *Wycliffe Bible*, 1382–1395, Genesis 9, v. 18–27.

———. *The Dore of Holy Scripture*. London: John Gough, 1540.

Wyndham, Thomas. John Hamilton Moore (ed.). *A New and Complete Collection of Voyages and Travels … Including … Voyages and Travels … With the Relations of Maghellan, Drake, Candish, Anson, Dampier, and All the Circumnavigators, Including … the … Voyages and Discoveries …* London: John Hamilton, 1785.

Wynter, Sylvia. 'New Seville and the Conversion Experience of Bartolomé de Las Casas: Part One.' *Jamaica Journal* 17:2, 1984, pp. 25–32.

Yeshiva, University Museum. *The Sephardic Journey 1492–1992*. New York: Yeshiva University Museum, 1992.

Youings, Joyce A. *Sixteenth-Century England*. London: Allen Lane, 1984.

Young, Brigham. *New York Herald*. 4 May 1855, p. 8.

Youngs, Frederick A. *The Proclamations of the Tudor Queens*. Cambridge: Cambridge University Press, 1976.

Yungblut, Lara Hunt. *Strangers Settled Here Amongst Us: Policies, Perceptions, and the Presence of Aliens in Elizabethan England*. 1996, new edition, London: Routledge, 2003.

Zabous, Chantal J. *Tempests After Shakespeare*. New York/Basingstoke: Palgrave, 2002.

Zinnemann, Fred et al. *A Man for All Seasons*. Columbia Pictures, 1966.

Index

Aaron (character), 131, 250, 265
Academia, 'established', 1–5
Ackame (Abercrombie), John, 7,
   272; burial of, 155; children of,
   154–156
Ackame, Penelope, 155
'Adam's Will', 39–44, 219
'Adoration of the Magi' (as
   depicted in art), 168, 277–278,
   283–284, 324
adventurers: 'acts of terror', 15,
   40; East African patronage, 42;
   international ports used, 40;
   limitations on trade of, 38
'Aethiopia(n)', 31, 108, 135;
   positive connotations, 136;
   see also Ethiopia
Africa: civilisations Eurocentric
   historians' denial, 67; colonial
   rule, 5; early modern
   pluralistic, 175
African-centred, ix, 1–3, 67, 77,
   126, 234
Africans: blacknesse explanations,
   94; colour perceptions, 28;
   community membership, 37,
   44; definition of 'English born',
   74; English-Iberian link, 25;
   'enemies of the world', 86; 'folk
   devils', 133; term use of, 1–2
Africanus, Julius, 175
Africanus, Leo, 90–91

Agrippa, Heinrich Cornelius, 53,
   70, 228
Al Zanata, Tariq Ibn Ziyad,
   23–24, 208
Al-Mansur, Ahmad, 171
Albion, legendary giant, 99
Alexander VI, 68
Alfred, King of Wessex, 229
Ali, Duse Mohamed, 2
Almeda, Elizabeth, 120
Almoravids, 24
Alvarez, Pero Pedro ('negro
   e forro'), 26, 42, 158;
   manumission, 26
Ambrose of Milan, 102
Ambrosiaster, 97, 101
American Declaration, 143
Americas, the, 5; African women as
   'chattels', 151, 163
Anger, Jane, *Protection for
   Women*, 53
Anglo-Spanish conflicts, 45; Wars,
   19, 43
Annius, 72–73; anti-African Ham
   version, 68–69, 78, 144; critique
   of, 110; genealogy, 69, 92,
   100; Ham-patricide fiction, 70;
   theological, absence, 166
anti-Semitism, 56; English
   pamphlets, 48
Antony, 'a poor old …', 165
Aquinas, Thomas, 72

Somebody told a lie one day. They couched it in language. They made everything black ugly and evil. Look in your dictionary and see the synonyms of the word *black*. It's always something degrading, low and sinister. Look at the word *white*. It's always something pure, high, clean. Well I want to get the language right tonight. I want to get the language so right that everybody here will cry out, 'Yes I'm Black and I'm proud of it! I'm Black and I'm beautiful!'[1]